JESSIE BE

Jessie Benton Frémont as painted in 1856 by Thomas Buchanan Read. *Courtesy of the Southwest Museum, Los Angeles.*

A BIOGRAPHY

JESSIE BENTON FREMONT

PAMELA HERR

University of Oklahoma Press
Norman and London

Library of Congress Catalog Card Number: 88-40213

ISBN: 0-8061-2159-9

Paperback edition published by arrangement with Franklin
Watts, Inc., by the University of Oklahoma Press, Norman,
Publishing Division of the University. Copyright © 1987 by
Pamela Herr. All rights reserved. Manufactured in the U.S.A.
First printing of the paperback edition, 1988.

For my parents,
Eugene and Phyllis Staley

CONTENTS

PREFACE

Jessie Benton Frémont was fond of quoting her own version
of Portia's lines from Shakespeare's *Julius Caesar:*

> Being so fathered and so husbanded,
> should I not be stronger than my sex?

As a nineteenth-century woman, she felt compelled to define
herself first as daughter and wife. But as the quotation suggests, she was indeed "stronger than her sex," and for me one
of the fascinations of her life has been to track the surge and
ebb of her personality as she burst into the public sphere,
then retreated to the confines of her woman's role. Yet because she sought to legitimize her ambition and energy, and
camouflage them even from herself, by channeling them into
her husband's career, I have found him invading my manuscript as he did her life. This is a biography of Jessie Frémont,
but also of a marriage to a compelling yet elusive man, a
marriage far more complex and troubled than has generally
been known.

Jessie Frémont was a Victorian woman, and the repres-
sions and reticences of her time shaped—and warped—her
life. One cannot help but speculate on what she might have
become had she lived today, with her brilliant verbal skills,
her managerial ability, her shrewdness, idealism, and drive
directed, for example, into politics. As it was, her life spanned
three-quarters of the nineteenth century, and she not only
witnessed, but also struggled to influence, many of its major

movements and events. Because she was more intimately connected with the history of her era than most women, I have tried to write something of a "life and times"—to give a sharp sense of the period as it affected this unusual woman, to suggest what it was like to be talented, ambitious, and female in nineteenth-century America.

Though John Charles Frémont and Thomas Hart Benton have merited comprehensive biographies, Jessie Benton Frémont's life has been treated less seriously, in sentimentalized and semifictionalized accounts. In trying to remedy this lack, I have made use of much previously unknown or little explored material. Of major importance were the more than a hundred letters from Jessie Frémont to her close woman friend, Elizabeth Blair Lee, in the Blair-Lee Papers at Princeton; the McDowell Papers at the University of Virginia and at Duke; the John Gutzon Borglum and Vinnie Ream Hoxie papers at the Library of Congress; the William Carey Jones Papers at Stanford; and Jessie Frémont's civil war letters to Thomas Starr King at the Society of California Pioneers and to Elizabeth Peabody at the Massachusetts Historical Society.

Many people have been generous in their help to me over the past six years as I worked on this biography. I am especially grateful to Mary Lee Spence, coeditor of the invaluable *Expeditions of John Charles Frémont*, who commented perceptively on the manuscript and offered further insights during several conversations; to Yosemite historian Shirley Sargent, who read my Bear Valley chapter and welcomed me to her home at nearby Yosemite to share her research on the Frémonts; and to Virginia Jeans Laas, cobiographer of Samuel Phillips Lee, who shared pertinent transcripts of Elizabeth Blair Lee's letters to her husband in the Blair-Lee Papers.

I also want to thank C. Venable Minor of Redart, Virginia, for permission to use and quote from the McDowell Family Papers at the University of Virginia and the following institutions for permission to quote from letters and other documents in their collections: Bancroft Library; Trustees of the Boston Public Library; Brown University Library; California

State Library; Clarke Historical Library, Central Michigan State University; Chicago Historical Society; Rare Book and Manuscript Library, Columbia University; William R. Perkins Library, Duke University; Eastern Kentucky University Library; Houghton Library, Harvard University; Huntington Library; University of Kentucky Library; Massachusetts Historical Society; Missouri Historical Society; Library of the New York Botanical Garden; New-York Historical Society; New York Public Library; Park-McCullough House, North Bennington, Vermont; Historical Society of Pennsylvania; Princeton University Library; Mabel Smith Douglass Library, Rutgers, the State University of New Jersey; Society of California Pioneers; Southwest Museum; Special Collections, Stanford University Library; George Arents Research Library, Syracuse University; Virginia State Library; Washington University Libraries, St. Louis; and the State Historical Society of Wisconsin.

I am also greatly indebted to Judith Quinn and John Kessell for their sensitive reading of the manuscript for style as well as content; to Robert Becker, who introduced me to the resources of the Bancroft Library and gave valuable advice on the manuscript; to Frémont biographer Ferol Egan for reviewing the chapters relating to Frémont's early career and the expeditions; and to Donald Mayall, Eugene Staley, Robert Reid, Peter Carroll, Bruce Bennett, and Wallis Ammerman Menozzi, who commented helpfully on various chapters and drafts. I also want to thank my agent, Fred Hill; my editor at Franklin Watts, Ellen Joseph; and Carolyn Mann, Sylvia Denys-Wenger, Jay Fliegelman, Ed Holm, Valerie Mathes, Carl Briggs, and Augusta Fink, for their generous help.

My deepest gratitude goes to Tanna and Robin Herr for their continued faith and encouragement, and to Barton J. Bernstein for his wise and insightful reading of several versions of the manuscript and for his steady care.

Pamela Herr

Palo Alto, California

JESSIE BENTON FREMONT

PROLOGUE: THE VIEW
FROM LOS ANGELES

IN THE LAST DECADE of the nineteenth century, an old woman—tiny, white-haired, and frail—lived out the remaining years of her life in a modest brown-shingled house given to her by a committee of California women. She had been one of the most extraordinary women of her time. Even now visitors remarked on the keenness of her mind, the wit and dazzle of her conversation. But for the most part, Jessie Benton Frémont lived quietly, privately: reading, writing (still hoping to earn a few precious dollars with her skillful pen), relishing such everyday pleasures as the scent of violets in her garden, the soft glow of her acacia trees at sunset.

Her Los Angeles home contained only a small portion of the memorabilia of her rich life, for poverty had long since forced her to sell most of the beautiful furniture, paintings, and objects she once owned. Still, she managed to save three portraits. These dominated the house.

The first was of her father, Senator Thomas Hart Benton of Missouri, a large, powerfully built man with a dark cloak thrown across his broad shoulders. Arrogant, flamboyant, brilliant, in his prime he had been the Senate's most influential spokesman for Jacksonian democracy and western expansion; in his declining years, a raging, wounded lion, prophesying civil war as he went down to electoral defeat for his stand against the spread of slavery.

The second showed a strikingly handsome man in his mid-seventies, with a full head of white hair, a trim beard and mustache, and keen, hooded eyes that glanced warily out of the elaborate gilt frame. This was her husband, the controversial, enigmatic John Charles Frémont—explorer, gold-rush millionaire, presidential candidate, and bankrupt.

The third portrait was of Jessie herself. Painted when she was in her early thirties, it showed a deceptively serene young woman in a gauzy white dress with a pale blue scarf tied at her open collar. She had a full oval face, finely arched brows over luminous brown eyes, and abundant dark hair swept back and caught at the nape of her neck. Though the mole by her mouth gave the portrait a touch of realism, its conventional nineteenth-century lines scarcely suggested the robust mind, the passionate heart, the energy and ambition behind the smooth young face, for Jessie Frémont was a heroine too spirited for her age, too gifted to be readily contained within the narrow image of proper Victorian womanhood.

The favorite daughter of Thomas Hart Benton, she was early given "the place a son would have had" in her father's heart.[1] Growing up in Washington during the boisterous years of Jacksonian democracy, relishing the freedom of the frontier during long stays in St. Louis, and exposed to a life based on slavery at her genteel mother's family estate in Virginia, Jessie became a rebellious adolescent who chafed at the restraints of Victorian girlhood. While in reluctant attendance at Miss English's Female Seminary, she met John Charles Frémont, a dashing army surveyor who was born illegitimate. "There was no room for reason" in their headlong romance.[2] Jessie was just seventeen when she defied her family and scandalized Washington society by eloping with the young explorer.

What followed was a life of extremes, of glittering successes and bitter failures, of wealth, power, and poverty. Soon after her marriage in 1841, Jessie collaborated with her husband in writing the best-selling accounts of his western explorations that catapulted him to fame and made his scout, Kit Carson, a legend. At the height of the gold rush, accompanied only by her six-year-old daughter, she crossed the Isthmus of Panama by dugout and muleback to join her husband in California, where their mines brought them a fortune in gold. In 1856, with "Frémont and Our Jessie" as a slogan of the antislavery North, she became the first presidential candidate's wife to play an active part in a political campaign.

Though Frémont gained the majority of northern votes, he was defeated nationwide. The family retreated to California, where Jessie's San Francisco salon became a gathering place for antislavery intellectuals like young writer Bret Harte. When civil war broke out, Lincoln appointed Frémont commander of the western region with headquarters in St. Louis. With Jessie's support, her husband issued a sensational proclamation that freed the slaves of Missouri rebels, only to have the more moderate Lincoln revoke the decree. Though Jessie rushed to Washington to defend her husband in a dramatic confrontation with the president, Frémont nonetheless lost his command.

By 1873, the Frémonts' gold-rush fortune was gone, and Jessie, aged fifty, took up her pen to support her husband and three children. During the next twenty years she churned out articles and books in a desperate effort to ward off poverty. "I am like a deeply built ship," she said during this difficult time. "I drive best under a strong wind."[3]

Slowly her dreams had crumbled. She had poured her energy into her husband's career, only to watch him stumble each time his fingers grazed the brass ring. Nonetheless, she remained in love with this reticent, elusive man. Even persistent rumors that he was unfaithful did not change her fierce devotion. When he died in 1890, her son feared she might kill herself. But as always her strength came through. She lived twelve more years, vibrantly alive to the end.

Jessie Frémont was an activist cast in a supporting role, living through a man the part she might have played herself. When, out of her abundant energy, she was tempted to act directly, she found herself thwarted and misunderstood. Critics called her "General Jessie," while Abraham Lincoln himself branded her a "female politician." Even her writing was affected. Though she dreamed of a "writing table and a room" of her own, she learned to pass off her work as mere scribbling, an offhand hobby that happened to pay.[4]

As a proud young woman, she believed she could shape her own destiny. Though she never gave up the attempt, she was gradually forced to accept that much of life was beyond her control. Her husband's career began with flash and brilliance but guttered out in a strange series of failures that she, a woman, could do little to prevent. In a letter to a friend she once acknowledged her dilemma. After quoting Tennyson's lines, "For man is man and master of his fate," she observed wryly, "That is poetry. When one is not man but woman, you follow in the wake of both man and fate, and the prose of life proves one does not so easily be 'master' of fate."[5]

During her last years in Los Angeles, with her father and husband dead, Jessie Frémont began to write her memoirs. In these fragmentary recollections, never completed or published, she revealed feelings and incidents she earlier found it prudent to suppress.

Among the major events of her life, she also recorded seemingly trivial moments, inconsequential yet somehow emblematic. And so she wrote of an episode that occurred nearly sixty years before, when her frantic parents, hoping to distract her from the young army surveyor who was already courting her, packed her off to attend a grand family wedding in Virginia.

She had written about the same Virginia wedding once before when, desperate for money after her husband's business failures, she ransacked her past for reminiscences tailored to the taste of the Victorian reading public. On that occasion she described it as a pageant of southern charm. This time she remembered it differently, recalling one scene so vividly that she could see again the distinct yellow color of her ruffled muslin dress.[6]

It had all begun innocently enough, she recalled. The scandal was unexpected.

She had been barely seventeen in June of 1841 when she arrived at her uncle's elegant estate for the wedding festivities. She had not wanted to come. She was a blooming young woman—exuberant, witty, impulsive, with a radiance that made gentlemen murmur of roses in full flower, or perhaps more perceptively, of the sharp-sweet taste of wild strawberries. Yet she sensed that her genteel and pious relatives found her high spirits improper and her cleverness alarming. Even her beloved father, who relished her spirit when she was a child, had begun to see her as a rebel. She knew she must be wary.

"We were a house party of thirty-five," she remembered so many years later. Uncles, aunts, and innumerable cousins overflowed the library at morning prayers and crowded the polished mahogany table for long, stately dinners. Jessie soon felt restless in the patterned social atmosphere, thick with family ties, until, amid the praying and tea-taking and decorous chatter, she discovered a cousin, a young West Point cadet named Preston Johnston, who felt as stifled as she did. The two even looked alike, as their relatives constantly noted, so much so that they could have been twins. "We *were* singularly alike," Jessie recalled, "but we grew tired of being stood side by side and freshly commented on by more cousins and more friends who kept up perpetual visiting." Exasperated by the fuss, Preston finally remarked, "I don't believe they would know us apart if we changed clothes." His words gave Jessie an idea.

That evening at a crowded party, two strangers slipped in among the crush of guests. One was a pretty girl in a yellow ruffled muslin dress, the other a slender young army cadet. At first, "no one detected us," Jessie said. Then their uncle, a stern, humorless man who suffered from chronic indigestion, looked across the room and saw the yellow-gowned girl standing alone. Learning that she was a stranger, he went over to find out just who she was. With a show of gallantry, he offered his arm. But when Preston, "not used to ruffles," gingerly extended his hand, the uncle spotted his strong, sunburned wrist protruding awkwardly from a frilly sleeve—and uncovered the ruse. Next he detected Jessie, disguised in Preston's cadet uniform.

Outraged at the impropriety—the sheer indecency—of their behavior, he called them "scandalous" and "immodest." As the two pranksters scurried away, onlookers clucked and smirked at the bold impudence of Senator Benton's favorite daughter, who dared to play the part of a man even in jest.

While the psychological implications of this incident would provide ample grist for a modern Freudian mill, Jessie Ann Benton, born in a time when a woman could act only through a man, returned to Washington more determined than ever to marry John Charles Frémont, whose impulsive and ambitious temperament was so like her own.

Yet the old woman in Los Angeles, recording that distant scene, must have felt that it revealed something important about the bright, ardent girl she had once been, and about the age in which she lived. She had longed not to be a man, but simply to act as a man could, freely and fully. But it was an era when the slightest blurring of roles could create a scandal. Her father had raised her like a son, encouraging her spirit and drive. But when she reached her teen years, even he expected her to conform. At first she had rebelled. But there was no place in nineteenth-century America for a clever, dominant, passionate woman. Slowly, sometimes painfully, she learned to compromise, to move adroitly about the airless velvet box in which she, like all Victorian women, was enclosed. But she was never wholly successful. Again and again she pushed rashly beyond its narrow confines. Each time she was condemned, just as when she put on a cadet's uniform as a lark at a Virginia wedding. The old woman, remembering that long-ago scene, was describing more than a prank. She was describing the pattern of her life.

1

*We see men who will aid the instruction
of their sons, and condemn only their
daughters to ignorance. "Our sons,"
they say, "will have to exercise political
rights, may aspire to public offices,
may fill some learned profession, may
struggle for wealth and acquire it. But
for our daughters," they say—if indeed
respecting them they say anything—
"for our daughters, little trouble or
expense is necessary. They can never* be
anything; *in fact, they* are nothing."

Frances Wright
Course of Popular Lectures
1834

*To think that all in me of which my
father would have felt a proper pride
had I been a man, is deeply mortifying
to him because I am a woman.*

Elizabeth Cady Stanton
to Susan B. Anthony
September 10, 1855

"THE PLACE A SON
WOULD HAVE HAD"

THE SENATOR WANTED A SON. Soon after Congress adjourned in May of 1824, Thomas Hart Benton hurried to his father-in-law's estate, Cherry Grove, in the Blue Ridge Mountains of Virginia, where his wife, Elizabeth, was awaiting their second child. Their first, born two years before, had been a puny, weak-lunged girl whom they named Elizabeth. This one would be called Thomas.

On May 31 the child was born. When he saw the robust brown-eyed baby, the senator was magnanimous, or so his second daughter was always told. "Two daughters," he proclaimed, "are a crown to any household."[1] Still, they named her for a man: Jessie, after Thomas Benton's father Jesse, changing the spelling slightly and adding Ann, for his mother, as a middle name.

Jessie Ann was a quick and energetic child. There were some who found her noisy, willful, and overly precocious, but her spirit delighted her father. "He made me a companion and a friend from the time almost that I could begin to understand," she recalled. "We were a succession of girls at first, with the boys coming last, and my father gave me early the place a son would have had."[2] It would be the central fact of her childhood.

Though Thomas and Elizabeth Benton would eventually have six children, including two sons, none ever replaced Jessie in her father's affection, for of them all, she was most like him. "I think I came into my father's life like a breath of his own compelling nature," she said, "strong, resolute, but open to all tender and gracious influences, and above all, loving him." She fiercely dismissed the possibility of rivals. "There were other sisters," she admitted, "but the first was an ailing, delicate child, and of the others, one was much too young, and another singularly unsympathetic."[3]

Jessie's older sister Elizabeth (whom the family called Eliza and later Liz) and her younger sisters, Sarah and Susan, would become charming, accomplished women, but as conventionally ordinary as their names. Her two brothers were less fortunate. The first, John Randolph, born when Jessie was five, was named for the brilliant, eccentric Virginia statesman John Randolph of Roanoke. He would grow into a fatally weak young man, an alcoholic "inclined to dissipation," who died of a sudden fever when he was twenty-two. The second, born when Jessie was seven and named for Elizabeth Benton's father, James McDowell, was a "doomed consumptive" who survived only four years.[4]

Jessie Ann was the only Benton child named exclusively for her father's side of the family, a fact that was strangely appropriate, for only she had his brash vitality. Full blown in both father and daughter was that combination of idealism and ambition, of passion and energy, that must find an outlet in practical action as inevitably as a river seeks the sea.

The Bentons had always been ambitious—a family on the make—eager, aspiring, tenacious. Jessie's great-grandfather, Samuel Benton, an Englishman who was probably the first of his line in America, was a shrewd, grasping, not overly scrupulous man who schemed his way to a large estate and political power in colonial Granville County, North Carolina. His oldest son, Jessie's grandfather Jesse, was evidently something of a misfit in the raw Carolina hill country where, like his father, he practiced law, farmed, and dabbled in courthouse politics, for he was a reserved and cultivated man who prized his fine library of books in five languages. Still, he had the Benton ambition. Americans were moving west in the late eighteenth century, and Benton saw opportunity there. He was among the founders of the Transylvania Company, a group of early-day developers with a grandiose plan for acquiring western land.

In 1775, Jesse Benton and his colleagues made the arduous trip over the Appalachian Mountains to wilderness Tennessee, where for ten thousand pounds' worth of trade goods, heaped tantalizingly in nearby cabins, they struck a bargain with the Cherokee Indians for a colossal domain—some 17 million acres, which included two-thirds of the present state of Kentucky and vast tracts in Tennessee as well. That it was illegal for a private company to purchase land from the Indians was ignored by lawyer Benton and his eager companions. Even as they dickered, the company's chief scout, Daniel Boone, began to hack out a rough trail through the Cumberland Gap. Soon the Transylvania Company's first wagon train of land-hungry settlers was following his lead into the virgin forests and rich grasslands of Kentucky, where, it was said, wild strawberries grew so lushly in the meadows that horses passing through were stained crimson to their knees with the juice.

Sometime during this period of western enterprise, Jesse Benton married. His bride was Ann Gooch, a tall, slender, vivacious young woman with blue eyes and a rich mass of wavy chestnut-colored hair. She was the niece and ward of Thomas Hart, a wealthy North Carolina revolutionary war patriot and partner in the Transylvania Company. Jesse and Ann settled on a North Carolina plantation, where Jesse continued to build his fortune in land, borrowing heavily for his incessant speculations west of the mountains.

In 1782, the Bentons' third child and first son, Thomas Hart Benton, was born. He grew into a tall, muscular boy with blue eyes, fair skin, and red-blond hair. He was bright and quick-tempered, an outdoor lad who loved to ride and hunt in the pine woods near his home. But Jesse Benton's health was slowly deteriorating, and during the bleak winter of 1790–91, when Thomas was eight, his father died of tuberculosis, a disease that would haunt the family for generations. He left his thirty-two-year-old widow with eight children, a debt-ridden estate, and vast but increasingly dubious land claims over the western mountains.

"I fancy my grandparents liked each other very much, and the parting was hard," their granddaughter Jessie wrote long afterward in an account of her father's family,[5] for in the weeks following her husband's death, Ann Benton collapsed. Her splendid chestnut hair turned a tarnished white. But her loss also brought out an unsentimental strength that would deeply impress Jessie when she knew her grandmother in later years. After negotiating a loan from her uncle, Thomas Hart, Ann Benton settled her husband's debts, put the reduced estate on a paying basis, and then turned her attention to her oldest son's future. Determined that he become a scholar and lawyer like his father, she used books from her husband's library to teach him law and history, and saw to it that he was tutored in Greek and Latin. By the time he was sixteen, she had saved enough to send him off to the new University of North Carolina at nearby Chapel Hill.

What happened next never appeared in Jessie's account of her father's family. Scarcely three months after he entered the university, Thomas returned home in disgrace, expelled as a petty thief. What mysterious pressure or desperate need caused him to steal small amounts of cash from his three roommates—the proof was convincing at the time—remains murky. The humiliation must have been excruciating. According to Chapel Hill legend, as young Thomas prepared to leave town, his fellow students gathered to jeer and taunt him. Turning toward them defiantly just before mounting his horse, he hurled back a memorable prophecy. "I am leaving here now," he told his tormentors, "but damn you, you will hear from me again!"[6]

The episode left him proud, prickly about his honor, and fiercely determined to prove himself. It also made him honest. In an era when men like Daniel Webster accepted cash payments in return for political favors, Thomas Benton was known for his scrupulous integrity.

The ugly incident must have haunted the family, for they soon fled west over the mountains to the new state of Tennessee, where a tract of 2,560 acres remained of Jesse Benton's western dreams. By 1801, Thomas was helping his younger brothers and the few family slaves sow corn and cotton and build a fortresslike house of stone and wood, for settlers still feared the Indians, whose trail passed by the edge of "Widow Benton's Settlement."

Thomas was too ambitious to remain a farmer for long. When frost blackened one cotton crop and poor market conditions reduced the value of another, he turned to his father's law books in earnest. By the time he was twenty-four, he was handling his first cases. Clever, aggressive, and unremittingly thorough in his work—a driven scholar—he soon had a flourishing practice. Traveling by horseback from one county courthouse to another, the burly young lawyer developed a gaudy speaking style—ornate, pugnacious, and massively factual. He became a friend and protégé of Tennessee lawyer-politician Andrew Jackson, fifteen years his senior, a poor boy from the Carolinas who, like Benton, had migrated to Tennessee. At twenty-seven, Benton was elected to the Tennessee state senate. Politically, he was a Jeffersonian democrat with an optimistic faith in the common people that would grow stronger as he moved west.

As Benton began to make his way in Tennessee politics, the family malady reasserted itself. One by one, three sisters died of tuberculosis. By 1812, Thomas too had developed the hacking cough, night sweats, and recurring fever that signaled the disease. In an era when treatment commonly consisted of bleeding with leeches and a near-starvation diet—goats' milk and Iceland moss was one prescribed regimen—Benton in desperation tried a different cure. While leading a regiment under Andrew Jackson during the War of 1812, he walked instead of riding, bathed daily in cold streams, and slept in the open air. By the time the march ended, "he had lost his cough, his sleeplessness, his despair," wrote his daughter Jessie, who turned his cure into a family legend. She also drew a moral. He learned, she said, that he had an "ally within himself on which he could surely rely—his own will."[7] Benton would pass this powerful optimism on to his daughter, a disturbing inheritance deeply at odds with the prevailing view that a woman must curb her will and submit to both man and fate.

In a region where every man carried a gun or knife and was quick to defend his "honor," it was perhaps inevitable that a man both as aggressive and as touchy as young Thomas Benton would become involved in violence. That his opponent was Andrew Jackson made the episode notorious.

The controversy began when Thomas's rambunctious younger brother Jesse became involved in a duel. When his shot went wild, Jesse panicked. Turning his back and crouching to protect himself, he was hit ignominiously in the buttocks by his opponent, William Carroll, whose second happened to be Andrew Jackson. When Thomas Benton learned that Jackson had helped make his brother the laughingstock of Tennessee, he was furious. Soon the two hot-headed men were bitter enemies. The climax came on September 4, 1813, when the lanky, lantern-jawed Jackson, accompanied by cronies and armed with a riding whip, a small sword, and several pistols, confronted the Benton brothers at a Nashville hotel.

"Now defend yourself, you damned rascal," Jackson challenged, brandishing his whip. Thomas reached for his gun, but Jackson drew first. Pointing his pistol at Benton, he forced him backward down a hallway. At that moment, Jesse Benton fired, and his bullet smashed into Jackson's left shoulder. Blood spurting from his wound, Jackson managed to get off a shot that grazed Thomas's coat sleeve before he fell to the ground. Thomas fired twice but missed, as a bystander threw himself on Jackson's body to shield him. A Jackson partisan fired wildly at Thomas, whose gun was now empty, while others slashed at Jesse and Thomas with knives. The brawl ended abruptly when the heavyset Thomas tumbled backward down a flight of stairs.

Jackson's wound was serious. As doctors worked desperately to stanch the blood, the Bentons and their supporters gathered outside in the square, calling taunts. Jackson's blood soaked through two mattresses before the flow was stopped, and he vowed revenge against the two brothers. "I am literally in hell here," Thomas wrote a friend soon afterward. "I . . . see no alternative but to kill or be killed; for I will not crouch to Jackson."[8]

Benton managed to hang on in Tennessee for two more years, but when Jackson led American frontiersmen to a stunning victory over the British at New Orleans in 1815 and became a national hero, Benton headed west again, this time to St. Louis in Missouri Territory. It would be ten years before the two men would be reconciled and several more before Benton, recognizing their deep political affinity, could support his old enemy for president. Eventually though, when the two had become staunch allies, Benton could even joke about the feud. "Yes, I had a fight with Jackson," he would say. "A fellow was hardly in fashion then who hadn't."[9]

About the time he moved to St. Louis, Benton was introduced to twenty-year-old Elizabeth McDowell of Cherry Grove, Virginia, by her uncle, army colleague James Patten Preston. She was a lovely brown-haired woman, deeply religious and steeped in the gentle manners of southern womanhood. At the same time she was "a ready and incisive talker," highly intelligent and well-read. The combination so enchanted the thirty-three-year-old Benton that he proposed almost immediately. But Elizabeth refused, explaining that she could never marry "a red haired man, a democrat, or a western man." It marked the beginning of a long, stubborn courtship.[10]

Born into an aristocratic southern family in 1794, Elizabeth was raised at Cherry Grove, her father's estate in Rockbridge County, Virginia. Unlike the restless Bentons, the McDowell family had lived contentedly for five generations in the Blue Ridge mountain valley where they first settled in 1737. Principled, fiercely independent Scotch-Irish, the

McDowells had been driven first from Scotland and then from their refuge in northern Ireland because of their dogged Presbyterianism. Fleeing both religious and economic persecution, they emigrated to America with a great wave of their coreligionists in the early eighteenth century.

During the revolutionary war, their Scottish hatred of the English made them gallant soldiers, but once the war was over, they returned to the tranquil life of their mountain retreat. Firmly established as landed gentry in western Virginia, the McDowells and their relatives, the Prestons, entered politics in a manner that managed to convey gentlemanly duty and noblesse oblige rather than vulgar ambition. Elizabeth McDowell's uncles, brother, and cousin all became Virginia governors, and numerous relatives served as senators, congressmen, and state representatives. Even as late as the 1880s, Jessie Frémont found that her "southern connection" still included two senators and six congressmen.

Elizabeth McDowell's own upbringing combined the ease and grace of upper-class southern life with the Calvinism of her family's Scotch-Irish forebears. The youngest of three children, she was, in her daughter Jessie's view, "indulged in every way."[11] As a young belle, she summered at fashionable White Sulphur Springs and wintered in Richmond, where her uncle, Benton's friend James Patten Preston, was governor from 1816 to 1819. Accompanied by a maid and footmen, she traveled in her own yellow-painted London-built carriage with an interior of scarlet leather.

The sheltered Elizabeth must have found Thomas Benton almost overwhelming, filled with a robust sexuality that frightened her. And she probably learned of his indiscretions: the cheating episode, the brawl with Jackson, perhaps even the rumor that he had a quadroon mistress in Tennessee. Moreover, to this delicately bred woman, frontier Missouri was "impossible."[12] Her life was comfortable and secure, and she had no taste for pioneering.

For the next six years Benton persisted, returning to see her again and again from his new home in St. Louis, where

he was quickly rising to prominence as a lawyer and newspaper editor. Though Elizabeth continued to turn him down,
she refused all other suitors as well. While the earthy Benton
may have alarmed her, the Virginia gentlemen she knew must
have seemed insipid in comparison. Yet in a time when women
considered themselves old maids at twenty-four, she no doubt
felt increasing pressure to marry. Perhaps she was fearful of
marriage itself or of her own loss of independence. Whatever
the cause, her decision was reluctant and painfully long in
coming. Elizabeth McDowell was nearly twenty-seven when
she agreed to marry Thomas Benton, and she gave her consent
only after he was elected senator from the new state of Missouri. To her more impetuous and venturesome daughter Jessie, who adored her father, the delay was always inexplicable.
She never quite forgave her mother the long hesitation.

Thomas and Elizabeth were married at Cherry Grove in
March 1821, and Benton whirled his new bride off to St.
Louis, where he combined a honeymoon with politicking.
Perhaps in spite of herself, Elizabeth found it all so heady
that she was soon writing home to urge her brother, James,
to emigrate to Missouri, an idea her mother gently but firmly
opposed. By the time the Bentons returned to Cherry Grove
in the fall, Elizabeth was pregnant. In the next twelve years,
she would bear seven children, including one that was still-
born.

Benton, nearly forty when Elizabeth agreed to marry him,
became a devoted husband and father. He insisted that his
growing family be with him as much as possible, so a caravan
of babies, nurses, and maids traveled regularly between
Washington, Cherry Grove, and his political base, St. Louis.
Despite Benton's devotion, Elizabeth's feelings are less clear.
She bore his children, accompanied him to St. Louis and
Washington, served as a gracious and dutiful wife. Yet her
daughter Jessie noted that she participated in his political
career reluctantly, that she was often ill, and that her true
home remained her parents' estate, Cherry Grove.

Jessie and her mother, so different in temperament, were

never close. Elizabeth Benton was an intelligent but unadventurous woman who preferred an ordered, tranquil life where voices were never raised either in joy or anger. She was a domestic woman with a "genius for home comfort," who ran her large household with smooth efficiency.[13]

Pious, domestic, and genteel, Elizabeth Benton was the very model of early-nineteenth-century womanhood. Even her poor health enhanced the image, for it was an age that considered frailty the essence of femininity. In contrast, Jessie's vigorous, direct, and emotional temperament resembled her father's, and it was with him that she felt real rapport. Beneath the profound differences between mother and daughter there also lurked a subtle rivalry for the same man. Jessie came to feel that she filled a place in her father's life that her mother had left vacant, that from earliest childhood she provided him with a companionship he could not find elsewhere.

As a child, Jessie loved to hear her father recall an incident that occurred when she was three, while he was campaigning to elect Andrew Jackson president. One day, as Benton would tell the story, Jessie and her five-year-old sister, Eliza, pranced into his Washington study to show off fancy new purple capes. But Benton was out, and Jessie, feeling restless, began to toy with a stack of foolscap covered with writing. Spotting some red and blue chalk on a nearby table, she tried to "write" on one of the sheets, licking the chalk as she worked to make her marks darker. Soon she had persuaded even the cautious Eliza to join in the fun.

When Thomas Benton entered the room some time later, he was horrified to find his two daughters sprawled on the floor, their mouths smeared with chalk, covering page after page of a speech he had just completed with red and blue marks. In the thundering voice he ordinarily reserved for his political enemies, he demanded, "Who did this?"

Eliza began to wail, but precocious Jessie planted herself firmly in front of her father and asked, stalling, "Do you really want to know?"

The senator did.

"It's a little girl that cries 'Hurrah for Jackson!' " she replied with awkward grammar but a triumphant smile.

Amused by her pluck and quick wit, disarmed by her understanding of his political sympathies, Benton caught her up in his arms and gently explained that she had scribbled all over the final copy of his latest speech. But his anger was gone. "By what flash of instinct did I go straight to the hidden spot in my father's armor?" Jessie asked herself long afterward. "Did he even then feel the germ of that instinctive sympathy which made us one?"[14]

2

If [parents] would give their daughters the same mental training they do their sons, they would not be converted into slaves so handily

Jane Swisshelm
Letters to Country Girls
1853

WASHINGTON
CHILDHOOD

THE BENTON FAMILY was celebrating. At Dawson's Number Two, the Capitol Hill boardinghouse where the senator and his wife lived with their three young daughters, more than a hundred friends had gathered to toast the inauguration of the new president. "Here was a perfect levee," exclaimed one guest. All were "happy and rejoicing—wine and cake were handed in profusion."[1]

Earlier that warm March day in 1829, most of the Benton guests had been among an immense crowd of jubilant citizens who watched tall, gaunt Andrew Jackson, dressed in a plain black suit and black cravat, take the oath of office as the seventh president of the United States.

Washington had never seen such a throng. For days beforehand people had poured into the little capital, overflowing its hotels and taverns, and exhausting its liquor supply. "It was like the inundation of the northern barbarians into Rome," wrote an alarmed opponent. "Strange faces filled every place, and every face seemed to bear defiance."[2]

At noon the president-elect, his iron-gray hair brushed stiffly back from his high forehead, appeared on the East Portico of the Capitol and bowed gravely to the cheering crowd. As if on cue, the clouds parted and the sun streamed through. "It is beautiful, it is sublime!" exclaimed the Bentons' friend Francis Scott Key as he viewed the scene from afar.[3]

The ceremony was short and dignified, but when the new president turned and bowed again, the jubilant crowd swarmed toward him, trampling the freshly planted flower beds and lawns of the Capitol in their eagerness to shake his hand or touch his clothing. Jackson managed to reach a waiting horse, tethered at the Capitol fence, mount, and head down muddy, rutted Pennsylvania Avenue. Behind him followed the people, a great procession of "country men, farmers, gentlemen, mounted and dismounted, boys, women and children, black and white."[4]

Tables of cake, ice cream, orange punch, and wine had been set up in the East Room for the presidential reception, but as thousands crowded into the White House, what had been planned as a decorous occasion turned into a melee. Cut glass and china were smashed and gallons of punch spilled on the carpets as citizens vied for refreshments, while others scrambled onto satin-covered chairs in their muddy boots to catch a glimpse of the new president. Only when tubs of orange punch were carried onto the lawn and the crowd was lured outside was order restored. "It was the People's day and the People's President, and the People would rule," reported one tolerant observer, but aristocratic Supreme Court Justice William Story was in despair. "The reign of King 'Mob' seemed triumphant."[5]

Ex-President John Quincy Adams, spending a day on a gloomy horseback ride in the country, would have agreed. Defeated for reelection by a man he regarded as a mere brawler from Tennessee, a nearly illiterate backwoodsman "who could not write a sentence of grammar and hardly could spell his own name," Adams scarcely understood the change that had occurred.[6] For the first time, a self-made man, a frontier politician, had been elected president of the United States.

One man who did understand was Thomas Hart Benton. With the election of Jackson, his political fortunes would change dramatically. Soon acknowledged as the president's chief spokesman in the Senate, Benton would become one of the most influential politicians in America, a vital part of a controversial and tempestuous era. As for Benton's four-and-a-half-year-old daughter Jessie, the election of Jackson would mean that her childhood years would be spent in the eye of the storm, close to the center of power. It would provide her with an extraordinary political education.

The Washington of Jessie Benton's childhood was not an impressive place. It was "as unlike the capital of a great country as it is possible to imagine," pronounced an Englishwoman come to view the new democracy. Though it had been laid out according to French planner Pierre Charles L'Enfant's grand design, it remained a rough skeleton—raw, half-built, far from filling out its visionary lines. The seven "theoretical avenues" radiating from the Capitol were in reality badly rutted paths connecting scraggly groups of houses and shops.[7] Even Pennsylvania Avenue, which linked Washington's two genuine showplaces, the White House and the Capitol, was unpaved and, like all Washington roads, mired in mud or clouds of dust, depending on the weather. Planted with Thomas Jefferson's still scrawny Lombardy poplars and lined with gambling and grog shops as well as shabby congressional boardinghouses, it was scarcely the grand boulevard its planner envisioned. Slave pens bordered the unkempt, swampy Mall, and foreign visitors were quick to point out the hypocrisy of a nation that preached liberty in the halls of Congress while slaves were bought and sold nearby.

With a population of twenty thousand, Washington was still a country town. Pigs rooted in the roads for sewage, cows grazed near public buildings, and government bureaucrats—there were some six hundred—rode to work by horseback from their homes in Georgetown. Even elegantly attired diplomats were forced to jump ditches and cross muddy fields as they made their ceremonial rounds. For the city's poor, living in shacks and hovels, sanitary conditions were appalling, and even the more prosperous residents hauled their water from public wells and dumped their slops in open ditches.

Many found Washington's residents as crude as their city. Drinking, gambling, dueling, and brawling competed with politics as pastimes. At the gambling houses that lined the north side of Pennsylvania Avenue, men were lured to play faro by free food and drink. One congressman reportedly lost thirty-five hundred dollars, a year's salary, in one unlucky night.

The House of Representatives was itself no model of decorum. Congressmen lolled about "in the most unseemly attitudes, a large majority with their hats on, and nearly all, spitting to an excess that decency forbids me to describe," wrote one horrified Englishwoman.[8] Members from the new western states, with their frontier manners and eccentric clothing—Congressman Davy Crockett of Tennessee sported a panther-skin vest—particularly amazed staid easterners. The Senate was generally considered more sedate, but even there arguments often came to blows, perhaps intensified by a brew called "Switchel," a concoction of molasses, ginger, and water liberally "flavored" with rum that was constantly dispensed during debates.

Visitors were also shocked at the freedom of Washington women, who were often seen on the arm of someone not their "husband, father, nor . . . brother." Oblivious to the advice that no husband would be happy "whose wife was fond of gadding," they flocked to the Capitol to hear Henry Clay speak in the Senate or Daniel Webster argue before the Supreme Court, located in seedy quarters in the Capitol basement. At the countless teas, dinners, and receptions of the Washington season, they were noted for the scantiness of their dress and the cleverness of their conversation. "They lace up too tight and expose their shoulders too much," a newcomer wrote home to his New England wife. "On the whole," he concluded, summing up the Washington scene, "if there is more extravagance, folly, and corruption anywhere in the world than in this city, I do not wish to see that place."[9]

Young Jessie Ann Benton often accompanied her father to the White House, scrambling up the stairs behind him to the second floor, where they would find Andrew Jackson in his rocking chair, drawn close to a blazing fire. Though tall south-facing windows flooded the room with sunlight, the White House was cold and damp, aggravating the aging president's rheumatism and the ache of old bullet wounds.

With his thin, deeply lined face and grave blue eyes, the president seemed a melancholy old man to Jessie, burdened by cares, still grieving for his wife, who had died just before the inauguration. Sensing his loneliness, Jessie would sit patiently beside him while he stroked her hair, trying not to squirm even when, in the intensity of political talk, he would absentmindedly grip her hair so tightly it would hurt.

The two frontier politicians had formed a powerful alliance. Jackson could count on Benton to defend his policies in the Senate against the formidable opposition of Daniel Webster, Henry Clay, and John Calhoun. Fifty years old in 1832, Jessie's father was an impressive-looking man: massive, vigorous, fastidiously neat in his double-breasted frock coat with high black neck stock and a pince-nez swinging from a gold chain. Though he was recognized as one of the most erudite men in Congress, his long, laboriously researched speeches, generously larded with statistics and classical allusions, seemed both tedious and bombastic to his opponents. Arrogant yet genuinely idealistic, Benton relished his role as representative of the frontier West. "Nobody opposes Benton but a few black-jack prairie lawyers," he would proclaim. "Benton and the people, Benton and Democracy, are one and the same, sir; synonymous terms, sir."[10] Never lukewarm in his feelings, he was an aggressive opponent when aroused, and his anger was legendary.

Yet Benton the politician and Benton the family man were two different creatures, for the man his enemies called "the Missouri demagogue" was courtly and affable with his friends, gentle and tender with his wife and children. In fact, his character softened so markedly that he was known as "the public lion and the private lamb." Even bitter political enemies like John Quincy Adams were disarmed by his obvious affection for his family.

Although many congressmen, considering Washington unsuitable for family life, left their wives and children safely in their home districts, the Benton family regularly stayed in Washington while the Senate was in session—ordinarily from December to early March or, in alternate years, until July.

Curious, impulsive, and ceaselessly energetic, Jessie was inevitably the leader, the prankster, the troublemaker among the Benton brood in their crowded boardinghouse rooms. "I was called 'Tom-boy,' " she admitted, "and never had an untorn dress."[11] Yet under her father's approving eye, she flourished. Still, it was perhaps to spare Elizabeth Benton's fragile nerves, as well as because he relished his daughter's company, that Thomas Benton took Jessie with him on his political rounds.

Jessie regularly accompanied her father to the Capitol. While Benton attended to his senatorial duties, he would "pasture" her in the Library of Congress, then housed in the Capitol between the House and Senate. Under the kindly eye of the congressional librarian, she was left to browse among the books and folios in the comfortable reading room, cozily furnished with sofas, mahogany tables and desks, and a Brussels carpet. The core of the library was Thomas Jefferson's four-thousand-volume collection, purchased from the destitute ex-president at a bargain price. Jessie could inspect Jefferson's books, with marginal comments in his own round, delicate hand, but she most enjoyed the library's volumes of Audubon bird plates and portfolios of French engravings. At home, too, she was a companion to her father. "At all times I had the right . . . to go into my father's library, where walls of books rose to the ceiling on every side." If she was quiet, she could stay as long as she liked.[12]

When Jessie and Eliza reached school age, Benton employed a series of tutors to give them lessons. Still, he supervised their studies himself, giving particular emphasis to history, geography, writing, and languages. In a time of rote memorization, he condemned "parroting" and insisted that his daughters discuss and question their work. Pinpointing the mental character of each, he nicknamed the dutiful Eliza "Memory" and the more speculative Jessie "Imagination," for while Eliza plodded steadily ahead, Jessie "would leap to conclusions."[13] Her mother, noting her second daughter's penchant for causes, called her "Don Quixote."

During the winter of 1835–36, when Jessie was eleven, they were joined in their studies by their cousin Sally, the bright, earnest daughter of their mother's brother, James McDowell, Jr., of Virginia. Fourteen-year-old Sally was soon writing home with news of French, guitar, and dancing lessons. Like Jessie, she doted on Thomas Benton. "Uncle Benton is very, very kind," she told her mother, "and I believe loves me more and more each day."[14]

Benton supervised his children's health as thoroughly as he did their education, and the regimen he devised for them was considered eccentric, even outrageous, by friends and relatives. His daughters wore sturdy high-topped walking shoes rather than fashionable slippers, ate plain meals without rich sauces or desserts, and slept, well-bundled in woolen nightgowns and blankets, on fresh straw mattresses, with windows wide open summer and winter. Benton even installed an exercise ring on the nursery ceiling for Eliza, whose stooped shoulders and tubercular cough concerned him. After several years of daily swinging, she was nearly as robust as Jessie.

Despite their plain diet, dinner at five, the usual hour in Washington, was a convivial meal. Dressed in fresh clothes, the Benton children would gather in the parlor at least fifteen minutes beforehand to await their father's return from the Senate. The Bentons shared a table with other boardinghouse tenants—congressmen like Franklin Pierce and James Polk— as well as frequent guests—Jacksonians James Buchanan, Martin Van Buren, and the brilliant Washington *Globe* editor Francis Blair and his family. The talk was always lively, and children could participate. Even strictly raised Sally, shy and proper, found herself joining in one spirited discussion on dueling before she suddenly remembered her place. Jessie, passionate and alert, was less hesitant. "Anything agreeable we saved to tell then," she remembered, "and were listened to."[15]

Despite her exposure to Washington's crude glamour, Jessie's childhood world, bound by her father's love, was warm and secure. In Jacksonian America, many parents, particularly passionate democrats like Thomas Benton, rejected the puritan doctrine of infant depravity for the more optimistic view that children were innocent creatures who should be allowed to develop freely, guided by love rather than fear. The results were controversial. "Baby citizens are allowed to run wild as the Snake Indians," reported a shocked foreigner. English writer Harriet Martineau, more sympathetic to the new democracy, admitted that American children could be "spoiled, pert, and selfish" but found they had "the advantage of the best possible early discipline; that of activity and self-dependence."

Most observers agreed that American boys were "much more spoiled than the girls," for it was the male child who benefited most fully from the new optimism.[16] While boys were urged to become ambitious and self-reliant in order to succeed in an increasingly open and competitive society, girls, relegated to the domestic sphere, were still taught the virtues of purity, piety, and passivity.

Jessie was an exception. Given a son's place, she was encouraged to be active, independent, and resourceful. The fact that her father preferred her high spirits to her sister Eliza's docility reinforced these traits. Yet even within her own family she faced opposition. At Cherry Grove, her mother's Virginia home, she was the misfit, the child who did not quite belong.

3

Now little girls should never climb,
And Sophy won't another time
For when upon the highest rail
Her frock was caught upon a nail,
She lost her hold, and sad to tell,
Was hurt and bruis'd—for down she fell.

Rhymes for the Nursery
1837

Thomas Hart Benton. *Courtesy of Southwest Museum, Los Angeles.*

THE LESSONS
OF GEOGRAPHY

EVERY OTHER YEAR, when Congress adjourned in July, too late in the season for the long trek to St. Louis, the Benton family traveled south to Cherry Grove for a six-month stay. To Elizabeth Benton it was always a journey home, for she never lost her deep attachment to "Mama" and "Papa" and the Blue Ridge mountain valley where the McDowell family had lived for five generations. Jessie made the journey less easily, for Cherry Grove, despite its comforts and country pleasures, was an alien world.

Traveling first to Fredericksburg, Virginia, by public coach, they were met by trusted McDowell family slaves, bringing "Cinderella's Pumpkin," the elegant yellow carriage Elizabeth Benton had used as a young belle. Crowded into the carriage, with a mule-drawn baggage wagon following behind, they traveled through the Virginia countryside, stopping en route to visit relatives at their great estates before following the winding road up into the cool heights of the Blue Ridge.

Descending into Rockbridge County, the narrow, isolated valley where Cherry Grove was located, the road was so steep that the back wheels of the carriage had to be locked with special brakes to take the weight off the horses. Though wolves howled on the ridges, the valley itself was pastoral, checkered with rolling fields of grain, peach and apple orchards, and upland meadows where cattle grazed. Its inhabitants were hardworking Scotch-Irish like the McDowells, earnest, moral people who clung tenaciously to a stern Calvinist faith.

The McDowells were among the valley's most prosperous citizens as well as its first settlers. They still owned the land they had acquired a hundred years before, a tract whose boundaries, at least in Jessie's childhood imagination, extended "from the intersection of the two streams to the tops of all the mountains in sight." By Jessie's day, their way of life had become "fixed and unchanging." Among them, she observed, "everything had so long been going along in an established way that it was small wonder they believed in predestination."[1]

Cherry Grove was a sizable estate, a self-contained community supplying most of its own needs. The large white house, approached through a double row of cherry trees, was surrounded by well-manicured lawns and formal gardens where peacocks strutted. Nearby, masked by tall privet and holly hedges, were the quarters of the household slaves. Beyond fields of grain and tobacco, on a ragged street a mile from the house, stood additional slave cabins as well as shops where the estate blacksmith, cobbler, wagonmaker, and weavers worked.

At Cherry Grove, the Benton children followed a well-regulated routine, supervised by an assortment of nurses and governesses, with a black "mammy" for the youngest. The day began as it ended with family prayers, then lessons for Jessie and her sisters with a governess. Meals were dignified formal affairs, presided over by Grandfather James McDowell, a tall, stern man who disliked Jessie's "sudden, noisy ways." Her grandmother, in contrast, was warm and gentle, "feeling her yoke yet bearing it as inevitable" in her husband's somber household.[2]

In the grave, upright McDowell family, Jessie was considered wild and unmanageable. Adventurous, boisterous, rebellious, she seemed unable to resist bouncing on plump feather beds, sliding on polished wood floors, putting an occasional toad down her strict English governess's back, or when she was older, reading forbidden novels aloud to the overseer's daughter.

When relatives visited Cherry Grove, Jessie and her sisters, wearing starched white linen dresses, frilled pantalets, and dainty slippers laced with ribbons, would be exhibited for family scrutiny. Jessie always felt reproved. As soon as she could, she would change back into the sturdy leather shoes her father preferred, not only because she could run and play in them but because she knew her conservative southern relatives scorned them as "Jefferson shoes," worn only by poor whites and slaves. Jessie, who dimly understood that her father shared Jefferson's more egalitarian views, returned to them proudly, as a badge of her own emerging convictions.

Jessie felt more comfortable outside the orderly house, playing with her sisters in the oak grove or climbing one of the giant sycamore trees on the estate. Whenever she could, she escaped her governess's supervision to play with the slave children, hunting for duck eggs, climbing the cherry trees to their tops for the best fruit, playing seesaw with a board improvised over a fence. When she stayed with her uncle, James McDowell, Jr., and his family on their nearby estate, she and a boy cousin would sometimes slip away to the slave cabins in the evening. Taken onto the cook's generous lap, she would listen to banjo music and songs of freedom in a promised land.[3]

While slavery existed in both Washington and Missouri, it was at Cherry Grove that Jessie experienced a way of life based on the system. Her Grandfather McDowell owned forty slaves worth thirteen thousand dollars when he died in 1835. Yet the McDowell family was deeply ambivalent about slavery, for their religious principles caused them to question the system. Elizabeth Benton was the most opposed. When she inherited slaves from her father, she gave them their freedom, Jessie explained, "because of her conscientious feeling on the subject. . . . then maintained them and their children until they were self-supporting."[4]

Sally's father, scholarly, Princeton-educated James McDowell, Jr., shared his sister's convictions, and as a young state legislator spoke out publicly against slavery. In the summer of 1831, when Jessie was seven, the bloody Nat Turner slave rebellion panicked the South. The following winter, during an extraordinary debate in the Virginia legislature, McDowell and other reformers attacked slavery and urged a system of gradual emancipation.

Spectators thronged the state capitol designed by Thomas Jefferson to hear Patrick Henry's grandson deride "that Fanfaronade about the natural equality of man" and McDowell present a moving rebuttal. "You may place the slave where you please—you may dry up . . . the fountains of his feeling, the springs of his thought . . . you may yoke him to your labors as the ox which liveth only to work and worketh only to live . . . you may do this and the idea that he was born to be free will survive it all."[5]

Though a resolution condemning slavery was passed by a slim majority during this unique legislative session, no concrete steps were taken to dismantle the system. The proslavery forces grew stronger as the South's slave-based cotton economy prospered, and men like McDowell fell silent. Nonetheless, Jessie's later abolitionism was firmly rooted in her experience at Cherry Grove and in her mother and uncle's early opposition to slavery.

Jessie was happiest when her father was at Cherry Grove, for then her world expanded. "I stuck to him like a pet doggie and trotted everywhere with him." They often went hunting in the country fields far from the house, Jessie hurrying to keep up with his long strides, proud to carry the game bag where the still-warm quail were stored. At noon they would settle under a spreading apple tree to lunch on biscuits and apples. Leaning against her father's shoulder, she would listen dreamily as he read tales of daring and adventure from Homer or the *Arabian Nights*.[6]

As Jessie grew older, she longed for a larger, freer life than Cherry Grove allowed. Slavery weighed on her heart, while the constraints of young ladyhood seemed to tighten around her with each passing year, like the bruising corsets she would soon have to wear. To run, to shout, to climb trees—all were forbidden activities for a proper young woman.

Yet Cherry Grove was only one of Jessie's worlds. St. Louis, her western home, offered an alternative. From the moment the specially hired coach jolted to a stop at their Washington door and the Benton family clambered aboard, Jessie relished this expedition to the frontier, where the possibilities of life seemed as boundless as the prairie that stretched westward beyond town, farther than the eye could see.

Their journey began in solitude as the lone coach rumbled across Maryland toward the sparsely settled Alleghenies. They entered the mountains just as spring touched the land and found the region like a wild garden, thick with cedar, pine, oak, and beech; blooming with rhododendron, azalea, and mountain laurel. In sheltered nooks they sometimes glimpsed the fresh green of early wheat and the pink of peach trees in bloom, but settlements were few, and the road led mainly through dark pine forests.

Yet even here the careless expansionism of nineteenth-century America had left its mark, for they could see felled trees lying scorched and mutilated by the road, and desolate farmhouses abandoned by settlers who had moved farther west. "America," remarked Englishwoman Frances Trollope, who traveled the same route in 1830, "is a vast continent, by far the greater part of which is still in the state in which nature left it, and a busy, bustling, industrious population, hacking and hewing their way through it."[7]

During the day, when the family stopped to rest, Benton often pulled out a small English valise filled with books and maps—a kind of portable schoolroom—that always accompanied them on their travels. The senator made few concessions to youth, and some of the books he used were difficult for the children to understand. "Yet we grew into them," Jessie said. "Especially we never got away from Plutarch and the *Iliad*. The gods and goddesses descended on us everywhere."[8]

At Wheeling, already grimy from coal dust, Jessie caught her first glimpse of the Ohio River, blue and limpid in the spring sunlight. Here the Bentons boarded the first of a series of steamboats that would take them on a long, roundabout journey to Louisville and New Orleans, then back upriver to St. Louis.

On board Jessie found the full panoply of American types, from gamblers and adventurers to Yankee peddlers, immigrant families, and slave dealers with their chained human cargo. Conditions aboard were often far from luxurious. "I would infinitely prefer sharing the apartment of a party of well conditioned pigs" than be confined to the cabin of a Mississippi steamboat, pronounced Frances Trollope. "My bed had two sheets . . . measuring seven-eighths of a yard wide," complained artist-naturalist John James Audubon. "My pillow was filled with corn-shucks. . . . When it rained outside, it rained also within."[9]

The early steamboat was a male domain. The few women who ventured aboard were isolated and protected, remaining, except for meals, in the ladies' cabin, apart from the roistering, high-spirited, often reckless and violent life of the boat. Meals could be convivial occasions for talking with all manner of people or the crude repasts reported by Mrs. Trollope, who condemned "the total want of all the usual courtesies of the table." If steamboat manners were rough, they were often deliberately so, if only to emphasize the equality of frontier life. In these regions, observed an Englishman, "no white man can appear without disgrace in the capacity of servant to another."[10]

Though the social dangers of steamboat travel might be debatable, the physical dangers were not. Storms, floods, fires, fog, exploding boilers, collisions, and the constant menace of hidden sandbars, snags, sawyers, and floating debris all made the journey a risky venture.

Jessie was only eleven months old when she was taken aboard her first steamboat. During the many subsequent journeys of her childhood, sheltered though she was, surrounded by family and nursemaids, she still saw much of this vigorous, rough life, with its constant danger and casual violence. In a time when girls were raised to be prim, squeamish, and faint-hearted, it reinforced her taste for adventure and gave her a clear-eyed toughness she would never lose.

Floating down the Ohio, Jessie felt released. She noted that "life seemed easier and more gay" than in the well-regulated, "strictly English atmosphere" of the East.[11] Stopping at Louisville to visit relatives, she found her Kentucky cousins chattering of Paris dresses and the theater, of Mardi Gras and winters in New Orleans.

When the steamboat entered the swift, tawny Mississippi, the landscape grew desolate, with only an occasional squatter's cabin to break the flat monotony of the swampy shoreline. Approaching the Gulf, Jessie could see slaves laboring in the fields of the great sugar and rice plantations that lined the river, and in New Orleans itself, she could glimpse the thronged auction house where men, women, and children were bought and sold.

The Bentons customarily spent two to six weeks in New Orleans, where the senator had legal business, before heading back upstream. If there were no mishaps on the river, they would spot the high limestone bluffs of St. Louis just twelve days after leaving New Orleans.

To Jessie, St. Louis was a "blossoming town" where life seemed a continual celebration. Even with her eyes closed, she could recognize it in the late spring, when the fragrance of wild plum and crabapple "embalmed the air," and "everywhere was the honeyscent" of the locust trees.[12]

Founded in 1764 as a French trading post, St. Louis passed into American hands in 1803 as part of the Louisiana purchase. When Thomas Benton arrived there in 1815, it was largely a French community of two thousand inhabitants, where taxes could still be paid with panther, wolf, or wildcat skins in lieu of cash. By the time of Jessie's childhood in the 1830s, however, it had become a boomtown. The burgeoning fur trade, the opening of the Santa Fe Trail to the Southwest, and the growing river traffic inaugurated by the steamboat had transformed it into a thriving commercial center swarming with life "from its thronged river-bank out through to the Indian camps on the rolling prairie back of the town."[13]

To Jessie's curious and romantic eye, one of the fascinations of frontier St. Louis was its exotic mix of people: painted, blanketed Indians; weathered mountain men in fringed deerskin; Mexican traders in sombreros, red silk sashes, and silver spurs; old French farm women wearing white caps, wooden shoes, and full red petticoats. On the crowded levee she could hear the chant of the black stevedores as they loaded goods onto steamboats, stacked two and three rows deep in the harbor, and catch the sound of laughter and talk as trappers, traders, and riverboatmen in town on a spree caroused in the dram shops that lined the river bank.

The Bentons' St. Louis home was an ample, two-story house overlooking a main square. Broad galleries, screened by locust trees, ran its length on both stories. As soon as Thomas Benton arrived in St. Louis, he established his headquarters on the shady lower gallery. Ensconced in a comfortable settee with a work table and "colony" of chairs nearby, he conducted his political affairs and received a constant stream of visitors.

Many were from the frontier, for Benton's passionate interest was the West, and his dream a nation stretching to the Pacific. American exploration of the immense territory beyond St. Louis had officially begun when Meriwether Lewis and William Clark made their epic four-thousand-mile journey to the Pacific in 1804–1806. Since then fur trappers and traders and an occasional exploring party had penetrated the area between. Still, it remained largely Indian country—a vast region of deserts, mountain ranges, and endless plains. Year after year on the Benton gallery, Jessie listened as mountain men, frontier soldiers, and missionary priests who had lived among the Indians gave her father firsthand information about the mysterious and alluring land that lay between St. Louis and the Pacific.

To Jessie, the most impressive of Benton's visitors was old William Clark himself. A dignified but friendly man who wore

his gray hair loose to his shoulders, he served as superintendent of Indian affairs with headquarters in St. Louis.

Every spring Indian bands rode their canoes down the
Missouri to see Clark in St. Louis. When Jessie was eight,
she attended one of their ceremonial dances at Clark's headquarters, but as the music and dancing grew wilder, she uncharacteristically burst into tears and had to be carried away
and comforted. That year she also saw the old Sauk warrior,
Black Hawk, trudging about the prison yard of the army barracks near town, dragging a ball and chain. Defeated in a last
desperate effort to prevent his people's forced removal from
their Illinois homeland, he seemed "captive but not subdued,"
though he was nearly seventy and weak with fever.[14]

In St. Louis, Jessie studied Spanish with an elderly Spanish soldier. To learn French, she and Eliza were sent to a
small French girls' school not far from their home. Jessie's
grandmother, the widow Ann Gooch Benton, who lived in
their St. Louis house, encouraged her reading. A forceful,
intellectual woman, she urged Jessie to leave domestic pastimes like sewing to others and attend to her books instead.

In the late summer of 1832, when Jessie was eight, she
sensed a change in the air. The bright sweetness of life in St.
Louis "seemed to chill over." "*C'est le cholera,*" people whispered as they waited in dread. For ten years this first nineteenth-century pandemic had made its way across a vulnerable
world. As cases developed in St. Louis, the Missouri *Republican* blamed the disease on "shameful inattention" to cleanliness among the populace. Smugly it claimed, "The sickness
. . . is confined to imprudent and uncleanly people, and slaves."[15]

As the death toll mounted, among black and white, prudent and imprudent alike, Jessie saw wagons piled with coffins
jolting across the square. She was no longer allowed to attend
school or play with her friends. The family diet was reduced
to boiled rice and mutton. Then the disease struck Elizabeth
Benton.

In the hush of the sickroom, if standard medical advice
of the day was followed, Jessie's mother was dosed with opium

and calomel, a mercury poison, and bled with leeches as her fever rose. Somehow she recovered, surviving both the disease and the treatment. For Jessie it was "one brush of the dark angel's wing."[16]

Returning in the fall to her Washington home, leaving behind the usually bawdy, lighthearted town with its strange blend of old French and raw American, Jessie plunged again into another world. Almost inevitably, as she moved from one closed circle to another, participating in each as only a child can, she acquired a broad tolerance, an early wisdom, and an independent spirit. Such qualities would make for a difficult adolescence.

4

*School is the place and time
to humble the pride; to subdue
the temper; and bow the will,
and govern the heart, and thus
make you tolerable to yourself,
and lovely in the eyes of others.*

Rev. John Todd
The Daughter at School
1853

*If there is any one thing on
earth from which I pray God
to save my daughters, it is
a girls' seminary.*

Elizabeth Cady Stanton
Eminent Women of the Age
1868

MISS ENGLISH'S
FEMALE SEMINARY

B Y THE TIME JESSIE reached her teen years, Washington, the skeleton city, was putting on flesh and even a few feathers and a bit of glitter. Congressional families and diplomats were settling there in greater numbers during the latter 1830s, and the social pace was hectic. "The gaiety is increasing and so is luxury and European habits, hours and fashions," lamented one old-time Washingtonian.[1] Residents grew accustomed to the sight of the new Russian ambassador, Count Alexander de Bodisco, bowing showily to the populace as he made his daily journey to the Capitol in a white coach gleaming with varnish and brass and drawn by four jet-black horses. Jessie herself, when she was barely a teenager and still in girlish sashed muslin dresses, attended a lavish children's party at Bodisco's Georgetown mansion, where the favors included tiny white kid gloves and satin bags filled with bonbons.

The tempo was liveliest during the winter season, when Congress was in session. Dancing and whist were in vogue at parties, where fashionable women wore red and purple silk-velvet gowns and extravagant hats. A new dance, the waltz, was catching on, though many agreed with a shocked New England congressman who wrote home to his family, "I do not think the dance would be tolerated in the North nor ought it to be."[2]

While visitors continued to marvel at the extraordinary mix of Jacksonian society, it was generally conceded that the White House had become almost elegant. Guests were served fine wines and French cuisine, though Jackson himself, suffering from chronic indigestion and diarrhea, usually dined on bread, milk, and vegetables even in company.

It was an era of bitter partisan battles, and the nation was divided into two camps, Whig and Democrat. "Abusing Gen. Jackson and marveling at [his] undeserved popularity" had become the fashion, observed a wealthy New Yorker. To Democrat Benton, the issue was clear. "There are but two parties . . . founded in the radical question, whether PEOPLE or PROPERTY shall govern? Democracy implies a government by the people. . . . Aristocracy implies a government of the rich. . . . and in these words are contained the sum of party distinction."[3]

Even Jessie felt the repercussions of party rancor. Her mother's cousin, Senator William Preston of South Carolina, was a bitter opponent of Benton, and his daughter treated Jessie and Eliza with cool contempt. Still, Elizabeth Benton insisted that her children behave politely when they met. Eliza readily complied, but Jessie, who made her father's political battles her own, found it difficult even to be civil. Cousin Sally reported that whenever Mrs. Benton was not there to supervise her, "Jessie's vanity" made her "act in such a way as would be extremely disagreeable to her Mother were she by."[4] All her life, Jessie would remain a partisan. Fiercely loyal to the causes and people she believed in, she would find it almost impossible to forgive an enemy.

On March 4, 1837, a cold, bright day, the Benton family watched from a side window of the Capitol as Jackson's hand-picked successor—shrewd, unflappable Martin Van Buren—took the oath of office on the East Portico. But it was Jackson, looking old and feeble but contented, whom the crowd had come to see, and when he rose to go, it was for him they cheered. Benton himself was close to tears. "For once," he said, "the rising was eclipsed by the setting sun."[5]

Jessie, entering her teens as the Jackson presidency drew

to a close, had imbibed her father's democratic faith. She was also beginning to bloom. Several suitors had already approached her parents for her hand in marriage, and it was clear that she would soon have the pick of Washington. But these early proposals alarmed the Bentons, and in 1838 they decided to send the exuberant Jessie, along with her sister Eliza, to a fashionable girls' boarding school to keep them from thoughts of marriage for a few more years.

Miss English's Female Seminary was located on the heights of Georgetown, three miles from Washington. With a staff of twenty-five teachers, some forty-five boarders, and more than twice that many day students, it was the capital's leading girls' school, patronized by the daughters of its political and social elite.

From the first Jessie despised the school. "It was a favorite place for the daughters of Senators and members of Congress and army and navy people, and there was no end to the conceit, the assumption, the class distinction there." She found that the democratic ideals she had absorbed from her father and from her long stays in frontier St. Louis were at odds with this "society in miniature," where rank and wealth dominated even on the playground. While the more malleable Eliza "gave in to the current," Jessie "rashly" made friends with the girls she liked, regardless of their parents' social standing. She also found the curriculum dull in comparison with her lessons at home under her father's supervision. "I am afraid I did not study much," she admitted. Miserable in the narrow, elitist atmosphere, she "learned nothing there."[6]

Jessie's alienation reached a climax over the election of the school's May Queen. One of Jessie's special friends was Harriet Williams, the daughter of a government clerk with a large family to support. Tall, beautiful, and good-natured, Harriet could play as heartily as Jessie and was as disaffected a student. With Jessie as her impromptu campaign manager, Harriet was voted May Queen by the girls, but the teachers and principal nullified the vote, ostensibly because of Harriet's "constant, repeated, and unconcerned indifference . . . to her studies." To Jessie's disgust, they named in her place "a pretty scared girl—who could not even dance."[7]

Jessie was outraged by the injustice, which she was convinced was based more on Harriet's humble social position than on her scholarly lacks. "Raising my hand for permission to speak, and getting it, I gave the astonished principal my opinion of the whole proceeding," she recalled. But when a "snaky little teacher" suggested that Jessie must be sick, the principal took the hint. "You have a fever, Miss Jessie Benton," she announced. "You will go to the infirmary, and take a dose of senna," a bitter-tasting purgative. "I had to go," Jessie remembered with feeling, "and take the great cup of senna."

This schoolgirl tempest had an ironic sequel. Some time after Jessie's protest, Washington buzzed with the news that Harriet Williams, the deposed May Queen, was to marry none other than the splendid Russian ambassador, Count Bodisco, whose dining room contained so much gold plate that one dazed guest found it "like dining in a gold mine."[8] Then, Jessie observed, "came one of those shameless revolutions in conduct. . . . The girl who had been held not worthy to be Queen of May became all that was desirable as the fiancée of a foreign minister, and from all—teachers and scholars—came a chorus of flattery."

Jessie, chosen to be the first bridesmaid, was taken out of school for the festivities. The wedding party was a strange mixture of youth and age. While the eight bridesmaids were teenagers like Harriet, most of the groomsmen were distinguished older men. Bodisco himself was a short, ugly man in his sixties, with a heavy, wrinkled face, shaggy whiskers, and a brown wig. Jessie's partner was tall, courtly Senator James Buchanan of Pennsylvania, a silver-haired bachelor much sought after by the ladies despite a slight defect in one eye that made him look at people sideways "like a poll-parrot."[9] Sixteen years later, he would run against John Charles Frémont for the presidency.

The wedding was the high point of the Washington season,

reported and gossiped over up and down the eastern seaboard. The ceremony took place on a warm April day in 1840 at the bride's simple Georgetown home. Crowds gathered in the street beforehand to watch the notables arrive: diplomats and generals, congressmen, cabinet members, even the new president, suave, dapper Martin Van Buren.

When the wedding party assembled at last, the guests saw a lavish tableau. In the center stood the sixteen-year-old bride, golden-haired and beautiful in a heavy white satin and silver lace Russian wedding dress with a diamond-sprinkled coronet on her hair. Next to her was Bodisco, his stout body encased in a glittering velvet and lace court uniform spangled with medals and ribbons. Beside them was graceful Henry Clay, a late-night gambling partner of Bodisco, who was to give the bride away. Around them ranged their attendants, including the polished Buchanan and dark-haired Jessie in a glistening white brocade dress "built" by the fashionable Mrs. Abbott, "Milliner and Mantua-maker from London."

At the reception and dinner following the ceremony, Jessie continued to play out her role, acquitting herself so well that Bodisco announced that she might "come frequently to spend a Saturday with the bride." But fifteen-year-old Jessie was exhausted by the excitement, the strain, and the confusion she felt over the marriage itself. More and more she sensed that her lighthearted friend had sold herself to an ugly old man who would provide lavishly for her and her family in return. The ceremonial exchange of youth and beauty for money and position, so wholeheartedly endorsed by the cooing chorus from Miss English's, seemed a crass business transaction in which a young woman had bargained for her fate.

Brooding over the marriage, Jessie took action. One morning she seized a pair of scissors and impulsively chopped off her long, dark-auburn curls. Then she rushed in to confront her father. Passionately she told him that she wanted no more "society." She begged only to stay at home "to study and be his friend and companion," as the French writer, Mme. de Staël, had been to her father.

Benton was horrified. Blind to his own ideals in the words

of his adolescent daughter, he saw only that she was rebellious and willful, and that her jagged mop of hair was decidedly unattractive. While he had delighted in her spirit and energy when she was a child, and had given her the attention and education most men reserved for their sons, he now expected her to be a proper young lady. "Then I learned," Jessie recalled wryly, "that men like their womenkind to be pretty, and not of the short-haired variety."

At fifteen she had reached a crisis in her life. She must now enter the narrow sphere of womanhood, where there was no place for a rebel raising the issues that had absorbed her father in his political career, no room for an American Anne Louise de Staël, living among men as an intellectual equal. The new America that Jacksonians like Thomas Benton had helped create contained a paradox. While its young men found expanding opportunities and greater freedom to do and be what they chose, girls like Jessie confronted a shrinking world. In colonial times women had been vital economic partners with men, sharing in the work of farm and shop. But as America became increasingly urban and industrialized, more and more women were relegated to a domestic role, docile guardians of the hearth, dependent on men for their fate. If, like Harriet Williams, a woman sought money, position, or security, she must marry it. If, like Jessie, she dreamed of action or adventure, she must also find it through a man. Women, Jessie was discovering, were acceptable only as adjuncts to men, in their roles as daughters, wives, and mothers. "Stay within your proper confines and you will be worshipped," nineteenth-century clergymen warned American women. "Step outside and you will cease to exist."[10]

5

Do not suffer your hand to be held or squeezed, without showing that it displeases you by instantly withdrawing it. If a finger is put out to touch a chain that is round your neck, or a breast-pin that you are wearing, draw back, and take it off for inspection. Be not lifted in and out of carriages, on or off a horse; sit not with another in a place that is too narrow; read not out of the same book; let not your eagerness to see anything induce you to place your head close to another person's.

Eliza W. R. Farrar
The Young Lady's Friend
1836

Why have women passion, intellect, moral activity—these three—and a place in Society where no one of these can be exercised? Marriage is but a chance, the only chance offered to women to escape and how eagerly it is embraced.

Florence Nightingale
1859

THE YOUNG
LIEUTENANT

WHILE JESSIE ANN BENTON'S ardent spirits were precariously contained behind the walls of Miss English's Female Seminary, a handsome, somewhat mysterious young southerner arrived in Washington to await an appointment with the United States Corps of Topographical Engineers.

John Charles Frémont was born in Savannah, Georgia, on January 21, 1813, the illegitimate first child of a desperate and passionate union between a faded Virginia belle and an itinerant Frenchman.[1] His mother, Anne Beverley Whiting, could claim descent from an aristocratic Virginia family proud of its ancestral connection to George Washington. Anne's father had been a wealthy landowner, who in his prime was a prominent member of the House of Burgesses. After his death, when Anne was still a baby, her mother remarried. When her new husband began to waste the family fortune, Anne, the youngest, was sent off to live with a married sister, who found it difficult to provide for her.

By the time she had become an attractive teenager, her relatives were eager to marry her off. Their candidate was Major John Pryor, an aging revolutionary war veteran and man of means, whose thriving enterprises included Richmond's finest livery stable and a prosperous amusement park. The fact that Pryor was old enough to be Anne's grandfather seems not to have deterred the matchmakers. The disparate couple were married in 1796, when Anne was about seventeen.

Pryor seems to have been a crude, gouty old man, who was probably impotent. Nonetheless, this loveless arrangement had lasted twelve years when a destitute French adventurer, Jean Charles Fremon (his son would later add both the *t* and the accent) arrived in Richmond to seek work.

A Royalist during the French Revolution, Fremon had been en route to Santo Domingo when an English man-of-war captured his ship and took all French citizens prisoner. His incarceration in the British West Indies was benign enough, however, to enable Fremon to earn money by weaving baskets and painting frescoes on the ceilings of the island's most elegant homes. By 1808, he managed to reach the United States, where he found work as a French teacher in Richmond.

In June 1810, the slender, darkly handsome emigré rented a cottage on the Pryor property. There he met Anne Pryor, past thirty, childless, and trapped in a loveless marriage. Heedless of the consequences, she grasped for happiness. Eventually rumors of the liaison reached her elderly husband.

In July 1811, John Pryor confronted his wife and Fremon with his suspicions. The next day the two lovers fled Richmond, while Pryor published a melodramatic notice in the Virginia *Patriot*. Renouncing responsibility for his wife's debts, he furiously condemned "the vile and insidious machinations" of her lover, "an execrable monster of baseness and depravity, with whom I have recently discovered she has for sometime past indulged a criminal intercourse."[2]

As Richmond blazed with the scandal, the two outcasts headed south. "We are poor," Anne wrote her brother-in-law, "but we can be content with little, for I have found that happiness consists not in riches."[3] By fall they reached Savannah, where Charles eked out a living as a dancing and French instructor while Anne took in boarders. It was in such difficult circumstances that their first child, John Charles, was born.

During the next few years, the family drifted from town to town as Fremon *père* sought work. Two more children were born. Then about 1818, when John Charles was five, his father died. The bereft family eventually settled in Charleston, South Carolina, where Anne probably continued to take in boarders.

Here in this bustling seaboard city, Charley, as he was then called, put down what shallow roots he could.[4] The next years must have been difficult for the slender, dark-haired boy. Money was a constant problem, and the stain of his illegitimacy remained. He grew up an outsider, with both the freedom and insecurity that brought. A part of him yearned for acceptance and for the stability of normal family life. Yet inevitably, he felt resentful toward a society that branded him a bastard. He became a loner, skeptical of rules and deeply wary of authority, relishing his independence and cautious in sharing his feelings.

Young Charley was nonetheless an exceptionally bright and attractive boy, with gray-blue eyes, olive skin, and the natural dash of his French father. When he was fourteen, a Charleston lawyer who had taken him on as a clerk thought him clever enough to send to school under Dr. John Roberton, a distinguished Edinburgh scholar. Frémont impressed the learned Scotsman as well. Under Dr. Roberton's tutelage, he learned Greek and Latin with extraordinary rapidity. "Whatever he read, he retained," wrote his admiring teacher.

In 1829, when he was sixteen, John Charles entered Charleston College, ostensibly to study for the ministry. But as Dr. Roberton himself observed, "When I contemplated his bold, fearless disposition, his powerful inventive genius, his admiration of warlike exploits, and his love of heroic and adventurous deeds, I did not think it likely he would be a minister of the Gospel."[5]

At Charleston College, John Charles at first excelled, particularly in mathematics, and his classmates later remembered both his agile mind and reserved manner. But while young John Charles was quick, he was also restless and impatient with discipline. Moreover, at seventeen he had fallen "passionately in love," as he himself put it some fifty years later in his memoirs. The girl was Cecilia, the raven-haired daughter of a large French-speaking family. Neglecting his studies, he sailed on Charleston Bay or roamed the nearby woods, hunting and picnicking with Cecilia and her brother and sisters. "Those were the splendid outside days," he mused.

But the college authorities did not see the splendor. Three months before his scheduled graduation, John Charles was expelled for "habitual irregularity and incorrigible negligence." To the impulsive, love-struck young man, it hardly seemed to matter. "I smiled to myself when I listened to words about the disappointment of friends—and the broken career. I was living in a charmed atmosphere and their edict only gave me complete freedom."[6]

Though John Charles shrugged off his expulsion, he soon needed to find a job. Again his bright charm came to his aid, for he was singled out by one of Charleston's most prominent citizens, the urbane, politically powerful Joel Roberts Poinsett, a trustee of Charleston College. Jeffersonian in his wide scientific and philosophical interests, Poinsett had recently returned from a tour of duty as the American ambassador to Mexico. Impressed with the quick-witted and likable young man, Poinsett arranged a position for him as a mathematics instructor on the naval sloop *Natchez*, bound for a South American cruise.

John Charles found life aboard ship tedious and confining, however; and when he returned, Poinsett helped him find more congenial work on a geographical survey in the Carolina and Tennessee mountains. It seemed like "a kind of picnic" to John Charles as he tramped through the summer woods, taking time to savor the fragrance of the white azaleas that bloomed along the mountain streams. Part of the pleasure may have been another romance, for later, during the bitter 1856 presidential campaign, his opponents brought out a gossipy story about a South Carolina girl whom John Charles had courted and then abandoned that summer. "I had every opportunity of seeing the *love* exhibited by the couple, on very many occasions," claimed a woman who lived nearby at the time. "He was engaged to her, and deserted her without cause, and the family was very much distressed." During these bachelor years, John Charles, compellingly attractive, left a trail of such flirtations. "I never knew a more fortunate man in my life," sighed a young colleague who had far less success with women. "He steers through life like a Portuguese man-of-war over the crests of the waves . . . & I should be mistaken very much if he is not in love already again."[7]

In the winter of 1836–37, John Charles was hired as a surveyor for a reconnaisance of the Cherokee lands in Georgia. Sometimes accompanied only by a local guide, he traveled on horseback through the dense forests and fertile valleys of the region, where only an occasional Indian settlement broke the solitude. As he tasted the joys of wilderness travel, he felt he had discovered his life's work.

He applied for a commission with the United States Corps of Topographical Engineers, a war department agency engaged in exploring and mapping the unknown regions of the United States. By early 1838 he was in Washington to await his first assignment. He found the frowsy little capital depressing, "a lonesome place for a young man knowing but one person in the city." He felt restless in a town that, unlike Charleston with its generous vistas of the sea, had no spot "where a stranger could go and feel the freedom of both eye and thought."[8]

His first stay was mercifully short. With the aid of his single Washington acquaintance, Joel Poinsett, who had become secretary of war in the Van Buren administration, the French-speaking John Charles was named assistant to Joseph Nicolas Nicollet, an eminent French scientist-explorer employed by the Topographical Corps to survey and map the region between the upper Mississippi and Missouri rivers. In the late spring of 1838, John Charles joined Nicollet in St. Louis for the start of two successive expeditions to the northern plains. His pay would be four dollars a day, with an additional ten cents a mile for expenses.

Survey work in the 1830s was a makeshift science. The equipment was primitive and the work tedious. Nonetheless, for John Charles it was all a glorious adventure. The suave yet warmhearted Nicollet treated him with fatherly affection, while the vastness of the frontier gave scope to his wanderlust. Washington had stifled him, but in the western wilderness he felt at home. He relished the nights on the open prairie, the camp-fire talk of the French-speaking voyageurs who accompanied the expedition, his first sight of a buffalo herd, moving like a dark sea.

John returned to Washington in late 1839, hardened by two seasons in the wilderness. His immediate task was to assist Nicollet in preparing the great map that would display the results of their explorations. As they began work, curious congressmen, hearing of the elaborate project, dropped by to observe the proceedings. Thomas Benton, a leading advocate of western exploration and settlement, was among the most interested.

Stopping to chat with the twenty-seven-year-old surveyor in his workroom, Benton spoke of the need for a far more ambitious survey—one that would probe the lands west of the Missouri River to the Rocky Mountains and even beyond to the Pacific Ocean. As Benton talked, "The thought of penetrating into the recesses of this wilderness region filled me with enthusiasm," John recalled. "I saw visions."[9]

Thomas Benton was impressed by the young surveyor who had earned the confidence of Nicollet. Soon he was among those invited for informal evenings at the Benton home. While John began to share in exhilarating talk about the West with Benton and his colleagues, fifteen-year-old Jessie remained cloistered in her Georgetown school. It was several months before they met.

"I went with the eldest of the sisters to a school concert in Georgetown, where I saw her," John said of their first meeting. "She was then in the bloom of her girlish beauty, and perfect health effervesced in bright talk which the pleasure of seeing her sister drew out. Naturally I was attracted. She made the effect that a rose of rare color or a beautiful picture would have done."[10]

Jessie was equally drawn to the intense young lieutenant with the glamour of the West still in his eyes. Months passed before they saw each other again, when Jessie came home from school on vacation. Seeing her radiantly happy among her family—for Jessie was always elated to escape Miss English's—John began to fall in love.

Looking back after many years of marriage, he tried to recapture his first impressions of Jessie. "Her qualities were all womanly," he recalled, "and education has curiously preserved the down of modesty. . . . There had been no experience of life to brush away the bloom." She had, he wrote, "a soul so white" that it gave him "instant pleasure." But he saw more than modesty and purity; he recognized intelligence and imagination as well. "She had inherited from her father his grasp of mind, comprehending with a tenacious memory," but with it a quickness of perception and imagination that Benton lacked. At the same time her open warmth ensnared him. He found in her "a tenderness and sensibility that made feeling take the place of mind." Gradually, to the lonely and ambitious young man "came a glow . . . which changed the current and color of daily life and gave beauty to common things."[11]

Part of the enchantment was Jessie's warm family life. The Bentons had at last moved into a home of their own, ending years of make-do accommodations in congressional boarding-houses. Located on C Street near Capitol Hill, it was spacious and comfortable, with a grassy rear garden enclosed by walls garlanded with ivy and scarlet trumpet vine. Years later Jessie would still remember winter evenings in this much-loved house, recalling the dark mahogany furniture gleaming in the fire-light, "the shaded lamp and the glitter of the tea-equipage, the fragrance of the large plants of rose-geranium, and the delicate bitter of chrysanthemums."[12] For John, the warm and lovely Jessie, the intimacy of the family circle, the exciting talk of western exploration with the powerful senator from Missouri all must have been dazzling indeed.

To Jessie, poised on the farther edge of childhood, impatient with the restraints of school and home, the dashing young explorer offered a new world. Through him, the future beckoned—romantic, adventurous, alluring. Perhaps she sensed that here was a man who could cross the rivers and mountains and plains that were only words in her father's mouth. She may have dreamed that he would carry out, as she, a woman, could not, her father's vision of a nation stretching to the Pacific. Perhaps she already knew that she had found a hero-worth-the-making in John Charles Frémont. It was not without reason that her perceptive and fond father had nicknamed his favorite daughter "Imagination."

Jessie's childhood had been deeply secure, and she was open and optimistic because of it. John, in contrast, had been bruised; he was quieter, more wary. But beneath her surface exuberance and his restraint was the same willingness to act on impulse and passion. John, an outcast at birth, could thumb his nose at society. In Jessie, he found a woman who was not afraid to do the same. "And so it came," John said of their headlong romance, "that there was no room for reason."[13]

But Jessie was very young, and her parents feared her involvement with a poor army surveyor of dubious family background. The fiction of the day was filled with cautionary tales about girls who were led astray by men like dashing Lieutenant Frémont. "In affairs of love, a young heart is never in more danger than when attacked by a handsome young soldier," a popular author warned her readers. "Oh, my dear girls," she pleaded, "listen not to the voice of love, unless sanctioned by paternal approbation."[14]

Alarmed by their daughter's romance, the Bentons attempted to limit her meetings with John. But "parental approbation" meant little to Jessie, and the two continued to meet, alike ardent and impetuous. For Jessie, who savored the egalitarianism of Jacksonian Washington and the western frontier, and rejected the elitism of Cherry Grove and her Georgetown school, her love for John was not only a passionate impulse but a political statement, the only kind a young woman could make.

The climax of their courtship came the following spring. The newly elected president, William Henry Harrison, had died after just a month in office. For John and Jessie, Harrison's funeral procession on April 4, 1841, provided a convenient pretext for what John later called his "red letter day." Since his headquarters overlooked the funeral route, John invited the Benton family to view the cortege from his workrooms. "The working tables had been carried up to another floor," Jessie remembered, and the room filled with flowers and potted plants. John, "radiant with health and joy" in his best uniform, hurried about, bringing fresh logs for the fire, passing tea and cakes to his guests. Somehow, amid the talk and bustle and somber music in the street, he and Jessie managed to speak privately and pledge their love.[15]

The next day an elated John sent all the flowers that had decorated his workroom to Jessie's mother, a gallant gesture that only confirmed Elizabeth Benton's worst suspicions and galvanized her into action. Long afterward, Jessie explained what she believed had followed: "The Secretary of War, Mr. Poinsett of South Carolina, was friendly with my mother and Mrs. Poinsett was even more so. To her went my mother and frankly stated the case—my extreme youth, only sixteen— and the need for gaining time to dispel the impression" the young lieutenant had made on her willful daughter. The Poinsetts agreed to help, and a plan was concocted. Not long afterward, John "was astonished by orders detaching him from his duty on the map, and directing him to proceed without delay to make a survey of the Des Moines River in Iowa."[16] Nicollet, who was in poor health, protested the sudden removal of his chief assistant. He too suspected a plot, but nonetheless John had to go.

Jessie was treated with equal dispatch. While John gloomily prepared for the six-week survey, she was hustled off to Virginia to attend the wedding of her cousin and schoolmate, Sally McDowell, who was marrying middle-aged congressman Francis Thomas of Maryland. And so it was that while John headed west, Jessie, defiant at her parents' strictures and restless among her staid Virginia relatives, dressed up in her cousin Preston's cadet uniform and created a family scandal.

By the second week in July she was back in the capital. Soon Nicollet, sympathetic to their cause, was writing the banished John with thinly veiled news of her. "Everyone here . . . asks for you," he reported, "even at Mr. B——'s, each time I go there. The young ladies arrived the day before yesterday. . . . *Everything is fine, you are happily and impatiently awaited.*"[17]

The Bentons, hoping their daughter's passion was temporary, extracted a promise that she wait a year before marrying. In their eyes, John was an insignificant young lieutenant with neither money nor proper family credentials. They believed the radiant and clever Jessie could make a far better match.

But nothing could deter the two young lovers. When John returned in early August, "the grass had not grown under his feet," Jessie said.[18] They continued to meet as best they could. Perhaps they strolled together in the public gardens just east of the Capitol, a favorite spot for flirtation. They may also have found a sympathetic friend in Maria Crittenden, the wife of Kentucky Senator John J. Crittenden, who, according to one story, allowed them to meet secretly in her home.

While Jessie's head was full of her clandestine romance, she was launched in Washington society. In early October she wore her first Paris gown (handed down from a New Orleans cousin) to a great White House ball given by the new president, John Tyler, in honor of the young Prince of Joinville, son of King Louis Philippe of France. But if the Bentons hoped to distract their daughter, they failed in their purpose. In the days following the ball, she and John took matters into their own hands.

Elopements were not uncommon in nineteenth-century America, for, like the Bentons, many parents raised their children in relative freedom, then attempted to restrict them when they seemed on the verge of an unsuitable marriage. "An elopement to me was the crowning grace of a girl's life," wrote the irrepressible Peggy Eaton, a tavernkeeper's daughter who had caused a scandal herself by her affair with and marriage to Andrew Jackson's secretary of war. Jessie, too spirited to conform to the narrow propriety of the time, clearly felt the same way. Nearly twenty years later, she relished remembering how "all Washington was horrorstruck" by her runaway marriage.[19] Still, at the time, she must have felt she was stepping over a precipice.

The immediate problem was to find someone to perform the ceremony, for few would be willing to risk the well-known temper of the father of the bride. John first approached a Protestant minister, who flatly refused to marry them. Next he consulted Washington's popular mayor, William Seaton. The genial Seaton must have been puzzled by the young man's visit, for John spoke only in the most general terms about a possible marriage ceremony, without mentioning names. But Seaton, who knew the Benton family and may have suspected that Jessie was the bride, also turned him down. In desperation, John went to a Catholic priest, Father Joseph Van Horseigh of Washington's Saint Peter's Church. He agreed to perform the ceremony.[20]

How and where it was done remains a mystery, for John and Jessie revealed few details about their wedding, particularly after John was unjustly accused of being a secret Catholic during his 1856 presidential campaign. In a letter that year to a close friend who asked whether the marriage had been a civil or religious ceremony, Jessie replied vaguely, "Civil contract only, I should say. It was in a drawing room—no altar lights or any such thing—I was asked nothing but my age—& the whole was very short."[21]

Jessie Ann Benton and John Charles Frémont were married on October 19, 1841,[22] a date they doubtless chose because Senator Benton had just left on a trip to Kentucky and St. Louis. After the ceremony seventeen-year-old Jessie returned to her home alone. The deed was done, but they had yet to contrive a way to tell her parents.

"The possiblity of an accidental discovery is very strong!"

a young colleague wrote John in early November. "Why don't you go, manly and open as you are, forward and put things by a single step to right . . . only act now and you will *soon* get over little disturbances which might arise at first. Nothing very serious *can* happen now more to you—the prize is secured."[23]

John's friend was right that the marriage could not long remain secret, for the Benton name made the story irresistible. Gossips whispered and the scandal spread. According to Jessie's cousin and schoolmate Rachel Walker, John and Jessie had intended to keep the marriage secret for a year but "forgot that after the license had been drawn, it was obliged to be recorded. It was found out the very next day."[24]

Inevitably the news reached Elizabeth Benton. When she heard the story, she must have confronted Jessie, still living uneasily at home, and wrung the truth from her. She also rushed word of the crisis to her husband in Kentucky. In early November, Benton abruptly canceled plans to go on to St. Louis and hurried back to Washington to deal with his wayward daughter.

The senator was furious. He had expressly forbidden Jessie to marry, and she had defied him. Doubtless there was a scene when the angry senator summoned John to the house. Perhaps, as one family legend relates, Jessie—proud, scared, defiant—clung to her new husband and repeated the words of Ruth, "Whither thou goest, I will go. . . ."

Benton remained unmoved. Refusing to condone the marriage, he ordered them both from the house. Although Elizabeth Benton begged that he at least allow a second Protestant ceremony, he refused even that. John and Jessie fled first to Baltimore, or so relatives gossiped, and then returned to stay at Gatsby's Hotel or John's lodging or a boardinghouse on Capitol Hill.

While the blame for an elopement usually fell on the man, Thomas Benton saw it differently. When he placed their marriage announcement in the Washington *Globe* on November

27, he reversed what was an inviolate sequence by putting the bride's name first.

> On the 19th ult., in this city, by the Rev. Mr. Van Horseigh, Miss Jessie Ann Benton, second daughter of Col. Benton, to Mr. J.C. Frémont of the United States Army.

When someone at the *Globe*, possibly Benton's friend, editor Francis Preston Blair, questioned the order, Benton was said to have thundered, "Damn it, sir! It will go in that way or not at all! John C. Frémont did not marry my daughter; she married him."[25]

While the senator raged, Elizabeth Benton pleaded for a reconciliation. Friends and relatives pointed out that Second Lieutenant Frémont was not such a bad catch. "Mr. Campbell thinks Col. Benton's daughter has married a reputable young man, who will be able to support her (he belonging to the Engineer department & getting a salary of two thousand a year)," one Benton relative reported to another.[26]

Jessie's schoolmate Rachel Walker could scarcely believe the senator would banish his beloved daughter. "I am told that Col. Benton is very angry with them both and that she does not visit her Father, but I think it must be a mistake for Col. Benton is more devoted to Jessie than any one of his other children." But James McDowell III, not much older than Jessie herself, believed that his rebellious cousin had gotten just what she deserved. "It is a sad & distressing business," he wrote primly to his father. "I anticipated nothing else from her ungovernable passions."[27]

6

Woman's true greatness consists in rendering others useful, rather than in being directly useful herself, to make others seen and known, and their influence felt.

Dr. William Alcott
*The Young Wife, or
Duties of Woman in
the Marriage Relation*
1837

THE MAKING
OF A HERO

JANUARY 1, 1842, dawned clear and unseasonably mild. Ex-President John Quincy Adams, who had stayed on in Washington as a congressman from Massachusetts, noted in his diary that the weather was the finest of any New Year's he had spent in the capital. As a result, he reported, President John Tyler's New Year's Day reception "was thronged with visitors beyond all former examples."[1]

For Priscilla Tyler, the new president's pregnant young daughter-in-law, it was an exhausting occasion. "I never felt so tired in all my life," she wrote her sister, "standing up for three hours and shaking hands with I don't know how many thousand people." Still, she found the scene impressive. "At half past eleven we ladies took our station at the upper end of the Blue Room while father [John Tyler] stood in the centre (we being the lesser lights), to receive the foreign ministers and the Cabinet, who made their appearance half an hour before the crowd."

Prominent among the diplomats were Russian Count Bodisco and his schoolgirl bride, Harriet, now the mother of eight-month-old Nicholas. Bodisco looked "unusually hideous," Priscilla noted tartly, while Harriet resembled a milkmaid in her fresh-faced beauty. "I can imagine her dropping a curtsy like the maid in the song, with, 'My face is my fortune, sir, she said'; and her face really has been her fortune as regards a fine house, fine carriage, and fine clothes—and fine husband, too . . . for nothing could be finer than Mr. Bodisco's uniform.

It is perfectly dazzling in its magnificence, his whole breast glittering with orders."

At noon the White House was thrown open to the public. "The crowd rushed in—men, women and children—a very orderly crowd, though, and nicely dressed," Priscilla related, no doubt thinking of Jackson's more raucous receptions. "A little after the first rush of the 'sovereign people' came the ladies and their respective escorts."[2]

While Priscilla Tyler was observing the scene within, a huge, awkward-looking carriage caught the attention of the crowd still waiting outside. As it lumbered toward them, many recognized it as the famous "ark," the carriage of Ferdinand Hassler, eccentric director of the U.S. Coast Survey. But when it lurched to a stop and its doors opened, it was not the elderly Hassler who emerged, but Thomas Benton's daughter Jessie and the man she had defied her father to marry. Hassler, a friend of the young couple, had loaned them his carriage for the occasion.

"It took some nerve to drive up in the ark among the holiday crowd," John recalled, not only because the carriage itself was glaringly conspicuous but because their elopement, just two and a half months before, was still the talk of Washington, a city Martin Van Buren once branded "the gossipingest place in the world." Andrew Jackson had been even blunter: "I had rather have live vermin on my back than the tongue of one of these Washington women on my reputation."[3]

Everyone in the gawking crowd knew of Senator Benton's stormy opposition to his daughter's marriage. Some had heard harsher tales as well—of John's illegitimate birth and his parents' scandalous liaison—stories that would haunt John and Jessie throughout their married life. To most Washingtonians, Senator Benton's daughter had made a reckless marriage, giving up the wealth and prestige that could so easily have been hers for the mere glint in the eye of a Frenchman's bastard.

To arrive so conspicuously in the ark was to defy such talk, and certainly on that springlike New Year's Day, Jessie felt more than equal to the attention. Like her flamboyant father, she had an instinct for drama, a talent for playing the scene. Besides, she was deliriously happy. After weeks of anger and recrimination, her father had accepted her marriage, at first grudgingly, then with increasing warmth.

Thomas Benton had been both stunned and hurt by his favorite daughter's marriage. But as the senator slowly reconciled himself to her choice, he found that she remained devoted to him as well. While Benton's love for his daughter was intense, he was an emotionally healthy man, warm and generous in his affections. Gradually he had begun to regard John as a part of the family, and even to glimpse in him the qualities and possibilities that Jessie had seen long before.

And so, as John and Jessie descended from the ark that New Year's Day, the throng outside the White House saw a gloriously happy couple, dazzling in their good looks, touched by scandal yet in some way glamorized by it. Young and untried though they were, they had already begun to display the dash, the bravura, the sense of their own image that would eventually make them one of the most celebrated couples in America. Jessie, dressed stylishly in a blue velvet gown with a narrow hooped skirt and matching bonnet topped with three lemon-yellow ostrich feathers, walked proudly beside her husband, handsome in his dress uniform. Radiant, a touch defiant, they entered the White House, ready to face not only the crowd within but the future as well.

They found the reception rooms jammed. Above the din of a thousand conversations, the Marine Band, playing in the vestibule, struggled to make itself heard. Secretary of State Daniel Webster was there, so majestic in appearance, despite his drinking and debts, that he seemed like "a cathedral in britches" to one admirer.[4] There were other notables as well: the brooding John Calhoun, already obsessed with southern rights; General of the Army Winfield Scott, an American Bodisco in his bemedaled uniform; and of course Thomas Benton, always suave and courtly on such social occasions.

Though Jessie suspected that she and John were of as much interest that day as any politician or general, she was more stimulated than frightened by the attention. Greeting the presidential family and chatting with Washington acquaintances, she was already showing herself to be a witty and entertaining conversationalist. Yet she was only seventeen in January of 1842, and though her talk was engaging and her political insights astute, she was still too young to be labeled "clever," that deeply amibivalent word that was as much a curse as a compliment to a nineteenth-century woman.

Making the rounds of the White House that day, it was clear that Jessie had much to give the young man by her side. Her contacts, her political knowledge, her personal charm were a valuable dowry. In marrying John, she had drawn him into the circle of power, where the future promised more than even an ambitious topographical engineer might once have dreamed possible.

In return, John had more than a little to offer. Despite the scandal in his background, his reserved and courteous manner, lightened by a French grace, attracted all who met him. His piercing eyes, chiseled features, and lithe body suggested the hero to an era steeped in the poetry of Byron and Shelley and the exploits of Napoleon. Moreover, he was, as one woman remembered years later, "quite simply the handsomest man in Washington." There were even some, privy to government gossip, who looked at him that day with a certain respect, for it was already rumored that he would soon play a prominent part in his father-in-law's western plans.

Later that same day, John and Jessie joined the Bentons for a festive family dinner. Soon the senator steered the conversation to talk of the West. Almost comfortable now with his new son-in-law, he spoke, as so often in the past, of the need for a series of exploring expeditions that would trace and map the two-thousand-mile route that lay between the Missouri frontier and the Pacific.

Though fur trappers and traders had roamed the West since the 1820s, their expertise remained in their heads, scarcely known to the outside world. Typical of such men was Kentucky-born Kit Carson, a daring and resourceful mountain man with a photographic memory for terrain. At seventeen, Carson had fled a tedious apprenticeship with a Missouri saddlemaker to join a Santa Fe–bound caravan. By his mid-twenties he had driven cattle to Chihuahua, trapped beaver in the Rockies from Taos north nearly to the Canadian border, and made his way across the southern Arizona desert to hunt game in California's interior valleys. But Carson, like most mountain men, was illiterate. His vast knowledge was unrecorded. If Benton's dream of western settlement was to be realized, detailed descriptions and accurate maps compiled with the latest cartographic instruments were essential. These things John, superbly trained by Nicollet, was well prepared to provide.

Originally Benton and his western colleagues in Congress had hoped that Nicollet himself would lead an initial expedition, with John as his assistant. Recently, however, it had become clear that the aging scientist, who had been ill for months, was in no condition to travel. And so Benton, doubtless encouraged by Jessie, turned to John. Now, on New Year's night, he could tell them the good news. Everything had been arranged. As chairman of the Senate Committee on Military Affairs, which controlled funds for the Topographical Corps, he had been able to include funds in its budget to finance a four-month expedition to the Rocky Mountains. Moreover, he assured them, John would be named its head. It was a rare opportunity, one that would bring John—and Jessie—a first taste of fame.

John would set out in the nick of time, for emigrants were already heading west on their own. Just a month and a half before, in November 1841, the first sizable California-bound group—thirty-two men, an eighteen-year-old woman, and her baby daughter—had managed to reach the San Joaquin Valley after a harrowing journey. Traveling with only the vaguest directions, they had been forced to abandon their wagons in the sandy wastes beyond the Great Salt Lake and eat their pack animals for food as they struggled to find their way over the Sierra Nevada. "Our ignorance of the route was complete," one of them later confessed. "We knew that California lay west, and that was the extent of our knowledge."[5] Even before their incredible venture, small groups of pioneers, guided by what fur trappers or friendly Indians they could find, had followed a more northerly route to the rich Willamette Valley in the Oregon Country. But until these routes were described, mapped, and publicized, only a hardy few would dare follow.

Yet such journeys were the beginning of a powerful tide, a mass migration that would impel thousands of restless pioneers westward in the next decade. Benton, one of the first national leaders to sense this surge in the making, was determined to foster it with all his formidable resources. One of them was now his new son-in-law.

The situation in the West was potentially explosive. The Oregon Country, an enormous region extending northwest from the Rocky Mountains to the Pacific, was held in uneasy joint occupancy by Great Britain and the United States under an 1818 treaty. The area was dominated by the Hudson's Bay Company, England's great fur-trading firm, while American interests were represented by a scattering of missionaries and farmers. Benton saw clearly that whichever nation first settled the region in large numbers would win it. "Emigration is the only thing which can save the country from the British," he warned the Senate in 1843.[6]

South of the Oregon Country lay Mexico's vast realm, including California and much of the Southwest. Here, too, events were moving toward crisis. In 1836, American settlers in Texas, who outnumbered Mexican residents ten to one, had proclaimed themselves a republic and named Sam Houston their president. Now they were clamoring for American annexation, a move Mexico vigorously opposed. Fearful of provoking war, the U.S. government was hesitating, but Mexico's large, loosely held empire had begun to seem both desirable and ripe for the taking.

From that New Year's night in 1842 when John learned he would head an expedition west, Jessie shared in his work. She had already served an apprenticeship as occasional secretary and research assistant for her father. Now, with John, she eagerly took a far larger role.

One of their first joint efforts was the long-overdue report of the Des Moines River survey, which John had been sent on so suddenly the previous summer to separate him from Jessie. Ironically, when John submitted his report in the spring of 1842, it was in Jessie's handwriting. Brief and factual in tone, it nonetheless had flashes of charm and interest unusual in a government document, qualities that foreshadowed the Frémonts' later collaborations. Amid data on vegetation, rock structure, and river depth was a fleeting picture of a road "fragrant and white with elder" and a vivid glimpse of an Indian encampment by a river, with its blanket tents draped over the branches of low-hanging trees.[7]

The spring passed quickly as John and Jessie busied themselves with preparations for the expedition. Relations with the Bentons grew steadily warmer, and sometime during this period, the young couple moved into a cozy room overlooking the back garden in the Bentons' commodious C Street house. About this time Jessie found she was pregnant. Her baby was due in November, just after John was scheduled to return from his western journey.

John left for the West on May 2, 1842. For Jessie, passionately in love, the parting was hard. Elated though she was by his great opportunity, she felt bereft. After the intense intimacy of their first months of marriage, he was suddenly gone, "gone into the silence and the unknown, how silent, how unknown it is impossible to make clear."[8] She could expect no word from him until his return in the fall, unless a chance trader or trapper encountered him at some river crossing or forest encampment and agreed to carry back a letter.

Pregnant and lonely, Jessie grew more listless each day as the heat of the Washington summer intensified. Thomas Benton observed his daughter with growing concern, and one morning he summoned her to his study. Indicating the library table where she had once done her schoolwork, he suggested that she resume her place there. "You are too young to fritter away your life without some useful pursuit," he told her. He needed information about Mexico, and she could aid him in his research by translating portions of Bernal Díaz's *Conquista de la Nueva España*, a firsthand account by one of Cortés's lieutenants. Though Jessie suspected that her father's request was something of a pretext to keep her mind occupied, she eagerly accepted.[9]

In the weeks that followed, Jessie joined her father each day in his study. As they exchanged scraps of talk and gossip between work sessions, their old intimacy returned. At the same time, the exploits of Cortés, resplendent in his gaudy plume of feathers, must have fueled her already vivid imagination and taught her how her own husband's ostensibly scientific expedition could be turned into a glorious adventure.

Then tragedy struck the Benton household. Elizabeth Benton had always been a delicate woman: frail, nervous, suffering from insomnia. Now, approaching fifty, she began to have painful headaches. When her elderly physician was called, he ordered that she be bled. Benton watched uneasily as his wife grew weaker with each treatment. Finally, knowing that some younger physicians opposed the procedure, he urged that the bloodletting be stopped. But Elizabeth herself pleaded that it be continued. By the time she had been bled thirty-three times, she had suffered a paralytic stroke that left her unable to eat or speak. Fortunately, at this point, her physician himself fell ill, and a young doctor was called to replace him. He stopped the bleeding.

For three days Elizabeth Benton lay in a coma, hovering between life and death. When at last she regained consciousness, she could speak only haltingly.

She had suffered brain damage. For the next few months she required constant care. The young doctor appointed Jessie and a servant to share nursing duties. Each day Jessie would try to coax her feeble, despondent mother to eat a little from a savory dish of asparagus or sweetbreads, or take a sip from a cup of beef bouillon.

Benton was deeply affected by his wife's condition. Instructed by the doctor to keep up her spirits, he would go into her room with a cheerful face, Jessie recalled, "then bolt to his own room to give way to the strong man's agony at the realization of the ruin that had befallen that now speechless, emaciated woman." Little was left of the lovely southern woman he had married; the woman, he told Jessie, who had been "my pride." Once Jessie saw him break down. He had just carried his wife to her bed from the couch where she spent the day, when she struggled to speak to him. "So good . . . so kind," she murmured in her broken voice. Benton fell on his knees and wept.[10]

Though Elizabeth Benton lived twelve more years, she was never completely well again. Several months after her stroke, Benton wrote to her brother, James McDowell, Jr., that her nerves were still "much shattered," and she had "tendencies to vertigo." A family friend remembered seeing her sitting helplessly in an armchair, "scarcely recognizing anyone."[11] Another recalled an occasion when she came into the parlor, her mind wandering and her dress in disarray, while Benton was talking with some political associates. Gently and without embarrassment, he had taken her arm and introduced her to each one in turn.

In late August, Benton was forced to go to St. Louis on business. Now more than ever, Jessie was alone. As summer turned to fall, she tended her mother and longed for John. Her baby was moving strongly inside her, and she was afraid John would not return in time for its birth. Her mother's collapse, her father's despair, the dangers of the West that John might encounter, and the risks of childbirth itself all burdened her spirit. Yet she was young and strong. Her childhood had given her a sublime optimism that was not easily shaken. Despite her cares, she awaited the future more in eagerness than dread.

On October 29 John arrived at last, jubilant over the success of his expedition. He had crossed the plains to the Rockies, raised a flag on one of its highest peaks, and surveyed South Pass, the great gateway to the Oregon Country.

Two weeks later, on November 15, 1842, eighteen-year-old Jessie gave birth to a healthy daughter. She was named Elizabeth, after Jessie's mother, but everyone called her Lily. Like most women of her time, Jessie had her baby at home. Though a doctor was no doubt in attendance, there would have been little to relieve the pain of labor but whiskey and smelling salts. Evidently Jessie was brave, for not long afterward John, writing to his mentor, Nicollet, announced the birth of "a fine little daughter, eleven days old today," and added, "Jessie is sitting up and has got through with her sickness very well indeed."[12]

According to family tradition, Jessie, like her father before her, had wanted a boy. John consoled her. One day as she lay recovering from the birth, he came into the room and with a flourish spread the tattered flag he had raised on a Rocky Mountain peak across her bed. Jessie treasured his gift. When she was an old woman living in Los Angeles, it was still among her most precious possessions.

Jessie's joy over John's return gave way to concern as he struggled to begin the government report that would describe the expedition to the American public. But "the horseback life, the sleep in the open air," had unfitted him "for the indoor work of writing," as she tactfully explained the problem. His head ached, he had nosebleeds. Every start proved false. Convinced that he could never write the report, he was ready to give up. At this point Jessie intervened. She suggested that he recount the journey and she write it down for him. Desperate and discouraged, John agreed. "I was let to try," she said, "and thus slid into my most happy life work."[13]

Jessie's mother, still weak from her illness, protested the arrangement. She was afraid such strenuous mental exercise so soon after childbirth would make Jessie sick. Benton, however, had no such qualms. He was delighted that the report would now progress with her energetic help. It was quickly arranged that while Jessie worked, baby Lily would be cared for by a family servant, who probably served as wet nurse as well.

John and Jessie soon settled into a daily routine. "Every morning at nine I took my seat at the writing table and left it at one. Mr. Frémont had his notes all ready and dictated as he moved about the room."

"I write more easily by dictation," John himself explained. "Writing myself I have too much time to think and dwell upon words as well as ideas." He soon discovered that Jessie made a valuable sounding board, for they were now so close that she seemed like his own "second mind." They would often pause to talk over a point. The result, he found, was "a form of discussion impossible except with a mind and purpose in harmony with one's own and on the same level."[14]

Jessie—intelligent, perceptive, devoted—made an ideal collaborator. The hours she had spent on her father's gallery in St. Louis, listening to the tales of mountain men, missionary priests, and frontier soldiers gave her an immediate understanding of her husband's journey. As John watched her expressive face, listened to her comments, and answered her questions, the expedition began to come alive on paper. Jessie could visualize the little band of adventurers, some two dozen men in all, starting out across the prairie on horseback, with their mule-drawn carts, laden with supplies and surveying equipment, trailing behind. Most of the men were French-speaking voyageurs, roving mountain men toughened by years spent hunting beaver in the western wilderness. Their guide was thirty-two-year-old Kit Carson, short and broad-shouldered, with steady blue eyes and a gentle manner. Though he already had a reputation among fellow trappers (Kit "wasn't afraid of hell or high water and his word was as sure as the sun coming up"), he was unknown outside that small circle. John had met him by chance on a steamboat near St. Louis, where Carson had gone to leave his young daughter for schooling after the death of her Arapaho mother. Learning that John was looking for a guide, he offered his services. John hired him at a hundred dollars a month.

The choice was a fortunate one. The modest, steel-nerved Carson would be indispensable to John on his three major expeditions, and their friendship would be deep and loyal. "With me, Carson and Truth mean the same thing," John said. "He is always the same—gallant and disinterested." In turn Kit came to feel that he owed more to John "than to any other man alive."[15]

From their starting point near present-day Kansas City, the men headed northwest across the Kansas-Nebraska plains, following the North Platte and Sweetwater rivers into the Rockies. As John described the four-month journey to Jessie, what might have been only a scientific treatise became an adventure story as well.

Despite the hardships and dangers, John loved the wilderness West, and his joy permeates the narrative. Twenty days out they encountered their first buffalo. "When we came in view of their dark masses," he remembered, "there was not one among us who did not feel his heart beat quicker. . . . Indians and buffalo make the poetry and life of the prairie and our camp was full of their exhilaration." He gloried, too, in the beauty of the prairie, with its clumps of wild roses, sunflowers, and glinting silver sage, just as later he reveled in the "savage sublimity" of the Rockies.

As they moved into Indian country, the tension increased, and at the first Indian alarm, Kit Carson began his long ride into American mythology. "Mounted on a fine horse, without a saddle, and scouring bareheaded over the prairies," John recalled, "Kit was one of the finest pictures of a horseman I have ever seen." The description of Carson reflected a romantic vision of the journey that John and Jessie shared, a vision that transformed a ragtag band of men into knights on a heroic quest. Even the Indians shared in the glamour. To John they were both noble and menacing, and their presence gave the story much of its vitality.

By August 8, the expedition reached South Pass in the Wyoming Rockies, 950 miles from their starting point. Their main work was done. Still, John could not resist a last glorious gesture. For three days he and a few of the men struggled up what they mistakenly believed was the highest peak in the Rockies. "I sprang upon the summit," John exclaimed, "and another step would have precipitated me into an immense snow field five hundred feet below." Here he unfurled the flag he later gave to Jessie, took barometric readings, and exulted that he stood where no man had trod before. Then, as if on cue, a lone bee winged its way into the scene. Nimbly, John turned it into a symbol. "It was a strange place, the icy rock and the highest peak in the Rocky Mountains, for a lover of warm sunshine and flowers," he mused, "and we pleased ourselves with the idea that he was the first of his species to cross the mountain barrier, a solitary pioneer to foretell the advance of civilization." Swiftly he clapped the bee between the pages of his notebook and made it immortal.[16]

Such was the climax of the story. A month and a half later, John heard the tinkle of cowbells from settlements across the Missouri and knew he was home.

While John, with Jessie's help, turned the expedition into a splendid adventure, his German cartographer, squat, red-faced Charles Preuss, recorded a different version in his private journal. To the gloomy Preuss, the food was bad, the cooking worse, the ground hard, and the mountain men a mere rabble. He found the prairie monotonous, the Rockies disappointing in comparison with the Alps, and the touted climb to the highest peak disagreeable. "No supper, no breakfast, little or no sleep—who can enjoy climbing a mountain under these circumstances?"

Preuss also pricked the budding heroes. Carson, he wrote, exaggerated the Indian danger "in order to make himself important," while Frémont was a "childishly passionate man." "There was such a hurry this morning," Preuss recorded, "that Frémont became angry when my horse urinated. He whipped its tail when it had only half-relieved nature."[17] But Preuss kept his sour realism to himself. It was the Frémonts' story that reached an American public eager to believe in the romance of the West.

John and Jessie labored over the report through the winter of 1842–43. By March 1, their manuscript was in the hands of Colonel John J. Abert, chief of the Topographical Corps. The next day, Lewis Linn, Benton's friend and fellow senator from Missouri, rose in the Senate to praise the report and move that it be published as a senate document. The following day a print order of a thousand copies was approved. Jessie was soon reading proofs. "This too I mastered; all the queer little signs that must be accurate, and behold! Mr. Frémont's first book was finished."[18] It was accompanied by an excellent series of maps drawn by Preuss, the first accurate maps of the region ever published.

The report was a unique document. Previous accounts of the West had been either dryly scientific or exciting but factually unreliable. In contrast, Frémont's report combined accuracy with narrative power. It was both a keenly observed description of a western journey by a trained scientist and a dramatic adventure story buffed to a high literary polish. It was also a practical guidebook for the emigrant, with detailed, day-by-day information about terrain, the best campsites, and the availability of water, fuel, fodder, and game.

How much of the report was Jessie's and how much her husband's has remained a controversial question. While John's observations and experiences formed its solid core, Jessie's hand can be seen in the graceful style, the skillful pacing, and the vivid scenes and vignettes that make it so readable. Without her sharp eye for a good story, the report, if completed at all, would have been another dry treatise, to be filed and forgotten. Though Jessie herself, admittedly with a hint of Victorian coyness in her words, called the report "Mr. Frémont's book," she also made very clear that her own drive, enthusiasm, and talent were essential to its completion. Significantly, while John found writing an ordeal, Jessie discovered in it her "most happy life work."

The report was an immediate success. Newspapers throughout the country were soon printing excerpts. Passed from hand to hand, read and discussed, it touched the restless heart of America. The flower-strewn prairie, the majestic mountains, Carson on horseback, Frémont raising the flag on a snowy peak, the solitary bee—all entered the dreams of a nation on the move.

The poet Henry Wadsworth Longfellow, listening to his wife read the report aloud over several winter evenings in Cambridge, found it so enthralling that he considered writing an epic poem about the journey. "Frémont has particularly touched my imagination," he wrote in his journal. "What a wild life, and what a fresh kind of existence! But, ah, the discomforts!"[19]

For younger, less established men, the lure of Frémont's West proved irresistible. In Cincinnati, one seventeen-year-old boy found "the glowing pages of Frémont's tour to the Rocky Mountains . . . so alluring to my fancy that my parents were persuaded to let me go westward." On an Ohio farm, another boy, who would become the California poet Joaquin Miller, was similarly stirred. Years later he remembered (with a poet's license) the report's effect on him. "I fancied I could see Frémont's men hauling the cannon up the savage battlements of the Rocky Mountains, flags in the air, Frémont at the head, waving his sword . . . with unknown and unnamed empires at every hand. It touched my heart when he told me how a weary little brown bee rested on his knee. . . . I began to be inflamed with a love of action, adventure, glory, and great deeds away out yonder under the path of the setting sun."[20]

Such responses, multiplied by the thousands, rippled across the nation. The report struck a deep chord in the American psyche and gave direction to a pent-up energy ready to burst forth. The solitary bee would soon become a swarm.

7

Where is the true sphere of woman?
Where is the seat of her dominion?
*My answer is—*HOME*! Much to be de-*
plored is any circumstance which
draws a woman from this sacred sphere.
I care not whether it be fashion or
fanaticism, pleasure or politics.

Godey's Lady's Book
1844

WAITING

E VEN BEFORE THE FIRST REPORT was published, Jessie was helping John prepare for his second western journey. By now most of his correspondence was in her hand, for, as she justified a task she clearly relished, "second lieutenants cannot indulge in secretaries."[1] This expedition would be far more ambitious than the first. Its main purpose was to survey and map the Oregon Trail region from the Rocky Mountains west to the Pacific. It would be the most important exploring expedition since Lewis and Clark's epic journey nearly forty years before.

In the early spring of 1843, while Senator Benton traveled to Kentucky on business, Jessie and John shepherded Elizabeth Benton, Lily, and the rest of the family over the familiar stage and steamboat route to St. Louis, where Jessie planned to stay during John's absence. In St. Louis, John hastened to buy supplies and hire men for the expedition. Though experienced voyageurs again formed the core of his party, and Preuss once more served as cartographer, John was persuaded to take on several gentlemen-travelers, dreamy-eyed novices like Harvard-educated Frederick Dwight (who would manage to lose two horses before the expedition had been gone a week) and frail young Theodore Talbot (who carried a volume of Byron's poetry in his pack). While eighteen-year-old Talbot was venturing west, Jessie would assume the task of corresponding with his doting mother, a widow waiting anxiously in Washington for news of her only son.

In early May, hurrying to depart, John sent a belated request for weapons to Colonel Stephen Watts Kearny, the austere commander of the Third Military Department headquartered just outside St. Louis. His list included thirty-three carbines, five kegs of rifle powder, and a mountain howitzer, a small but unwieldy brass cannon, along with its carriage and five hundred pounds of ammunition. His party would be traveling through Indian country, he explained, and needed the howitzer for defense.

Though Colonel Kearny was known as a stern disciplinarian, he was also an old friend of the Benton family who had known and liked Jessie since her childhood. Putting friendship before military scruples, Kearny ordered Captain William Bell of the St. Louis arsenal to issue the weapons at once, without waiting for the customary approval from the War Department. Captain Bell reluctantly complied, but the situation was irregular and he was disturbed. Two days later the punctilious captain wrote the Ordnance Office in Washington to question the procedure.

While Captain Bell's fateful letter made its way east, John said his last good-byes to Jessie. On May 13 he set off by steamboat for Westport, four hundred miles up the Missouri (at present-day Kansas City), where his expedition would rendezvous for the long journey west.

For Jessie it was a wrenching departure. Only six months had passed since John had returned from his first expedition, and it was hard to let him go again. She knew she had only to say the word and her father would arrange a job for him in Washington. Yet she was willing to endure eight months of separation for what she saw as a noble cause, conceived by her father and carried out by her husband. "Self-renunciation lies at the root of great work," she wrote long afterward, "and this was to be my part in being of use to my father."[2] Jessie did not so readily admit to the budding ambition that also motivated her sacrifice. She had savored the brief taste of glory the first journey had brought. Now she wanted the full cup.

Meanwhile, Bell's letter had reached Benton's political enemy, acting Secretary of War James Madison Porter. Predictably, Porter was indignant. "This whole proceeding appears to have been singularly irregular," he informed Frémont's chief, Colonel John J. Abert of the Topographical Corps. If Frémont needed weapons he should have requested them "through the regular channels, and *in season*. Putting off the application to the last hour was ill-advised." Porter also condemned Kearny and Bell. "Order, regularity, and system must be preserved," he declared. "I cannot sanction the proceeding."[3]

Soon afterward a long official envelope from the Topographical Bureau arrived in St. Louis for John. "I was so much a 'business member' " of the enterprise, Jessie recalled, "that I was directed to open all mail and forward only what related to the expedition." The letter was from Colonel Abert, and when Jessie read it, she was appalled. Many years later, she summarized its contents as she remembered them. "It was *an order* directing Mr. Frémont to 'return to Washington and explain certain things in his fitting out the expedition. That it was a peaceful geographical survey, not one requiring a howitzer. That meantime another officer would be sent out to take charge of his men.' "[4]

The actual letter, though far less extreme than Jessie claimed, was nonetheless harsh. The usually placid Abert, spurred on by the secretary of war, was angry about the howitzer. "Now Sir what authority had you to make any such requisition," he demanded of John, "and of what use can such a piece be in the execution of your duties. . . . The object of the Department was a peaceable expedition . . . to gather scientific knowledge. If there is reason to believe that the condition of the country will not admit to the safe management of such an expedition . . . you will immediately desist . . . and report to this office."[5]

To Jessie, Abert's letter seemed to jeopardize the entire mission. She saw it as an attempt by jealous rivals to remove her husband from command. "The Report had given immediate fame to Mr. Frémont—then why not the same to another officer? I felt the whole situation in a flash, and met it—as *I* saw right. I had been too much a part of the whole plan for the expeditions to put them in peril now—and I alone could act. Fortunately my father was off in the state attending to his political affairs. I did what I have always since been glad to remember."

Jessie rightly suspected that a duplicate of Abert's letter had been sent to the frontier, in case the original did not reach John before he left St. Louis. Afraid that he would receive the copy and turn back, Jessie wrote a quick note of her own, urging him to start on his journey at once. *"Only trust me and Go,"* she pleaded. Then she sent for Baptiste Derosier, a French Canadian voyageur who planned to join the expedition at the last moment. When Derosier arrived, Jessie explained that she had an urgent message for her husband. "How long will you need to get ready?" she asked.

"The time to get my horse," he replied. Since Derosier would remain with the expedition, he suggested that his brother go with him to carry back a reply.

"Say nothing of this, Derosier," Jessie warned as he hurried off.

In what seemed like a "marvelously short time" to Jessie, waiting tensely in St. Louis, Derosier's brother returned with a message from John. "I trust, and GO," she reported his terse reply.

When Thomas Benton returned to St. Louis in mid-June, he backed up his daughter's defiance by firing off a testy letter to Abert "condemning the recall, repulsing the reprimand which had been lavished upon Frémont, and demanding a court-martial" to clear his name. Seven months later the senator took a fuller revenge. Wielding his power as chairman of the Committee on Military Affairs, he blocked acting Secretary of War Porter's senate confirmation, forcing him to resign. Jessie was jubilant. "I am rejoiced to see," she wrote gleefully to a friend, that Porter "was rejected contemptuously by the Senate."[6]

For the rest of her life, Jessie would boast of her part in the howitzer fracas. She was convinced that if she had not stopped the letter, "the grand plan [for western expansion] ripening and expanding from Jefferson's time . . . would have fallen before petty official routine."[7]

Jessie wrote several accounts of the incident during her lifetime, each more dramatic than the last. They reveal much about her character. In the first place, Abert's letter was far less threatening than her alarmed reaction would suggest. He did not mention replacing John with another man, as she later claimed, nor did he order John to report to Washington unless the expedition was in danger. There is even reason to question whether Abert's letter, dated May 22 from Washington, could have reached St. Louis in time for Jessie to get a message to John before he left the Westport vicinity a week later. If Jessie's message was delivered *after* John started on his own, she did not save the expedition as she liked to think. In exaggerating the threat to the expedition and her own part in averting it, Jessie revealed herself to be not only a fiercely devoted daughter and wife but a woman chafing at her domestic role, who relished the moments when she felt she had played a real part in the masculine world.[8]

By now Jessie, John, and Thomas Benton had formed a powerful alliance. "We could count on each other—my father, Mr. Frémont and I, as one," she said. Together they planned the first two expeditions without clearly revealing their larger purposes to the government, which at the time was reluctant to push westward expansion. "I . . . had full knowledge of the large scope and national importance of these journeys," Jessie wrote later, "a knowledge as yet strictly confined to the few carrying out their aim. Even to the Secretary of War, and to Mr. Frémont's immediate commander [Abert], they were only geographical surveys to determine lines of travel."[9]

But such power bred arrogance, a disdain that at times allowed this formidable trio to believe they were above ordinary reckoning. Thomas Benton was one of the most influential politicians in America. As his favorite daughter, Jessie grew up believing that she too was exceptional. As for John, he had deeply ambivalent feelings about authority. Rejected by conventional society during his boyhood, he found it easy to join the Bentons in the conviction that they could disregard normal constraints.

This conviction would be a key factor in the singular volatility of his career. It was already evident in his disregard for any kind of real accountability to the Topographical Corps, not only in planning his expeditions but in keeping financial records as well. Colonel Abert's continual pleas for authorizations beforehand and receipts afterward is a minor but persistent theme in their correspondence.

Such arrogance is often double-edged. John was at his best in the wilderness, where daring and improvisation were necessary qualities. The first two expeditions would have been far less successful under the command of a more ordinary man, a "mere martinet—line and rule—officer," as Jessie dismissed such types.[10] Yet there is a fine line between healthy dissent and arrogant disregard for authority. Daring can become recklessness, and independence, contempt for the rights of others. At times throughout their lives, John and Jessie would cross that line. Believing themselves immune from ordinary consequences, they eventually paid a heavy price. Ironically, the first installment was linked to the cumbersome brass howitzer, for the exacting Colonel Stephen Watts Kearny, who had disregarded normal procedures to get the howitzer for Frémont, never forgot the embarrassment the freewheeling young explorer had caused him. Three and a half years later, when the two found themselves chief actors in the takeover of California, Kearny would have little tolerance for Frémont's willfulness, and they would clash head on.

But waiting in St. Louis in the late spring of 1843, Jessie was still a passionate nineteen-year-old who ached for her absent husband. During the weeks following his departure, she found what comfort she could in reminding herself that he would be home again by New Year's. Meanwhile, there were always visitors eager to hear her talk of her husband's grand adventure.

St. Louis was obsessed by the West. As the wife of the celebrated Lieutenant Frémont, Jessie found herself a center of attention not only among fond relatives and friends but among the trappers, traders, soldiers, and politicians who came to see her father. The town swarmed, too, with restless emigrants, many of them spurred to go west by the first report. That May, as Jessie began her vigil for John, a thousand pioneers would begin the long trek west on the trail he was mapping. Most headed for Oregon, but a daring few, like John himself, would be drawn south to remote and beckoning California.

In September two Indians brought Jessie a letter from John, written June 26 from the Kansas-Nebraska prairie. All was well, he assured her, although heavy rains had slowed their pace across the plains. They were in buffalo country at last, and amid the endearments he must have mentioned the herds he had seen, herds so immense they covered the whole face of the land. Perhaps it was fortunate for Jessie's peace of mind that John wrote when he did and not a few days later, for they were entering a region of barren sand hills, where they would be forced to drink the putrid water of buffalo wallows, rancid with urine and excrement. "O! that some over dainty connoisseur might taste of it!" exclaimed an already toughened Theodore Talbot in his journal.[11]

"They had gotten on very prosperously as late as the 26th of June," Jessie reported cheerfully to young Talbot's mother in Washington a few days later. Her son, Jessie assured her, would be home by New Year's.[12] But as fall turned to winter, Jessie's confidence began to fade. Elizabeth Benton collapsed with an attack of chills and fever that required her daughter's constant care. Jessie was further depressed to learn that Joseph Nicollet, the French scientist who had looked so fondly on her romance with John, had died, alone and distraught, in a Washington hotel room. Meanwhile, Thomas Benton had returned to Washington to attend Congress, leaving Jessie without his warm support. During the first expedition, she had worked alongside him, translating Díaz's *Conquista de la Nueva España*. This time there would be no similar challenge to her vigorous intelligence. While her husband plunged into the western wilderness, she would remain cloistered with an invalid mother, a small child, and servants to do the daily work that might have provided some outlet for her active nature. Her round of visiting and church-going, of letter-writing and reading, provided little relief from the essential passivity of her role. Her task, so alien to her buoyant temperament, was simply to wait.

In late November, eleven of John's men unexpectedly returned to St. Louis, bringing further news of the expedition. One of them, Henry Lee, had been entrusted with a packet of letters, and Jessie must have been bitterly disappointed when he confessed that in swimming a river en route home he had lost them all. Nonetheless, he gave her a firsthand account of the expedition, which she soon passed on to Adelaide Talbot. "They had had perfect success in all their undertakings," Jessie assured her, "but when they arrived at Fort Hall [a British fur-trading post in what is now Idaho], Mr. Frémont found he could not procure provisions enough & therefore gave permission to ten [eleven] of the least useful of the party to return."[13]

Jessie was determinedly optimistic in her letter to Adelaide Talbot, but the report of scarcity disturbed her. Actually, Henry Lee had spared her the grimmer details. He had not told her, for example, that John and some of the men, detouring to explore Utah's mysterious saltwater lake, had been so close to starvation that they had been forced to dig roots and slaughter one of their horses for food.

By the time Jessie received Lee's report, John had crossed through the rugged Snake River region and reached British-held Fort Vancouver on the lower Columbia, near present-day Portland. Though his mission was now officially complete and his orders were to return home by the Oregon Trail, John could not resist a detour. Disregarding his instructions, he resolved to head south toward the vast, unexplored Great Basin of Nevada, Utah, and New Mexico. It was a daring choice, one that would keep Jessie from seeing her husband for many more months.

By the Christmas season the expedition was moving south into Nevada. On December 25, John woke to the crack of gunfire and the boom of the howitzer as the men greeted the day. Later, in a festive mood, they celebrated with coffee laced with sugar and some of their carefully hoarded brandy.

New Year's Day was far gloomier. They had reached the western edge of Nevada's Black Rock Desert, a cold, desolate region of poor grass and soil so rocky that their animals could scarcely hobble on their lacerated hooves. They were wandering now, unsure of their whereabouts or destination. John had hoped to find a way east across the Great Basin, but he saw that such a journey in winter would be risky for both men and animals. There was talk in camp of heading for California, but between them and that golden land lay the massive, snow-covered Sierra Nevada.

Once New Year's had passed, Jessie began to make each day a vigil. "From the moment I open my eyes in the morning until I am asleep again I look for him," she wrote Adelaide Talbot. If she ventured out of the house during the day, she raced home to ask if he had come. In the evening she made a ritual of preparing for his arrival. "I put a strong light every night in my window. Every night I made the little table pretty and put on it the food he would be sure to need."[14]

January passed with agonizing slowness. By the end of the month her nerves were frayed, and she had headaches so severe that she took to her bed. Though her mother and older sister Eliza were often sick, Jessie prided herself on her splendid health. But now, forced to wait helplessly, she too succumbed to illness, the most acceptable way for a woman of her time to express anxiety. Yet from the beginning she recognized her headaches as psychosomatic, caused, she admitted, by "sickness of the heart."

Elizabeth Benton, perhaps reluctant to give up the role of family martyr, downplayed Jessie's symptoms. "My own Mother says I am too young & too perfectly healthy to know all the miseries that attend a separation, & that if I were older and in a nervous state of health this incessant disappointment would wear me out," Jessie confessed to Adelaide Talbot. Even John's mother, with whom Jessie dutifully corresponded, seemed determined to outmartyr her. "My poor mother-in-law has but one living thing to love," Jessie told Adelaide Talbot. "She says, '[John] Charles is all that the grave has left me,'—and should anything happen to him how utterly desolate must she be." Among such lugubrious women, Jessie tried valiantly to remain optimistic. "It is very fortunate for us all that I have elastic spirits," she wrote earnestly to Mrs. Talbot, "for being here I hold a very responsible place & the letters I write my Mother[-in-law] & yourself are I know guides to your thoughts & exert an influence over your feelings." Yet her own anxiety continually seeped through. "For the last two weeks I had become so excited & unhappy for every day, every hour indeed brought a fresh disappointment."[15]

On the last evening in January, Jessie received an unexpected visit from Robert Campbell, a wealthy St. Louis merchant who had supplied John with provisions and advanced him money for his expedition. For twenty years Campbell had been in the fur trade, first as a trapper in the western mountains and then as a supplier in St. Louis. Now he had come to reassure Jessie.

Spreading a map before him, he painstakingly traced the expedition's route home and estimated the day John and his men would reach each spot on the map. "They may have a *tedious* journey," he told her, "but I assure [you] *not a dangerous* one." According to Campbell's calculations, they would reach St. Louis in February. Jessie was elated to have such news from a man she trusted, but Elizabeth Benton was skeptical. "Ma says I believe because it is what I want to hear," Jessie wrote Adelaide Talbot with girlish candor, "and although I do not think so yet perhaps it is the case."[16]

On that same January evening, John and his men were huddled around a campfire on the eastern side of the Sierra Nevada, far from the homeward route Robert Campbell traced for Jessie. Two days before they had been forced to abandon the howitzer in heavy snow; that evening they had killed the camp dog for food. Before them loomed the great mountains, their steep flanks dark with pines, their peaks shrouded in clouds of snow.

A dozen Washo Indians sat with them around the fire. Gesturing forcefully in sign language, the Washos warned them that the mountains were impassable in winter. Instead, they suggested retreat to a nearby fish-stocked lake to wait for spring.

But John was obsessed with California, lying green and golden less than a hundred miles over the mountains. Kit Carson, who had been there fourteen years before, had often described its rich grasslands, plentiful game, and balmy climate. Now, camped in this frozen wasteland, John could not resist its lure.

The next day he announced his decision. They would plunge westward over the mountains. With one great effort they would be "in the midst of plenty."[17] It was the decision of a hero or a fool, a man willing to disregard orders and risk lives in pursuit of his own vision.

For Jessie, waiting in St. Louis, the next months were painful. In February, Elizabeth Benton again collapsed, and for ten days Jessie nursed her continually. Then Lily came down with whooping cough. With sickness in the house and no word from John, Jessie grew more distraught.

In March, there was more bad news. Jessie learned that her father had been injured while attending an outing on the warship *Princeton*. President Tyler, his cabinet, and an assortment of dignitaries including seventy-six-year-old Dolly

Madison, had all been aboard for a gala cruise down the Potomac, climaxed by a demonstration of the navy's huge new gun, "The Peacemaker." All went well until the final shot. "I saw the hammer pull back," Benton recalled, "heard a tap— saw a flash—felt a blast in the face, and knew that my hat was gone; and that was the last that I knew of the world, or of myself, for a time of which I can give no account." When he regained consciousness, Benton saw "two seamen, the blood oozing from their ears and nostrils, rising and reeling near me." The disaster killed several people outright, including the secretaries of state and the navy. Benton, who only moments before the explosion had moved away from the gun, suffered a ruptured eardrum that left him permanently deaf in that ear. Though his brush with death sobered him, the senator retained his exuberance. A month after the accident, Congressman John Fairfield noted that Benton had acquired a new trick. By holding his nose, Fairfield reported, Benton could "force the air through his ear, making a noise equal to the wind coming from bellows."[18]

When she learned of her husband's accident, Elizabeth Benton hastened to join him in Washington. Jessie planned to go with her, but at the last minute she could not bear to leave St. Louis, where John would return first from his journey. Still, she dreaded the wait alone. "I think I shall have to resort to some desperate remedy such as plain sewing to relieve the nervous state I shall fall into," she confessed ruefully to Adelaide Talbot.[19]

By late April Jessie was in better spirits. "The advancing season cannot fail to bring them," she wrote Adelaide Talbot with some of her old buoyancy. "The locust trees by my windows are covered with white blossoms. They look as if they had come forth to meet a bridegroom. I am sure I feel more like a bride than I ever expected to do again, only Lily makes an unusual addition to the wedding party."[20]

In mid-June word reached Washington that the expedition was in California. Their mountain crossing had been a month-long ordeal. "The starvation and fatigue they had endured rendered them truly deplorable objects," reported Captain John Augustus Sutter, the genial Swiss entrepreneur who welcomed them at his Sacramento Valley ranch. John and his men "had a dreadful time" in the mountains, Thomas Benton informed his brother-in-law, James McDowell, Jr., in Virginia. "It required a talent for command to keep 25 men in order in such circumstances, and so far removed from law & civilization," he added with almost fatherly pride.[21] The news of their ordeal was carefully kept from Jessie, who nonetheless sensed from the extra concern of friends and relatives that something had gone wrong.

As the fragrant spring turned to summer, Jessie felt more alone than ever. At dusk couples strolled the shadowy streets while piano music drifted from open windows, where young women played for their beaux. More than a year had passed since she had seen John, and she had no idea where he was or when he would return. Lily was sick again, and her own head throbbed continually. "My usual pain in the head," she called it.[22]

In early August, Jessie went to stay with a St. Louis cousin, Anne Potts, whose husband was slowly dying of tuberculosis. On the morning of August 7, "we were roused by a message from my elder cousin," Jessie recalled, "to ask if Mr. Frémont really *had* arrived?" When Jessie questioned the messenger, she learned that Gabriel, the Benton coachman, claimed to have seen John the night before. Gabriel "insisted he had been waked by a lot of gravel thrown into his room through the open window; that in the moonlight he saw the Captain 'in his uniform and thin as a shadow.' " At first Gabriel had taken the gaunt figure for a ghost, but once he was convinced it was John, he explained that Jessie was at her cousin's helping to care for her sick husband. Learning this, the man hurried off into the night.

Like everyone else, Jessie was skeptical of Gabriel's tale. Her hopes had been dashed so many times that she was wary now. Besides, "poor Gabriel occasionally drank, so he was held guilty of that this time. . . . But it put us all astir."

While Jessie passed the next few hours in guarded antic-
ipation, Lily's nurse assumed the worst. She was sure John
was dead, and Gabriel had seen his ghost. She "mourned
accordingly," Jessie said, "when—enter ghost!—in the life,
but not in the flesh, for he was awfully worn." It was John,
home at last, "thin, brown, and as hungry as I had foreseen."

Later Jessie pieced together the rest of the story. Reluctant to disturb the Pottses at night, John had gone off to await
the dawn. "The only green spot with trees was the open
ground in front of Barnum's hotel," Jessie explained, "and
there he sat on a bench watching for the slow stars to grow
pale. One of the hotel people seeing the uniform came out
and hospitably offered a room when he recognized Mr. Frémont." Exhausted, John slept until late morning.[23]

As the news spread that John was home, friends and relatives crowded into the Pottses' house to welcome the returning hero. But John and Jessie longed to be alone, and
John—or so the family story goes—scarcely stopped to greet
his well-wishers before gathering his young wife in his arms
and carrying her off to bed.

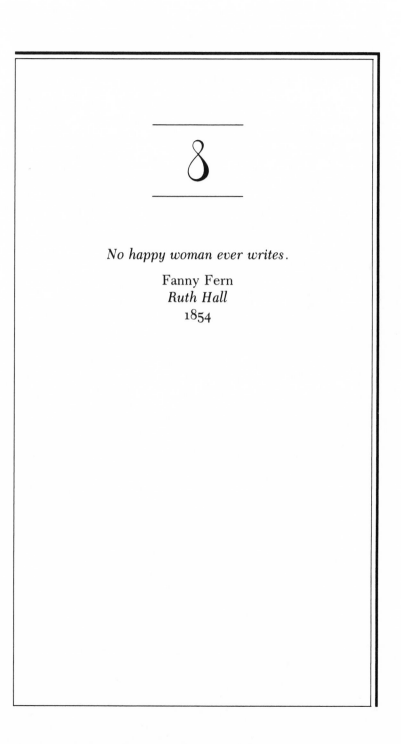

8

No happy woman ever writes.

Fanny Fern
Ruth Hall
1854

"THE HAPPY WINTER"

J ESSIE AND JOHN remained in St. Louis for less than two weeks before setting out for Washington, where they planned to spend the winter. By late August 1844, they had settled contentedly into their old room in the Benton house on C Street, with its familiar view of the back garden, lush now with scarlet trumpet vine in rampant bloom. For Jessie the next nine months would be so filled with happiness that in later, more trying years she would remember them with wistful longing. Yet from the beginning she knew her time with John would be brief, for he was already talking of a new expedition to the West. His intentions were so firm that he had left his pack animals to pasture on the frontier instead of selling them, so they would be ready for another journey in the spring.

John and Jessie soon set to work on the expedition report. For Jessie, this plunge into activity would be a crucial factor in her contentment that winter. After fifteen months of anxious waiting in St. Louis, with no outlet for her restless energy, her talent and drive were again put to use. "Now followed a time of work so delightful in itself, so useful, so undiluted by any drawbacks, that it stands in my memory as 'the happy winter.' "

But John had become a celebrity, and they were besieged by visitors. There were so many, all eager to hear him talk of Oregon and California, that they found it impossible to work in the Benton home. Eventually they contrived a solution. "There was a good small house within a square from us," Jessie explained, "and this Mr. Frémont rented." Joseph Hubbard, a young Yale-trained astronomer who would help with map calculations, was installed on the ground floor, while John and Jessie reserved the upstairs for their workroom. Hubbard protected them from interruptions. "Only my father had the privilege of coming up," Jessie said.

They soon settled into the same disciplined routine that had been so effective in writing the first report. Bolstered by its success and the intense curiosity the second expedition had aroused, they planned a far more elaborate account, one nearly three times as long. Since it was to be presented to Congress by March 1, they had only six months to complete the job. "It was my great reward," Jessie said, coating the truth with proper wifely piety, "to be told that but for me the work could not be done."[1]

From the beginning their focus was California, for John had returned inspired by it. The terrible midwinter climb over the Sierra only made it gleam more brightly in his memory as he described it to Jessie. He had risked his own and his men's lives to reach it, and it had more than met his expectations. Even Charles Preuss, the expedition's sullen German cartographer, had been entranced. "It is true," Preuss wrote wonderingly of the Sacramento Valley in his diary, "this valley is a paradise. Grass, flowers, trees, beautiful clear rivers, thousands of deer, elk, wild horses, wonderful salmon." Both he and John dreamed of settling there one day. Farming, Preuss noted, would be easy. "The lazy Spaniards just scratch the surface with a spike instead of plowing the ground, yet everything grows wonderfully." Even the Indians seemed manageable. "To be sure," he wrote, "they all go naked because it is eternal spring." But they seemed eager to please. "At a dance with which the Indians entertained us," he claimed, "one had painted his penis with the Prussian national colors."[2]

For four hours each morning John and Jessie labored over the report. Punctually at one, a nursemaid arrived with two-year-old Lily in tow. While the maid prepared tea, Jessie had a chance to stretch her legs before they settled down to a lunch of cold chicken, beaten biscuits, and fruit. Afterward there was time for play with Lily, though John, who left home when she was only six months old, found it hard to become reacquainted. "She was fully jealous of him [and] would not be friends," Jessie admitted. "I don't know you," Lily told him. "Maybe if I do I will like you—maybe not?"

"But I am your father," John would reply, laughing, perhaps to cover his own uneasiness.

"I have my grandfather," Lily responded firmly. "I like him."[3]

After months in the wilderness, John found fatherhood awkward and domesticity a strain. Long afterward, Jessie confided to a friend that during these years he seemed to lack "parental instinct." Away five out of the first eight years of their marriage, he remained a wanderer at heart, "only a guest—dearly loved & honored but not counted on for worse as well as better." Like Lily, Jessie relied on Thomas Benton for the stability her husband could not provide. Each time John left on a new expedition, "we 'closed ranks' and became once more the compact family."[4]

But this was the "happy winter," and to Jessie everything seemed better, not worse. After their romp with Lily, she and John would go off together for a brisk walk to the Potomac. Strolling along its banks in the crisp fall air, they were blissfully happy. "A slight rain, we did not mind—only a rain storm," Jessie recalled. "It seems now there was never any bad weather."[5]

Despite their preoccupation with the report, John and Jessie found time each evening to join the family for a leisurely dinner. As always, Thomas Benton presided grandly over the family table, which often included Washington friends or visitors from out of town. Benton himself was especially fascinated by California. When historian-politician George Bancroft, soon to be secretary of the navy, spent an evening at the Benton home listening to John describe his journey, he too was impressed. "His account [was] enough almost to make you think that the Garden of Eden was the other side of the mountains," Bancroft wrote to his wife. "I had no idea that there [was] so beautifully picturesque and inviting a region: destined you may be sure to be filled by Yankees."[6] Even hidebound New Englander Daniel Webster was curious enough to invite John to dinner to talk about California.

Another interested figure was the shrewd new British ambassador, Richard Pakenham, who entertained Senator Benton, his celebrated son-in-law, and other Washington notables at a sumptuous bachelor dinner that winter. While John was no doubt asked about his journey to the Pacific, the conversation must have skirted uneasily around the subject of Oregon, still held jointly by the two nations. The situation was tense. For years American and British diplomats had dickered over a final boundary settlement near the forty-ninth parallel [the northern border of present-day Washington state], but as more American settlers reached the region, expansionists pushing for additional territory made "Fifty-four Forty or Fight" a national slogan. California, loosely held by weak Mexico, was also looming as a source of contention between the two powers, and Ambassador Pakenham must have viewed John's enthusiasm with alarm. "California, once ceasing to belong to Mexico, should not fall into the hands of any Power but England," Pakenham had written his government two years before.[7]

Though the talk at the ambassadorial table was necessarily guarded, the display of food was not: the nine-course meal included soup, bass, sweetbreads, chicken, canvasback duck, boiled ham, oyster pie, saddle of mutton, ice cream, and cake. But if the lavish spread was there to suggest the awesome power of the British Empire, it was nonetheless ineffective in thwarting America's westward impulse. While the politicians enjoyed the British feast, farmers in the Mississippi Valley, discouraged by hard times, huddled by their fires and talked of the rich soil and mild climate of the Pacific Coast. As for John Charles Frémont, he would return from the dinner to work again with Jessie on the report that would convince so many of them to head west.

The Oregon controversy was one of the two great issues that swirled around Jessie and John that winter. The second was Texas. Since Texas had declared itself an independent republic, American citizens, lured by free land, had poured into the region, quadrupling its population by 1844. Texas was eager for statehood, but some Americans, particularly in the North, were reluctant to comply, both because it could lead to war with Mexico, who still claimed Texas, and because it could mean the extension of slavery into the Southwest, where under Mexican law it had been prohibited. The situation was complicated by the fact that the new Texas Republic claimed an immense chunk of land between the Nueces River and the Rio Grande, land that was not part of the original Mexican province of Texas.

Although Senator Benton favored eventual statehood for Texas, he regarded its claim to the Rio Grande as plain theft— "the seizure of two thousand miles of a neighbor's dominion." In a massive, three-day senate speech in May 1844, Benton argued that the immediate annexation of Texas, with its bloated claims to Mexican territory, would bring war with Mexico, a war "unjust in itself—upon a peaceable neighbor—in violation of treaties and of pledged neutrality—unconstitutionally made." Moreover, though Missouri was a slave state, Benton's antagonism to slavery had grown. "I am Southern by my birth; Southern in my affections, interest, and connections," he proclaimed, but "I will not engage in schemes for [slavery] *extension* into regions where . . . a slave's face was never seen." For the sixty-two-year-old senator, it was a fundamental shift.[8]

Benton's Texas speech caused a sensation. Afterward, his longtime enemy, John Quincy Adams, serving as a congressman from Massachusetts, came forward to shake his hand; while Andrew Jackson, dying in Tennessee, took it as a sign of his old friend's "derangement," caused, he suspected, by the *Princeton* explosion.[9]

Like Benton, former President Martin Van Buren, the Democratic front-runner in 1844, refused to endorse immediate annexation. But such scruples contradicted the new national mood, and the Democratic Party turned to dark-horse candidate James Polk. The party platform, like Polk himself, was boldly expansionist, endorsing the annexation of Texas, with its extended boundaries, and defying the British by advocating the "re-occupation of Oregon."[10] When the opposition presidential candidate, Whig leader Henry Clay, failed to support immediate annexation, the nation elected Polk president in a close popular vote. In expansionist-minded Missouri, Benton campaigned loyally for Polk while maintaining his own position on Texas. Though Polk received an overwhelming vote in Missouri, Benton was elected to his fifth senate term by a dangerously narrow margin.

The Texas question marked the beginning of a deep split in the Democratic Party between the growing antislavery wing represented by Benton, Van Buren, and Washington *Globe* editor Francis Blair, and the moderate faction of Polk and James Buchanan.

As if to underscore such changes, in January following the election, Thomas Benton paid an unexpected New Year's call on John Quincy Adams, "the first in a period of twenty-five years of a common residence of him and me in this city," as Adams carefully noted in his diary. Two days later Adams returned the visit. Benton's "wife and three daughters were there," he observed, "and Lieutenant Frémont, his son-in-law." A short dumpy man with a bald pink scalp and weepy eyes, Adams seemed a lonely, aloof figure, still embittered by his defeat at the hands of the uncouth Jacksonians. But in slavery—"the great and foul stain upon the North American continent"—he had found an issue that evoked his moral fervor. Adams opposed the annexation of Texas with equal zeal; seizure of territory rightfully part of Mexico would turn America into "a conquering and warlike nation," he warned.[11] As Benton edged toward this view, the two enemies found common ground at last. As for Jessie, watching the shift in party alliances and absorbing the political talk, she too began to ponder the issue of slavery as well as the morality of America's continental thrust.

In mid-February, as the ice thawed on Washington's swamps and ponds, the president-elect and his wife arrived in town and settled at Coleman's Hotel to await the inauguration. The Benton family promptly paid a call.

James Polk, former Speaker of the House and governor of Tennessee, was a staid little man with steel-gray eyes and a tightly compressed mouth. Though Polk resented Benton's disloyalty over Texas, his manner with the Bentons, as with everyone, was polite but guarded, for Polk was a suspicious, humorless man who kept his own counsel. Like Thomas Benton, he was of North Carolina Scotch-Irish stock, and like Benton, he had migrated to Tennessee, where he made his way in politics as a protégé of Andrew Jackson. Polk had been a sickly child, but he demonstrated an unexpected toughness at seventeen, when he had a gallstone removed in a dangerous experimental operation. Strapped on a wooden table, given brandy to dull the pain, and held down while the cut was made, young Polk survived the ordeal without anesthetic. Though Benton judged Polk mediocre and Francis Blair later dismissed him as a "little mole,"[12] the president would surprise them both; for his doggedness would keep him firmly in command as president, well able to thwart the plans of Benton, John, and Jessie.

Polk's inauguration on March 4, 1845, was marred by a driving rain, and John Quincy Adams noted with sour satisfaction that the new president was forced to give his address "to a large assemblage of umbrellas." Polk played the expansionist theme full stop. Days earlier, Texas annexation had been approved by Congress and signed into law by outgoing President John Tyler. Mexico's reaction was expected to be heated, but Polk nonetheless spoke exultantly of the new state. Oregon too evoked his defiance. "Our title to the country of the Oregon is 'clear and unquestionable,' " he told his audience. "Overbearing and aggressive," fumed the London *Times* when the speech reached England, "the clearest *causa belli* which has ever yet arisen between Great Britain and the American Union."[13] Polk did not, of course, mention California, but in a rare burst of candor, he confided to George Bancroft, his new secretary of the navy, that one of the aims of his administration was to acquire it from Mexico.

It was at this crucial moment, just as Texas became a part of the Union and a determined new president gazed resolutely westward toward Oregon, California, and the Southwest, that John and Jessie completed the second report. By March 1, 1845, they delivered it to the Topographical Bureau, and soon afterward Congress ordered twenty thousand copies of an edition that would combine the first and second reports.

In six months of intensive effort, they had produced both a classic in the literature of exploration and a powerful piece of propaganda that would encourage thousands to head west. More than any other work of its time, it dramatized the West and made it both alluring and accessible to a generation of restless Americans.

The second report is a superb blending of the technical and the intimate. Jessie's influence began with its style, at its best a limpid, direct, seemingly effortless prose. As required of a topographical survey, the bulk of the report consists of scientific data: a mass of detail about the geology, climate, soil, and plant and animal life of the immense region the expedition traversed. Yet what could have been tedious becomes intriguing even to the general reader because the transparent prose renders the journey in such telling detail. John had curiosity and a keen eye: his smallest observations are firmly grounded in the particular. The camus root he sampled among the Snake Indians was sweet, "having somewhat the taste of preserved quince." A succulent buffalo cow Carson shot for the men's supper had "fat on the fleece two inches thick"; the arrows of the southwestern desert Indians were "barbed with a very clear translucent stone, a species of opal, nearly as hard as the diamond."[14]

If such specifics are the backbone of the report, its lifeblood is its human story. Here Jessie's contribution was vital. Without her concern for the human response—for the intimate details of how the men felt, what they ate, where they slept—the report, like most of its kind, would have been another lackluster government document, valuable as science but not as story. What Jessie did was encourage John to infuse his observations with feeling. Far more than the first report, the second is a subtle and at times brilliant synthesis of the scientific and the personal.

The report falls naturally into four segments: the journey to Oregon, dominated by the pioneers moving west on the Oregon Trail; the trek south to the Nevada desert, climaxed by the terrible Sierra crossing; the idyllic California interlude; and finally, the journey home across the hostile southwest landscape.

"Trains of wagons were almost constantly in sight," John observed of their first days on the trail. Some hundred pioneers headed west in 1842, the year of the first expedition, but a year later there were nearly a thousand, accompanied by a hundred creaking wagons and five thousand livestock. In the fertile Bear River valley northeast of the Great Salt Lake, the expedition suddenly came upon a scene "that went directly to our hearts," John recorded. "The edge of the wood, for several miles along the river, was dotted with the white covers of emigrant wagons." Smoke rose lazily from camp fires, children romped in the grass, and herds of cattle grazed nearby.[15] Such scenes of domesticity on the trail were as seductive to some readers as the tales of Indians and buffalo were to others. Families yearning to head west, yet wary of its dangers, were reassured that within the western landscape were oases of human scale, gardens in the wilderness.

John kept a constant eye out for such spots. "The soil of this country is excellent," he observed of the grassy prairie east of Pike's Peak. "Water excellent; timber sufficient; the soil good," he assessed the Bear River valley itself. In the mountainous Oregon Country he found the soil fertile and the grass excellent, though he admitted he had "never seen a wagon road equally bad."[16] Such passages would be read with scrupulous attention by potential emigrants, including Mormon leader Brigham Young, moored precariously at Nauvoo, Illinois, and looking for a western sanctuary for his people.

Yet there was an anguished underside to the westward movement that Jessie understood more easily than John. Most of the women who went overland traveled with young children; a fifth were pregnant on the trail.[17] For these women, the journey could be a bitter trial, an uprooting that shattered the domestic cycle of their lives and threatened the family itself. Young women unencumbered by children often traveled with joy and curiosity; mothers made the trek with more mixed emotions. Jessie herself was deeply sensitive to what she later called "the constantly recurring domestic tragedy of emigration," for she intuitively understood "what loneliness, what privations, what trials of every kind" it involved.[18]

John was lured by the wild, not the domestic West, and there is a tension in the narrative between the West of potential settlement—a West Jessie might live in—and the West of poetry and adventure that John preferred. To him the high point of the first leg of the journey was the detour to explore Utah's Salt Lake. When he sighted it at last, an inland sea "stretching in still and solitary grandeur," he was elated. "I am doubtful if the followers of Balboa felt more enthusiasm when, from the heights of the Andes, they saw for the first time the great Western ocean."[19]

The narrative follows the men northwest through the Snake River valley, "a melancholy and strange-looking country—one of fracture, and violence, and fire." As they reached Oregon, the landscape changed. There were "nutritious grasses and dense forest," and an Indian economy based on the salmon.[20] On November 1, they woke to see Mount Hood glowing in the sunlight. But John was restless in this incipient garden, and he decided to head south into the unknown. By late January, lost and disillusioned, the expedition faced the frozen Sierra.

The narrative assumes a new sweep and power as the men, dwarfed by the snow-covered ranges, made their painful way west. For three weeks, the march continued. By the time it was over, half of their sixty-two mules were dead, and the men were so weak some could scarcely walk.

"Every thing is getting green," John exclaimed of their descent into verdant California. "Butterflies are swarming; numerous bugs are creeping out . . . and the forest flowers are coming into bloom." A sense of rapture pervades this segment of the report—a California idyll. "Our road was now one continued enjoyment," John wrote of their journey south through California's Central Valley.[21]

The account of the two-thousand-mile journey east, skirting the southern rim of the Great Basin, stands in stark contrast to the soft pleasures of California. But almost as if designed to break the monotony of the desert trek, the men encountered two Mexicans whose comrades had been killed and horses stolen by Indians. The narrative becomes western melodrama as Kit Carson and French Canadian voyageur Alexis Godey gallop a hundred miles in thirty hours to ambush the Indians and retrieve the horses. When they returned victoriously to camp, two bloody scalps dangling from Godey's gun, Preuss alone was disgusted. John and countless readers relished this episode in the burgeoning Carson legend.

By the time the men reached northwestern Colorado, they were in familiar territory again. On June 12, "we had the first glad view of buffalo," John wrote, "and welcomed the appearance of two old bulls with as much joy as if they had been messengers from home."[22] Emotionally, for John and Jessie as well as for the reader, the long journey was over.

Despite her inevitable fatigue, Jessie was more depressed than relieved when the report was finished, for it meant the end of work she thrived on. John would soon set out on another expedition, while she remained at home, frittering away her time and energy, waiting for his return. She would have been even more dispirited had she known that it was the last report they would write together. "The happy winter"—that brief time when love and work not only coexisted but merged—would never come again.

9

Separate and individual triumphs are the lot of few women, and those few are rarely happier for them; but collateral triumphs she may have without number. How few have been the distinguished men who have not acknowledged that their deepest obligations have been to a wife, a sister, or, above all, a mother! Let the mind of every girl, especially of every girl of talent, be sedulously directed to this cheering view of female influence.

Godey's Lady's Book
1842

THE VAGARIES
OF REPUTATION

WHILE JOHN AND JESSIE were still at work on the second report, they were also making preparations for the third expedition. Initially, the government had authorized only a short excursion to the Rockies, with a return the same year in October. "Long journeys to determine isolated geographical points are scarcely worth the time and the expense," Colonel Abert had warned John in February 1845.[1] But when the Polk administration assumed power in March, the expansionist vision became national policy.

Polk's cabinet included two men who soon became involved in plans for the third expedition. The first, Secretary of State James Buchanan, Jessie's escort at the Bodisco wedding, was a long-standing family friend and political ally. By now Buchanan was a prim old bachelor, still wearing his spotless white cravats, still flirting harmlessly with the ladies. Though "the girls plagued him almost to death," according to one congressman, there was something sexless about Buchanan, a lack of passion and will. "The first thought that one had in looking at him," remarked Varina Davis, the nineteen-year-old bride of Congressman Jefferson Davis of Mississippi, "was how very clean he was." Even the staid Polk, exasperated by Buchanan's fastidiousness, pronounced him "an old maid." The only thing Buchanan was sure about, Polk sourly suspected, was that he wanted to be president.[2]

The second was a man more to Jessie's taste: scholar-turned-politician George Bancroft, the administration's resident Harvard-trained intellectual. Bancroft was a New

England rebel who had rejected the conservative politics of Boston for Jackson's rough populism. Brilliant and intense, Bancroft was oblivious to social niceties, but Jessie much preferred his sharp, odd talk to Buchanan's bland polish.

During the winter of 1844–45, John, Jessie, and Thomas Benton often discussed the third expedition in long fireside talks. Now Buchanan and Bancroft joined in these conversations, and with their support, John's new journey became not a tame excursion to the Rockies but a bold expedition to the Pacific, where Oregon and California's fates hung in the balance. In early April, Colonel Abert sent revised and far more generous instructions, allotting John additional funds, time, and men for his expedition. Indicative of John's new power, his request for a howitzer, this time made properly to the War Department, was immediately approved and instructions sent to the punctilious William Bell, still head of the St. Louis arsenal. But again there were problems, for the cannon, perhaps by deliberate bureaucratic delay, did not reach John's rendezvous point until after the expedition had departed.

In May the administration-backed newspaper, the *Union*, noted that the expedition planned "to go through to the Pacific Ocean," while Abert again augmented John's orders, giving him the freedom to make "more distant discoveries." This sudden vagueness from the usually precise Abert suggests that the new administration intended to give John considerable leeway because of the volatile situations in Oregon and California. Though the administration hoped to purchase California from Mexico and gain Oregon by an agreement with England, its stance was determinedly expansionist. "The march of the Anglo-Saxon race is onward," proclaimed the *Union* in early June. "The road to California will be open to us. Who will stay the march of our western people?"[3]

John himself was eager to be off. "I am making every effort to get out at the end of this month," he wrote botanist John Torrey in April, "but am very much pressed by business. I find it difficult to restrain my impatience when I see every thing coming into bloom & remember how many beautiful things for us [lie] beyond the Mississippi."[4] For Jessie, who took down his words, it must have been hard to record her husband's enthusiasm for the journey, which to her meant the loss of his company and the work she loved.

Their last few days together were hectic. "I have not been able to find a single quiet hour among my friends," John wrote Torrey the night before his departure, again in Jessie's hand.[5] They had only that day finished correcting the last proofs of the report and returned them to the printer. Torrey's botanical notes, which alone remained to be seen through the press, would be left for Jessie to supervise, along with John's increasingly voluminous correspondence.

On May 15, 1845, John headed west once more. As always, his departure left Jessie despondent, clinging to dreams of his return, when they would be together again, working on a new report. Yet she knew the silence would be less complete this time. John was now well known, and she would be able to follow his adventures, albeit belatedly, in newspaper reports and government dispatches as well as occasional letters.

A month later she could read in the *Union* of his arrival in St. Louis. "The talented and enterprising explorer of the West," as one correspondent called him, had caused a sensation. So many eager young men had clamored to accompany him on his expedition that John had called a public meeting in a large tobacco warehouse to explain the duties of the sixty men he planned to hire. The warehouse proved too small for the enthusiastic crowd that came to hear him, and he was forced to move outside. As he began to speak, the boisterous men surged forward, breaking the fence he was standing on. Mounting a wagon, he tried again, but the shouting and shoving became so great that he gave up and retreated to a nearby hotel. Eventually, John managed to hire sixty men, all expert shots experienced in wilderness travel, but many hundreds were turned away.[6]

All summer long Jessie monitored the swell of enthusiasm for Frémont and the West. The newspapers continued to note his progress, and when the combined first and second reports were published in midsummer, the excitement reached a peak. In Washington both the *Union* and the opposition *National Intelligencer* printed long excerpts, and newspapers all over the country followed suit. The initial government printing of twenty thousand copies quickly disappeared, and in the next few years, at least twenty-two issues and editions—including five in Europe—were printed by private publishers.[7] The reviews were as enthusiastic as the public response. "The name of Frémont is immortalized among the great travelers and explorers," exclaimed the *Southern Literary Messenger*, "and will doubtless survive as long as those of the Sierra Nevada and the Sacramento."[8]

The report's style was singled out for praise. "Simple, clear, unassuming, beautifully graphic; describing what was seen precisely as seen," pronounced the *Union*. The *Democratic Review* agreed. It found the account "seldom paralleled in the annals of adventure, and never surpassed by anything that we have read." The *Review* ranked Frémont's journey above Lewis and Clark's, whose discoveries lacked "the breadth and variety which distinguish his." Frémont's report, it added pointedly, was an "immense collection of geographical, botanical, geological, and meteorological information, mixed up with the details which would enable a general to march an army, or an emigrant to move his family to Oregon."[9]

It was perhaps not coincidental that, in the same issue, *Review* editor John O'Sullivan coined a striking new phrase— "manifest destiny"—to justify that curious mixture of idealism, longing, and greed that would fuel America's expansion to the Pacific lands described in such haunting detail in the second report. As for the emigrants—those men and women who would carry out that destiny along with their own private dreams—they read the report avidly, for both the information and the inspiration they needed on the long journey west.

"In the winter of 18 and 46," pioneer Mary A. Jones remembered, "our neighbor got hold of Frémont's *History of California* [the combined reports] and began talking of moving to the New Country & brought the book to my husband to read, & he was carried away with the idea too. I said *O let us not go.* Our neighbors, some of them old men & women, with large families, but it made no difference. They must go. . . . We sold our home . . . and what we could not sell . . . we gave away & on the 7th day of May 1846 we joined the camp for California."[10]

Many emigrants carried a well-thumbed copy en route and compared their progress with Frémont's. Some used it almost like a Baedeker, occasionally with contrary results. Near Soda Springs in Idaho, where the gas from the natural springs had given John a kind of nineteenth-century high, a disappointed pioneer confessed that he felt "none of the giddiness or nausea mentioned by Frémont, though I breathed it time and again for a considerable time." For those who remained behind, the report was also useful. "Mother and I have been reading Frémont to become acquainted with your route and distances," a New York farmer wrote a brother who had gone west. Others read it for sheer enjoyment. "I have never been so delighted with any Book in my life," exclaimed one enthusiast. "When I have not been reading it myself my friends have, and I really believe it is being read all the time by some one of them."[11]

The overwhelming response to the report left Jessie almost giddy. "Its popularity astonished even me, your most confirmed and oldest worshiper," she wrote John in June 1846. "Lily has it read to her (the stories, of course) as a reward for good behavior. . . . Father absolutely idolizes Lily; she is so good and intelligent that I do not wonder at it. And then you should see his pride in you!" Jessie had received countless letters of praise as well. "If I begin telling you the sincere compliments from people whose names are known in Europe as well as America I would need a day."[12]

Yet at least one perceptive reader had reservations. Ralph Waldo Emerson, reading the report at Concord, detected a preoccupation with image, with what he called a "passion for seeming." "The stout Frémont," Emerson recorded in his journal, "is continually remarking on 'the group,' on 'the picture,' &c. 'which we make.' [His] passion for seeming must be highly inflamed, if the terrors of famine & thirst for the camp, & for the cattle, terrors from the Arapahoes & Utahs, anxieties from want of true information as to the country & the trail, & the excitement from hunting, & from the new & vast features of unknown country, could not repress this eternal vanity of *how we must look.*"[13]

Frémont's "passion for seeming," for "how we must look," was in part the result of his collaboration with Jessie. In telling her his story, he saw it again through her admiring eyes, a distancing that is reflected in the prose. In the years to come, many would regard such self-consciousness as posturing, as the too careful nurturing of a reputation. Already a few had detected an unseemly eagerness for glory in the young explorer. "He appears to me rather selfish," Dr. George Engelmann of St. Louis wrote fellow scientist Asa Gray, who in turn suggested that Frémont wanted "all the scientific glory." But it was the cynical Preuss who suspected that John was after far more than scientific renown. When Carson and Godey killed and scalped the two Indians on the journey home, John's spirits had soared. "I believe he would exchange all [scientific] observations for a scalp taken by his own hand," Preuss observed.[14]

With Jessie's help, John had created an image that at times in the next years seemed to control his actions. Made a hero by the reports, he felt obliged to live up to the image. Eventually some would charge that for both him and Jessie, reputation—"this eternal vanity of how we must look"—had become more important than truth.

Belying such accusations, John, in an introduction to the combined reports, generously acknowledged the help of such scientists as Torrey, Hubbard, and Preuss himself.[15] Yet nowhere did he mention his most important collaborator. He was not ungrateful. Jessie herself would have been alarmed at such public recognition. The work she had done was questionably appropriate for a woman; to acknowledge it openly would only compound the crime. For the present she would remain unheralded, anonymous except as the wife of that "talented and enterprising explorer of the West," Captain John Charles Frémont.

"The Potawatomi Indians paid a visit of respect, yesterday, to Col. Benton, at his residence," the *Union* reported on November 6, 1845, six months after John's departure. The Benton family greeted them in the parlor, though Lily, just turning three, shrank in terror from the strange buckskin-clad men, adorned with beads, feathers, medals, and paint. After a brief speech by Half Day, the Potawatomi leader, "the conversation became general," the *Union* account continued, "and was participated in by members of Col. Benton's family— among whom, we are tempted to remark, was the accomplished lady of a gallant young officer who has already, by his distinguished service to the government in the wilds between the Missouri and the Pacific, achieved for himself a reputation which will be as lasting as it is enviable."

The *Union*'s discreet reference to Jessie as "the accomplished lady of a gallant young officer" was as close as she could properly come during these years to public recognition in her own right. Just twenty-one and brimming with youthful energy, she would continue to channel that drive into her husband's career. Over the years, it would be his reputation, not her own, that would absorb her. Whatever rewards she would reap would come through him. And if he stumbled, so would she.

But in the fall of 1845, reading the *Union* account, Jessie would have little reason to ponder the word *reputation* or its vagaries, although two years later she might have found it fraught with meaning. As she began her third vigil for John, such reportorial flattery merely assuaged her loneliness and fed her dreams. Only the howitzer incident, when she acted so fiercely to defend her husband against what she saw as the envy of lesser men, might have warned her of the dangers ahead, for John would return from California with his reputation tainted by controversy. While some would hail him as the hero who conquered California, others would brand him a grasping opportunist, posturing for glory. Such attacks would profoundly alter Jessie's view of the world. While she would try to dismiss them as the result of envy, they would provide her with a lifelong task: the defense of that fragile commodity that was hers only indirectly, her husband's reputation.

To the *Union* and other newspapers that picked up the story, Jessie, Lily, and the Potawatomi were only a splash of color amid the serious news of the day. The Potawatomi had come to Washington to protest their forced removal from their Iowa land to a reservation farther west. When Half Day reproached the president at a White House meeting, Polk listened politely to his "red children," as he and the press persisted in calling them, but remained unmoved. To him, as to most white Americans, the Potawatomi were only a minor obstacle in the nation's continental thrust. Their claims were easy to brush aside with trinkets and another treaty. The claims of England and Mexico were more disturbing. Just the week before, Polk had invited Senator Benton to the White House to discuss the situation in the West.

The two politicians had been at odds since their disagreement over Texas, but now they were determined to be cordial. "His manner and conversation were altogether pleasant and friendly," the president noted afterward in his diary.[16] Their talk first focused on Oregon. Benton, who for years had steeped himself in the details of the border controversy, was far less bellicose than Polk. Benton pointed out that England's title to the region north of the forty-ninth parallel was stronger than America's, a view that Polk, who claimed "all Oregon" in his election campaign, was still reluctant to concede publicly.

The conversation then turned to California. The Polk administration hoped to purchase the province from Mexico, but two weeks before, the government had received alarming news from Thomas O. Larkin, the energetic Yankee merchant who served as American consul at Monterey. In a letter dated July 10, Larkin warned that Mexican troops, rumored to be partially financed by Great Britain, would soon arrive in California to beef up Mexican rule. "There is no doubt in this Country," Larkin wrote, "but the Troops now expected here in September are sent on by the instigation of the English Government under the plea, that the American settlers in California want to revolutionize the Country."[17]

The usually reliable Larkin would prove alarmist. Mexico itself was in such political and financial turmoil that the anticipated troops would never reach California; while England, though intrigued by the demi-paradise on the Pacific, would ultimately decide it was not worth a contest with the United States. But to James Polk, speaking to Benton on an October afternoon in distant Washington, Larkin's ominous dispatch only confirmed his belief that England wanted California. The president was determined to prevent them from taking it. Benton agreed, although as long as California remained a part of Mexico, he saw no reason to intervene militarily, for he was convinced that California would eventually join the United States as a natural result of emigration. Inevitably, the two men also talked of Benton's celebrated son-in-law and "his intention to visit California before his return," but of the details of this part of their conversation, Polk's diary is mysteriously silent.

Captain Frémont was on the president's mind six days later when he met with thirty-three-year-old Marine Lieutenant Archibald H. Gillespie, who was about to set off for California on a secret mission provoked by Larkin's July dispatch. Fluent in Spanish, the tall, vigorous Gillespie had been provided with fake papers to enable him to cross Mexico rather improbably disguised as an ailing merchant traveling for his health. Gillespie carried a secret letter for Larkin, which he was to memorize and destroy before reaching Mexican soil, as well as a letter of introduction from Buchanan and a sealed packet from the Benton family for John Charles Frémont.

The letter to Larkin reflected the administration's alarm over British intentions in California. Discreetly worded by Secretary of State Buchanan, it appointed Larkin "confidential agent" at a salary of six dollars a day and urged him to use "the greatest vigilance in discovering and defeating any attempt" by a foreign power to seize California. Although the United States did not intend to interfere with Mexican rule, Buchanan wrote, it would "vigorously interpose" to prevent a British or French takeover. At the same time, Larkin was to encourage the Californians to secede from Mexico and join the United States, though he was to use only peaceful means to accomplish this.[18]

By early November, Gillespie was on his way. His meeting with Frémont six months later in the southern Oregon wilderness would have far-reaching consequences not only for the ambitious explorer and his devoted wife, but for California as well.

Gillespie's mission was only one part of the action the administration set in motion after receiving Larkin's dispatch. At the same time, American troops, already stationed in disputed Texas territory, were ordered closer to the Rio Grande, while Secretary of the Navy Bancroft reaffirmed his previous order that the Pacific fleet seize California ports in case of war with Mexico. Bancroft may have displayed the American hand most clearly when he forwarded copies of the Texas constitution, conveniently translated into Spanish, for distribution among the California populace.

As Gillespie set out on his fateful mission, Jessie settled in for another long winter without John. Her mother was again seriously ill, and the fear of another attack kept the whole family on edge. At times Elizabeth Benton would seem almost well, receiving friends in the parlor, taking an airing in her carriage, even walking a few blocks in mild weather on Senator Benton's arm. Then, unexpectedly, she would be felled by epileptic-like convulsions in which, as Benton described them, she saw "the gloomy image of death before her."[19]

Her mother's unstable condition kept Jessie at home much of the time, reading, caring for Lily, attending to her own and John's correspondence. The confinement seemed to suit her mood, or so she assured her husband. "Mother's health . . . gave me a reason for staying at home quietly as I wished, and I have read so much that is improving that you will be very pleased with me." She had received a daguerreotype of him from his mother. "It hangs over the head of my bed and is my guardian angel, for I could not waste time or do anything you did not like with that beloved face looking so kindly and earnestly at me."[20]

Jessie naturally gravitated toward friends who understood her lonely state. She often saw her old correspondent Adelaide Talbot, whose son, Theodore, was again with John, but her closest friend was Elizabeth Blair Lee, whose husband, a naval officer, was frequently at sea. "I never said so much about myself to any one . . . before," Jessie confided to her "dear Lizzie."[21]

The two women had much in common. Lizzie's father, Francis Preston Blair, had been Thomas Benton's closest friend and political ally since Jackson's time. Like Jessie, Lizzie had sat at Jackson's knee when her father, a member of his Kitchen Cabinet, conferred with the president; and like Jessie, she had acquired a zest for politics. Both women possessed charm, wit, and an inner strength some inevitably regarded as excessive.

There were differences, however. While Jessie had a robust vitality, Lizzie was a frail creature whose health appeared so precarious that for many years her doting family believed she should never marry. Lizzie was also far less of a rebel, and when she did fall in love, she waited patiently until the Blairs gave in and allowed her to marry Samuel Phillips Lee. Gracious, restrained Lizzie seemed to like Jessie almost in spite of herself, for though she found Jessie "very amusing and bright witted," at times she seemed "very wanting in taste"—too outspoken, passionate, and ambitious to be quite proper. Jessie herself hinted at such differences in a letter to Lizzie written while both husbands were away. "Is there any thing as selfish as grief, dear Lizzie," she wrote. "You feel nothing so much as Mr. Lee's absence & here I am lamenting to you Mr. Frémont's when I pity you more than myself. I am so much healthier for one thing & then it is with me a sort of penance to wipe out the past—but you are delicate and with you there is no atonement to make—you have been good always."[22]

Until Polk's election, Lizzie's father, the brilliant Blair, had been the fiercely combative editor of the Democratic Party newspaper, the Washington *Globe*. Along with Benton and Van Buren, Blair represented the more radical northern wing of the party, and he shared their scruples about Texas. Like them, he had been only lukewarm toward party candidate Polk, and it was this lack of enthusiasm that caused his downfall. One of Polk's first acts as president was to force his resignation.

The Blairs retired to a country estate, Silver Spring, five miles from Washington. Francis Blair was a skinny little man—all bone, gristle, nerve, and brain, as one friend said—but his energy was formidable. Soon he was planting stands of chestnut and pine, laying out lavish vegetable and flower beds, as well as a vineyard and peach orchard. He also indulged a taste for construction. Along a woodland stream he installed rustic grottoes and bridges, stone baths, a summerhouse shaped like an acorn, and an ingenious water-powered mill that cut hay, threshed grain, pulverized corn, churned butter, and even washed clothes.[23]

Silver Spring was a joyous place: the grounds a trifle overstuffed but nonetheless enchanting, the food delicious, the political talk invigorating. There was even a bevy of ponies for children like Lily to ride. It was here that Jessie came whenever she felt lonely or depressed, or simply needed a change. The hospitable Blairs kept an upstairs room especially for her, and at times she preferred it to her own in Washington, for it held no haunting memories of John. "I didn't much like to come away," she wrote Lizzie after a day at Silver Spring. "It would have been much more agreeable to me to have gone to *my own* room up stairs & stayed there quietly than to have returned to the one here which always reminds me that it was not always mine alone."[24]

Despite her quiet life that winter, Jessie found herself on the fringes of controversy when the marriage of her cousin and former schoolmate, Sally McDowell, erupted into a full-blown scandal.[25]

There had always been something unsettling, unsavory even, about Sally's husband, Maryland politician Francis Thomas. "Every time I see him I fear more than ever that your fancy for him will become so great as to induce him to marry you," Jessie's sister Eliza had warned Sally long beforehand. "Heaven forbid that ever such an event should happen."

Eliza's fears were well-founded, for Francis Thomas proved an unstable, neurotically jealous husband. Not long after the wedding, he charged a Maryland physician with giving him poisonous drugs to "debilitate, disable, and derange" him. At the same time he accused Sally of sexual liaisons both before and after her marriage. One of them, he claimed, was with Benton's colleague, Senator Lewis Linn of Missouri, who had since died.

Sally and Mrs. Linn had not liked each other. "She is a great fat woman," Sally confided to her mother. "Everybody attributes her sickness, fits & all to a dissipated winter, an excitable & constantly excited mind, imprudent eating, & most of all to tight-lacing." At one point Mrs. Linn had accused Sally of having an affair with her husband, a man evidently known for his "excesses." Though she later retracted the charge, this was the seed from which Francis Thomas's obsession sprouted.

When Thomas's slurs reached Benton, the senator was outraged. "Our dear Sally's character requires no evidence from any quarter," he assured her anxious father, James McDowell, Jr. Soon Thomas was denouncing Benton himself as an "unscrupulous demon" who had connived at Sally's seduction by Linn, then schemed with Mrs. Benton "to persuade and prevail upon an unsuspecting . . . man" to marry the tarnished girl. Thomas became so obsessed by this theme that he spewed out a fifty-two-page pamphlet of dark bombast in which he made his charges public.

At a town meeting in Virginia, Sally's supporters attested to her purity and virtue, but Benton and McDowell decided that only by suing Thomas for libel could they redeem her reputation. Marshaling his formidable forces in defense of "injured innocence," Benton vowed to "crush *in toto* this blasted wretch."

The courtroom was packed when the case came to trial in November 1845. Thomas, recently retired governor of Maryland, faced James McDowell, the incumbent governor of Virginia, as well as the burly and implacable Benton, the distraught Sally, and Jessie and her sisters, who were to testify as character witnesses for their cousin.

The trial proved an anticlimax, for the case, mired in technicalities, was repeatedly postponed. Then in March 1847 came a stunning breakthrough. Thomas's three lawyers announced that, as a matter of conscience and without their client's permission, they were withdrawing from the case. They were convinced that Thomas's charges were "mental delusions" and Sally totally innocent.

Gradually the scandal faded. Thomas dropped into obscurity, only to surface again twenty years later as a congressman, while Sally, granted a divorce, married a distinguished Protestant clergyman and lived to an uneventful old age. For Jessie, the gossip and innuendo, the newspaper stories and the sensational trial, would be only a taste of what she would encounter when John returned from California. Then she would endure another public trial centered on "reputation," one far more disturbing to her than Sally McDowell's anguished Victorian melodrama.

10

Woman should not be expected to write,
or fight, or build, or compose scores;
she does all by inspiring man to do all.

Ralph Waldo Emerson
Journals
1841

"I HAVE NO SYMPATHY
FOR THE WAR"

SALLY MCDOWELL'S TRIAL was a savory tidbit for Washington gossips, but as the winter passed, it could not compete with speculation about Mexico. The news was ominous. Though torn by revolution, Mexico remained determined not to yield territory to the United States. In December 1845, Mexico rejected Polk's emissary, authorized to offer up to forty million dollars for California and as much of the Southwest as he could get. By late March 1846, American troops were camped on the north bank of the Rio Grande, their cannons pointed across the muddy stream at Mexican forces massing at Matamoros. But many Americans, including the Benton family, still doubted American claims to the region. Even among the troops there were skeptics. "We have not one particle of right to be here," a colonel on the Rio Grande confided to his diary. "It looks as if the government sent a small force on purpose to bring on a war, so as to have a pretext for taking California and as much of the country as it chooses." The opposition *National Intelligencer* agreed. "Is there to be no mercy, no shame? . . . We talk familiarly of California as presently ours, of New Mexico as a pear nearly ripe to fall into our hands. Helpless, distracted, covered with the disgrace of suffering such things, Mexico lies a victim-people, at our mercy, with nothing to hope but to see her provinces torn from her, one by one."[1]

Benton worked diligently to prevent a clash. Secretaries Buchanan and Bancroft called often to discuss the impending crisis, and Jessie found herself more intimately involved when

Buchanan brought dispatches from Mexican agents to the Benton home for translation. Either Benton or New York Senator John Dix, both of whom knew Spanish, would give Buchanan a rough, on-the-spot translation. Later Jessie or Eliza would furnish him with a polished written copy.

The official state department translator was Robert Greenhow, a scholarly Virginian whose clever and alluring wife, Rose, was an ardent southerner and confidante of John Calhoun. Long afterward Jessie would claim that the formidable Rose had been passing information to the British during those years, and that Buchanan, suspecting a leak but too timid to confront her, avoided the issue by taking his secret dispatches to the Bentons for translation. Jessie and Rose, similar in temperament but at odds politically, evidently disliked each other from the first. Even then Jessie may have suspected that Rose was already whispering in Washington drawing rooms that her husband, as a boy in Richmond, had attended the dancing school of a disreputable Frenchman named Charles Fremon, who soon ran off with another man's wife.[2]

While troops massed on the Rio Grande, more than a thousand pioneers—another kind of army—gathered on the Missouri frontier to begin their journey west. Some heading for Oregon defied British claims by scrawling "54° 40'" on the canvas tops of their wagons. Others, bound for California, showed a similar bluster. "If our government declares war," reported a correspondent, "and would authorize the emigrants to make the conquest of California, they would soon do so." The leader of one wagon train had a more benign remedy. Announcing the birth of twins to a couple in his train, he asked, "If we continue this way, how long will it take to people California?"[3]

In early May 1846, just as the Mexican situation reached a crisis point, Jessie learned that John had reached California. Writing on January 24 from Yerba Buena, as the tiny hamlet on San Francisco Bay was then called, he told her he planned to travel north past Klamath Lake to the Willamette Valley, hoping to find a better wagon route to Oregon. He intended to complete his work quickly. "So soon as the proper season comes, and my animals are rested, we turn our faces homeward," he promised. "Many months of hardships, close trials, and anxieties have tried me severely, and my hair is turning gray before its time. But all this passes, *et le bon temps viendra.*" Jessie allowed the *Intelligencer* to publish John's letter, and it was quickly reprinted in other newspapers, whose readers were evidently eager to read more about the gallant captain and his brave men.[4]

Just as Jessie received John's letter, stunning—yet inevitable—news reached Washington: Mexican troops had crossed the Rio Grande and ambushed an American patrol, leaving sixteen casualties. "American blood had been shed on American soil," announced the administration-backed *Union*. Two days later, President Polk summoned Benton to the White House to approve his war message to Congress. But the senator was deeply disturbed. "He left without satisfying me that I could rely on his support," Polk recorded grimly in his diary.[5]

Benton faced a dilemma. Like many congressmen, Democrats as well as Whigs, he felt that the American forces were on Mexican soil. Yet if he refused to vote funds and more troops now that American soldiers had been attacked, he would be charged with disloyalty. That evening Benton returned to the White House. For nearly an hour Polk listened while Buchanan and the secretary of war pressured Benton to change his position. But the senator seemed adamant. The next morning, in a last ditch effort, Francis Blair was summoned from his Silver Spring retreat to reason with his old friend. Blair was blunt. Unless Benton supported the war, he would be a "ruined man" politically.[6] At last, Benton caved in. That afternoon he voted with all but two of his senate colleagues to approve Polk's war resolution.

At almost the same moment, the Oregon controversy came to a head when England offered a new compromise at the forty-ninth parallel. This time Polk, with the Mexican War on his hands, was more willing to deal, and a treaty, firmly backed by Benton in the Senate, was quickly signed, adding Oregon,

Washington, and Idaho territories to the nation. Meanwhile, young men swarmed to the recruiting offices as the nation cheered its first victories at Palo Alto and Resaca de la Palma.

Amid the patriotic frenzy, Jessie received disturbing news about John. In a clipping from a Mexican newspaper, she read that his expedition had been driven in disgrace from California. The episode had occurred in early March, two months before the United States and Mexico had gone to war. After reading the news, Jessie spent an anxious night. The next day Secretary Buchanan allowed her to see State Department dispatches about the incident, just received from American consul Thomas Larkin.[7]

From Larkin, Jessie learned that California officials feared that John's expedition—to them a sinister band of sixty rough men bristling with weapons—had been sent not on a peaceful topographical survey but to stir up a Texas-style revolt among the American settlers. Nonetheless, they had given John at least tacit permission to winter in California, with the understanding that he remain away from all settlements. Instead, the expedition had meandered dangerously near Monterey, ostensibly botanizing and grazing their stock but as probably waiting for news that the United States and Mexico were at war. Alarmed, the Californians abruptly ordered them out of the country.

John reacted with impulsive bravado. Stationing himself and his men on a peak in the nearby Gabilan Range, he built a crude log fort and defiantly raised the American flag. Californian General José Castro, whose flair for the theatrical equaled John's, responded with an impassioned call for volunteers to "tame the ulcer, which . . . would destroy your independence and liberty."

As armed Californians gathered on the plain below, John scribbled a dramatic note to Larkin, which Jessie now read among the consul's dispatches. "I am making myself as strong as possible in the intention that if we are unjustly attacked we will fight to extremity, . . . trusting to our country to avenge our death. . . . We have in no wise done wrong to the people or the authorities of the country, and if we are hemmed in and assaulted here, we will die every man of us under the Flag of our country."

Messages continued to fly as Consul Larkin used all of his considerable tact to soothe the prickly pride of both the young explorer and the California general. But Frémont's position was untenable. He was a foreigner in California, subject to its laws and with no orders from his own government to defy them. "My sense of duty did not permit me to fight them," he wrote Jessie afterward, "but we retired slowly and growlingly before a force of three or four hundred men. . . . For my own part," he added, "I have become disgusted with everything belonging to the Mexicans."[8]

The incident at Gabilan would rankle and fester. It left John, a man deeply sensitive about his image, angry and embittered. "I felt humiliated and humbled," he confessed to his father-in-law.[9] At the same time, it confirmed the Californians' fears about American intentions and left them more suspicious than ever about the motives of army captain John Charles Frémont.

Jessie's greatest concern as she read Larkin's dispatches was her husband's safety, and she seized with relief on the consul's view that much of the Californians' ferocity had been bluster. Writing five weeks after the incident, Larkin was confident that John "could if he pleases present himself in Monterey (without his party) at any time." Even more reassuring was Larkin's news that John was on his way north to Oregon and would be home again in September.[10]

On June 11, John's dramatic note to Larkin, written from a California mountaintop, appeared in the *Union*, no doubt at the instigation of Jessie and her father. To an America at war with Mexico, his stand seemed doubly heroic. His conduct against the Californians' "unwarranted" attempt to drive him from the country, the *Union* editorialized, "was marked alike by courage and discretion."

John's stand against the Californians may have influenced the senator, for he was gradually drawn into the war. Over the summer of 1846, Polk consulted with Benton frequently about an overland march to seize the Southwest and California, and it was Benton's suggestion that Colonel Stephen Watts Kearny, the St. Louis friend who had helped John procure the troublesome howitzer, be named commander of the troops that would march west. Benton also proved adept at more arcane intrigue when in June he arranged that Polk send the experienced Santa Fe trader James Magoffin to dicker for peace with the New Mexico governor. Magoffin was "of generous temper, patriotic, and rich," Benton remarked, and he did his task well. When Kearny's troops reached the New Mexico capital in August, they found no resistance. Bribery was suspected. Benton conceded as much after the war, when he steered a special bill through Congress awarding Magoffin thirty thousand dollars for "secret services" to the American government.[11]

Jessie may have known something of this, but to her, Magoffin's journey meant a chance to send a loving letter to Bent's Fort in Colorado, where John would stop on his way east. "I hope that as I write you are rapidly nearing home," she wrote on June 16, "and that early in September there will be an end to our anxieties." She congratulated him on his recent promotion to lieutenant colonel and assured him that it was "entirely a free will offering of the President's, neither father nor I nor anyone for us having asked or said we would like it."

So your merit has advanced you in eight years from an unknown second lieutenant, to the most talked of and admired lieutenant-colonel in the army. Almost all of the old officers called to congratulate me upon it, the Aberts among them, and I have heard of no envy except from some of the lower order of Whig papers who only see you as Colonel Benton's son-in-law. . . . I had to publish almost all your letter, and like everything else you write it has been reprinted all over the country. . . . Editors have written to me for your biography and likeness, but I have no orders from you and then you know it would look odd to leave out your age, and you never told me how old you were yet.

How old are you? You might tell me now I am a colonel's wife—won't you, old papa? Poor papa, it made tears come to find you had begun to turn gray. You must have suffered much and been very anxious. . . .

Mr. Magoffin has come for the letter and I must stop. I have not had so much pleasure in a very great while as today. The thought that you may hear from me and know that all are well and that I can tell you again how dearly I love you makes me as happy as I can be while you are away. . . . Farewell, dear, dear husband. In a few months we shall not know what sorrow means.[12]

Jessie's letter glows with love and pride in her husband, but there is an uneasiness beneath the surface. At times she seems too eager to praise, too ready to reassure. She knew that John's childhood had left him deeply insecure, anxious to prove himself and abnormally sensitive to slights. She must have sensed that his precarious pride had been rubbed raw by the humiliations at Gabilan, and to soothe that wound, she added the balm of wifely flattery. Jessie had become the keeper not only of her husband's public reputation but of his private image as well.

Over the steamy Washington summer, Jessie watched the papers anxiously for further word from California. Solid news finally arrived in early September, when she learned that on July 7, the American fleet had raised the flag at Monterey and claimed the province for the United States. There were also vague and garbled reports that sometime earlier a group of American settlers had seized the northern town of Sonoma and proclaimed a republic. Somehow, John was involved. Over the next few months, Jessie would piece together the chain of events that had made her husband a revolutionary.

After his March humiliation at Gabilan, John had retreated slowly northward, distracted from his brooding by the glories of the California spring as he rode through fields of poppies in golden bloom. In early May the dawdling expedition reached the remote shores of Upper Klamath Lake in southern Oregon, where they again hesitated before heading northwest over the still snowy Cascades. It was at this moment that Archibald Gillespie, the marine lieutenant sent west by Polk six months before, rode out of the forest.

"How fate pursues a man!" John would exclaim years later, though others would say that fate had not so much pursued as that John had paused, waited, even courted it, first in his wanderings near Monterey and now at Klamath Lake.[13]

Gillespie himself had reached Monterey on the sloop-of-war *Cyane* in mid-April, before the Mexican War began. After giving Consul Larkin his secret instructions, Gillespie dallied only long enough to attend a grand fandango in his honor, where the Californians were hospitable but wary of the tall, red-headed gentleman who claimed to be traveling for his health. "We found it difficult to believe that the government of the United States would send a ship of war solely to bring a young invalid to California," one woman shrewdly observed.[14]

Gillespie was already on his way north to find Frémont when a messenger on horseback overtook him at Yerba Buena with fresh news from Larkin. The consul reported that yet another American warship had reached Monterey. Its captain believed that the United States and Mexico were probably at war and that the Pacific fleet would receive the news "by the next Mail (Six or eight days)." In Larkin's opinion, "Our flag may fly here in thirty days."

"Glorious news for Capt. Frémont," replied American Vice-Consul William Leidesdorff, with whom Gillespie was staying in San Francisco. "I think I see him smile."[15]

When Gillespie reached Frémont two weeks later on May 9, Larkin's report was uppermost in his mind. The two young adventurers, meeting by a remote Oregon lake, must have felt that great events were at hand. Yet what exactly transpired between them has remained the subject of intense speculation.

Gillespie brought with him Buchanan's brief letter of introduction, the Benton packet, and what news and instructions he carried in his head. Two years later in a semiofficial account of the episode, John stated that Gillespie told him "he had been directed by the Secretary of State to find me, and to acquaint me with his instructions, which had for their principal objects to ascertain the disposition of the California people, to conciliate their feelings in favor of the United States, and to find out, with a design of counteracting, the designs of the British government upon that country." These, in effect, were Larkin's instructions as well. But even in this recounting, John injected a mysterious note. While Buchanan's letter of introduction seemed a mere formality, its delivery by a secret messenger in the Oregon wilderness suggested to him a purpose "intelligibly explained to me by the accompanying letter from Senator Benton, and by communications from Lieutenant Gillespie."[16] Over the years, this hint of a hidden meaning in Benton's letter would blossom into a story of a secret message in family code urging John to act at once to take California. But given the senator's clearly expressed views against an armed takeover, it is unlikely that he would have gone beyond Buchanan's instructions to Larkin and Gillespie. Far more considerate of Mexican rights than the administration, and convinced that American settlement would naturally and inevitably bring California into the Union, Benton would have seen no reason to force the process unless England intervened.

John and Gillespie talked late around the camp fire that

first evening in the Oregon woods, and when at last the marine lieutenant slept, John continued to read the treasured packet of letters from home and debate his course. In his excitement he neglected to post a guard, and when he too rolled into his saddle blanket and fell into exhausted slumber, Klamath Indians, who had been trailing Gillespie, lunged out of the darkness and killed three of his men. In the next few days, Kit Carson led a revenge party against the Klamaths, killing a dozen and burning a nearby village.

Shaken, sobered, the expedition turned back toward California, for John wanted to be on the spot for whatever might occur. Yet he was clearly uneasy. "We certainly commenced our voyage when some malicious and inauspicious star was in the ascendant," he wrote Benton en route, "for we find enemies and difficulty everywhere." Edward Kearn, the expedition's artist and cartographer, afterward put it more crudely: "What we were to return to Cal. for no one knows (but to return was sure of creating a row with the yellow bellies)."[17]

As the expedition rode into the Sacramento Valley, they encountered an atmosphere of rumor and alarm. California officials, perhaps in response to Frémont's Gabilan stand, had issued a proclamation in April forbidding foreigners to buy land and threatening their expulsion "whenever the government finds it convenient."[18] Now American settlers—there were some eight hundred in the valley—hastened to Frémont's camp, reporting that General Castro was forming an army to drive them out and even inciting the Indians to burn their wheat fields.

General Castro had indeed gathered soldiers at Santa Clara in the South Bay, either to attack the settlers, defend himself against an expected American revolt, or vanquish his southern California rival, Governor Pío Pico, as the latter firmly believed. John, wary of the Indians and embittered by his humiliation at Gabilan, listened indiscriminately to the settlers' talk and neglected to check their stories with a knowledgeable observer like Larkin, who was convinced that with time and diplomacy Castro could be persuaded to accept American rule.

In late May, John reached the Marysville Buttes, a cluster

of peaks jutting out of the valley sixty miles north of Sutter's Fort. Here he paused, unsure whether to take the lead against Castro, as the settlers and his men urged, or remain neutral until he knew his country was at war. Though the United States had declared war on May 13, the news had not yet reached California.

At this critical moment, John received a batch of newspapers, out of date but still prized in remote California, from the solicitous Larkin. "In one you will find a pretty Bee story [from] your published Books of Travels," the consul told him. "In another paper you will read of a visit paid by some Indians with a long name to Col. Benton. Had a talk with Mrs. Frémont, and tried to make acquaintance with your child, but the little one declined an introduction. . . . One of the papers contained a long story of a Governor," Larkin continued, "who it appeared married . . . one of Col. Benton's Kinsfolks, which caused some trial, where Mrs. Frémont and two sisters attended Court as witnesses. All the Herald's and other papers have something to say about California, half of them relative to the gallant Capt. Frémont and Lady."[19]

Poised on a butte above the Sacramento Valley, unsure whether to act or wait, John read of Jessie, Lily, and the Potawatomis, of Sally McDowell's marital troubles, and of his own past explorations, already the stuff of legend. How should a man, eager to prove himself yet hesitant to compromise his government, behave? And the "Lady"—how would she feel if he failed to seize the moment and make it his own? The situation was delicate, and John confused and uncertain. He was a courageous man but temperamentally impatient, with little talent for complexity. By acting he would not only redeem his honor, besmirched at Gabilan, but enhance it as well. He was, of course, well aware that he would be on his own. As an army officer, he was duty-bound to remain neutral until he learned his country was at war. He admitted as much two years later in his semiofficial account. His action in California, he stated, was "without expressed authority from the United States, and revolutionary in its character."[20]

John would claim at the time that he moved only to protect

his party and "justify" his character,[21] but neither the settlers nor his own men were in serious danger from the Californians, bombastic in rhetoric but otherwise circumspect. In reality, he overreacted to a situation that required more tact than daring. It was his own image, not the Californians, that had him cornered. In the end he acted because action was irresistible to a man of his character: impulsive, daring, romantic, inclined to disregard rules and scruples—and profoundly insecure. He made his choice not out of any clear consideration of the facts or his own conscience but for the sake of his reputation, his fatal "passion for seeming," for "how we must look."

"On the 6th of June I decided on the course which I would pursue, and immediately concerted my operations with the foreigners [Americans] inhabiting the Sacramento valley," John wrote Benton afterward.[22] Four days later, a small group of the settlers, with John's behind-the-scenes support, captured nearly two hundred horses being driven south from Sonoma to Castro's camp at Santa Clara. At dawn on June 14, 1846, the same band, augmented to more than thirty, seized the small garrison town of Sonoma and took four of its leading citizens prisoner. Amid the rhetoric and a liberal sampling of General Mariano Vallejo's brandy, they raised a crude flag with a grizzly bear painted on it and declared themselves a republic.

It was a sordid enterprise, or so thought Rosalía Vallejo Leese, sister of one prisoner, wife of another. The men were the dregs of the American community, a band of "horse thieves, trappers, and run away sailors," wearing hats of wolf or coyote skin, felt or grimy straw, and greasy buckskin or blue cloth breeches. Many had no shirt or shoes. To her their flag was equally contemptible: "a piece of linen about the size of a large towel . . . painted [with] a red bear and a lone star."[23]

When Thomas Larkin, working quietly in Monterey to win over the Californians, heard the news, he was surprised and dismayed. "I can hardly believe it and do not understand the affair," he said. He would remain convinced that the Bear

Flag Revolt provoked the Californians to resist the American occupation more strongly than if they had been treated diplomatically.[24]

Captain John B. Montgomery of the warship *Portsmouth*, waiting at Yerba Buena, was also surprised, but unlike Larkin, he cheered from the sidelines. "The capture of the horses and the surprise at Sonoma were master strokes," he wrote John, "but should have been followed up by a rush upon Santa Clara, where Castro . . . might have been taken by thirty men." While Montgomery himself had to maintain "a strict neutrality," he confessed his sympathy with "the gallant little band" who had taken Sonoma.[25]

Montgomery's enthusiasm may have encouraged John to become more conspicuously involved. On June 23, acting on reports that Castro's troops were about to attack Sonoma, John rushed with nearly a hundred men to protect the little capital. Finding no enemy, they marched to Yerba Buena and back, while some fifty Californians scampered south across the bay. By the Fourth of July, having fought no battles, John and his troops were at Sonoma again for a triumphal celebration, complete with a reading of the Declaration of Independence and a festive fandango. The next day John publicly accepted command of the rebels, now swollen to more than two hundred men, and began to plan the further conquest of California. But additional unauthorized glory was thwarted five days later when word at last came that the United States and Mexico were at war, and the American navy had raised the flag at Monterey and Yerba Buena.

The province was quickly taken. "We simply marched all over California from Sonoma to San Diego," reported a member of Frémont's battalion, now mustered into American forces under naval commodore Robert Stockton, "and raised the American Flag without opposition or protest. We tried to find an enemy, but could not."[26] On October 30, Jessie could read an enthusiastic report in the *Intelligencer* from an American seaman who had witnessed John's triumphal entry into Monterey. In his admiring eyes, Rosalía Leese's motley crew had become heroes. "Colonel Frémont's party arrived here yesterday," he wrote on July 20. "They . . . are the most daring and hardy set of fellows I ever looked upon. They are splendid marksmen, and can plant a bullet in an enemy's head with their horses at a full gallop. . . . They never sleep in a house, but on the ground, with a blanket around them, their saddle for a pillow, and a rifle by their side."

To most Americans reading such accounts, John seemed an ideal hero, dashing and romantic. But there were questions as well, mainly from those who opposed the war with Mexico and regarded the Bear Flag Revolt as an extension of the same predatory ethic. Though this dissent would swell in later years, there was already enough to cause Thomas Benton to write an elaborate defense of his son-in-law's part, perhaps as much to explain it to himself as to the public.

Benton argued that in the Bear Flag uprising, as well as earlier on Gabilan Peak, John had acted in self-defense. He was a scientist-explorer who "knew nothing of the war" until Castro's threats forced him to "turn upon his pursuers and fight them instantly . . . to seek safety for his party and the American settlers, by overturning the Mexican government in California." Basing his explanation solely on John's letters, Benton did not cite the threat of an imminent British takeover as motivation for John's actions. Eventually, however, for him as well as John and Jessie, it would become the chief justification for John's part in the Bear Flag uprising.[27]

It was a dubious pretext. The U.S. fleet, hovering off the coast, had already been instructed to act in case of a British move. Moreover, though British ships were nearby, they had orders—unknown, of course, to the Americans—to remain neutral. Larkin, who had feared British action the year before, had since become convinced that there was no danger and had so written Gillespie and Frémont before they acted.[28]

With the publication of his defense of Frémont, the senator was fully implicated in the war. "You know what my position has been," he told Polk the day after it appeared, "but let Bygones be by-gones. . . . Now I will give you any support in this war in my power." That evening Benton appeared at the president's regular Tuesday evening reception with Jessie on his arm.[29]

Despite her father's involvement, Jessie continued to have mixed feelings about the war. In this she reflected the curious ambivalence of much of the opposition. While many condemned the blatant seizure of Mexican territory, even the most ardent moralist tended to view American expansion to the Pacific as inevitable and American character and institutions as superior to Mexican. Even war opponent Henry Thoreau, in retreat at Walden Pond, noted with deliberate symbolism that whenever he went for a walk, his natural inclination was to head southwest. And while many condemned the war as unjust, few suggested returning a prize like California to Mexico. Americans like Jessie and her father would have preferred to gain California and the Southwest by purchase, by persuasion, or by emigration. But when a country is as weak as Mexico, purchase may be close to bribery, persuasion not far from coercion, and emigration merely slow invasion. The shrewd old Russian ambassador, Count Bodisco, saw this ambiguity clearly. Russia, he laughed, was in the habit of taking ten times the territory of Texas, "but the main point was to do it in a genteel way."[30]

Jessie's views were, of course, complicated by John's involvement. Though she questioned the war, her husband had become one of its heroes, and in time she would become his chief apologist. But in the early months of 1847, she still saw his course as personal rather than political, motivated by his sense of honor. "Fighting is not his aim," she wrote John Torrey in late March, "& though he threw all his energy into the affair last July & August yet it was as if revenging a private insult for he knew nothing of the war. Of course as an officer, real insults to the country would be felt, & such by him in the same manner, but in my private opinion, there was no necessity for blood to wipe out the insult offered by Mexico."

Jessie was close to the truth. The danger from Castro was exaggerated and the British threat illusory. Scarcely investigating either, Jessie's husband had acted for far more personal reasons. Anxious to redeem himself for Gabilan and hungry for further glory, it was indeed honor, image, reputation, that made insurrection irresistible to John Charles Frémont.

Jessie was clearly impatient with soldiering and eager to have her husband home. Her latest news from California, she told Torrey, was not from John, who was "several hundred miles in the interior," but from Commodore Stockton. In late September, the Californians had rebelled, as Larkin had feared, and retaken much of the southern part of the province. To Jessie, Stockton's dispatches were "vexatious—because they require more assistance from Mr. Frémont" in reconquering the country. She hoped the arrival of General Kearny and his dragoons, marching overland from Santa Fe, would free her husband from the war.

With the passage of time, Jessie's views would change drastically. Forty years later, she would exalt her husband as the conqueror of California. But in the early spring of 1847, Jessie still had grave doubts about the war with Mexico. And she did not hesitate to speak for her absent husband as well. "As you may perceive," she told Torrey in all candor, "I have no sympathy for the war, nor has Mr. Frémont."[31]

11

Be not led away by all you hear and read now-a-days about the rights of women and their intellectual equality. There is nothing more dangerous for a young woman than to rely chiefly upon her intellectual powers, her wit, her imagination, her fancy.

Godey's Lady's Book
1844

"A NEW AND
PAINFUL EPOCH"

TWO MONTHS LATER, on May 8, 1847, the nation celebrated a year of victories in the war with Mexico. In
Washington, Miller's Confectionary did a brisk business
with a new flavor of ice cream called "Palo Alto" in honor of
the war's first battle, while a giant banner across Pennsylvania
Avenue proclaimed, "Our country—may she always be right;
but right or wrong, our country." In the evening thousands
flocked to the Navy Yard to see the fireworks, then moved
on to the Capitol, where a great bonfire of tar and turpentine
barrels shot flames forty feet high. Though the prudent president, fearful of fire, had forbidden the illumination of government offices, the White House itself, as well as most stores
and homes, glittered with candles or the new gas lights. With
the curious ambiguity the war evoked, even the offices of the
National Intelligencer, whose editorials daily condemned the
war, blazed with celebratory light. Many people also displayed
special transparent pictures in their windows—patriotic designs and mottoes painted on tissue paper that, lit from behind, glowed like stained glass. Some honored the war's heroes: Winfield Scott or Zachary Taylor, Jefferson Davis or John
C. Frémont. One depicted the goddess of liberty with a map
of Mexico spread at her feet.

At the Benton house on C Street, Jessie too laid aside her
doubts about the war and, with her sisters' help, installed
three windows of transparencies. In the central window the
words "Santa Fe, Chihuahua and the Missourians" celebrated
the victories of the Missouri troops who were marching south-

west under General Kearny, while the two side windows proclaimed the victories at Buena Vista and Cerro Gordo. Upstairs, in a more personal celebration, Jessie hung the cherished flag John had planted on a Rocky Mountain peak and later given to her.[1]

Senator Benton, politicking in Missouri, was soon speaking proudly of his daughters' patriotic display, pointing out with his customary flamboyance that it was he who had taught them to honor the state he represented. Despite such puffery, Benton continued to suggest that the Mexican War could have been avoided. Although he never blamed Polk directly, it was yet another indication that the two stubborn politicians had not resolved their differences. In early March, when Jessie's older sister Liz (called Eliza as a child) married New Orleans lawyer-editor William Carey Jones, the president himself escorted the bride to the supper table. But it was an ephemeral gesture in a friendship that had long been strained. When Jones appeared at the White House to ask Polk for a government job, the president, plagued by office-seekers, turned him down, grumbling to his diary that he had no intention of appointing a man who had once worked for an opposition newspaper, though he fully expected "a violent outbreak" of protest from his formidable father-in-law.[2]

Still, it must have been with some surprise that Polk, after a long morning of paperwork, opened his office to visitors at one o'clock on a June afternoon and discovered Senator Benton's second daughter, Jessie, among the usual crowd of petitioners. With her was a short, unprepossessing man with curly brown hair, mild blue eyes, and fair skin freckled and burned by the sun. Though the stranger bore himself with natural dignity, he looked hot and uncomfortable in his black broadcloth suit, starched shirt, and silk cravat.

When the president greeted Jessie, she introduced the man as Kit Carson, her husband's guide on his three western journeys. Carson had just ridden east from California, bringing dispatches for the government as well as a long letter from Frémont, which he now handed to the president. Carson,

Jessie told Polk a trifle pointedly, had been waiting to see him for several days, hoping to talk with him about the situation in California.

Polk must have stiffened at her words. During the past six weeks, unsettling reports had reached Washington that Commodore Robert Stockton of the navy and Brigadier General Stephen Watts Kearny of the army were quarreling over command in California, and that John Charles Frémont had sided with Stockton. Jessie too had heard the rumors, but it was not until Kit Carson reached Washington that she learned just how deeply her husband was involved.

Less than three months after the American flag was first raised at Monterey, defiant Californians had retaken Los Angeles and other southern settlements. By early December 1846, American forces had recaptured San Diego and, under the pugnacious Stockton, were preparing to march on Los Angeles. Meanwhile, Frémont, with four hundred emigrant volunteers, was moving south from Monterey to aid him.

At that strategic moment, General Kearny, accompanied by a hundred weary dragoons, arrived overland from New Mexico. Blundering into premature battle with the Californians at San Pascual near San Diego, his exhausted men were badly mauled and Kearny himself wounded. His position remained precarious until Stockton sent help. When the two commanders joined forces, they managed to cooperate only long enough to retake Los Angeles. Frémont was still a few miles from the scene when the fighting ended, but the defeated Californians, wary of Stockton's harshness, chose to surrender to John instead. On January 13, 1847, they signed the generous peace terms he offered. Seven months before, John had begun the conquest of California on his own. Now, without consulting his superior officers, he completed it.

Once the three leaders gathered in the rain-drenched pueblo of Los Angeles, their quarrel erupted in earnest. Kearny's orders stated that if he conquered California, he should set up a civil government. Stockton argued that since California had already been taken and a government established (the insurrection being only a temporary setback in his eyes) long before Kearny arrived, Kearny's orders no longer applied. Far from being a conqueror, Kearny had to be rescued after San Pascual and had contributed only sixty of the nearly six hundred troops who retook Los Angeles. When Kearny challenged this view, Stockton angrily threatened to have him recalled.

John was caught in the crossfire when Stockton appointed him governor of California, while Kearny, who claimed he planned to make John governor at a later date, issued a direct order that blocked him from accepting Stockton's offer. At this point John was forced to make a crucial decision. In strictly technical terms, his duty was to obey Kearny. Though he and his men had been temporarily serving under Stockton, he was a lieutenant colonel in the army, and his direct superior was Brigadier General Stephen Watts Kearny. Moreover, common sense and general practice suggested that the army, not the navy, was the appropriate force to administer a new territory.

But Jessie's husband was not an army man by temperament or training. Independent, irreverent, and careless of authority, in a situation so murky he was not likely to be swayed by the scrupulous technical argument. And so it was perhaps inevitable that on January 17, 1847, after a night of reflection, John Charles Frémont informed General Kearny that he would not obey his order. "Until you & Commodore Stockton adjust between yourselves the question of rank, where I respectfully think the difficulty belongs, I shall have to report and receive orders as heretofore from the Commodore."[3]

Furious at Frémont's defiance, Kearny retreated to Monterey to await government clarification of his orders, while Stockton retired to his ship in San Diego harbor. Alone in Los Angeles, John moved into a two-story adobe befitting a new governor, entertained the citizens with lively fandangos, and began to sign himself "J. C. Frémont, Governor of California."

The intentions of the Polk administration remained unclear until mid-February, a month after John's confrontation with Kearny, when orders finally reached California giving Kearny definite authority to form a civil government. John had stated that he would obey Stockton until the government made clear who was in command, but strangely, Kearny did not immediately send him the new orders. John had been foolish to side with Stockton, but Kearny, in forcing him farther out on a limb, showed himself to be harsh and vindictive.

Increasingly anxious about his position, on March 22, John set out on a dramatic horseback ride to Monterey to talk with Kearny. It was at this crucial meeting that he might have saved himself. Kearny was not eager to tangle with his old friend Benton, and he knew the Polk administration would also want to avoid a conflict. But it was not in John's nature to grovel or in Kearny's to forgive. The meeting was a disaster. John accepted Kearny's authority only grudgingly, while Kearny and his fellow officers went out of their way to humiliate him. Kearny and his staff had already reached an ominous conclusion about John's motives—one that Jessie would soon see repeated in the eastern press. Frémont's stand, smirked Kearny's surgeon, was based on his "thirst for Glory, and Stockton's—I won't say what—but I only wish I could marry a Senator's daughter."[4]

When she learned of the situation from Kit Carson, the senator's daughter was deeply disturbed. But now, as she faced the president, she encountered a blank wall. "Mrs. Frémont seemed anxious to elicit from me some expression of approbation of her husband's conduct," Polk recorded, "but I evaded." To the narrow, literal-minded president, Frémont's duty was clear. "In truth I consider that Col. Frémont was greatly in the wrong when he refused to obey the orders issued to him by Gen'l. Kearny. I think Gen'l. Kearny was right also in his controversy with Com. Stockton. It was unnecessary, however, that I should say so to Col. Frémont's wife." Bidding for time, the habitually close-mouthed Polk hoped that Stockton and Frémont would yield gracefully to Kearny's authority, settling their quarrel "without the necessity of . . . a Court Martial."[5]

Though Jessie's meeting with the president left her unsatisfied, Carson's quiet faith in her husband did much to ease her mind. She had not seen John for two long years, and it was comforting to talk with a man who had left him only three months before. This was Carson's first visit to the East, and everyone was eager to meet the bold frontiersman made famous by Frémont's reports. Carson was astonished by his sudden fame. Strangers stopped him on the street to shake his hand, and society hostesses vied to display him at their tables. At the War Department, where he delivered dispatches, even the bureaucrats were impressed. The stir in Washington was only the beginning. Over the next years, magazine and newspaper stories would transform him into a tall man of magnificent proportions; and in the innumerable dime novels that followed, as he rescued damsels from naked savages and gunned down outlaws, he would come to define the western hero—tall, noble, taciturn, and properly bashful with the ladies.

Jessie herself was not immune to such romanticism, and she relished the stories she coaxed from the modest Carson. She was probably the author of a long account of his exploits that appeared in the *Union* that June. "I have my reasons for thinking that 'tis written by Jessie," Lizzie Lee told her husband. "She is a smart woman."[6]

Despite her delight in Kit's company, Jessie remained concerned about John. Determined to help her husband, she and Kit called on the president once more. Again, Polk was evasive. Though Jessie understood that the administration was trying to smooth over the controversy, she felt the situation had become too serious for such tactics, for there were reports that Kearny planned to arrest both Stockton and Frémont for mutiny. "We should not be surprised," announced the Pittsburg *Gazette* with bland satisfaction that May, "to hear of their trial, and even summary execution."[7]

Though Jessie had no way of knowing John's or Kearny's plans, she was restless in Washington. "She looks thin & is sad," Lizzie Lee noted. "She seems tired of her courage & is now really pining for her husband." When Carson with naval officer Edward Beale headed west again on June 15, carrying government dispatches to California, Jessie and Lily seized the opportunity to travel with them as far as St. Louis, where Senator Benton was staying. "Be under no uneasiness about either of them," the senator wrote John when they arrived. "They are both my children, & will share all my cares and affections equally with the rest. They are both exceedingly well, and have no want but that of your return."[8] When Kit Carson left St. Louis for California, Jessie gave him a miniature portrait of herself to take to John.

As she waited through the hot summer days, Jessie grew more disturbed. Rumors abounded but there was little solid news. She found it a strain to see people and pretend nothing was wrong, but even more agonizing to be alone. More than anything, it was her helplessness that undid her. By day she managed to cover her fears, but at night they overwhelmed her. She became "convulsed and frantic," Benton recalled, "the heart bursting, the brain burning, the body shivering; and I, her father, often called, not to witness, but to calm, this terrible agitation."[9]

In August she heard new and more reliable reports that John was under arrest. Overcome by anxiety, she insisted on going to the frontier to meet him. Though Benton must have protested a young woman traveling alone by steamboat, Jessie's fears had crystalized into resolve, and even her formidable father chose not to stand in her way.

"I went up the river alone to what is now Kansas City," she recalled of that terrible time.[10] The town was little more than a steamboat landing, a cluster of crude frame and log buildings on a bluff. Inquiring among the roustabouts and traders, she learned that John was traveling east with General Kearny's party and was expected there at any time. "There was no way to learn more." She found a log cabin to stay in, and there she passed the next days, brooding in the stifling late summer heat. Then one evening, just as the sun faded from the river, she heard the rapid trampling of many horses and knew "the long waiting was over."

When she saw him at last, riding among his men, she sensed at once that something was terribly wrong. He was dressed not in his accustomed army uniform but in the broad-brimmed sombrero, riding pants, and scarlet sash of the native Californian. To Jessie his strange clothing seemed a silent message of defiance. But it was his haggard face that revealed the wounded man.

When Jessie cried out and ran to him, he jumped from his horse and took her in his arms. But as she clung to him, she sensed that he was stunned, not so much by the shock of seeing her as by something else, something so painful that he could not bear to tell her. Sensitive to his feelings, she did not probe, but when, needing to be alone, he made an excuse to look after the horses and disappeared into the dusk, she turned to his longtime companion of the trail, Alexis Godey, to learn what was wrong.

Godey confirmed what she had seen in John's face. The day before at Fort Leavenworth, General Kearny had placed John under arrest and ordered him to report to Washington for a court-martial. Godey also told her of the humiliating march east from California, "the long indignation" of being forced to travel in Kearny's wake though shunned by the general and his party.

John and Jessie headed downriver on the *Martha*, still surrounded by his loyal men who, Jessie said, "had learned not to trust a General of the Army any more than they would have trusted a revengeful Apache." General Kearny, grim-faced and taciturn, had preceded them to St. Louis, and speculation about "the rival heroes" was soon so feverish that the Missouri *Republican* urged its readers to remain calm until all the facts were known. Nonetheless, John and Jessie found many supporters in St. Louis. Though Benton's political opponents eagerly sided with Kearny, most people felt an instinctive sympathy for the young explorer caught in a power struggle between two crusty old commanders. As the case won national attention, it was John—and Jessie—who caught the public imagination. Their reunion at Kansas City had already been noted by the press. When Frémont's "young and amiable spouse" at last met her "soul's lord," the New York *Herald* informed its readers, "the meeting, after a separation of more than two years, was a joyous one." The same newspaper predicted that the court-martial would make Frémont "ten times more popular than ever."[11]

The press continued to note their progress as they made their way by steamboat to Kentucky, where they joined Thomas and Elizabeth Benton at their Woodford County farm. Yet all but the most partisan papers still refrained from taking sides. Most praised both Kearny and Frémont for their gallantry in California and regretted that troublemakers on both sides had turned a "misunderstanding of their . . . instructions," as one Washington columnist defined the issue, into a "disgraceful wrangle." One of these meddlers, the same correspondent suggested, was Senator Benton.[12]

The senator was indeed spoiling for a fight. When John and Jessie reached Kentucky, they found him eager for a showdown with Kearny. By this time Benton's own son, seventeen-year-old Randolph, had become a bitter disappointment to him, for the bright and talented boy had turned into a surly and belligerent young man with a serious drinking problem. Benton's difficulties with Randolph intensified his ties to John, who had become, as Jessie said, his spiritual heir, carrying his dreams into action.

Because of his illegitimacy and his father's death when he was five, John himself felt deeply ambivalent about authority. While he yearned for a father's love, he resisted the control that implied. With certain warmly paternal men like his early mentors, Joel Poinsett and Joseph Nicollet, John related as a beloved son, but other men—grim figures like Kearny and General Castro—evoked his anger and defiance. Now, with the blustering but affectionate Benton, he seemed, at least temporarily, to find the father he both longed for and resisted.

In Kentucky, John and Jessie spent many hours discussing the case with Benton. The senator was confident of victory. "I have a full view of the whole case—Kearny's as well as yours—and am perfectly at ease. You will be justified, and exalted; your persecutors will be covered with shame & confusion."[13] By September 12 they were on their way up the Ohio on the *Josephine*, cheered by Benton's optimism as well as supporters they met en route. But their fragile optimism was shattered when they reached Washington.

John received an urgent message that his mother was dangerously ill, and he set out at once for South Carolina. That same week, as newspapers proclaimed American victories at the gates of Mexico City, Jessie was stunned to learn that her lively and irreverent cousin, Preston Johnston, had been killed at the battle of Contreras. Only six years before, Jessie had worn Preston's cadet uniform as a prank at Sally McDowell's wedding. Now Preston was dead, Sally embittered, and Jessie herself much changed from the buoyant, headstrong young girl who had eloped that long-ago October day.

For John too, childhood ties were severed that week, for when he reached Aiken, South Carolina, where his mother had been spending the summer, he learned that she had died just hours before he arrived.[14] Traveling by train, he accompanied her body across the state for burial at Charleston. With his nerves raw from the humiliations of the past six months, the journey home must have been especially hard to bear, evoking painful memories of a mother struggling to support three bastard children and of a young boy who never quite belonged.

While John was in the South, Jessie displayed a new fierceness on his behalf. Convinced that a court-martial would clear

him of wrongdoing, she was determined to see that all witnesses were present for the trial. On September 21 she boldly
wrote the president, enclosing a newspaper report that two
potential prosecution witnesses who had served on Kearny's
California staff were being ordered to Mexico. "After reading
it," Jessie informed Polk, "you will see the manifest injustice
to Mr. Frémont of letting his accusers escape from the investigation of the charges they have made against him." There
were also rumors that Kearny himself would be sent to the
war. "You have the power to do justice & I ask it of you that
Mr. Frémont be permitted to make his accusers stand the
trial as well as himself. Do not suppose Sir, that I lightly
interfere in a matter properly belonging to men," she added
to justify her audacity, "but in the absence of Mr. Frémont
I attend to his affairs at his request."[15]

When John returned from Charleston, there was little
time for healing as he and Jessie prepared for the bitter fight
for his reputation. From Kentucky, Benton bombarded them
with advice and encouragement. The senator had decided to
handle the case himself. "I shall be with you to the end," he
assured them, "if it takes up the whole session of Congress."[16]

When Benton returned to Washington in mid-October,
he immediately called on President Polk. Despite their differences over the war, the two men managed a "long & pleasant" conversation about Mexico. Only when Benton brought
up the court-martial did the strain emerge. Benton spoke
emotionally about the case, but Polk, as usual, was unre-
sponsive.[17] Three days later, the president received a visit
from yet another overwrought Benton, seventeen-year-old
Randolph.

The senator's son was in a frenzy as he burst into the
president's office to demand that he be appointed a lieutenant
in the army. Polk managed to get the agitated boy to sit down
and then, speaking quietly to calm him, began to explain that
there were no vacancies. But Randolph would not listen.
Leaping to his feet, he shouted that both his father and the

secretary of war had also refused to help him. "He left my office in quite a passion," Polk recorded, "& very rudely, swearing profanely as he went [out] of the door."[18]

The commotion amazed visitors waiting to see the president, and one of them, writer T. S. Arthur, swore he smelled liquor on Randolph's breath. Others concurred, although Arthur's testimony alone might have been suspect, for he specialized in temperance fiction and would soon write the celebrated *Ten Nights in a Bar-Room.*

Polk's encounter hardened the harassed president against the Benton clan. "I have always been upon good terms with Col. Benton," he observed, "but he is a man of violent passions and I should not be surprised if he became my enemy because all his wishes in reference to his family and their appointments to offices [are not gratified], and especially if I do not grant his wishes in reference to Col. Frémont's trial." A week later, on November 2, Polk marked his fifty-second birthday. Perhaps because the court-martial began that day, he was feeling glum. "I have now passed through two-thirds of my Presidential term," he noted sourly, "& most heartily wish that the remaining third was over."[19]

Twenty-three-year-old Jessie found the days before the trial even more difficult than did the beleaguered president. Still reeling from the sudden change in fortune and pained by the anguish John felt, she marshaled all her love, sympathy, and tact to support him in his ordeal. Now more than ever, she was lover, friend, and family. Taking her cue from her father, she clung to the belief that the court-martial would vindicate John. And this time she found relief from her anxiety in work. She participated in strategy sessions that were as likely to take place at the tea table as more formally in her father's library. While Liz's still-unemployed husband, lawyer William Carey Jones, gathered documents at the State and War departments, Jessie was pressed into service as secretary and copyist for her father, who was preparing arguments and evidence with his usual relentless energy.

When Francis Blair dropped in on the Benton household, he found the senator *"cram* full of Frémont." Benton swore that he would see the case through, even if President Polk decided to hold the trial in hell. If there were any justice, Jessie added dryly, General Kearny would be there already.[20]

Jessie was changing. The buoyant young woman who believed she could control her own fate was growing cynical. The court-martial marked what she would call "a new and painful epoch" in her life, from which, like a tender plant hardened by its first winter, she would emerge a stronger and far more formidable woman.[21]

12

As a general rule a modest woman seldom
desires any sexual gratification for
herself. She submits to her husband,
but only to please him; and, but for the
desire of maternity, would far rather
be relieved from his attention.

Dr. William Acton
*The Functions and Disorders
of the Reproductive Organs*
1862

[Some speak] as if the female must be forced
to the creative act, apparently ignorant
of the great natural fact that a healthy
woman has as much passion as a man.

Elizabeth Cady Stanton
Diary
Sept. 6, 1883

John C. Frémont, 1856. *Courtesy of California State Library, Sacramento.*

"THE PROUD
LONELY MAN"

THE DAY WAS DAZZLING, unusually warm for November, as the parade of carriages and horse-drawn omnibuses jolted through tawny fields to the army arsenal two miles from town, where the court-martial would begin at noon. But if Jessie, wearing a wine-red dress as a sign of her own optimism, found the weather encouraging, she must have been less sure once she entered the shabby courtroom, where the sun, glinting feebly through small high windows, scarcely pierced the cavernous gloom.

The room was crowded with friends and supporters, as well as army and navy officers, the press, and the merely curious. All eyes were on the two antagonists, Frémont and Kearny, "both handsome men and both looking very well," as one reporter observed in his dispatch that night.[1] Superficially, Kearny was the more impressive of the two: tall, ramrod straight, graying, distinguished. In contrast, John seemed young and so slender he appeared almost delicate. Like Kearny, he was courteous and composed, his feelings, hidden by a deep reserve, revealed only occasionally in the intensity of his glance. The press also noted the vigorous presence of Thomas Benton, corpulent but still powerful-looking, and his aide, William Carey Jones, as well as the thirteen career army officers, impressive in their uniforms touched with gold and silver, who would act as judge and jury.

The court met briefly that first day, and it was not until the next morning that the charges were read: mutiny, disobedience of the lawful command of a superior officer, and conduct to the prejudice of good order and military discipline. Afterward Jessie listened as John gave his plea, "Not guilty," and the most celebrated court-martial of its time began.

The courtroom was tense as the prosecution called its first witness, Stephen Watts Kearny. Questioned by the judge advocate, Kearny moved quickly to a crucial scene, the January 17 meeting in Los Angeles when John refused to obey his order. At first, as Kearny told the story, he had been almost fatherly to the young explorer, but when John remained obdurate, he had turned grim. "I told him that Commodore Stockton could not support him in disobeying the orders of his senior officer, and that, if he persisted in it, he would unquestionably ruin himself." Then Kearny offered the court an explanation for John's conduct that Jessie would later call perjury. Frémont had informed him, Kearny said, that Stockton planned to name him governor. "I told him Commodore Stockton had no such authority," Kearny continued. "He asked me if I would appoint him governor. I told him . . . that as soon as the country was quieted I should, most probably, organize a civil government and that I, at that time, knew of no objections to my appointing him governor. He then stated to me that he would see Commodore Stockton, and that, unless he appointed him governor at once, he would not obey his orders."[2]

This was damning testimony. Kearny was suggesting that John was not just a rash young man with poor judgment but an unprincipled schemer bargaining for the governorship—a man who sided with Stockton only because he would make him governor the sooner. To Jessie, Kearny's testimony was unforgivable.

As the court-martial continued, Jessie's days took on a regular shape. The court met daily except Sundays from ten to three. Afterward she would huddle with John and her father to prepare for the next day's session. John conducted his own defense, since Benton, a civilian, could not speak in a military courtroom. Nonetheless, the senator was the driving force, totally, relentlessly absorbed. All questions and arguments had to be presented to the court in writing, a process "irksome and binding to the last degree," said Jessie, who must have done much of the copying.[3] Before the case was over, Benton's arguments reportedly covered more than eight hundred pages of foolscap.

Despite such efforts, the trial went badly for the defense almost from the beginning. Benton's strategy was to broaden its scope to consider not just whether John had disobeyed Kearny, for clearly he had, but the underlying question of who had supreme authority in California at the time. But when John tried to probe this larger issue during his cross-examination of Kearny and other witnesses, his questions were ruled irrelevant by the court, who time and again limited the testimony to the narrow issue of whether he had disobeyed Kearny's orders. "The scope of the inquiry [was] kept exactly to the matter in hand," Jessie observed, "and in this Court-martial the following illogical result occurred: Colonel Frémont was tried for acts growing out of his appointment as Governor of California by Commodore Stockton. If his Commission as Governor was legal and just, and Commodore Stockton in the right, so were Colonel Frémont's acts. The question could only be determined by a trial of either Stockton or Kearny." But since the army could not try the navy, John had become the scapegoat.[4]

As the trial wore on, Commodore Stockton seemed the one man who could extricate John from his dilemma. In late November the commodore arrived at the arsenal, full of the cheerful bluster that made Consul Thomas Larkin much prefer him to the stern, aloof Kearny. "I will tell all about my conduct," he announced to the press. "I will tell everything, if I have an opportunity. I want the truth to come out."[5]

But his charm soured when he took the stand to present a long, rambling account justifying his own conduct in California. When he still had not reached the question of John's conduct by the end of the second day, the court cut short his testimony. Later, under cross-examination by the judge advocate, Stockton was vague and forgetful. When asked under what authority he established a civil government in California, his reply was feeble: "Well, I do not think I had any . . . I formed the government under the law of nations."[6]

Before he left California, Stockton had been eager to best Kearny. "I have taken my gloves off and they will find Commodore Stockton the same man he was twenty years ago," he bragged to a friend. But by the time he took the stand, the two men had reached an understanding. "Colonel Benton will be very disappointed in the testimony of Commodore S as I think when he hears it," Kearny confided to his brother-in-law the week before Stockton testified.[7] Through an intermediary Kearny had sent Stockton a conciliatory letter, and the commodore had replied in kind. A rapprochement was to the advantage of both. Stockton would redeem himself in the eyes of the military establishment, while Kearny would disarm the one person who might save John.

Jessie, of course, was well aware that the case was not going as her father had planned. Once Stockton had failed them, a series of witnesses passed through the courtroom, but restricted to the narrow question of John's disobedience, they could add little to the defense. Benton himself was so outraged by the court's recalcitrance that just before Christmas he temporarily turned the case over to Jones and refused to attend the proceedings.

The weather too had turned bitter. Washington's poor foraged for driftwood along the Potomac, while in the drafty arsenal, where the meager courtroom fire scarcely cut the chill, one of the judges suggested moving to warmer quarters or, better yet, postponing the trial until summer. The press was also complaining. "The impression made upon us is, that the case ought never to have been brought to trial," announced the New York *Herald*. "Frémont ought to have apologized to Gen. Kearny, and the whole matter ought to have been settled, instead of being blazed about the world as it is now."[8] Kearny alone seemed in good spirits, feted by fellow officers and entertained by Washington hostesses like the shrewd and charming Rose Greenhow, who was vocal in her support of the general.

For Jessie, it was an anxious time. She was suffering from a lingering cold that verged on pneumonia. Moreover, she was pregnant. It must have been with mixed feelings that she realized she was carrying a child, for the present was painful and the future obscure. Nonetheless, she and the family celebrated the Christmas season with determined optimism, and New Year's callers found their wassail bowl the most generous in town.

As the trial dragged into January, the public lost interest in the case. The testimony seemed both tedious and trivial. But on January 8, a little more drama was wrung from the scene when General Kearny unexpectedly lost his composure. "On my last appearance before this court," he suddenly charged, "Thomas H. Benton . . . sat in his place, making mouths and grimaces at me . . . to offend, to insult, and to overawe me."

Hastily, the presiding judge tried to smooth things over, murmuring that while he had not seen the incident, he certainly regretted it. By this time Benton was on his feet, massive and implacable. "On or about the first day of General Kearny's examination before this court," he told the startled courtroom, "he fixed his eyes upon Colonel Frémont, fixedly, and pausingly; and looked insultingly and fiendishly at him." One of the judges tried to interrupt, but Benton stopped him. "When General Kearny fixed his eyes on Colonel Frémont, I determined if he should attempt again to look down a prisoner, I would look at him. . . . I did to-day look at General Kearny when he looked at Colonel Frémont, and I looked at him till his eyes fell—till they fell upon the floor."[9]

Furious at this insult, Kearny published a vigorous denial in the *Intelligencer.* Senator Benton, he swore, had never outstared him. As usual there were rumors of an impending duel. The two were "quarreling . . . like an infant school," complained one observer. But in the Benton household the wrangling was soon pushed into the background as the family celebrated a romance that had bloomed amid the rancor of the court-martial. Jessie's sister Sarah was marrying Richard Taylor Jacob, a well-to-do Kentuckian who had served in Frémont's California Battalion and come to Washington as a defense witness. On January 17, 1848, the young couple were married in the Benton home. But political antagonisms affected even the nuptial celebration. Ten months before, when Liz Benton married William Carey Jones, President Polk himself had escorted the bride to the supper table. This time he was conspicuously absent. Instead, Sarah's escort was opposition leader Henry Clay. Secretary of State Buchanan, still friendly with the Benton family, also attended, but the rest of the Polk cabinet was not in evidence. As father of the bride, Benton was at his most ebullient, and even the *Herald*, which routinely chastised the bombastic senator for his excesses, conceded that he was "one of the kindest and best fathers who ever lived."[10]

Meanwhile the trial was winding down, and on January 11, 1848, it recessed for twelve days to allow the defense to prepare its final summation. Again it was Benton who dominated. "I have never seen our good friend roused to such a pitch of cool fixed, reflecting, desperate resolution," Francis Blair exclaimed. Benton had read him part of the text, and Blair pronounced it "the clearest, most logical legal pointed battery of well-arranged facts" he had ever heard.[11]

When the court reconvened on January 24, the room was once again crowded with military officers, congressmen, and "a goodly sprinkling of the fair sex." For three days John, looking composed but intense, read the closely reasoned document, a statement the press conceded was masterly. "If it was a crime in me to accept the governorship from Commodore Stockton," he concluded, "it was a crime in him to have bestowed it. . . . I am now ready to receive the sentence of the court."[12]

Five days later the court reached a harsh verdict. The judges found John guilty of all three charges and sentenced him to dismissal from the army. However, seven of the thirteen recommended "lenient consideration" or "clemency" to the president. Four among them also jointly pointed out that Frémont had been caught in a struggle between two superior officers, a dilemma that might have confused even a more experienced soldier.

After several acrimonious cabinet meetings, where Buchanan was outspoken in his support of Frémont, President Polk reached his own decision. He dismissed the most severe charge, mutiny, but sustained the other two. Then, because of Frémont's "meritorious and valuable services" to the nation, he waived his dismissal from the army. "Lieutenant Colonel Frémont will accordingly be released from arrest, and will resume his sword, and report for duty."[13]

John and Jessie reacted with fury. Without hesitation John refused to accept Polk's pardon, since it would "admit the justice" of the verdict against him. To John there was no honorable alternative but resignation from the army. Polk, Buchanan, and others urged him to reconsider, but as Jessie explained, "he felt the injustice too keenly" to change his mind. Senator Benton agreed. "Neither Mr. Frémont nor my Father were of natures to compromise with a wrong," Jessie said. She might have added that neither was she.[14]

To Jessie, at least in hindsight, the court's verdict seemed inevitable under the circumstances. "The trial before the Court being upon technicalities could only have a verdict based on them," she said, "but the case was, at the same time, tried before the public on the *facts*, and its verdict was unanimous and overwhelming in upholding Colonel Frémont." Though she exaggerated the public enthusiasm, most Americans prized individualism too much to condemn the young explorer under such confusing circumstances. While Kearny, Benton, and the Polk administration were all variously blamed for the situation, John himself was not. "Most men in the place of Frémont would have done precisely what he did," claimed a *Herald* columnist.[15] To most people, the verdict seemed out of proportion to the crime, especially in light of John's daring explorations and his part, still unexamined, in acquiring California. Ironically, if John had emerged victorious in the court-martial, he would have been condemned as the son-in-law of a powerful man. By losing, he became a popular hero.

Despite such public support, Jessie was shattered. After all the hardships John had endured—the cold, hunger, danger, the long absences from home—he had been brutally humiliated by those he served. Jessie ached for her proud, reserved husband. Though he kept his anguish deep inside, she saw it in every gesture and glance, and heard it behind every word.

John wanted to escape the poisoned atmosphere of the East, to begin a new life in California. Within days of resigning from the army, he was sending seeds and vine slips by sea for a ranch he had purchased there. Though his relations with Benton were still warm, he may also have wanted to distance himself from his affectionate but overbearing father-in-law. But Jessie, pregnant with their second child, feared "the ordeal of being uprooted and transplanted."[16] Although she loved John intensely, her emotional security was still centered on her father and her familiar Washington world. For the first time in her life, she dreaded the future.

During the spring the Frémonts busied themselves with a "geographical memoir" of the third expedition, a brief topographical essay to accompany the map of Oregon and California that Charles Preuss was preparing. But Jessie had reached her breaking point. The long ordeal of the court-martial, her pregnancy, and her fears for the future combined to overwhelm her. One evening, as she worked with John on the memoir, she suddenly fainted. When she regained consciousness, it was clear she was severely ill. The doctor ordered complete rest.

During her collapse, Jessie experienced a profound readjustment. She had been a willful and optimistic young woman, a senator's daughter who believed she could shape the world to her own desires. Now she was forced to recognize that events outside her control could change her life. A world she believed bountiful and good suddenly seemed malevolent, filled with ambitious, predatory men who could wound her and her husband, and thwart their dreams. Even her powerful father had been helpless against them. "All the teachings, the examples of my twenty-three years, had been so in contrast with this experience that I really tried to believe the worst—not the best—of the human race," she recalled. Her disillusionment drove her to reflect on the meaning of life and human experience. Was it ultimately good or evil, she wondered. When she questioned various acquaintances, their replies confirmed her own doubts. "Of all I asked, only one person . . . answered without hesitation, *Good*. This was my father."[17]

By late May she was recovering. "For some months I have been unwell," she wrote John Torrey, "& since the last of April I have not left my room, but have had a battle with a violent bilious fever, which like Bunyan's fight with Apollyon was the dreadfullest fight I ever had. Like him, however, I have gained the victory & I am more than willing not even to remember it."[18]

But remember it she did. Bunyan's pilgrim fought with the angel of the bottomless pit. Jessie wrestled with a similar demon of despair. Looking back, she believed she emerged with a strengthened faith in the ultimate benevolence of the universe. But she also lost her innocence. She became stronger, fiercer, less forgiving, and far less sure that the world would go her way. At times in the future she would try to shape it to her needs; on other occasions she would practice a painful resignation.

Meanwhile John managed to finish what he had come to call that "cursed memoir" but his heart was not in the task and it was a perfunctory effort.[19] He was now waiting for Congress to approve funds for a full-scale report as well as for a new expedition to the West.

On July 24, 1848, Jessie gave birth to their second child, a boy. To celebrate the closeness of father and husband, he was named Benton Frémont. The baby was sickly, suffering from spasms in which blood rushed to his head, and Senator Benton feared he had " 'the Court-Martial,' a family disease."[20]

Less than three weeks later, the Frémonts' hopes for a salaried future were dashed when the House refused to fund either a third report or a new western expedition. Meanwhile, as if to rub salt in their wounds, President Polk had nominated General Kearny for an honorary promotion. Enraged, Benton poured out his accumulated fury in a long, venomous senate speech that occupied parts of thirteen days. "Human crime can rise no higher," he cried of Kearny's deeds.[21] But the Senate disregarded the old man's harangue and on August 9 confirmed the promotion.

In early August, amid these congressional rebuffs, Kit Carson arrived in town, again bringing dispatches from California for the government. His renown was now such that he was accompanied on his ride east by an admiring young army lieutenant with journalistic aspirations who would soon turn their horseback interviews into articles for *Harper's*. Carson arrived just in time to stand as godfather when three-week-old Benton was christened at Washington's Episcopal Church of the Epiphany on August 15. But Carson's quiet concern for the child unnerved Jessie. With painful honesty, he told her he feared her baby would not live.[22]

Carson brought not only official dispatches from California but newspapers and letters as well, and it was probably from his pack that the New York *Herald* obtained and on August 19 printed a long letter from California. Buried in a wordy paragraph on the region's mineral resources, the writer mentioned that gold had been discovered on the south branch of the American River, not far from Sutter's Fort. But the news, if noticed at all, was dismissed as just another California tale, and when Jessie and John set off for St. Louis and the Kansas frontier in September, they had no inkling that the gold discovery would change their lives.

Though Benton's power was waning, the indefatigable senator helped John obtain private financing for a new western expedition from St. Louis investors interested in building a railroad from St. Louis to the Pacific. One of John's chief tasks would be to locate a potential railroad route through the Rockies that would be passable even in winter.

Jessie, with Lily, the new baby, and a nursemaid, accompanied him to the frontier. They went first to New York, where John supervised the shipment of sawmill machinery for his California ranch, then took the steamer *Saratoga* from Buffalo.

The Frémont family kept to themselves, though they did confide to one sympathetic passenger that they were little more than emigrants, going to California to make a new start.[23] John would journey overland during the winter, while Jessie and the children, traveling via the Panama route, would join him there in the spring.

By October 3 they reached St. Louis and boarded the *Martha* for the last leg of their journey to the frontier. As the steamboat churned up the Missouri, ten-week-old Benton became dangerously ill. Suddenly, on October 6, he died. Stunned, Jessie clung to her dead child, unable to accept what had happened. "Grief was new to me then and I could not bear to give him up." Two days later when the steamboat docked at Westport, she was forced to leave his body on board, in the care of a cousin, to be returned to St. Louis for burial.[24]

The grieving family continued on to Boone Creek, a few miles away, where the expedition would make final preparations for their journey. Major Richard Cummins, the amiable old Delaware Indian agent, generously provided them with a room in his rambling log-cabin house, but by day Jessie preferred to stay near her husband at the Boone Creek camp. While John plunged into activity to relieve his sorrow, Jessie was made comfortable in a roomy tent under a tall, browning cottonwood tree. "I sat watching all the many preparations for the long winter journey, I the only idle one: weak from undermining illness and heavy at heart for all that had come and what might yet come to us both."[25] Touched by her grief, the men tried to pamper her. One shot wild quail and grilled them over the fire for her lunch. Another sketched her tent with its fading cottonwood tree and gave it to her as a present.

On October 20, 1848, John and his thirty-three men set out for the West. It was perhaps the hardest parting Jessie had known, for she was no longer the buoyant and trusting young woman she had once been. John too had changed. Since the court-martial, his reserve had deepened. He was no longer the exuberant young adventurer, eager to head into the wilderness he loved, but a stricken thirty-five-year-old man with graying hair and bitter memories. The journey, unsponsored and underfunded, was a job, not a joy. When he reached Bent's Fort in Colorado a month later, he confessed as much in a letter to Benton. "I think that I shall never cross the continent again, except at Panama. I do not feel the same pleasure that I used to have in those labors, as they remain inseparably connected with painful circumstances." He was no longer willing to undergo hardship and danger when the rewards could be so bitter. "I will drop into a quiet life," he told Benton.[26]

After the men and loaded mules disappeared in a cloud of dust, Jessie walked with Major Cummins through the deserted camp, where the coals of their breakfast fires still glowed. Winter was in the air, and the cottonwood was bare of leaves. As they returned to Cummins's house, he pointed out the den of a wolf who had been killing his sheep. Jessie shuddered when he told her that his men had found her cubs the night before and killed them all.

That evening, exhausted by sorrow, Jessie fell quickly to sleep. "I was awakened by a sound full of pain and grief, and wild rage too," she recalled, an eerie sound, the wolf searching for her cubs, that seemed to echo her own despair. Slipping back into sleep, she was reawakened "by a big dark object, rough-coated, and close to me." John had ridden back for a last good-bye. They clung together, closer now than ever, in a world that had turned hostile. They had only one passionate hour and a moment to share a cup of tea before John rode off again into the night. For Jessie it was enough. "Unexpected joy is always so keen that . . . it seems to hold enough to reconcile one to the inevitable."[27]

Her journey downriver to St. Louis was nonetheless bitter, as she mourned for her dead child and for John, riding into the silent wilderness, and brooded over the injustices of the court-martial. Convinced that the long horror of the trial had weakened her during her pregnancy, she blamed General Kearny for her baby's death.

Immediately after the trial, Kearny had been sent to Mexico, where he was stricken by yellow fever and a debilitating dysentery. In the late summer, he returned to St. Louis, gaunt, feeble, his skin a sallow yellow. On October 31, he died. Immediately after his death, Kearny partisans spread the story that the Frémonts had sought a reconciliation with the dying general. Long afterward, Jessie chose to leave a far different impression. When she returned to St. Louis from Westport, she explained, Dr. William Beaumont, who was her physician as well as Kearny's, told her that Kearny wanted to see her to ask her forgiveness. She refused. "There was a little grave between us I could not cross," she said.[28]

Jessie returned to Washington profoundly depressed. She had promised to meet John in California in the spring, but she dreaded leaving her familiar world. To John, California meant escape from a hostile East. To Jessie, it was the severing of a comforting web of lifelong ties.

The plan was for Jessie and Lily to take the new government-subsidized mail steamer to Chagres, on the east coast of Panama, transfer to dugout and muleback for the isthmus crossing, then catch a second mail steamer at Panama City on the Pacific Coast for the voyage to San Francisco.

The perils of the journey alarmed her. She knew the isthmus crossing was dangerous, for cholera, malaria, and yellow fever lurked in the jungle. Chagres had "wretched facilities for travelers," the *Intelligencer* announced in late December. "Its climate for strangers is as bad as miasma and fever can make it." Reports trickling east from San Francisco were also unsettling. "Vice of every kind and in the most horrible forms prevails here," wrote one correspondent.[29]

To assuage her anxiety, Jessie threw herself into a frenzy of preparations. For want of a better authority, a friend who had been to China was consulted about clothes, and a seamstress employed to sew dozens of cool dresses and chemises. "We busied ourselves with preparations for the heat of the tropics," Jessie remembered, "with refreshing my Spanish, and I, for my part, chiefly, in reconciling myself to the fact that in a few months I should be cut loose from everything that had made my previous life."[30]

It was a hard winter for the Benton family. When Francis Blair dropped by, he thought the senator looked thin and white, while Elizabeth, who tottered into the parlor to greet him, seemed "the very ghost of her former self." Jessie too was unwell, though long, hopeful letters from John improved her mental state. Still, at least one letter must have disturbed her. "Both Indians and whites here report the snow to be deeper in the mountains than has for a long time been known so early in the season," he wrote from Bent's Fort in November, "and they predict a severe winter." Nonetheless, he remained determinedly optimistic. He expected to reach California by early January, where he would await her arrival.[31]

Ever since she and John had agreed to meet in California, her family and friends opposed the plan. Secretary Buchanan, who still had a warm spot for her, paid a call especially to dissuade her from what he bluntly called "a cruel experiment."[32] Over the long winter, the pressure continued, and even her father tried to convince her that she should postpone her journey until conditions were less dangerous.

Jessie herself was torn. For the first time in her twenty-three years, she would be on her own. "I had never lived out of my father's house, nor in any way assumed a separate life from the other children of the family. . . . I had never been obliged to think for or take care of myself, and now I was to be launched literally on an unknown sea, . . . everything absolutely new and strange about me, and undefined for the future."[33]

But John's sad, worn face haunted her. Despite her own fears and her family's pleas, despite the very real perils of the journey, she was determined to go. "I saw only the proud lonely man making a new start in life, but for me quite alone."[34]

13

*It is no place for a woman to live
and I would not have my family here
for all the gold in the mountains.*

Charles Winslow
San Francisco
June 19, 1849

*My husband grew enthusiastic and
wanted to start immediately, but I
would not be left behind. I thought
where he could go I could, and where
I went I could take my two little
toddling babies. I little realized
the task I had undertaken. If I had,
I think I should still be in my log
cabin in Missouri.*

Luzena Stanley Wilson,
Forty-niner

VOYAGE TO
EL DORADO

O N JANUARY 24, 1848, while Jessie and John were still immersed in the court-martial, a thirty-five-year-old carpenter named James Marshall, supervising the construction of a sawmill on the south fork of California's American River, reached down into the freshly dug tailrace and picked up a handful of metallic flakes that glittered like gold.

The news traveled slowly. By late summer a few reports had trickled east. In September the Frémonts' friend, naval officer Edward F. Beale, arrived in Washington from California, carrying gold nuggets in his pocket and a letter from Thomas Larkin confirming the discovery. Beale's news made a brief splash in the papers, but when he called on the president, Polk evidently suspected he was speculating in San Francisco real estate and spreading the story merely to increase his profits.

Tales of California gold continued to reach the East that fall. "Your streams have minnows in them, but ours are paved with gold," one Californian boasted to an eastern newspaper. Men were picking up nuggets just like "1,000 hogs, let loose in a forest, would root up ground-nuts."[1] But such western braggadocio was largely ignored until early December, when a detailed report from California's military governor reached Washington.

Governor Richard Mason admitted that he had not believed the stories himself until he toured the diggings in mid-summer and found nearly four thousand men at work, taking out a combined thirty to fifty thousand dollars a day in gold.

Entire crews were jumping ship when they reached the coast, and his own soldiers were deserting daily. "I have no hesitation now in saying," the governor solemnly concluded, "there is more gold in the country drained by the Sacramento and San Joaquin rivers than will pay the cost of the war with Mexico a hundred times over."[2]

The governor's report convinced even the skeptical president, and in his annual message to Congress, he made the news official. But it was the generous sample of gold that Mason enclosed—nearly four thousand dollars' worth jammed into a tea caddy—that provided the final proof. Put on display at the War Department, it created a sensation. "We are on the brink of the Age of Gold," exclaimed Horace Greeley's New York *Tribune*. All a man needed to make a fortune in California was "a stout pair of arms, a shovel, and a tin pan."[3]

By the time Jessie arrived in New York on March 14 to take the Panama steamer, the city was in a frenzy of gold fever. Living out her own private drama in the spring of 1849, she found herself caught up in a great male adventure as thousands abandoned their farms, shops, and families to head for California. Ships of the most dubious seaworthiness were refurbished for the voyage to Panama or around the Horn. By mid-April three hundred ships had left New York harbor. Overland companies were also forming. For $110 a man could join the Kit Carson Association, which promised him two mules, three months' provisions, and a guided journey across Texas to California. Many in the Midwest simply banded together, loaded up their farm wagons, and headed out across the plains. By the end of the summer, more than a hundred thousand argonauts would reach El Dorado.

The dream had its props and costumes. Gold-seekers equipped themselves with flannel shirts, corduroy or Kentucky denim trousers, broad felt hats, and high boots, garnished with a formidable array of pistols, knives, and rifles to meet all romantic contingencies. Every forty-niner had his pan, pick, and shovel, carried in a canvas or rubber sack. Some also succumbed to more elaborate contraptions like Bull's

Concentric Gold Washer or a patented portable bellows and forge for smelting gold on the spot. Many also carried Frémont's reports, repackaged for the gold-rush trade as *The California Guide Book* or *Oregon and California*, with added notes about the gold region. For sickness there were patent medicines like Gay's California Canchalagua Compound ("for what is wealth compared with health?") and for loved ones left behind, daguerreotypes of the expectant gold-seeker furnished by Mathew Brady's studio on Broadway "at lowest prices."[4]

While this exuberant cast dressed and equipped themselves for their California adventure, Jessie steeled herself for exile. "I was much in the position of a nun carried into the world for the last time before taking the veil," she said of her journey to New York. She and Lily were accompanied by Senator Benton, her sisters Liz and Sarah, and Sarah's husband, Richard Taylor Jacob. Since it was deemed unthinkable that Jessie travel so far without male protection, Jacob, suddenly found to need a sea voyage for his health, had been drafted to escort her. A servant was also considered essential. From among the Benton household staff, a young black woman whom Jessie especially liked had been delegated to accompany her, "each of us . . . considered a victim selected for a sacrifice." But when they reached New York, the young woman's fiancé and friends protested her departure so vigorously—even claiming that she was being carried off to California to be enslaved—that she became frantic. "When she appealed in tears to us to decide what she should do, we told her to stay." A replacement was hastily found. "To go without any servants was the right course," Jessie said in retrospect, "but we had never heard of that sort of thing, so my Father took for me a 'middle-aged respectable New England woman'" who came highly recommended. "I barely looked at her, and saw she was a hard, unpleasing person to my mind; but the steamer sailed next day, and there was no time for any choice. She was only an item in the many griefs that seemed to accumulate on me at this time."[5]

The morning of March 15 was gray and dismal, with a light snow falling, as Jessie's little entourage made its way to the wharf where the steamer *Crescent City* was docked. They found it swarming with forty-niners, strutting in their red flannel shirts and boots, and carrying their precious sacks of mining tools. Among them was at least one future millionaire, a young Connecticut clock and notions peddler named Collis P. Huntington, who shrewdly suspected that in California there was more money to be made in goods than in gold. But what was most striking and most typical about the *Crescent City's* nearly three hundred fifty passengers was that aside from Jessie and Lily, their new servant, and a sedate-looking Irish woman traveling with her husband, every one of them was male.

As the Benton family made their way on board, stevedores tumbled bales and boxes up the gangplank, mates shouted orders to deckhands, and peddlers cried their wares. Alongside the steamer, a man floated in the icy water, advertising a "patent life preserver." To Jessie, immersed in her own private agony, it was all a blur. Somehow she endured the tearful good-byes, the promises to write, and the final words of advice from her beloved father. As Thomas Benton left her at last, Jessie heard someone whisper to him, "It is like leaving her in her grave."[6]

When everyone had gone, Jessie remained in her cabin, numb with grief, while six-year-old Lily, in tears, clung to her. Dimly they heard the farewell shouts of the passengers and the answering calls of those on shore over the throb of the engine. Moving down the river and out to sea, the steamer began to pitch and roll, but Jessie scarcely noticed. When the captain, solicitous toward the senator's woebegone daughter, stopped by and counseled that she go to bed early since it was too rough to walk on deck, she found it a relief to take his advice. Jessie tucked Lily into her berth, then climbed in beside the sobbing child to comfort her.

Lily had at last fallen asleep and Jessie herself was half-dozing when their new servant came silently in. "I became aware someone was examining my face with a light and some instinct made me pretend to be asleep," Jessie remembered. "In the mirror . . . I saw my new maid take off her wig of plainly dressed dark hair and show herself to be years younger with light hair. She then opened my trunk, took out collars, cuffs, handkerchiefs, a little armful, and went softly out of the room. Instantly I was up . . . and locked the door. She beat on it in vain. I called loudly for help."

When Jessie told the captain what had happened, he placed the servant under guard in another cabin. Long afterward, Jessie learned that the woman was a known thief, but the person who recommended her had hoped that in a new land she would reform. "I was sacrificed in the experiment," Jessie said sourly.[7]

To make matters worse, her assigned protector, Richard Jacob, was so seasick he could not leave his bed. Jessie moped about her cabin until the captain discovered she was not seasick herself and urged her up on deck. "I loved it at first look. I had never seen the sea, and in some odd way no one had ever told me of the wonderful new life it could bring."[8] From then on Jessie spent her days on deck, but as they neared Chagres, the captain grew increasingly concerned about the thin young woman and small child in his care.

They reached Chagres on March 24, nine days out of New York. As the steamer rolled offshore beyond the breakers, a tender so small it seemed a mere toy to Jessie approached. Behind it came a swarm of dugout canoes manned by dark, naked men.

In the confusion of loading passengers and baggage into the tender, the captain pleaded with Jessie to return to New York. Thousands of men were already stranded at Panama City waiting for transportation to California, but every ship that reached San Francisco lost its crew to the gold fields and could not return to the isthmus. Panama City, he told her almost angrily, with its heat, disease, and restless men, was no place for a woman or a child. But Jessie was determined to go on. Despite her fears, she and Lily clambered down into the lurching little boat.[9]

The tender carried them only a few miles upriver, where they changed to dugout canoes for the three-day, forty-mile journey to Gorgona. While other passengers scrambled to hire canoes and crew, Jessie, Lily, and Richard Jacob were ushered into the steamship company boat, a larger, more stable model, with a palm-leaf canopy for shade. For the isthmus crossing they had been consigned to the care of a company employee named Tucker, a longtime captain in the mahogany trade, who later confessed to Jessie that he had dreaded the assignment, for his wife had warned him that a Washington lady would be sure to make trouble about the dirt, the heat, the food, and especially the naked Indians. He had been relieved when he met her to find that she was only "a poor thin pale woman and not a bit of a fine lady."

Jessie invited the steamer's other woman passenger to join her in her relatively commodious boat, while over her protests, the thieving servant also claimed a place. As the native crew poled them upriver against the stiff current, the oppressive heat, the rank smells of rotting vegetation, and the strange sounds of the jungle engulfed them. Monkeys shrieked and great flocks of parrots whirred by. Alligators slithered through the water. Jessie glimpsed flaring crimson and violet blossoms in the vine-choked trees and brilliant butterflies with iridescent wings. When they neared the bank, the trees enclosed them, "so matted by masses of flowering creepers that we seemed at times to glide along an aisle of flowers through a great conservatory."

Jessie's pampered entourage stayed each night at one of the camps built for the American engineering team surveying the isthmus for a projected railroad. Jessie fully appreciated the fresh tea, clean boiled rice, and airy tents equipped with cots made up with linen sheets when she saw the forty-niners camped haphazardly along the riverbank or sleeping in crude huts.

On the last day of their river journey, Richard Jacob, impatient when the crew dallied in getting the boat off a sandbar, jumped into the water to help. "We did get off sooner than usual," Jessie recalled, "and he was very triumphant about it, when suddenly his eyes rolled back in his head and he fell prostrate from sunstroke just as we reached Gorgona." That night it seemed doubtful he would live.

Jacob survived, but his illness forced them to remain for several days in the small tropical outpost. On the hills around town Jessie discovered hundreds of stranded Americans living in what she called "apologies for tents" while they waited for transportation to California. Among them she saw women and children surviving on meager salt provisions brought from home, and often ill from the anxiety of their situation, if not from malaria, cholera, or yellow fever.

As something of a celebrity, Jessie was invited to breakfast with the town *alcalde*, who lived in a thatched-roof, mud-and-twig-walled house that to her resembled "a magnified vegetable crate." When the meal was served, she managed to remain unperturbed, although the main course, baked monkey, looked like "a little child that had been burned to death."

After several days at Gorgona, it was clear that Richard Jacob would have to return east by the next Chagres steamer. The American surveying team at Gorgona begged Jessie to go with him. All the careful plans for her protection had collapsed, and when her escort, Captain Tucker, left her in Panama City, she would be completely on her own. Nonetheless, she decided to push on.

The twenty-mile journey over the mountains to Panama City seemed "a *distance* not a *road*" as they traveled through jungle and swamp and over mountains on wretched, underfed mules. Dead mules littered the route, and as they neared one, the vultures flapped heavily away.

Jessie watched everything, half-fascinated, half-appalled. Captain Tucker was elated that she seemed neither sick, tired, nor afraid. "As there were no complaints or tears or visible breakdown, he gave me credit for high courage, when the fact was that the whole thing was so like a nightmare that one took it as a bad dream—in helpless silence." Still, she could not deny the strange joy she felt when, cresting the last mountain, she gazed westward to the Pacific.

Following an ancient stone roadway, they descended into the walled city of Panama, where crumbling stone houses leaned so far over the narrow streets they nearly blocked the sky. Jessie and Lily established themselves in one of the innumerable hotels hastily opened to accommodate the flood of forty-niners, but their canvas-walled rooms let in every noise and smell. They were grateful when an aristocratic Panamanian widow, Señora Arcé y Zimena, whose nephew Jessie had known when he was the Panamanian ambassador in Washington, insisted that they stay at her home.

Jessie and Lily were soon ensconced in a cool, shadowy second-floor room with high ceilings and tile floors, furnished with a blue damask sofa, grass hammocks for sleeping, and crystal chandeliers. From their balcony overlooking the main plaza, they could see the cathedral with its inlaid mother-of-pearl spire, the customs house, and the jail, where the guards held frequent cock fights. "I became, in spite of myself, expert in judging these," Jessie said.[10] Soothed and cosseted by Señora Arcé, she sank gratefully into the languid, protected life of upper-class Panamanian women.

Every day more boats arrived at Chagres, disgorging men bound for California. They poured into Panama City, until there were several thousand forty-niners, frustrated at being stopped in their path to sudden fortune. Jessie encountered them as she walked along the sea wall, anxiously scanning the horizon for the long-overdue steamer. As the rainy season began, the men grew more discouraged. Many were stranded without money. Some sickened and died of mysterious tropical diseases.

With each passing day, Jessie too became more uneasy, not only about her own precarious situation but for John as well. Disturbing rumors had reached Panama that his expedition had met disaster in the mountains. Nonetheless, she was unprepared for the letter she finally received, dated January 27 from Taos, New Mexico.[11]

"I write to you from the house of our good friend Carson," John began. "This morning a cup of chocolate was brought to me while yet in bed. . . . While in the enjoyment of this luxury, then, I pleased myself in imagining how gratified you would be in picturing me here in Kit's care. . . . But I have now the unpleasant task of telling you how I came here. . . . I have an almost invincible repugnance to going back among scenes where I have endured much suffering."

John then described his fatal winter journey to the San Juan Mountains in the southern Colorado Rockies, where incessant snowstorms bewildered his party and prevented them from finding the pass they sought. John blamed the guide, Old Bill Williams, an experienced but eccentric mountaineer in his early sixties who "proved never to have in the least known, or entirely to have forgotten, the whole region of country through which we were to pass. We occupied more than half a month in making the journey of a few days, blundering a tortuous way through deep snow." By mid-December their situation was desperate. Ahead lay not the snowless plain Williams had promised but impenetrable ranges of snow-covered mountains. "It was impossible to advance, and to turn back was equally impracticable," John wrote. "We were overtaken by sudden and inevitable ruin."

John sent Williams and three other men to get help at the nearest settlement in New Mexico, while the rest remained behind. They had rations—macaroni and bacon—for only two weeks. As the days passed, the waiting men grew despondent. One lay down in the trail and froze to death.

After sixteen days without word from Williams, John, accompanied by Preuss, Godey, and two other men, set out on a second attempt to find help. Six days later they stumbled across Williams's group, living skeletons floundering in the snow. One man had already died, and both Preuss and John suspected that the others, half-crazed, were living off his flesh.

"In starving times no man who knew him ever walked in front of Bill Williams," Kit Carson later said.[12] Eventually, John's rescue party reached a settlement, and Godey hurried back with provisions and mules for the remaining men. Before he reached them, eight more had died of cold, hunger, and exhaustion. In all, one-third of John's expedition perished in the snow.

Later several survivors would charge not Williams but John himself with responsibility for the disaster. But it is significant that not only the experienced Alexis Godey but Preuss, the skilled cartographer who never wrote a kind word about John in his private diary if he could help it, also blamed Williams. "Bill's vacillations showed that he was not very much at home, at least in these parts," Preuss observed. "In crossing the second chain, Bill definitely missed the promised *good* pass." When the expedition realized the full horror of their predicament, Preuss recorded, "that old fool Bill lay down and wanted to die."[13]

Though Williams may have been a poor guide, perhaps too old to remember what he had once known so well, John, as the expedition leader, nonetheless bore the final responsibility. It was foolhardy to venture across the Rockies during the worst winter in memory, against the advice of both settlers and Indians. And it was rash to push stubbornly ahead, when a wiser leader might have turned back. John no doubt remembered his equally risky Sierra crossing, from which he emerged a hero. Haunted by the court-martial, and ultimately by his illegitimacy, he felt compelled to prove himself once more.

Writing to Jessie from Carson's warm Taos home, John wanted only to forget the tragedy, to escape his anguish and guilt. More than ever, California seemed a refuge. "We shall yet enjoy quiet and happiness together—these are nearly one and the same to me now. I make frequently pleasant pictures of the happy home we are to have. . . . I have it all planned in my own mind."

Stunned though she was by the tragedy, Jessie was deeply

relieved to know John was safe. Yet her own situation seemed more precarious than ever. She was stranded in a strange tropical city. The rain poured in torrents, and the mosquitoes had become almost unbearable. The walls of her room were so damp that water ran down them in rivulets.

One morning an acquaintance brought her a fresh newspaper account of John's mountain disaster. That evening, when he returned with yet another report, "he found me where he had left me in the morning—sitting upon the sofa, with the unopened paper clasped in my hand, my eyes closed, and my forehead purple from congestion of the brain, and entirely unable to understand anything said to me." The doctors diagnosed her ailment as "brain fever." To her, "it was a relief to become too ill to think."[14]

Jessie's lungs were infected, and she was coughing blood. Señora Arcé summoned both her own Panamanian doctor and, in deference to Jessie's nationality, an American doctor as well. The Panamanian advised a closed room, bleeding, and hot drinks, while the American advocated fresh air, blistering, and iced liquids. "These two, with their contradictory ideas and their inability to understand each other fully, only added to the confusion of my mind, and became part of my delirium," Jessie said.[15] Fortunately, leeches were unavailable, but her chest was rubbed with croton oil, furnished from the medicine chest of a British warship in the harbor, to produce the requisite blisters.

Somehow the crisis passed. Her cough and fever dwindled. Eventually she was well enough to walk again along the ramparts of the city at sundown. More informal now, she sat on one of the huge old Spanish guns pointing out to sea, talking with the American men she chanced to meet. She found them more discouraged, desperate even, and, like everyone else she encountered, convinced that she should turn back. This time she was ready to agree.

In the hours before dawn on May 6, Jessie was startled awake by the echoing boom of a great gun, followed by excited shouts. Hurrying to her balcony, she saw forty-niners pouring into the moonlit plaza, laughing, cheering, crying. The long-awaited steamer *Oregon* had arrived from San Francisco. In the midst of the excitement, another gun boomed. There was a hush, then shouts of joy. A second steamer, the *Panama*, had arrived from around the Horn.

As Jessie watched, she saw two men push through the crowd. "I heard my own name and caught sight of a familiar face and uniform." "Mrs. Frémont here!" she heard the man say as he turned into her entrance. "What a crib for a lady!"[16] It was naval officer Edward Beale, just arrived on the *Oregon*. He was traveling east again with government dispatches and carrying a lump of gold worth two thousand dollars.

Though Beale would tell the Panama *Star* that California soil was "so strongly impregnated with Gold as to be inexhaustible,"[17] he stressed another aspect to Jessie. Talking with her that day, he described the chaos of San Francisco—the few women, the lack of housing and servants, the gambling and wild abandon of the city. Moreover, Beale had learned that John had injured his leg during his mountain ordeal and was expected to return east for treatment. Now Beale urged her to do the same. She and Lily could leave for Chagres with him the next morning. In a few days they would be on the Atlantic steamer, bound for New York.

Jessie was torn. It would be so easy to give up and travel home by government escort. But she had promised to meet John in San Francisco, and she believed he would keep his word. She had endured so much, she wanted to see the journey through.

When she told Beale her decision, he was angry at her stubbornness. As for Jessie, the choice exhausted her. "After this I did no more deciding, but let myself go with the current."[18]

On May 18, after nearly two months on the isthmus, Jessie and Lily boarded the crowded *Panama*, bound for San Francisco.[19] Built for mail rather than passengers, the steamer had accommodations for only eighty, though it now carried four hundred forty-niners. Food was in short supply, and Jessie found the ship's steward was "reserving the canned provisions to sell for his own benefit. For a piece of gold he would sell a little can of vegetables or preserved meat."

Her hot, airless cabin revived her racking cough, so a tentlike room was rigged up for her on the quarterdeck by draping a large flag over the boom. "Everybody contributed something to make me comfortable: one a folding iron camp bedstead—some, guava jelly—some, tea." Jessie shared her tent with Lily and one of the few other women on board. Around them slept hundreds of men, their places on the deck marked in chalk.

Gradually Jessie was drawn into the life of the ship. She found her fellow passengers a fascinating lot. There was William Gwin, an ambitious Tennessee-born politician who openly bragged that he would become California's first senator; ebullient Sam Ward, bon vivant, friend of Longfellow and brother of Julia Ward Howe, going to California to recoup a lost fortune; and Major George Derby, a puckish army officer, later known as the comic writer John Phoenix, who kept the whole ship entertained with his nightly skits and plays. Even the steerage passengers were invited to the upper deck for such inspired efforts as "The Rescued Maiden," a wild spoof with "the maiden," "the ravisher," and "the rescuer" all played by men. Jessie herself ignored eastern propriety long enough to serve as mistress of ceremony for a series of comic tableaux devised by Derby.[20]

En route to Panama, Jessie had been tense and fearful, careful to keep her distance from the forty-niners who jammed the steamer. But on the isthmus, as she shared the vicissitudes of dugout and muleback, as well as the long wait in Panama City, the Victorian East became remote—another country— and she began to enjoy their company. For her the journey had become a passage into a male realm, an exhilarating place she had occasionally known with her father and with John when they worked together on the reports. But her new openness seems not to have gone uncensored. Several months later, Theodore Talbot encountered a British army captain who had been on the *Panama* with Jessie and was evidently disturbed by her informality. "[He] does not admire her," Talbot noted tersely in his journal.[21]

Jessie discovered that almost everyone on the *Panama* kept a journal. She herself felt no such need: "Everything burned itself in its own image on my mind." When a school of whales cavorted into view and every man reached for his notebook, she sent out scouts to find out what it was that people were writing. "I was sure the greater number would put, 'This morning . . . we met the leviathan of the deep disporting himself in his native element,' or, 'Glorious sight! huge monsters at play!' I was sure very few would call a whale a whale."

Jessie's scouts coaxed the unsuspecting diarists to reveal their entries. When the returns were in, " 'the leviathan' had it by an immense majority; very few whales." Most forty-niners still saw with eastern eyes, applying ornate and inappropriate rhetoric to a new and far different scene. Jessie, as a woman with more radical changes to make, had learned more quickly than they to call a whale a whale.

During the early part of the voyage, Jessie buried her fears about John and let the days drift by. But when the ship reached the mud hamlet of San Diego, where she would learn whether he had reached California or returned east, she was so tense that she closeted herself in the stuffy cabin to await the news alone.

At last came shouts, footsteps, and a brisk knock at the door. "The Colonel is safe!" a man called. "It's all right now!" Joyously, Jessie threw open the door as what seemed like half the men on the ship crowded around her, sharing her happiness. John had reached Los Angeles several weeks before and was riding north to meet her in San Francisco.

The last days on board passed quickly. Though its passengers were exuberant, the *Panama* was running out of coal. Nearing San Francisco, it began to burn its own planking to keep up steam.

Early on the morning of June 4, 1849, as mist and fog swirled around the ship, it steamed through the narrow strait Jessie's husband had named the Golden Gate. As it entered the bay, men crowded to the rails, peering eagerly into the fog. Among them stood Jessie and Lily, waiting for their first glimpse of El Dorado.

14

I would much prefer that a wife of mine should board in a respectable bawd house in the city of New York than anywhere in the city of San Francisco.

Robert Effinger
Forty-niner

And only think of such a shrinking, timid, frail thing as I used to be. I like this wild and barbarous life. Here, at least, I have been contented.

Louise Clappe
Rich Bar, California
1851

CALIFORNIA
METAMORPHOSIS

IT WAS A BLEAK SCENE that emerged through the chilling mist. In the harbor Jessie saw hundreds of ships, abandoned by their crews, swinging eerily with the tide, and beyond, on the shore, a chaos of tents, shanties, and shacks perched haphazardly on the slopes of barren, windswept hills. As the steamer approached, she saw that the beach was swarming with men.

Jessie was wild to see John again, and when a dozen boats came out to meet the steamer, she searched each one for his familiar face. Her heart sank when she realized he was not aboard any of them. A man from one of the boats introduced himself as William Howard, a local merchant. Howard explained that John had not yet arrived in San Francisco, although he was expected any day. Meanwhile, he could provide her with a place to stay.[1]

Shivering in the damp sea air, she and Lily were rowed close to shore, then carried through the surf by sailors and deposited on the beach, where rough, bearded men stared at them with open fascination. Traveling along the crude trails that passed for streets in the makeshift city, they glimpsed crowded gambling tents where music blared and men shouted raucously. The harsh wind cut through their clothes, and blew sand and grit into their hair and eyes.

Howard had arranged rooms for them in what was probably the most elegant accommodation in town, the Leidesdorff house, a solid adobe with veranda and garden, which a group of prospering merchants were paying sixty thousand dollars a year to rent. Inside, Jessie was amazed to find thick carpets, fine furniture, and even a piano, although there was no wood for a fire. In California, she discovered, "luxuries of every kind were to be had, but there were wanting some necessaries."[2]

During the next few days, as Jessie waited uneasily for John, she saw more of the raw new city. There was a frenzy, a fever, in the air. Men daily spilled out of ships and headed for the diggings, while others returned with bags of gold to spend on a spree. Goods from every corner of the world were piled in the streets and in flimsy tent stores. Housing was so scarce that men would pay a dollar a night to sleep in a straw-filled packing crate. Jessie received a flood of visitors, who regaled her with tales of sudden wealth, as much from speculation in town lots or merchandise as gold. San Francisco society, she learned, consisted of a scant sixteen ladies. The occasional woman she glimpsed in a gambling tent or riding horseback astride like a man was not, of course, included in this select company.

Ten long days passed before John appeared and Jessie could hold him in her arms again. Though he looked lean and tan, she could see traces of the past year's tragedies in his face; and his leg, badly frostbitten during his Rocky Mountain journey, still pained him.

They had so much to tell each other, it was hard to know where to begin. Jessie learned that John's sawmill at San Jose would soon turn a handsome profit, since lumber was in sharp demand in San Francisco. Moreover, Las Mariposas [The Butterflies], a seventy-square-mile ranch in the Sierra foothills near Yosemite Valley that John had given Thomas Larkin three thousand dollars to purchase for him before the gold rush, was not the worthless tract they feared. On a hunch, John had hired a group of experienced Mexican miners to prospect it for him, and they were finding gold.

Jessie had her own tales to tell, and though she tried to downplay the hardships of her journey, Lily told him bluntly that her mother had almost died in Panama. To John, Jessie seemed achingly frail, and in the fog and harsh winds of San Francisco, her lungs had begun to hemorrhage again.

An immediate move to a warmer spot seemed essential. They decided on Monterey, a hundred miles to the south, where the gentler climate and backwater drowsiness could be expected to soothe both her lungs and her psyche.

When they arrived by steamer on June 20, Jessie found a village of red-tiled adobes nestled in the curve of the bay, with fragrant pine-scented hills rising behind. It was a tranquil, sunny place, occupied by old California families and a small garrison of American military officers. One of them was the future Civil War General William Tecumseh Sherman, a tubercular youth "thin to gauntness, and not considered more likely to live" than Jessie herself.[3] Aside from the American officers, Monterey was a town of women, children, and old men, for virtually every able-bodied man had gone to the diggings.

Housing was scarce, but the Frémonts managed to rent a wing of the adobe villa of Señora José Castro, wife of the California general who had driven John from Gabilan Peak three years before. Castro himself was in Mexico, but the señora proved hospitable. She and her children occupied one wing; and a flour merchant rented the long central section, once a ballroom, for his warehouse. The Frémonts settled into the second wing, where a generous window overlooked the bay. The rhythmic roll of the surf became a background to their contentment. Lily was soon playing happily with Señora Castro's daughters in the large walled garden bordered by hedges of pink roses.

Though Jessie was delighted with her quarters, she found that domesticity was not easy in gold-rush California. "It was barely a year since the gold had been discovered, but in that time every eatable thing had been eaten off the face of the country, and nothing raised. I suppose there was not a fowl left in the northern part of the state, consequently not an egg." Even potatoes were a luxury. "Housekeeping, deprived of milk, eggs, vegetables, and fresh meat, becomes a puzzle."[4]

Jessie managed on canned meats, pasta, and rice purchased in San Francisco, supplemented by freshly baked bread sent over by an American officer's wife; a daily cup of milk for Lily furnished by Señora Castro, who owned the only cow in town; and occasional baskets of cabbages and carrots grown by the military governor himself, who delivered them with such gallantry that it seemed he was bringing her roses.

It was an endless problem to have clothes laundered or wood chopped for the stove. "We have been in despair how we should get the sheets washed and the big tablecloths," moaned Lottie Wescott, wife of an army officer and mother of three, who, like Jessie, was trying to keep house in Monterey. Two California mission Indians, Juan and Gregorio, who had traveled with John on several of his expeditions, occasionally helped Jessie in the kitchen. Though she found their *guisado* of bird, squirrel, rice, and hot peppers tasty, she did much of the cooking herself. A man who met the Frémonts that summer found her "busily engaged preparing some corn to cook, for here every lady has to do her own work."[5]

Jessie furnished her Monterey rooms with a wayward charm dictated by what John could buy in San Francisco and send down by steamer: exotic bamboo couches, chairs, and carved, inlaid tables from China; rich oriental and French fabrics for cushions and drapes; and a fancy punch bowl for a wash basin. She laid straw matting on the floors and spread an enormous bearskin rug before the fire.

Although the few American women in Monterey welcomed Jessie, the native Californians were more hesitant. To them, "my name represented only invasion and defeat." But her genuine charm, as well as her knowledge of Spanish, honed by eight weeks in Panama, gradually softened their wariness, and they became "among the kindest people I knew there." Many forty-niners dismissed the Californians as slovenly, ignorant, and lazy; but Jessie found their houses "charmingly neat and orderly," and the women and children busy and contented in their secluded domestic life. She enjoyed

sitting with them in the intimacy of their shaded inner court-
yards, talking and sewing, admiring the embroidered linens
and bright satin dresses they pulled from painted Chinese
chests to show her.[6]

In warm, somnolent Monterey, Jessie's cough disappeared, and her natural vitality returned. Though housekeeping was not easy, the problem seemed almost irrelevant.
"We had the luxuries of life, if not its necessities. Youth, health
and exultant happiness can do without commonplaces."[7]

John too relaxed, and the shadow of the past year's tragedies left his face. He was exhilarated by his success at Las
Mariposas, where his gold deposits were proving far richer
than they dreamed possible. A vein of gold two feet across at
the surface, widening as it descended more than a mile into
the earth, had been discovered there. He showed Jessie the
samples: great chunks of reddish quartz thickly streaked with
gold.

They were visiting in nearby San Jose when the first con-
voy of Las Mariposas gold arrived. Since accommodations
were as scarce in San Jose as elsewhere, they were staying in
a single room whose floor John doused with scalding water
every morning to kill the day's supply of fleas. To Jessie it
seemed a delicious irony to be in such surroundings when
the buckskin bags arrived, each filled with a hundred pounds
of glittering dust and nuggets. Only then, seeing the gold,
touching it, running it through her fingers, did she begin to
understand just how fabulously rich they were. To her, the
gold meant not so much material possessions as independence. Never again would they be at the mercy of a fickle
government or a vengeful general. The gold, she believed,
would buy them their freedom.

They celebrated their new independence by taking long,
leisurely trips through the countryside, traveling in an ingenious carriage—a kind of early-day camper equipped with sliding leather seats that turned into beds—that had been shipped
around the Horn for them. There were no roads as such, so
they followed bridle paths or ox-cart tracks through the tawny

valleys of the Coast Range, "putting into San Francisco for news, or San Jose for soft weather." Sometimes Jessie rode horseback with a man's saddle down the steep mountain trails. To her, it was a blissful time. "The wild oats were ripe . . . the wild cattle were feeding about or resting under the evergreen oaks. . . . The sky was a deep blue, without a cloud."[8]

They were often accompanied by Ned Beale, the naval lieutenant Jessie had last seen on Panama under far different circumstances. Beale, who liked to sport a serape and jangling Chilean spurs, tried to train two spirited California horses to pull the Frémont carriage, but they bucked so relentlessly that Jessie insisted on mules, despite their lack of dash.

Nonetheless, they made a picturesque sight, like a scene from an opera to Jessie, who delighted in the display. John and Beale rode ahead, scouting the route, followed by the two Indians, Juan and Gregorio, resplendent in their embroidered Spanish riding outfits with red silk scarves tied beneath white sombreros. Jessie and Lily came next, comfortably ensconced in the carriage, with its leather curtains rolled up for the view. Behind trailed a string of pack mules, carrying food, cooking supplies, hammocks, and clothes packed in square leather hampers.

During their wanderings they often detoured to visit California families at their ranchos, where as many as four generations would gather to welcome them. Jessie was in her element as she arrived like a rural princess in her eccentric carriage with its colorful entourage. While there was something of the incipient grande dame in twenty-five-year-old Jessie, she was also a warm and open woman, unusually sensitive to the predicament of the Californians, whose culture was threatened by the gold-rush invasion. It was a way of life she valued. In St. Louis she had found French-Catholic culture an appealing alternative to the crabbed puritanism of the East that hobbled her own natural exuberance. In California she found a similar gaiety and passion. "Before we brought taxes and litigation upon them," she reflected later, "the Californians were a wholesome and cheerful people, going about their pleasures not sadly, as is the inherited wont of our nation, but making a joyful noise."[9]

Though both John and Jessie were temperamentally attracted to the warmth, gaiety, and pageantry of California life, they were still Yankees at heart, driven by ambitions that set them apart from the Californians. Even as they indulged in their summer camping idyll, their latent political dreams were aroused by talk of the coming constitutional convention at Monterey, the government to be formed, and the officials—governor, senators, representatives—to be elected. It was widely said that John Charles Frémont—California conqueror, senator's son-in-law, and gold-rush millionaire—could have his pick of offices.

California was in desperate need of a civilian government. As forty-niners poured into the region, the loose military regime of the conquest, administered by a handful of soldiers at Monterey, could not cope with the exuberant chaos. "Every man carried his code of laws on his hip," claimed one observer, "and administered it according to his own pleasure."[10] When Congress, unable to agree on whether California should be slave or free, failed to provide it with a territorial government by the summer of 1849, Californians took matters into their own hands. That August delegates were elected to a constitutional convention that would form a government and most probably ask for immediate statehood.

When the four dozen delegates reached tiny Monterey in early September, they found only a single grimy restaurant, with adjoining billiard parlor, but no hotels. Delegates doubled up in the flea-infested army barracks, crowded into private homes, or camped out under the pine trees, while local residents provided open house for the hungry men.

The Frémonts made a point of being in Monterey for part of the convention, although Jessie's country forays had rather ignominiously resulted in a case of poison oak so severe that for several weeks her legs and feet were too swollen for her to put on shoes.[11] Nonetheless, she managed to entertain delegates in her cozy rooms and do her part in keeping them well fed.

For Jessie, looking back, the crucial issue at the convention was slavery. She had confronted the question earlier that summer when a Texan, learning that she needed household help, offered to sell her a black woman. Shocked, Jessie had refused. The convention gave her a chance to reaffirm her views. She remembered most vividly a delegate bringing a group of fifteen men "to hear for themselves from me, that for no reason would I consent to own or use a slave." One tall, rough man was especially impressed with her self-sufficiency. "All these women here are crying to have 'suv-vents'— but if you, a Virginia lady, can get along without, they shan't have them—we'll keep clear of slave labor." Ruefully, Jessie admitted, "I should have liked my clothes ironed, otherwise I felt the need of nothing. In short, my pretty rooms were the headquarters of the antislavery party, and myself the example of happiness and hospitality without servants."[12]

Jessie overstated both the controversy at Monterey and her own influence. Before the convention there had been speculation that slavery would be a major issue, but when the vote was taken, the delegates, including known southern sympathizers, unanimously agreed to prohibit it in California. For most, the decision was more practical than moral. It had "nothing to do with slavery in the abstract," one man admitted. "Not one in ten cares a button for its abolition." What the forty-niners feared was slave competition in the gold fields. "All here are diggers, and free white diggers won't dig with slaves."[13]

While Jessie exaggerated the slavery controversy at the convention, in a larger sense she was right, for it was slavery that blocked Congress from providing a territorial government for California, and it would be slavery that would provoke a bitter national debate when California petitioned Congress for admission as a free state.

There was more than slavery on Jessie's mind that September, for with her eager support, John had decided to run for senator, a post to be filled by a vote of the new legislature meeting in December. It was doubtless to promote his candidacy that in early October, a week before the convention adjourned, the Frémonts and Ned Beale returned to San Francisco for a brief stay.[14] Jessie was stunned by the changes she found. Thousands of tents crowded the hills, while in the center of town, wood and even brick buildings had sprung up. "The sound of hammers never ceased." The harbor was a forest of masts, and the streets were clogged with carts, drays, and wagons. Shabby gambling tents had become virtual palaces, with glittering chandeliers, gilt mirrors, and polished wooden bars. Yet among the men who jammed the streets she saw many whose dreams had failed, men sick with fever or dysentery or loneliness, men who had returned from the diggings empty-handed or who had lost what they earned in one reckless night. Such men, sleeping in the streets and scrambling for food, lived "worse than hogs at home," said one forty-niner.[15]

John, with his abundant gold, quickly solved their own housing problem by purchasing an ingenious prefabricated house from China, with smooth wooden parts that fitted together like a puzzle. By late October the Frémonts were living in Happy Valley,[16] an outlying district rapidly filling with tents and shanties, that would later become the site of the Palace Hotel.

The fall days were warm and the nights clear. Blue lupine bloomed on the dunes, and there were sweeping vistas of the sea. "Our little house had but two rooms, but they were large and clean and we had what were luxuries—a wood fire burning in front of the cottage and clean food well cooked."[17] Jessie slept in a hammock, wrapped in a navy blue blanket. Two bundles of shingles made their dinner table. In the evening friends rode over the dunes to join them for an outdoor meal. To Jessie it was an exhilarating time. She enjoyed the bearded adventurers who had come to California as much to escape the cramped life of the East as to make their fortune. Like them, she felt released in the freewheeling, unformed atmosphere of gold-rush California.

In turn, the men must have found her enchanting: young, open, alive, no longer merely enduring but relishing this new world. Jessie, of course, recognized her privileged position. "I was a great feature," she said, "for any lady was a rarity." And at least one man who met the Frémonts in San Francisco found Jessie "the better man of the two, far more intelligent and more comprehensive."[18] It was an observation, both derisive and admiring, that would recur as the years wore on.

The Frémonts returned to Monterey just as the rainy season began. John soon rode off to Las Mariposas and San Jose, where the new legislature would meet in December, while Jessie remained behind with Lily in their rooms overlooking the bay. After the excitement of San Francisco, she found the seclusion wearing. The flour merchant loaned her his entire library: a large stack of *Merchants' Magazine*, five bound volumes of an illustrated London newspaper, and an edition of Byron's poetry. Jessie made the best of this random collection, but the days passed slowly. As the rain beat down, trapping her indoors, she felt restless and lonely. Again John was off making his future; again she was merely waiting.

One rainy night just before Christmas, she was startled to hear the sound of hoofbeats through the storm. There was a sudden knock at the door and John burst in, "dripping wet and brilliantly happy."[19] He had ridden seventy miles from San Jose to bring her the news. The legislature had elected him senator on the first ballot. They would leave for Washington on New Year's night.

Two weeks later, as the rain poured down, John carried Jessie across the flooded streets of Monterey to the wharf, where a boat took them out to the waiting steamer. Jessie was supremely happy. She and John had come to California as exiles. Now, nine months later, they were returning east in triumph. As they boarded the steamer, she scarcely noticed the rain, the wild sea, or the ache in her lungs that the damp weather had renewed. "I have found that it changes the climate and removes illness to have the ship's head turned the way you wish to go."[20]

Though Jessie only dimly understood it that New Year's night, the journey to California had changed her. "A man on coming to California could no more expect to retain his old nature unchanged than he could retain in his lungs the air he had inhaled on the Atlantic shore," remarked gold-rush reporter Bayard Taylor.[21] For the few women who reached California during the gold rush, his words were even truer.

Jessie had left New York a pampered, frightened young woman, anguished to leave her comfortable and familiar world. But the journey begun in fear had become a challenge and finally a delight. Though she had been sick, lonely, and afraid, she had not only survived but emerged far stronger. "I had done so many things that I had never done before that a new sense of power had come to me," she said.[22] Her California experience brought forth her latent courage and independence. What at first seemed banishment had become an escape from Victorian America, a release that put her in touch with her own buried powers. But there was danger lurking in Jessie's new strength, for she would now find it far harder to resume the narrow life she had once so reluctantly left behind.

15

*The more I see of men, the more I am
disgusted with them—they are rather
worse too, in California, than anywhere
else—this is the Paradise of men—
I wonder if a Paradise for poor* Women
*will ever be discovered—I wish they
would get up an exploring expedition,
to seek for one.*

Martha Hitchcock
to her sister-in-law
California
1851

BRIEF TRIUMPH

TWO MONTHS LATER, Jessie stood in a sumptuous New York hotel room and stared with dismay at her reflection in the ornate mirror. Her dark eyes looked enormous in her pinched, white face, and her dress hung shapelessly on her thin body. She wore shabby black satin slippers, a tattered straw hat anchored with an old crepe scarf, and around her shoulders a plaid shawl that had done service as an awning on their Chagres River dugout. Seven-year-old Lily looked equally bedraggled. Scarcely recognizable as the robust child who left Monterey on New Year's night, she wore a faded dress and a handkerchief knotted around her head to cover what was left of her hair, shaved close when she was sick with fever in Panama.

The journey home had been a long ordeal. During their twenty-day voyage to Panama, Jessie had become dangerously ill, possibly with malaria contracted when they stopped at the Mexican port of Mazatlán. Drugged with opiates, she was carried ashore at Panama City and taken to Señora Arcé's house, where she awoke to find John lying in an adjoining room, suffering from fever and painful rheumatism in his frostbitten leg. Lily soon joined them in their misery. Too sick to travel farther, the invalid family spent a month under Señora Arcé's solicitous care.

John and Lily were recovering, but Jessie was still weak from fever when they were forced to set out across the isthmus to catch the next monthly steamer at Chagres. Jessie made the journey in a makeshift stretcher improvised from a ship's hammock, rigged with canvas curtains, padded with a crimson silk pillow provided by Señora Arcé, and slung between two poles carried by Indian porters. The first night on the trail, dosed with quinine, coffee, and opium, she saw a vampire bat sucking blood from the neck of a white horse. Horrified, she tried to cry out to stop it but found she had no voice. Days later they reached the mouth of the Chagres River. When Jessie glimpsed the dark masts of the waiting steamer rising above the jungle foliage, she leapt joyfully from her hammock, only to collapse again with fever.

The voyage home was rough. Desperately ill, Jessie was lashed to a sofa in the main cabin to keep her from falling as the steamer pitched and rolled in the stormy sea. When the ship reached New York on March 8, 1850, the family emerged like the survivors of a shipwreck.

Once on shore, Jessie recovered rapidly. Several days at the luxurious Irving House, with gold to buy whatever she needed, allowed her to rest and refurbish the family wardrobe before they traveled on to Washington.

They found Congress in the midst of a bitter debate on California statehood that had widened to include the whole panoply of slave-tainted issues. Southerners, fearful of becoming a permanent minority in Congress, insisted that California and the other new territories acquired from Mexico be left open to slavery, while free-soil northerners protested any extension. Henry Clay, withered with age but still eloquent, proposed a compromise bill that included the admission of California as a free state balanced by a more effective fugitive slave law to placate the South. Daniel Webster rose to back Clay's plan, but John Calhoun, wracked with the tuberculosis that would kill him in less than a month, opposed it, grimly warning of disunion if the South's interests were disregarded.

To Thomas Benton and many northern legislators of both parties, even Clay's proposal conceded too much to the South. California, Benton proclaimed, should not be made "the scapegoat of all the sins of slavery." Tempers reached such a pitch in April, just after John and Jessie reached Washington, that Senator Henry Foote of Mississippi, already the veteran of four duels, drew a pistol on Benton in the senate chamber. "Let him fire!" Benton cried, tearing open his coat and shirt dramatically. "I have no pistols! I disdain to carry arms! . . . Let the assassin fire!" Excited senators surrounded the two men and managed to calm them both, while someone took Foote's gun and locked it in his desk.[1]

Despite the political tension, the Washington social scene spun on, and that spring and summer of 1850, John and Jessie glittered at its center. Though John's leg still pained him and he had occasional relapses of "Chagres fever," Jessie was in radiant health again. For her it was a time of vindication. She and John had slunk away to California to find a modicum of peace in exile. Now they had returned with both the political power of a senate seat and dazzling wealth. It was, she would say in retrospect, the "high tide" of life.[2]

She savored it all: the teas and visits, the parties and galas. She attended musicales at the British Embassy, dinners with the Prussian ambassador, and a memorable gathering at the home of Massachusetts Senator Robert Winthrop, where she chatted with Webster, Bodisco and Harriet (heavy now, a mountain of lace and jewels), and the poet Longfellow. She and John also attended "a dinner full of eccentricities" at the home of wealthy abolitionist Gerrit Smith, "a remarkable and good man" whose wife wore the controversial new bloomer costume—a short silk skirt with trousers—and dessert was served on plates depicting "the Horrors of Slavery."[3]

As the hot summer wore on, congressional tempers continued to rise. Southern extremists and northern abolitionists talked openly of disunion. The bitterness was so great that Washington hostesses were reluctant to invite political opponents to the same dinner party. Even within Jessie's own family there were ominous signs of polarization. While Thomas Benton was speaking out against slavery, his brother-in-law, James McDowell, Jr., a recently elected Virginia congressman, moved in the opposite direction. Nearly twenty years before, in the Virginia legislature, McDowell had condemned slavery as a moral evil; but now, when northerners quoted back his youthful eloquence, he explained that he had become convinced that slavery was "an indispensable institution" in the South. He could only plead for northern understanding to avoid a "monstrous struggle of brother with brother."[4]

That summer the moderates prevailed as, piece by piece, Congress passed a revised compromise plan. On September 9, 1850, California was admitted to the Union as a free state. The next day, Jessie watched from the senate gallery as John and William Gwin were sworn in as California's first senators. There was a brief contretemps when Senator Jefferson Davis of Mississippi, a thin, erect, tight-lipped West Pointer, tried to block their immediate admission; but his motion failed when other southern senators, anxious for harmony, joined in voting against Davis.

During the few weeks that remained of the session, John established the beginnings of an antislavery record by voting to abolish the slave trade in the District of Columbia (but not slavery itself, as more radical Senator William H. Seward of New York proposed) and against stiff penalties for those who harbored runaway slaves. He also introduced eighteen bills relating to California and came near dueling with the vitriolic Henry Foote of Mississippi when Foote accused him of introducing a certain land-claims bill mainly to protect Las Mariposas.

Through it all, Jessie was gloriously happy. She relished both the rough joys of politics and the familiar comforts of her old home. But her season of contentment proved achingly brief. When he was sworn in, John had drawn the short senate term, which meant he would have to stand for reelection the following year. In late September he resolved to return to California to campaign. Jessie had only five days' notice.

For her it was a bitter blow. Two months pregnant, she longed to stay in Washington. She dreaded another isthmus crossing with its inevitable bout of fever, more for her unborn child than for herself. But she had endured too many separations from John to bear another just yet. The family set off for California in early October.

As Jessie feared, the journey was difficult, and she again

suffered from fever on the isthmus. One fellow traveler, spotting the celebrated Frémont family spending the night along the Chagres River, was shocked to see them huddled in a squalid hut with its sides open to the rain and swarming mosquitoes.[5] Boarding the San Francisco–bound steamer at Panama City, Jessie discovered an old antagonist, Rose Greenhow, on board. Passionately southern in her sympathies, Greenhow had nursed John Calhoun on his deathbed, then left for Mexico with her husband. Now the couple were headed for California to help the French speculator José Limantour press his dubious claims to San Francisco real estate in what would later be branded the largest land fraud scheme in the state's history. On board Jessie was barely civil. "I never spoke to her after we left the ship," she reported to Lizzie Blair Lee.[6] On November 21, 1850, this disparate crew reached San Francisco.

Jessie found the city larger, richer, more garish. The wealthy lived in a splendor of gold ornaments and red plush upholstery, crystal chandeliers, and costly French furniture. But the freewheeling joy and optimism of the early gold rush had seeped away. There was greed in the air and a palpable desperation. Adventurers, schemers, frauds, and thugs preyed on the populace. Muggings and murders, whippings and duels were everyday occurrences.

Jessie, four months pregnant and wrenched again from her familiar world, longed for domesticity, and she soon cosseted herself in a house on fashionable Stockton Street near the main plaza, still lined with gambling halls and brothels. At first she feared the rigors of the journey might have harmed her unborn child, as she believed the court-martial had damaged little Benton. But she found herself surprisingly well. John, however, was suffering again from painful rheumatism in his leg. Uneasy in the political thickets, he set out warily for San Jose, where the state legislature would choose a new senator.

The political situation had shifted. John was the favorite of the native Californians, who counted on him to protect their land along with his own Las Mariposas, and of the first American settlers, who still celebrated his part in the conquest. But to many newcomers he represented the propertied few against the landless majority. Moreover, by declaring himself a Democrat and voting his antislavery convictions in the Senate, he had alienated the numerous Whigs in the state as well as both the moderate and proslavery members of his own party.

In San Jose that winter, the candidates dispensed champagne and roast duck with lavish abandon. But the opposing forces were hopelessly deadlocked. After 141 ballots, the legislature adjourned without electing a new senator. By late summer, John had given up hope of winning the seat. Politics had become "too costly an amusement in this country just now," Jessie explained to Francis Blair, though John expected to "come to it with renewed vigor by the next election."[7]

Neither John nor Jessie admitted disappointment over this defeat. Jessie, immersed in motherhood, seemed willing to wait for a more favorable moment. When Francis Blair expressed enthusiasm for John's political future, she had mixed feelings. "The only politics we hear come from you & that is as much as we want," she told the Blairs. "We are living so peacefully I don't care to trouble it with outer world jars." Most of all, she wanted John near her. "I would dissolve the Union sooner than let Mr. Frémont go away a year to Congress," she exclaimed.[8]

As for John, he may have been relieved by his defeat. He still dreamed of glory, but unlike his pugnacious father-in-law, he found no joy in the political battle. When Rose Greenhow encountered him in San Francisco that year, he spoke longingly of the "primitive life" he hoped to lead at Las Mariposas and "confessed himself utterly unsuited for the part he had been appointed to play upon the world's great stage—in which opinion," added the hostile Rose, "I heartily concurred."[9]

That same year in Missouri, Thomas Benton, running for his sixth senate term, faced the fight of his political life. Though the old warrior campaigned vigorously, with the energetic support of Francis Blair's sons Montgomery and Frank, his views were treasonous to many of Missouri's proslavery voters. Still he refused to moderate his stand. "I despise the bubble popularity," he declared.

Forty ballots were taken in the state legislature before the old man was defeated by a proslavery candidate. After thirty years, Benton's senate career was over. When the news reached Silver Spring, his friend Francis Blair had the "blue Devils."

But the sixty-nine-year-old Benton would not give up either his principles or his desire for office. He plunged again into Missouri politics and by 1852 had decided to run for a seat in the House of Representatives. "The d——d old Rip!" said a political rival. "He's got enough in him to make five Roman tyrants."[10]

In San Francisco, John was increasingly occupied with Las Mariposas, while motherhood—actual and incipient—absorbed Jessie's energy. When their baby was born on April 19, 1851, she anticipated a cozy domesticity. Named John Charles after his father, he was from the first robustly healthy. But Jessie's tranquility was shattered two weeks later, while she was still in bed recovering from childbirth.

Just before midnight on May 3, San Francisco was deliberately set on fire. So absorbed had Jessie been in her nursery concerns that she had ignored the defiant bitterness that provoked the city's fifth major fire. Men worked feverishly to contain the flames, but San Francisco, with its flimsy wooden houses, planked streets, and sea winds, was a tinderbox. "On and on through the long night it raged and roared," Jessie remembered.[11] Before it was over, the fire burned through a fourth of the city and destroyed the entire business district. The flames came so close to the Frémont house that its painted walls were scorched, and the grass shriveled and died.

Badly shaken, Jessie tried to return to domesticity, while John set out for Las Mariposas. Then one day in the yard she discovered a handbill warning that the city would be torched again. "This literally murdered sleep for me," she recalled. Meanwhile desperate San Franciscans formed a "Committee of Vigilance" to stop the disorder. On June 11, a huge crowd in the plaza hanged the first of four victims, a man who had stolen a shipping agent's cashbox.

Eleven days later, on a quiet Sunday morning, Jessie was alone with eight-year-old Lily and the new baby when she heard the warning bells again. This time the fire was closer, and friends insisted that she leave the house immediately. Carrying her baby, still wet from his bath, wrapped in her dressing gown, she was led away.

Taken to the house of a friend on an isolated hilltop, she found it crowded with distraught women and children. Together they watched the city burn. One French woman laughed crazily as she saw her house go up in flames, then turned to Jessie and exclaimed, "Madame, your house goes next!" As Jessie watched, her house burst into flames. When the fire had passed, only the chimney remained.

Eventually, Jessie managed to reestablish herself in another residence, but it was a barren, comfortless place, and she felt brutally uprooted. "Fire-bells seemed always ringing in my head, and often I awaked to find myself standing at a window or trying to get out from the house," she remembered. "I felt shipwrecked," she confided to Lizzie Blair Lee two months later. "I really had something like the blues."[12] Jessie had been nursing little Charley, but now her milk gave out, and she had to rely on a goat she purchased. Lily, delighted by the new pet, named it Robinson Crusoe.

Not long after the fire, a procession of English emigrants who were renting cottages from John came to see her. They explained that when the fire threatened her house, they had rushed over to help, only to find her gone. "They proceeded to save everything," Jessie recorded, "working with such cool method that mirrors, china and glass, several hundred books, furniture, even kitchen utensils, and all our clothing, were saved in good condition." Afraid that she might lack money, they even offered to pay a quarter's rent in advance.

When John returned from Las Mariposas, he found his house in ashes. People could tell him only that Jessie had moved "near Grace Church." Hurrying there, he gazed at the surrounding houses, bewildered until he spotted white muslin curtains tied with pink ribbons fluttering from an upper window. Recognizing both Jessie's love of frippery and fresh air, he knew he was home. Later, when Jessie told him how the English tenants had saved their furnishings, he agreed to sell them their rented houses at a bargain price.

John was now immersed in schemes to make money. He traveled restlessly about the state: south to Los Angeles, east across the Central Valley to Las Mariposas. He dabbled in real estate, wangled a lucrative federal contract to supply beef to the Indians at a price so high that the government for a time refused to repay him, and aggressively tended his Mariposas enterprise. He hired a phalanx of lawyers headed by his brother-in-law, William Carey Jones, to prove his shaky title, and he borrowed heavily to finance his operations. By August he had suffered "heavy losses in his gold experiments," Jessie reported to Francis Blair, "but his energy and real 'Bentonian industry' have brought him out of them." For a time John hoped to establish the family there. "I shall be on the Mariposas in the planting season," Jessie wrote Blair that August, "and if a decently honest commission comes to decide our land titles, my own hands will gather the fruits." Still, she resisted California's lure. "This is a residence—a 'location,' anything you like, but I shall always feel the house on C Street [in Washington] as my home."[13]

By October, with more complications than profits, John was growing weary of Las Mariposas. "I am certainly disposed to rid myself of the trouble of managing the property," he wrote David Hoffman, his London agent. Thomas Benton was also urging him to sell. Frémont "is not adapted to such business and it interferes with his attention to other business to which he is adapted," Benton wrote bluntly to Hoffman.[14] But when Benton found a buyer who offered a million dollars for the property, John backed off. New discoveries indicated it was worth far more. Though squatters had scavenged the surface gold, its real wealth was still locked deep in quartz rock that required men, machinery, and money to remove. Several of the mining companies that had leased land and hauled equipment to Las Mariposas had already failed, but John was convinced he could make it pay.

When Benton learned that John would not sell, he was furious. Not only did he believe that his impatient, impulsive, sometimes gullible son-in-law was temperamentally unsuited to business, but he viewed Las Mariposas as a tainted pursuit, far less worthy than politics, writing, or exploration. Ten years before, Jessie had linked her father and husband in an intense yet always uneasy alliance. Now, with their disagreement over Las Mariposas, it began to fall apart.

Jessie shared her father's scruples about money-making, and in California she showed little interest in displaying her new wealth. Instead she relished her self-sufficiency. Writing to Francis Blair in August, she boasted of making a cake that day "and very well too." Little Charley "has no nurse at all but myself," she continued, "and yet I teach Lily and sew (but I hate that) and keep house and all quite easily and pleasantly. As these last are merits hitherto unsuspected in me, even by myself, I glorify myself not a little." Yet she was eager to escape the rigors of California life. San Francisco seemed a precarious spot for a young family, while remote Las Mariposas, with its "Indians, bears, and miners," appeared equally threatening.[15] When John proposed a European voyage both to raise capital for Las Mariposas and to enjoy their new fortune, Jessie was delighted. Politics had proved a disappointment, and Washington, since her father's disenchantment with John, seemed less than welcoming. She was ready for self-indulgence.

16

*A party of travellers lately visited
a lonely hut on a mountain. There they
found an old woman, who told them she
and her husband had lived there forty
years. "Why," they said, "did you choose
so barren a spot?" She did not know;
"it was the man's notion." And during
forty years she had been content to act,
without knowing why, upon the "man's
notion." I would not have it so.*

Margaret Fuller
Woman in the Nineteenth Century
1845

THE RESTLESS
YEARS

E N ROUTE TO PANAMA, Jessie used her ready gold to pay an old sailor to drive off the rats and cockroaches "as long as dates" that invaded their cabin each night.[1] But at Panama, even gold could not lessen the dangers of the isthmus trek or Jessie's alarm when her ten-month-old baby, wrapped in a tablecloth, slung on a porter's back, and given chicken bones to suck, was carried off down a jungle trail. Not until evening, when she clambered off her mule at Gorgona, did she see him again, surrounded by Indian women and splashing happily in a large earthen bowl filled with river water.

After stopping briefly in New York, the Frémont family crossed the Atlantic on the comfortable old side-wheel steamer *Africa*, "safe from rats, and roaches, and . . . Chagres fever." They reached Liverpool on March 22, 1852, and London soon afterward. Their arrival caused a sensation among Las Mariposas investors, the London correspondent of the *New York Times* reported, for "ugly suspicions" about its real worth had been circulating. Perhaps as much to squelch such rumors as to indulge themselves, the Frémonts settled into a magnificent suite of rooms at the Clarendon, "as becomes a millionaire fresh from California."[2]

Despite such swagger, their situation was precarious. A network of loans, based on expected profits from Las Mariposas gold, supported their lavish style. But the mining enterprise itself was shaky. John's title had yet to be confirmed by the courts, and it was still unclear whether gold could be extracted from its quartz veins cheaply enough to make it profitable. Nevertheless, the flamboyant Frémonts, taken as the millionaires they appeared to be, were lionized by English society. Though Jessie later complained of their "terrifying" social schedule, she clearly savored this season of pomp and glitter. They were seen everywhere: at the Countess of Derby's assembly, at the Lord Mayor of London's dinner, taking tea with the Duchess of Bedford, driving in an elegant coupé in the park. Slender and glowing in a pale-pink satin dress trimmed with blond lace and artificial roses, with ostrich tips in her hair and pearls around her neck, Jessie was presented to Queen Victoria.

The splendor ended abruptly. On April 7, just as the glittering Frémonts entered a carriage for yet another evening out, John was suddenly seized by four policemen. Told only that he was arrested for fifty thousand dollars in debts, he was hustled off to jail. Jessie was left behind, outraged, frantic, and confused.

It was ironic that John's arrest had nothing to do with Las Mariposas. Since his days in the Topographical Corps, he had been habitually careless about finances. During the California conquest, he freely signed drafts totaling more than a million dollars in the government's name to obtain supplies for his California Battalion. But the government, questioning his accounts, had not yet repaid the drafts. Discounted and sold, some had reached England, where one purchaser, giving up hope for government reimbursement, had Frémont arrested to force repayment.

Distraught and embarrassed, Jessie reacted with characteristic passion. Unwilling to wait while others acted, she set out that evening to raise bail money herself. She appealed first to John's London agent, David Hoffman.[3]

Hoffman was an unfortunate choice, for John and his elderly agent had been quarreling. Hoffman was a nervous, excitable man and something of a ditherer. In the summer of 1851, John had authorized him to raise capital for Las Mariposas among European investors, but Hoffman moved too slowly to suit the impatient young entrepreneur. Hoffman, in turn, found John careless and inattentive to business, agreeing with an associate who called John a "spoiled child of fortune," too self-important "to be subject to the homely rule and restraint of methodical industry."[4] When Hoffman discovered that other agents, some authorized by Frémont and some not, were competing with him to promote Las Mariposas leases in Europe and that Senator Benton wanted to sell the estate at what Hoffman considered a scandalously low price, he issued a long, vituperative pamphlet denouncing them all.

That night, with her husband in jail, Jessie ignored such differences as she hurried to Hoffman's house, accompanied by another Mariposas aide, Gwinn Heap. Though it was nine o'clock and Hoffman was in bed with a cold, Jessie demanded to see him at once. Ushered into the parlor, she even refused to be seated. "No I want no *words*. I have no time for *that*," she exclaimed, according to Hoffman's version of the scene. "I want £4000 and must have it." When Hoffman explained that he had no such sum, Jessie was convinced he was lying. She swept angrily out of the parlor, then turned and lashed into the old man. "You are a great rascal—my father says so. . . . You talk too much and write too much. You cannot talk little."[5]

That same night, a wealthy American merchant living in London provided John's bail, and the next day the prisoner was released. Defending himself in a long earnest explanation, Hoffman predicted "total ruin" for Frémont if he continued to associate with the unscrupulous speculators who had begun to surround him. Hoffman's own side, backed by businessmen "of means and of high character," represented "Regularity and Harmony"; the other, only "madness and confusion."[6] But John ignored the old man's warning, choosing instead to join with younger, more adventurous men, as willing as he to disregard conservative business practices to make their fortunes.

While John's arrest was generally condemned in America, there was some sniggering at his expense. "The fate of Frémont is indeed deplorable," declared the *New York Times*. "Only a week ago, he was announced as the Lion of London, and here he is caged, forsooth, and put upon exhibition." John himself was bitter about his night in the "sponging house," as the jail annex was called. "If I was [as] great a patriot as you," he wrote his father-in-law, "I would go to jail and stay there until Congress paid these demands, now over a million, but my patriotism has been oozing out for the last five years." Instead he bluntly asked Benton to get him a diplomatic post abroad "to protect me from further arrests & help to pay expenses." The press expected the irascible Benton to rage against his son-in-law's imprisonment, but they assumed a family unity that no longer existed. While Benton did forward John's request to the president and the secretary of state, where it remained unfulfilled, it was California Senator William Gwin, calling the arrest "an outrage" to Frémont and "disgraceful to our government," who convinced Congress to settle the California debts John had incurred in the government's name.[7]

At this difficult moment, Jessie learned that her twenty-two-year-old brother, Randolph, had died in St. Louis of a sudden fever. For years Randolph had floundered. Reckless, unhappy, probably alcoholic, he was never able to settle on a course of study or a career. As Thomas Benton's only living son, perhaps he found the burden too heavy. By the time of his death, even the sympathetic Francis Blair had pronounced him "entirely a ruin."[8]

Grieving for her dead brother, embarrassed by her husband's arrest and by rumors of Las Mariposas irregularities, Jessie was anxious to leave England, where at any moment John might again be thrown in jail.

They fled to Paris, where they rented an elegant Italianate house on the Champs Elysées, with views from the Arc de Triomphe to the Tuileries and a garden sloping down to the Seine. Jessie settled gratefully into this opulent refuge, with its silk hangings, Sèvres china, and full retinue of servants. Even John, she said, found "a boyish satisfaction" in taking long walks in the rain for the pleasure of returning to such comfort.[9]

By early summer she was pregnant. In the "lotuslike oblivion" of her Paris life, she pampered herself with luxuries—satin boots, a black lace bonnet trimmed with fresh violets.[10] Fluent in French, she cultivated a friendship with an elderly French nobleman and Las Mariposas investor, Augustin Pelletier, the Comte de la Garde, who saw to it that the Frémonts received invitations to the court fetes and receptions of Louis Napoleon.

On February 1, 1853, Jessie gave birth to a daughter, whom they named Anne Beverley for John's mother. Nestled in luxury, Jessie seemed content with her Paris life, but John was restless. His fencing sessions, his daily horseback rides, his long tramps in the rain, even his occasional trips to England to disentangle his legal and business affairs, still gave him time to brood over the humiliations of the past: the court-martial, his disastrous winter expedition to the Rockies, his political defeat in California, his night in jail, the endless murky complexities of Las Mariposas. When Thomas Benton informed him that Congress had authorized several western surveys to determine the best route for a transcontinental railroad, John was galvanized into action. A plunge into the wilderness could relieve his own restlessness, please his prickly father-in-law, and redress the failure of his last expedition. As soon as Jessie was able to travel, they returned to America.

By late June 1853, the Frémont entourage—including two French maids—reached Washington. Jessie was delighted to see her parents and sisters again, to show off the new baby as well as two-year-old Charley, with his toddler's Franglais, and Lily, sturdy and serious-minded at ten. Then, in the muggy summer heat, little Anne became seriously ill. Jessie took her out to Silver Spring, where she hoped the cooler air would heal her. The Blairs cosseted them both, but Anne weakened rapidly. Lizzie was with Jessie the last wrenching night, as she held her baby in her arms and watched her fail. At dawn on July 11, five-month-old Anne Beverley died.

The intimacy of that painful night cemented the two women's friendship. As Lizzie, childless herself, shared Jessie's tragedy, a deep bond was forged. Over the next decade, Jessie would find she could express feelings and thoughts to Lizzie that she could not always share with John.

Like Jessie, John was stunned by their baby's death. With grim determination he turned to preparations for his western journey. There were already obstacles. Even before he left France, he learned he would not head one of the official surveys. Though Benton had pushed for his appointment, the new secretary of war, Jefferson Davis, disliked him on both personal and political grounds, and moreover opposed the central route he and Benton favored.

Both Benton and Frémont reacted defiantly. Though Jessie sensed a continuing coolness between the two that disturbed her, Benton was eager to promote the central route, "that 'American road to India' . . . a cherished vision of mine for thirty-eight years," while John was determined to prove himself on another winter expedition. Together they raised money for a private survey that would cross the Rockies in midwinter to establish the route's viability in all weather. Jessie felt little enthusiasm for the venture, but John seemed obsessed with redeeming his tarnished image. "To him it was a question of honor as well as of national advantage."[11]

In September 1853, John set out for St. Louis and the frontier, while Jessie and the children settled into a house in Washington just a few doors from her parents. "I . . . again began the waiting, and hoping, and fearing."[12] A month later she received an alarming telegram: John, too sick to continue, had left the expedition and returned to St. Louis.

Hurrying west by train, Jessie found her husband looking gaunt and worn, suffering again from inflammatory rheumatism in his frostbitten leg, with shooting pains to his chest and head. If she had doubts about the journey before, they were explicit now. "I would rather have Mr. Frémont at the fireside taking care of himself . . . than getting all the stupid laurels that ever grew," she wrote bluntly to Lizzie. "I think he has done enough—but *he* does not."

In St. Louis, John began to recover. By keeping him "still with his feet up," Jessie explained to Lizzie, Dr. A. Ebers, his German homeopathic physician, had "soothed the pain, uprooted the inflammation & Mr. Frémont, though greatly shaken, is again literally 'on his legs.' "[13] Despite Jessie's pleas, John was determined to return to the expedition, though he did agree to take Ebers with him.

Jessie accompanied John and the doctor upriver to Independence, where, saying good-bye, she felt again the familiar wrench of parting. Their marriage had been a series of leave-takings, whose purpose she had begun to question. Though she tried to understand John's restlessness and his compulsion to prove himself, it hurt her to think that he might need to escape her as well.

Back in Washington, facing another long winter alone, she tried to comfort herself with family life. But her mother was increasingly frail and her father depressed over his wife's illness, despite the fact that he had recently been elected a congressman from Missouri. When Francis Blair paid them a visit in November, he found Benton "labouring most strenuously . . . from dawn till dusk" on a massive account of his thirty years in the Senate, while Elizabeth sat mutely by his side, scarcely able to move from her chair without his support.[14]

The political situation was also dispiriting. Slavery in the territories had again become an issue with the question of statehood for Kansas and Nebraska. Both territories lay north of the line between free and slave states drawn in the Missouri Compromise of 1820, but that winter Senator Stephen Douglas of Illinois, a driving little man eager to gain southern support for his presidential ambitions, opened a Pandora's box by proposing to abrogate that long-standing agreement and allow the two territories to decide by vote whether they wanted to be slave or free.

In the North there were mass protests against his Kansas-Nebraska proposal, which to free-soilers seemed a sly scheme to smuggle slavery into the territories. Benton, who had entered the Senate at the time of the Missouri Compromise, was outraged. Francis Blair, roused from the bucolic pleasures of Silver Spring, swore to fight any such attempt to extend slavery. He and other Democratic and Whig free-soilers began to talk of forming a new party that would oppose any extension of slavery. But in Washington the proslavery forces dominated, and Democratic President Franklin Pierce, anxious to retain southern support, endorsed the Kansas-Nebraska Act. "I am heart-sick of being here," free-soiler William H. Seward wrote his wife that winter. "All, all [is] in the hands of the slave-holders." The New York senator's spirits rose, however, when he accompanied Benton on a visit to Jessie and found her in strong agreement with his views. "She is a noble-spirited woman. Has much character," he reported enthusiastically to his wife. "I am sure you would like her. She is very outspoken."[15]

The slavery issue only partially distracted Jessie from her concerns about John, and she was relieved to receive a letter from him written near Bent's Fort in late November, just before he headed into the Rockies. He was feeling so much better that he had sent Dr. Ebers back to St. Louis. "I am determined to carry out the enterprise through to the end," he wrote solemnly. "Our movement now will be a struggle with the winter."[16]

The expedition headed west over the rugged Sangre de Cristo Range. By December 14 they reached Cochetopa Pass in southern Colorado. Though the snow on the ridges was two feet deep, John found only four inches at the pass, proving, he believed, that it would make a fine railroad route. As the expedition pushed on into southern Utah, they were pounded by blizzards. Game and grass became ominously scarce. Struggling across the frigid wastes, they were forced to live on the meat of their mules as the animals dropped one by one. Haunted by memories of the tragic fourth expedition, John began to eat alone in his tent. One freezing night he called his men together and had them swear not to resort to cannibalism, whatever might happen. "If we are to die," he said, "let us die together like men."[17]

As the Washington winter dragged on, Jessie began to dwell obsessively on the dangers of the journey. She imagined the cold, hungry men lost in a frozen wilderness. By late January, she was convinced they were starving to death. Overwhelmed by anxiety, she could scarcely eat or sleep.

One frigid night in early February, as she was getting kindling for the fire, she suddenly felt John's presence beside her, laughing, touching her arm, whispering her name. Stunned yet strangely peaceful, she was convinced that "whatever he had had to bear was over; that he was now safe . . . and that in some way he himself had told me so."[18] That night, for the first time in weeks, Jessie slept soundly.

In early April, Almon W. Babbitt, a Mormon official carrying dispatches from Utah, reached Washington. En route Babbitt had stumbled across John and his exhausted men just as they found refuge in Parowan, a Mormon village in southwestern Utah. All except one man had survived their ordeal. Piecing together the dates, Jessie was convinced that John had reached Parowan on the very day in February when she felt his presence and knew he was safe.

To celebrate Babbitt's news, Jessie invited the Blairs to dinner to meet the Mormon elder, "if you will forget he has lots of wives and look upon him only as I do in his last character as friend . . . to Mr. Frémont." Still, she was disturbed by her father's reaction to the news. Benton seemed aloof, almost unfeeling, more concerned by what he evidently considered another bungled mission than by the suffering John had undergone. "Father shocked back & chilled all my feelings when I looked to him for sympathy [that] winter," Jessie later confided to Lizzie. Though she knew John was out of danger, her father's harshness unnerved her, and she remained uneasy. "When I have no more anxious thoughts pressing on my heart it will not ache," she told Lizzie, but until John returned, "I must rely on Dr. Ebers' 'ten globules' to give me the rest I need."[19]

While Jessie was learning of John's ordeal from Babbitt, Lizzie's brother Montgomery was talking with the explorer himself in San Francisco, where he had arrived in April after a two-month journey from Utah. He "is as fat as a buck—so much so that his clothes seem too tight for him," Montgomery wrote his wife in Washington. Montgomery Blair was a somber man, but like many others, he was captivated by John's reticent glamour. "He has travelled great distances afoot eating horses & mules that had given out & grown fat on them & makes no account of his hardships," he continued. To Montgomery, it seemed heroic rather than disingenuous that John downplayed his ordeal, and noble, "bespeak[ing] a very lofty ambition," rather than obsessive "that he should have accomplished all this himself without the help of the govt. & at his own expense."[20] A shrewd lawyer, Montgomery was eager to help John with his tangled Las Mariposas affairs. Years later he would bitterly regret his enthusiasm.

None of Montgomery's cheerful news reached Washington before John himself arrived by steamer in late May. "He was his own messenger," Jessie said. Their summer together was hectic, as John attempted to settle old accounts with the government and complete a brief expedition report before returning to California. Minimizing his hardships, he claimed that "the winter condition of the country constitutes no impediment" to a railroad.[21] By the end of August he was on his way via Panama to California and Las Mariposas, promising to return by Christmas. Again Jessie remained behind. Her mother was failing fast, and she and John agreed she should stay in Washington. Though she may only have suspected it when John left, she was pregnant again.

While John headed back to California, Thomas Benton set out for Missouri. Defeated in his bid for a second congressional term, he was deeply weary. En route west he stopped at a Virginia hot springs, seeking a cure for his persistent headaches.

While Benton was away, Elizabeth Benton's condition deteriorated. One day she struggled from her bed, and with Jessie's support, tottered into the adjoining book-lined study, where she so often sat while her husband worked at his desk. Touching his chair with what seemed to Jessie a look of fare-well, she unexpectedly spoke. "Good child—take care," she murmured. Then she clung to her daughter, weeping. Soon afterward, on September 10, 1854, a Sunday evening, sixty-year-old Elizabeth Benton died quietly in her bed.

Benton was anguished not to have been with her at the end. "After all my years of watching she looked for me in vain," he told Jessie when he returned to Washington.[22] Jessie could do nothing to comfort him. His sons had died, she herself had married. Her childhood rivalry with her mother had long since been replaced by pity and compassion, and she recognized that this silent, broken woman had been her father's real support.

Five months later, on an icy day in late February, tragedy struck again. A fire smoldering in a defective chimney in the Bentons' C Street residence suddenly spread, giving Jessie's sisters, Susy and Liz, and the servants barely time to escape. When word reached the Capitol, where Benton was attending a House session, he rushed home to find his house in flames. Hurrying over, Jessie saw him standing bareheaded among the crowd, watching it burn. Except for his own portrait, rescued by a neighbor, everything—furniture, books, the nearly completed manuscript of the second volume of his *Thirty Years' View*—was lost. "Like a full freighted ship it went down," Jessie said, "bearing the accumulated books and papers and family gatherings of us all." Though Benton had no insurance, it was the loss of personal things that was most wrenching: "the bed on which my wife died, on which I sleep; her clothes, which were in a trunk setting at the head of it; the articles which she prized most, around it—the last things I saw at night, and the first in the morning."[23]

Benton sought refuge with Jessie. That first evening their old rapport returned, as if the fire had burned away the surface tensions that marred their intimacy. "We talked, my father and I, brokenly, all that long night," she remembered. He asked her to take his portrait, the one thing that had been saved from the flames. When Jessie cried, he explained, "It makes dying the easier, there is so much the less to leave."[24]

Las Mariposas entanglements kept John in California far longer than he anticipated, and it was spring before he returned to Washington. Together again, he and Jessie pondered their future. With the help of able lawyers like Montgomery Blair, his Mariposas title had at last been cleared, and John now hoped to make his mines pay. He was also being mentioned as a possible presidential candidate. That April a group of southern Democrats, including several of Jessie's relatives, talked to them both about backing John for the presidency.

There were possibilities as well with the emerging Republican Party, which since the passage of the Kansas–Nebraska Act in May 1854 had been gathering converts from among northern Whigs and Democrats disillusioned with their own parties' tolerance of slavery expansion. Kansas itself had become a battleground as northern emigrants opposed to slavery vied with proslavery southerners to populate the territory and thus decide its future. Thomas Benton supported the antislavery settlers, but he rejected the idea of a new party backed by only one section of the country and based on a single issue. Even more vehemently, he opposed John as their presidential candidate. Though Benton remained unfailingly polite to his daughter and son-in-law, relations were strained. "I felt I was no longer in my place," Jessie said.[25]

Amid such tensions, thirty-year-old Jessie gave birth to her fifth and last child, a boy, on May 17, 1855.[26] He was named Francis Preston after Francis Preston Blair, who was growing closer to Jessie and John as their political views converged. The baby was "well but not strong," Jessie informed Lizzie in July, and she herself was still weak. Though she had nursed Charley herself, she hired a wet nurse for little Frank. Suffering from "neuralgia" that spread through the trunk of her body, she was forced to take opiates to relieve the pain.[27]

Perhaps as much to escape the coolness of her father as to bolster her own precarious health, Jessie took the children to Nantucket in August while John tended to business in Washington, Philadelphia, and New York. Despite the political possibilities, they planned to go to California in the fall, where John would personally supervise his mines. "Just before leaving for California I will come to see Father for a day," Jessie told Lizzie. At the same time she would say good-bye to the Blairs, "my only other friends" in Washington, which more and more seemed a hostile, southern city to her.[28]

At Siasconset on Nantucket Island, Jessie tried to forget political differences as she sat on the beach, watching the children play. Charley "goes barefoot with his drawers rolled up and practices climbing on all possible places," she reported to Lizzie, while Lily "takes her place at the end of the rope every day and enjoys the beating of the waves." Baby Frank was "fat and contented" and making "quite sensible faces and noises." His nurse was a "fine cow," she continued, "patient and silly," and submissive to the "despotism" of Marie, the French maid.[29] Despite such domestic diversions, Jessie felt lonely and uncertain of the future.

Toward the end of August, John came to see her. Politics was on his mind. Jessie's relatives and their southern Democratic allies had formally offered to back him for the presidency. At the same time a number of Republican leaders were urging him to run as the first presidential candidate of the new party.

At sunset, John and Jessie walked along the lighthouse bluff overlooking the sea, talking over their choices. With the Whig party hopelessly split on slavery, and the Republicans still too new to have a wide following, the Democratic candidate could be expected to win the presidency. But to keep its southern wing loyal, the Democratic nominee would have to support slavery extension into Kansas and Nebraska.

Night came, the moon rose, and still they talked. They both opposed slavery. But they knew that to join the Republican party meant the severing of family ties—"excommunication by the South; the absolute ending of all that had made my deep rooted pleasant life." Most of all it meant estrangement from Thomas Benton. John was willing to face such consequences himself. He knew it would be far harder for Jessie. "Should I be unwilling, he would not accept," she said.

In the end "there was only one decision possible." They would ally themselves with the new Republican party. "When in the small hours we went in," Jessie said, "the past lay behind me."[30]

17

Ye friends of Freedom, rally now,
And push the cause along:
We have a glorious candidate,
A platform broad and strong:
"Free Speech, Free Press, Free Soil,
Free Men, Frémont." . . .

Chorus:
We'll give 'em Jessie,
We'll give 'em Jessie,
We'll give 'em Jessie,
When we rally at the polls.

Republican campaign song
1856

What a shame women *can't vote!*
We'd carry "our Jessie" into the
White House on our shoulders,
wouldn't *we.*

Lydia Maria Child
August 3, 1856

THE SOUND
OF CHEERING

NOT LONG AFTER THEIR TALK, John set out for Washington to test the political waters. Still too weak to risk a journey, Jessie was forced to remain behind. Nonetheless, she did what she could from her island retreat. On August 27, 1855, she sat down to write Francis Blair: "Mr. Frémont has under consideration so important a step," she began, "that before taking it he wishes for the advice and friendly counsel which have heretofore proved so full of sagacity and led to such success." They were turning to him rather than her own father for support, she explained, because Blair's "exquisite good taste" would spare John "the shocks that Father with his different organization is dangerously apt to give."[1] Though Jessie's words were indirect, Blair, who knew and loved both father and daughter, no doubt understood that she already dreaded her father's explosive and earthy opposition to her political dreams.

Despite such concerns, John's Washington visit was a success. Francis Blair responded with all the enthusiasm Jessie had hoped for, and soon the feisty old editor plunged into the campaign to make John the Republican nominee. "I think of Frémont *as a new man*," he explained to a dubious Martin Van Buren. "He is brave, firm, has a history of romantic heroism . . . & has no bad political connections—never had— no tail of hungry, corrupt hangers on like Buchanan who will I think be the [Democratic] candidate."[2]

By mid-October the situation was so encouraging that the Frémonts abandoned their California plans and settled temporarily at the Clarendon Hotel in New York City. John ordered new clothes—a frock coat, a heavy overcoat ("of rough coarse material and loose make, without any velvet about it"), and a light dress coat ("no velvet on it either")—to wear on his political rounds, while Jessie began an elaborately conspiratorial correspondence with Blair and Lizzie in Washington. Fearful that their letters would be opened by the post office, controlled by the hostile Pierce administration, they used initials and code words to hide their meaning. "Mr. Frémont wants me to tell you that the result of Mr. B's intervening was all that could be wished," Jessie reported on October 21. "Everything is working well—in Quakerdom the spirit moves them in the right direction." Soon she announced that John would visit Washington: "The Turkey is getting restless and will make his next flight to the pines of Silver Spring—where he will be found the middle of next week." But even the Blairs were occasionally mystified by her cryptic phrases. "The Mr. B. to whom I referred . . . was our northern friend, and not Rip Van Winkle," she was forced to explain in the same letter.[3]

While there was a perceptible ground swell of support for Frémont among the leaders of the new party, Thomas Benton remained a formidable obstacle. Twice during November, Francis Blair went to talk with his old friend. For years Blair had considered Benton the man most qualified to be president, but now he hoped to persuade him to support his son-in-law. When he broached the subject, however, Benton firmly opposed both the party and the man. Frémont lacked political experience, he declared, while the new Republican party was dangerously sectional.[4]

For Jessie it was the beginning of a painful breach that would widen as John's candidacy gathered strength. At first she and her father tried to ignore their differences. In Washington, Benton drove himself to rewrite the manuscript of the second volume of his massive *Thirty Years' View*, which had been destroyed in the fire. Rising at dawn, he worked until midnight, with only a noon horseback ride for diversion. "I can labor as much now as at thirty," he boasted to Martin Van Buren.[5]

Despite his bravado, Jessie knew that her mother's death and her own drifting defection had left her father deeply depressed, and in early December she sent Lily to Washington for an extended visit with her grandfather. It meant a break in Lily's schoolwork, Jessie explained to Lizzie, "but no accomplishment she can acquire will give any one such happiness as her simple presence does to that lonely old man." Though Jessie's sister Liz and her husband, William Carey Jones, were living with Benton, Jones, an alcoholic, was "continually soaked with rum," as an associate put it, and Liz too distraught to give her father the comfort he needed. "I know I would do best of all," Jessie told Lizzie, "but how [to] reconcile opposite duties."[6] Nonetheless, she did manage a brief trip to see her father at Christmas. But her visit was a strain for them both. By the time she returned to New York, their once joyous connection was near the breaking point.

Meanwhile, she and John had rented a commodious house at 176 Second Avenue, in one of New York's most fashionable districts. Jessie found the neighborhood a trifle showy. "Hamilton Fish has quite a palace just by us," she wrote Francis Blair. The house itself was "bright and pretty within and without" and supplied with "water, fire and gas, all over it." They had prudently taken it for six months, she explained, "as that is the longest time for which I think we should make a decided move."

At first Jessie had little desire to socialize. "I make no visits and don't intend to go into that weary round," she confided to Blair.[7] Her box at the theater, where she went frequently to hear the great French actress Rachel, was her only indulgence, for she found New York society glittering but dull. "I have been to two parties," she told Lizzie. "The women were dressed within an inch of their lives and stupid as sheep— some of the men had sense but not many."[8]

Though the quest for the presidency was now the focus of their lives, they scarcely admitted it even to themselves during these first months in New York. Between political meetings, John attended to Las Mariposas business while Jessie, buttressed by her two capable French maids, turned her energy to managing her large household. Thirteen-year-old Lily was as "gay as a bird," she wrote Lizzie, "singing all the time and looking resolutely away from all but the bright side of everything." Pretty Nina Frémont, the seventeen-year-old daughter of John's dead brother, Horatio Francis, was more of a problem. Nina had been living off and on with the Frémonts for several years, and Jessie found her a burden— frivolous, moody, easily bored. Nina was "at a bad age for idling," Jessie wrote Lizzie that winter, so she intended to keep her busy with dancing and French lessons. More appealing was little Frank, who at six months had four teeth and was "as much a child of nature in most things as a young Indian. A regulation Mother would have nervous attacks at the state he gets his gowns into rolling on the carpet." But it was Charley, nearly five, with her own great brown eyes and warm, impulsive temperament, who was her favorite. "I think I love him better than I ever can Frank," she confessed, "for he is my own nursling and has a hundred faults that come with his Mother's milk—all of which he atones for to me with his loving nature. . . . I am not a fair judge," she admitted, "for I realize it is almost excusing my own self, so alike are we in temper."⁹

In late December, just after Jessie's Washington visit, Francis Blair hosted a dinner conference of Republican leaders at Silver Spring to plan a national strategy for the fledgling party. Among his guests were Frémont's shrewd, theatrically handsome political adviser, Massachusetts Congressman Nathaniel Banks, and proud, moralistic Senator Charles Sumner, who had once long ago unbent enough to note young Jessie Ann Benton's piquant "wild strawberry flavor."¹⁰ Tall, dignified Salmon P. Chase, recently elected governor of Ohio under the still-obscure Republican banner, was also there, as was the abolitionist editor Gamaliel Bailey, first publisher of *Uncle Tom's Cabin*. While the men dined on fresh produce from Blair's fertile acres (and left unrecorded whether they saw any irony in the fact that the meal was cooked and served by slaves), they discussed organizing a national Republican party on a free-soil platform and bandied about the names of candidates. Blair forcefully presented the case for Frémont: young, glamorous, untarnished by previous political entanglements. His guests went away intrigued.

With the New Year, the Frémont campaign accelerated as Blair and Banks spread the word among free-soil politicians. In early February 1856, the campaign was given a boost when Banks was elected Speaker of the House after a long and bitter debate, though some saw it as an ominous sign of national disunity that he was the first Speaker ever chosen without a single southern vote. On February 22 and 23, a conference to organize a national Republican party was held at Pittsburgh. Though the delegates ranged from arch-abolitionists to moderates like Francis Blair, they uniformly opposed the extension of slavery and condemned the Pierce administration for its pro-southern stand on Kansas. When Blair was chosen permanent president of the organization, it was clear that the Frémont candidacy was gaining ground.

"Mr. Frémont is very gay and pleased & all his plans seem prospering," Jessie informed the Blairs two weeks later. Politicians and journalists were constantly at the house, "this . . . meeting ground for conspirators." Newspapers had begun to tout John's candidacy and New York society to court them both. The invitations poured in, and the pace became frantic, but Jessie still viewed it all with a jaundiced eye. "Just here & just now I am quite the fashion," she wrote Lizzie. "5th Avenue asks itself, 'Have we a Presidency among us' and as I wear fine lace and purple I am in their eyes capable of filling the place. So I go out nightly—sometimes to dinner & a party both the same night and three times a week to the opera where I hold a levee in my box." Though the adulation was heady, it was also a strain, and Jessie longed for an honest talk with a real friend. "I am getting . . . artificial . . . for want of a heart warming such as you would give me," she told

Lizzie. "Mr. Frémont might as well go back to Washington for we only meet in company—and when we get home silence is a luxury." But she was clear-eyed about her priorities. She wanted the presidency. If John lost the nomination, she knew they would have a home life again, "perhaps more of it than we might like."[11]

As the enthusiasm for Frémont swelled, Jessie faced a private dilemma far more disturbing than the hectic pace of social success. "I am all dammed up—for want of sympathizing ears," she wrote Lizzie in mid-April. "Most about Father." The next day she poured out her feelings in a second letter to Lizzie.

"I have written constantly to Father. I always tell him whatever I think may interest him—never saying politics— but for four months I have not had a line from him nor from Liz except one stiff note." Jessie had tried to ignore her father's silence, but she was deeply troubled. Benton remained vehemently opposed to John's candidacy, and Jessie, loving both, was caught in the middle. "I know both my people too well ever to look for concession from either side," she told Lizzie. "And with Father this is only the expression of years [of] distrust of Mr. Frémont's judgment. Since the revoked sale of the Mariposas, nearly five years ago, Father has put great constraints on his temper and now he has what he considers a fair occasion for opposition."

Jessie blamed William Carey Jones for promoting the breach. "I can see his traces in many things—Liz is irretrievably alienated. . . . The dropping of water wears away stone and I think the constant dropping of insinuations by Mr. Jones has worn away much of Father's remaining regard for Mr. Frémont." Unwilling to attack either her husband or her father, Jessie vented her fury on Jones. "If *he* ever makes the chance," she told Lizzie, "I will get him apart from Liz and 'blow him sky high'—and I know all his vulnerable points."[12]

Blair and Lizzie had been urging her to go to Washington to see her father, not only because they understood her distress at this break, but because they still hoped she might persuade him to support his son-in-law. But Jessie dreaded facing her father. "I have made one thing a fixed resolve," she told Lizzie, "not to be hurt at heart any oftener than it is forced upon me. To go deliberately into agitation and pain is almost suicide." Moreover, if John lost, "it would be a mortifying thing to add to the other annoyances of a defeat, that of having appeared to conciliate for a purpose."[13]

A week later she was still distraught. Writing again to Lizzie, she confessed that more than a month before she had written her father to arrange a visit, but he had never replied. "He always drops me that way when he is offended with Mr. Frémont," she said bitterly. By now John also wanted her to go to Washington to attempt a rapprochement. She had not told him of her own reluctance. He "does not think how much I mind it and you must not tell him—but if I can help him in any way I will swallow my wounded pride and go."[14]

Four days later she reported happily to Lizzie that she had received "a very kind letter from Father who asks me to 'come on and bring the whole'—Mr. Frémont & Nina will stay at home but all my blood I will take to him. It has been a sore thing to me to see Father and Mr. Frémont arraying themselves against each other . . . so I go to keep peace." Unless she could heal the rift, Jessie anticipated much bitterness after the election, whatever the result. "If we succeed Father will be cold & proud . . . & if we failed his generosity would be very unacceptable to Mr. Frémont."[15]

As Jessie pondered a visit to her father, tensions between the North and South continued to build. The focus was Kansas. In the fall, antislavery settlers had set up their own government to rival a proslavery government elected with fraudulent votes. Instead of calling for new, fairly conducted elections, which would have resulted in victory for the numerically superior antislavery settlers, the Pierce administration doggedly supported the proslavery government. In April, against the counsel of his more cautious advisers, John sent an eloquent letter of support to the free-state governor of Kansas. "Frémont's letter . . . has hit fair," John Bigelow of the New York

Evening Post wrote Francis Blair. "In about a fortnight he will be the . . . most popular man in America."[16]

Northerners intensified their efforts to send more anti-slavery settlers to Kansas, while Missouri "Border Ruffians" attempted to drive them out by terror and intimidation. Henry Ward Beecher and his Brooklyn congregation dispatched twenty-five Bibles and an equal number of Sharp's rifles to the Kansas settlers. "There are times when self-defense is a religious duty," the charismatic minister proclaimed.[17]

The violence mounted. On May 19, Senator Charles Sumner began a venomous diatribe against the South for its "crimes" in Kansas. Three days later, as he sat alone at his desk in the senate chamber, Congressman Preston S. Brooks of South Carolina attacked him with a cane, beating him savagely until he fell bleeding on the floor. The same day, a proslavery mob invaded the free-state capital at Lawrence, pillaged its two newspaper offices, set fire to the main hotel and the governor's house, and looted shops and homes.

The North was outraged. Thousands attended "indignation meetings" to protest the attacks, while in Kansas, an austere fanatic named John Brown, maddened by the news, led a raid against proslavery settlers and murdered five men.

Jessie had postponed her journey to Washington several times, and when she reached the city near the end of May, it was in an uproar over Kansas. "Everybody here feels as if we are upon a volcano," one southern congressman exclaimed.[18] To make matters worse, she found that her father had already left for St. Louis. Though neither would have admitted it even to themselves, they had both maneuvered to avoid a meeting and the irrevocable rupture it might bring.

At the Benton house, Jessie found her sister and brother-in-law cold and distant. "That was a very bad visit I had to Washington," she wrote Lizzie afterward. "The disappointment of missing Father, the want of hospitality in the house and the fatigue were altogether too much." Returning to New York she suffered a "violent attack of neuralgia, beginning

. . . in cramping at the heart." As she often did, Jessie saw her illness as emotional in origin. The painful journey had affected her heart. "When I look at my strong frame & see how sound the covering is, I cannot realize that it is all so at the mercy of every agitation that touches too keenly that one little organ."[19]

Though Jessie did not see her father in Washington, he left her a message of sorts. The second volume of his monumental *Thirty Years' View* had just been published, and in its concluding chapter, Benton passionately condemned the sectionalism that was dividing the nation, "arraying one-half against the other." If not soon checked, he prophesied, it would destroy the Union.[20]

As if to underscore this view, on his way west Benton had stopped to attend the Democratic convention in Cincinnati, where a reporter observed him in his parlor at the Broadway Hotel, campaigning "hard and hot for Buchanan." Though Benton admitted that Buchanan possessed only "fair talents," he told visitors that the candidate was "a man of peace, sir— eminently a man of peace." Buchanan would indeed be a shrewd choice for the party, for he had been serving as ambassador to Great Britain during the entire Kansas–Nebraska controversy and so was less tainted by it than other contenders. By the seventeenth ballot the convention agreed, and Jessie's long-ago escort became the Democratic nominee. Buchanan endorsed the party platform, which supported the Kansas–Nebraska Act and asserted that Congress had no right to prohibit slavery in the new territories. He was, an antislavery reporter noted cynically, "a Northern man with Southern principles."[21]

Meanwhile, the Frémont candidacy was booming. In May 1856, confirming their own optimism, the family moved again, this time to a fashionable house at 56 West Ninth Street. By now party leaders like Thurlow Weed, the astute former-Whig boss of New York state, were working actively for Frémont; and Horace Greeley, the eccentric and visionary editor of the powerful New York *Tribune*, was edging toward commitment. Absentminded, gawky, the pockets of his baggy white coat bulging with copy, Greeley was an earnest reformer who embraced causes from mesmerism and phrenology to women's rights, trade unionism, and the abolition of slavery. A militant idealist who lived on vegetables and whole wheat bread, he was also a shrewd journalist with a witty, down-to-earth style, who had made the *Tribune* the most widely read newspaper in America.

In early June, two weeks before the Republican convention, Greeley assessed the front-runners. Seward and Chase, he admitted, were the most deserving candidates, but their extreme antislavery views frightened moderates who might otherwise vote Republican. As to the four less radical candidates, one had already endorsed Frémont, another was in poor health, and a third too old. By default only Frémont remained. He was young, attractive, and celebrated. "That must be a very dark and squat log cabin into which the fame of Colonel Frémont has not penetrated ere this," Greeley pointed out. Opponents might charge that Frémont was "incompetent, unqualified, undeserving &c.," he speculated. "Candidates thus assailed have rarely failed of an election."[22]

Greeley's backhanded endorsement reflected the lingering doubts of many incipient Republicans. "All would be well if F[rémont] were not the merest baby in politics," Greeley confided to a colleague. He was also concerned about Las Mariposas and suspected some "shabbiness" in the venture. Another would-be supporter, who called on the Frémonts just before the convention, found John shy and uncomfortable, as if politics were not his element. In contrast, Jessie, who did most of the talking, appeared "far more interested in his success than he." Despite such doubts, Frémont remained the front-runner. "There is no name which can find such favor with the masses," Greeley proclaimed not long after his first grudging endorsement. Frémont was "a man of the People, sprung from the working class," whose life was full of "patriotic and perilous achievement." Even his inexperience could be an asset. "We have had enough of third-rate lawyers and God knows what rate generals."[23]

When the first national Republican convention convened in Philadelphia on June 17, 1856, John and Jessie, as was customary, remained at home to await the results. Characteristically, John monitored his image. "My nerves seem to preserve their usual tranquility, & so far I am well satisfied with myself."[24]

While the candidate maintained at least a surface calm, the nearly one thousand delegates who assembled in Philadelphia's Music Fund Hall were under no such constraint. Shouting, stomping, applauding, they demonstrated a fervor and moral zeal never before seen at a political convention. The nine-point platform adopted by the cheering crowd condemned both slavery and polygamy, "those twin relics of barbarism," in the territories and urged the admission of Kansas as a free state. From the first, "Frémont fever" dominated the convention. Accompanied to Philadelphia by Lizzie, old Francis Blair, his skinny withered frame belying his vigor, campaigned everywhere for his candidate. There was a minor threat from the supporters of elderly Supreme Court Justice John McLean, but in a convention of young and ardent men, "old fogyism" had little appeal. On the second day of the convention, in the sultry late afternoon heat, forty-three-year-old John Charles Frémont received the Republican nomination on the first ballot. William Dayton, a New Jersey free-soiler, was chosen as the party's vice-presidential candidate, though former Whig Congressman Abraham Lincoln, who was making a name for himself as a speaker, received 110 votes on an informal first ballot. "Something in my bones . . . tells me Frémont is to be our next President," Greeley wrote exultantly to a friend.[25]

Jessie and John heard firsthand about the convention from Blair and Lizzie, who stopped to celebrate with them on their way back to Washington. "This house has people pouring in from all quarters from 6 oclk in the mng until late at night," Lizzie reported to her mother. Everyone was jubilant. The enthusiasm for Frémont, Blair wrote his son Frank in St. Louis, "I think will continue to rise and to spread until it carries him to the Presidency."[26]

During the next months such optimism seemed fully justified. A week after the convention, an immense throng crowded into the New York Tabernacle to celebrate Frémont's nomination, while thousands more, unable to enter the packed hall, held spontaneous rallies outside. The crowd was predominantly male: "here and there a lady," noted one observer, "but few and far between."

Amid shouts and thunderous applause, the first speaker reviewed Frémont's exploits. "He conquered California with 62 men. . . . He is the path-finder through the Rocky Mountains. . . . He also won the heart and hand of Thomas H. Benton's daughter."

"Three cheers for Jessie, Mrs. Frémont!" a voice cried, and the crowd applauded wildly.

"Let me tell you that is no small feather in his cap," the speaker continued. "I hold that no man who has not had the courage to marry a wife ought to be put up for the President." The throng roared at this obvious dig at bachelor Buchanan.

After the speeches, the songs, the innumerable hurrahs for "Frémont, Free Speech, Free Soil, and Free Kansas," the exuberant crowd poured out into the cool evening air and, marching five and ten abreast in a procession half a mile long, followed the martial blare of Dodworth's band up Broadway to the candidate's house on Ninth Street. But as they massed in front, a part of the Frémonts' stone balustrade suddenly gave way and crashed into the street. When no one was found to be hurt, the crowd took it as a good omen, and the stone shards quickly disappeared into their pockets as souvenirs.

Frémont appeared on the balcony and spoke briefly, and though few could hear what he said over the din, they clapped and cheered. Then someone began to call for Jessie, and it was taken up by the throng. "Mrs. Frémont!" "Jessie! Jessie! Give us Jessie!" they cried. It was unprecedented for a candidate's wife to appear before such a crowd, and one of the dignitaries with Frémont tried to discourage them, explaining that such occasions were apt to disconcert ladies. "Three more for Frémont and then disperse," he ordered.

The crowd hurrahed obligingly, then called more loudly for "our Jessie." "Give us Mrs. Frémont and we'll go!" they cried.

At last, well flanked by male escorts, Jessie appeared on the balcony. The crowd went wild, roaring their approval "as though all their previous cheering were a mere practice to train their voices for this occasion," one young participant remembered.

For Jessie, it must have been a strange and heady experience to look down at the sea of upturned faces, at the waving hats and handkerchiefs, as their cheers reverberated in her ears. Though her would-be protectors feared that such a crowd would disconcert a lady, Jessie herself was undoubtedly more exhilarated than disturbed. Despite the painful rift with her father, she wanted the presidency with all her heart.[27]

18

*This is election day and my brother
is twenty-one years old. How proud he
seemed as he dressed up in his best
Sunday clothes and drove off in the
big wagon with father and the hired
men to vote for John C. Frémont, like
the sensible "Free-soiler" that he is.
My sister and I stood at the window
and looked out after them. I said,
"Wouldn't you like to vote as well as
Oliver? Don't you and I love the country
just as well as he does, and doesn't
the country need our ballots?" She
looked scared, but answered in a minute,
" 'Course we do, and 'course we ought—but
don't you go ahead and say so, for
then we would be called strong-minded."*

Frances Willard
Journal
Wisconsin 1856

Jessie Benton Frémont. 1856. Lithograph by Leopold Grozelier, *Courtesy of
National Portrait Gallery, Smithsonian Institution, Washington, D.C.*

"FRÉMONT AND
OUR JESSIE"

THE NORTH RESPONDED to the "Frémont and Jessie" campaign with a fervor that astonished the politicians. It evoked the "devotion and dedicated zeal of a religious conversion," recalled one ardent antislavery congressman. It was "a moral earthquake," claimed feminist Eliza W. Farnham. In New England, Ralph Waldo Emerson and Henry Wadsworth Longfellow emerged from their studies to speak for Frémont, while the Quaker poet John Greenleaf Whittier turned out stirring poems for the cause. Even the reclusive Henry Thoreau conceded that "all good people are praying that . . . Frémont may be the man."[1]

In New York, where the four leading newspapers supported Frémont, the enthusiasm for the candidate was massive. Hastily assembled campaign biographies sold by the thousand, while at Mathew Brady's photography studio, portraits of Frémont were snapped up at three dollars each. Brooklyn poet Walt Whitman, whose *Leaves of Grass*, "that incongruous hash of mud and gold," as the poet himself called it, had been published the previous year to jeers and incomprehension, composed his own impassioned tract on the election. "You young men! American mechanics, farmers, boatmen, manufacturers, and all the work-people of the South, the same as the North!" he exclaimed, "you are either to abolish slavery or it will abolish you."[2]

In the West, Frémont rallies attracted immense crowds. Nearly sixty thousand people poured into Indianapolis to cheer a Republican parade, whose pièce de résistance was a large, flower-decked float carrying thiry-one girls dressed in white to represent the states, and one, in black, to represent "downtrodden Kansas." At a massive gathering in Cleveland, a speaker recounted how eighteen-year-old Jessie had withheld the government orders that threatened to stop her husband's second expedition, and the rally ended with three thunderous cheers "for the gallant wife of a gallant man."[3]

The enthusiasm for Jessie was unprecedented. Never before had a woman been featured in a political campaign. Republicans warbled "Oh, Jessie Is a Sweet, Bright Lady" (to the tune of "Comin' through the Rye") and "Our Noble Young Jessie, the Flower of the Land." They sported ribbons, buttons, and banners proclaiming "Frémont and Jessie" or "Jessie's Choice." Women wore muslin dresses in violet, Jessie's favorite color, tucked fresh violets in their hair or belt, and named their babies Jessie Ann.

The enthusiasm had several causes. At thirty-two, Jessie was a charmer—glowing, spirited, attractive—and her elopement still made a glorious story. Moreover, she was the daughter of Thomas Hart Benton, one of the most famous politicians in America. Equally important, the 1856 campaign coincided with the first tentative emergence of American women from the constraints of propriety, and Jessie, with her wit and clear intelligence, seemed to represent the best of the new woman, politically aware yet devoted to her husband and children.

Inspired in part by her prominence, countless ordinary women ventured for the first time to the fringes of a political campaign. In Illinois, one-time Whig Congressman Abraham Lincoln, waiting his turn to speak for Frémont, counted more than seventy mothers with nursing babies among the crowd, and at a Frémont rally in Paterson, New Jersey, a reporter observed that "a large portion of the audience was composed of women." In midwestern towns and villages singing clubs for Frémont were popular. "We must enlist music and the ladies in our cause," declared an Ohio supporter. At an enthusiastic Frémont meeting in Buffalo, a correspondent noted "a new feature in political gatherings . . . in the presence of some 400 ladies" among the cheering throng. "The ladies here," he reported, " 'go in' for Frémont and 'our Jessie.' "⁴

While most women hovered on the edge of political involvement, the 1856 campaign gave bolder women a chance to influence the national political process more directly. Women had been active in the antislavery movement since the 1830s, but even among male reformers there were many who believed women should not write for publication, speak before a mixed audience, or participate in meetings as equals. Abolitionist Elizabeth Cady Stanton first confronted the issue of woman's rights when she attended an 1839 antislavery convention in London, where she, Lucretia Mott, and other female delegates were banished to a curtained gallery. During the 1840s, when a few daring women began to speak publicly against slavery, the outcry against such "unsexed" women, even from within the abolitionist ranks, made them even more painfully aware of their constricted rights. They began to feel that they, like the slaves whose cause they defended, were the victims of male domination. This realization led abolitionists Stanton and Mott to organize the first woman's rights convention at Seneca Falls, New York, in 1848, where they proclaimed the startling doctrine that "all men and women are created equal."

Chafing that they could not vote themselves, such women supported the Republican cause. "Our hopes . . . rest on Frémont," Lydia Maria Child, the author of an influential essay against slavery, wrote to a friend. "I would almost lay down my life to have him elected."⁵ Elizabeth Cady Stanton, whose six young children kept her enmeshed in a sticky net of domesticity, fretted that she was forced to stay at home while her husband campaigned for Frémont.

Most active women focused on the Kansas issue because aid to the antislavery emigrants of "bleeding Kansas" fitted more easily within woman's traditional sphere than direct support of a political candidate. Lydia Maria Child wrote a dramatic story, "The Kansas Emigrants," that Horace Greeley published in the *Tribune* just before the election. Clarina Howard Nichols, a former Vermont newspaper editor who had settled in Kansas, was a paid lecturer for the New England Emigrant Aid Society. An eloquent speaker, she spoke fifty times on the Kansas issue during the 1856 campaign and often followed with a talk on women's rights.

Like most Americans, Julia Lovejoy, a Kansas minister's wife who wrote for eastern newspapers, condemned such "gadders abroad—these women-lecturers who are continually at the old theme 'woman's rights.' " Passionately abolitionist yet deeply concerned with propriety, she suggested more respectable ways "in which ladies in their own proper sphere" could promote the Republican cause. "Let little Misses and young ladies in their ornamental work for the parlor, have the names of 'Frémont and Jessie' wrought in choicest colors; let the matrons in the dairy-room, make a mammoth 'Frémont cheese,' to be eaten with a zest, at their annual State or County Fair."[6]

Julia Lovejoy's concern with respectability was well founded, for the opposition used the participation of women in the Frémont campaign to alarm moderate voters. The candidate's supporters, one paper indignantly declared, included "unsexed females [who] delighted in addressing mobs of men in strains of vulgar violence." At a Frémont rally in Indiana, another newspaper scornfully reported there were "two wagon-loads of ladies, one wagon filled with negroes, and fifteen colored gentlemen on horseback. Drunken Frémonters were plenty."[7] A widely reproduced lithograph depicted a disreputable group of Frémont supporters, including a cigar-smoking, pantaloon-clad woman demanding the right to vote and a witchlike crone inviting the candidate to the next meeting of the Free Love Association.

Jessie herself was careful to maintain a decorous public image, but behind the scenes, she threw herself unabashedly into the campaign. As was customary for presidential candidates, both Buchanan and Frémont remained quietly at home, answering mail, receiving visitors, penning an occasional public letter, while their supporters campaigned for them. As a new party, the Republicans had no established network of support, and there was much to do. Jessie supervised the campaign correspondence. "Quite at the beginning," she recalled, "I asked that all mail should pass through me and the few friends qualified to decide what part of it needed to reach Mr. Frémont." Stationing herself in the dining room, with fruit and coffee nearby and the daily mail heaped in market baskets, she dealt with the deluge with the aid of shrewd, energetic *Evening Post* editor John Bigelow and two assistants. As the campaign heated up, they saw many vicious letters and newspaper attacks, which Jessie scrupulously kept from John. "Enough for us to meet slanders and coarse attacks—they gave *me* all the pain intended." She and Bigelow agreed "that in this way only, could he be left quite himself, to meet the more or less friendly crowds who came daily to see him."

As the campaign intensified, Jessie grew increasingly protective of her sensitive husband. "A remarkably capable and accomplished woman," as Bigelow called her, she came to see herself as emotionally tougher. Accustomed to politics since childhood, "I was able," she and Bigelow agreed, "to look into the political cauldron when it was boiling without losing my head." By implication, John was not.[8]

Opponents were quick to exploit Jessie's unusual role, even suggesting that she might be "the real candidate" for the presidency. "At a Frémont rally in New Hampshire," the opposition Washington *Union* reported, "one of the banners bore the inscription 'John and Jessie,' and another ignored poor John altogether by the inscription 'Jessie for the White House.' It is evident," the *Union* concluded indignantly, "that our opponent fully sympathizes with the woman's rights movement."[9]

Jessie also worked with Bigelow to prepare a campaign biography, writing the first chapter (on John's childhood) herself and supplying Bigelow with information and a detailed outline for succeeding chapters. Rumors were already circulating about John's illegitimacy, so Jessie's task was a delicate one. In early July she traveled to Virginia to gather material on his mother, Anne Fremon, and her family history.

At Old Point Comfort, she located elderly Catherine Whiting Lowry, Anne Fremon's sister. From Catherine's recollections, Jessie pieced together a poignant tale of the forced marriage of Anne, "one of the most beautiful women of her day in the State of Virginia," to wealthy old John Pryor, a man "in every respect repulsive to the young creature who was sacrificed to him." But in her account for Bigelow, Jessie said nothing of Anne's desperate elopement with Charles Fremon, though Catherine Whiting had confided it to her in gripping detail. In Jessie's truncated version, the childless Pryors, after "twelve long years of wedded misery," simply agreed to separate and were promptly granted a divorce by the state legislature. "Not long after," Jessie neatly concluded her story, "both married again, Mrs. Pryor to Mr. Frémont, and Major Pryor, in the 76th year of his age, to his housekeeper."[10]

Despite her words, Jessie was actually unsure whether either could remarry. "The power to re-marry must be looked into," she noted to herself at the time."[11] Though Jessie uncovered the will of Anne Fremon's father, as well as elaborate genealogical material showing her relationship to George Washington, she could produce no record of a Pryor divorce, Anne's marriage to Charles Fremon, or John's birth.

The Bigelow biography, hastily strung together with Jessie's help, was published in installments in the New York *Evening Post* and read avidly in the North; forty thousand copies at a dollar each were sold in book form. But among opponents, the "mad climber of the Rocky Mountains," as the Savannah *Georgian* branded Frémont, was savaged.[12] The focus was his illegitimacy.

Jessie naively hoped her account would be accepted, but opponents tore it apart. The Richmond *Dispatch* dismissed it as "like a novel," and presented its own version in cynical but suprisingly accurate detail. Pryor, the *Dispatch* agreed, was no prize: a "disabled, stiff-limbed old soldier" who had married only to secure a woman to "mend his linens or sew on his buttons." Fremon *père* came off little better: "a small swarthy individual with," the paper hinted darkly, "some French peculiarities strongly developed." As for Anne herself, the *Dispatch* commented dryly, "our informant does not remember whether she was very beautiful or not." After his wife's flight with Fremon, old Pryor had indeed "assuaged his grief" in the company of another woman, but "certain it is that [he] was never divorced from his wife. . . . These incidents in the life of the progenitor of the free-soil candidate for the Presidency, show that he was at least a disciple of Free-love, if not of Free-soil."

The Charleston *Courier* further punctured the divorce story when it examined Virginia legislative records for the period and found "but two divorces granted, neither of which was Mr. and Mrs. Pryor." In a widely reprinted Richmond speech, Virginia Governor Henry Wise exploited the candidate's illegitimacy and linked his election to civil war. "Tell me," he asked, "if the hoisting of the Black Republican flag . . . over you by a Frenchman's bastard . . . is not to be deemed an overt act and declaration of war."[13]

Coupled with questions about John's background was the charge that he was a secret Catholic. In reality, John had been raised an Episcopalian and confirmed at Charleston's St. Paul's Episcopal Church when he was fourteen. But the fact that his father was French and that he and Jessie had been married by a priest fueled the story. John refused to discuss the issue publicly, arguing that it was a private matter, but Jessie wrote a number of letters attesting to his Protestantism and furnished facts to Republican newspapers to combat the stories. But it was the Reverend Henry Ward Beecher who handled the marriage aspect most ingeniously. "Had we been in Col. Frémont's place," he gallantly declared, "we would have been married if it had required us to walk through a row of priests and bishops as long as from Washington to Rome, winding up with the Pope himself."[14] Still, to those Americans who felt threatened by Catholic immigrants pouring in from Ireland and Germany, Frémont's rumored Catholicism was yet another potent factor against him. That year the anti-Catholic, antiforeign Know-Nothing party was also running candidates; and though the party, split into southern and northern factions, had little chance of success, its presence revealed deep prejudices that worked against John.

As the campaign escalated, it became clear that John was vulnerable in ways that the lackluster sixty-five-year-old Buchanan was not, and the opposition exploited his weaknesses unmercifully. Its strategy was to make Frémont appear unreliable, dangerous, the lodestone of fringe groups. His exploits in California, his disastrous winter expeditions, his complicated financial maneuvers, and his Mariposas claim were also scrutinized. For Jessie personally, the most piercing accusations were sexual. Rumors of her husband's amorous adventures circulated in the South and in California. The opposition Los Angeles *Star* claimed that while John was in Los Angeles as self-proclaimed military governor, he had kept "a public harem" where he lured local "sisters, mothers, and daughters."[15]

As the rhetoric accelerated, the rift between the North and South widened. For many northerners, the campaign had become a crusade, a passionate struggle between good and evil. "There is but one question," proclaimed Henry Ward Beecher, whose Brooklyn congregation had given him two months off to speak for Frémont, "Freedom or Slavery—for or against." Many Republicans saw the election as a last chance to prevent civil war. "If the Slave-Power is checked *now*, it will *never* regain its strength," wrote abolitionist Lydia Maria Child. "If it is *not* checked, civil war is inevitable."

Deeply threatened by northern opposition to slavery, southerners also talked of disunion. Many were convinced that Frémont and the Republicans intended not only to prevent the spread of slavery but to abolish it entirely. "The election of Frémont would be the end of the Union," Senator Robert Toombs of Georgia flatly proclaimed.

"All this talk about the dissolution of the Union is humbug—nothing but folly," gaunt, shrill-voiced Abraham Lincoln answered such threats at an Illinois rally. "We won't dissolve the Union and you shan't." But such bluster was hardly reassuring to moderate voters in both the North and the South, and Buchanan strategists shrewdly exploited their fears. If Frémont won, Buchanan himself asserted, disunion would be "immediate and inevitable."[16]

"I am horribly tired," Jessie confessed to Lizzie in July. Incessantly busy, besieged by callers eager to assess the candidate's wife, she was caught up in a "tide of interruptions" that swept away all private life. She continued to manage the campaign correspondence, consult with advisers like Bigelow, Greeley, and Thurlow Weed, report regularly to Blair and Lizzie, and wield the pen when John wrote letters. At intervals snatched from her work, she was also posing for a portrait by poet-artist Buchanan Read. Though she felt that she looked gaunt and worn, Read had made her radiant and almost girlish. It "resembles me 'as the dew resembles rain,'" she wrote Lizzie with a sigh.[17]

In mid-July the family managed to escape to bucolic Staten Island, where they rented a cool, comfortable farmhouse overlooking the water. Still, Jessie could not rest. She and John commuted regularly to New York by boat. Moreover, little Frank was fretful from teething, and Jessie herself was ailing, though, as she wrote Lizzie glumly, "I always get well again & this is only one of [the] ill turns that I am accustomed to." She was not only disturbed by the accelerating attacks on John but painfully hurt that her southern relatives had turned against her. "The whole family has dropped me," she wrote bitterly. Most wounding of all were the actions of her own father.[18]

After endorsing Buchanan at the Democratic convention in Cincinnati, Benton spent June and July campaigning in Missouri, where he was running for governor. The former senator was in the ironic position of supporting the Democratic party, whose platform and candidate endorsed the Kansas-Nebraska Act, and opposing the Republican Party, whose platform and candidate, like Benton himself, condemned it. But Benton had a larger purpose. "The good of the Union alone brings me out," he told a St. Louis crowd. "Our country is in a deplorable condition. Fraternal affection gone—sectional hate engendered—extreme parties in the ascendant. Violence overspreads the land; we open no paper without seeing blood." Convinced that a Republican victory would shatter the Union, he put all personal considerations aside. "I am above family, and above self when the good of the Union is concerned."

Proud, stubborn, obsessed, Benton achieved a kind of moral grandeur that summer as he stumped the state, traveling more than a thousand miles in all to speak to the huge crowds who came to hear him. Addressing a massive outdoor rally, he seemed a "crowned king" to one listener, "his majestic form . . . attired in a handsome tailor-made suit of broadcloth," his eyes sparkling, his face aglow as he plied his audience with wit, sarcasm, and earthy anecdote. "The old Roman," as Lizzie called him that year when she was feeling forgiving (and "Ole Bull" when she was not), seemed indefatigable. "According to the calendar, my age is 74," he told a constituent, "but when anything is to be done I am 35 years old, sir."[19]

For Jessie, torn between husband and father, Benton's stand was difficult to accept. In mid-August she grew more disturbed when he did nothing to counter an attack by Pennsylvania Senator William Bigler, a Buchanan associate who demanded a senate inquiry into John's financial transactions in California and implied an unsavoriness in his accounts.

"I am blazing with fever from the sudden anger I felt last night on reading Mr. Bigler's motion in the Senate," Jessie wrote Lizzie. "Mr. Frémont says if Father takes no notice of [the Bigler attack] & continues to work with them he will never speak to him nor shall any of his children." Nonetheless, Jessie was determined not to break completely with her father. "I will let it make no outward difference," she told Lizzie, "but I have just written a long letter to Cousin Sarah [Benton Brant] that she may tell it to Father—not what Mr. Frémont says—that I only tell you—you are my confessional—but telling her what I felt he ought to do."

The Frémonts were convinced that Buchanan was behind Bigler's insinuations, but John controlled his impulse to retaliate. "I suppose they wish to force him into some act of resentment," Jessie wrote. "I wish they could understand how useless that is. He considers himself as belonging to the greatest cause ever at stake since the Revolution & his whole life shows that he 'throws away his body' for his duty—in this case he 'throws away his heart' & lets them slander & attack, in silence—knowing how injurious violence would be & how inadequate anything but death would be as punishment to such slanderers. The best answer will be in the triumph of our party."[20]

But for Jessie such forbearance proved difficult. "I have a bad rebellious nature that is always escaping even when I watch it," she confessed to Lizzie. She was tempted to write directly to her father, "who could by one line set right this Bigler movement," but John was adamant against it. To him, "the breach is made now & he accepts it for himself & his blood—I am free to do as I choose for myself but nothing he says will atone to him for Father's causeless hostility, pushed far beyond the limits of political difference."

To make matters worse, baby Frank had been feverish from teething. "I have carried him so much that Mr. Frémont said this morning I looked like a 'wilted plant' and took me off with him to a private conference room down town, where by way of relaxation I copied letters to California & Pennsylvania. But a pen is less weight than Frank."

Her baby recovered, but Jessie remained troubled. Her situation was more difficult to bear because she could not share her feelings fully with John. She continued to protect him from the most slanderous attacks (those against his mother were "but vaguely known" to him, she told Lizzie), while she endured them all.[21] Even harder, she tried to conceal her own anguish at the widening breach with her father. Only to the Blairs did she express her true feelings.

In late August she again poured out her concerns in a letter to Francis Blair. "I cannot rest unless I do all I can think of to prevent this unnatural state of things which brings no advantage to Father & really hurts me." The conflict, she confessed, had again made her sick. "The pain in my heart lasted longer than usual & a general inflammation has followed making me tired & feverish. . . . You know this is an old wound," she told Blair, "for the opening of which politics are only an excuse. Father has absolutely disliked Mr. Frémont since the refusal to sell the Mariposas." She might have said that the wound was far older, as old as her elopement with John fifteen years before.

Jessie's doctor ordered "no newspapers, no ideas, no excitement of any kind. . . . I am to get well enough to go to town next week when the opera re-commences & lead a life steadily devoted to amusements disconnected with politics." But her letter, filled with campaign talk as well as concern about her father, showed she was not following his advice. John, in contrast, was "as gay as a boy," she told Blair. "We let him read no papers (unless you write them) and he has the pleasure of doing daily good work in the cause."[22] Despite the physical toll, Jessie seemed determined to bear the emotional bruises of the campaign alone. More and more she saw herself as a buffer between her husband and a hostile world.

Before Jessie's letter reached Blair, Lizzie decided to intervene. Jessie had asked for her sister Susan's new address, and Lizzie used that as an excuse to call on Thomas Benton, just back from his Missouri campaign, where he was losing his bid for the governorship. To Lizzie he looked thin but well. Despite his political intransigence, she wrote Jessie afterward, "still I cling to the Old Roman more in his defeat than if successful." Inevitably, the conversation turned to Jessie. "Your Father talked lovingly of you in his way," Lizzie wrote, "& when I said that your only annoyance was the Bigler attack . . . his face flushed & a few minutes afterward he said, 'You need not tell her Susan's direction. I'll do that' . . . & said he would send you a letter by the next mail."[23]

Lizzie's tactful call had its effect, and Jessie was soon joyfully reporting a letter from her father. "He only wrote of family matters but it was enclosed in a very kind note to Mr. Frémont (family altogether) which Mr. Frémont answered immediately." Yet the possibility of a permanent break continued to haunt her. When she learned that Benton had privately expressed "great indignation" at Bigler's charges, she still feared her blunt, outspoken father might be "worried into some depreciatory remark" about John, causing a new rupture between the two men. "Mr. Frémont has not my motives for indulgence," she told Lizzie.

Determined to preserve the fragile link with her father, Jessie went to see him in September. The visit was wearing, but they managed to avoid a crisis. Though Francis Blair himself was "in exceedingly ill humor" with Benton, he too did his part by having both father and daughter to dinner at Silver Spring.[24]

By the time of Jessie's Washington visit, the shape of the campaign had become clear. The middle states—Pennsylvania, Indiana, and Illinois—were pivotal. If Frémont swept New England and the upper North, and Buchanan the South, the candidate who triumphed in these three states would win the presidency. Since both Pennsylvania and Indiana held state elections in early October, a month before most other states, the results could serve as both bellwether and bandwagon for the winning candidate. By late summer, Pennsylvania, with its twenty-seven electoral votes, had become the focus for both parties.

"Urge every available man to go into Pennsylvania & speak," Jessie wrote the Blairs in mid-August. "The Democratic party will fill that state with documents of their own but the human voice will exercise a magnetic power which will undo their work."

The Democrats were spending lavishly in Pennsylvania, and Thurlow Weed now set to work to raise money for the Republicans. Teams of speakers hurried to the state. "If old Penn. is to be carried by only a few votes & I could change the votes of that few to Frémont, nothing would induce me to leave the field," Kansas lecturer Clarina Nichols reported from Pennsylvania. Nathaniel Banks urged the Frémonts to make a ceremonial visit to the state, but neither John nor Jessie was enthusiastic about this innovative idea, and the trip never occurred. "I want to fight with stronger weapons than courtesies & I will do mischief if I am let loose among opponents," Jessie explained.

The night of the Pennsylvania election, Jessie awaited the results with Francis Blair, "too wise to be entirely confident, but very hopeful."[25] Toward the end of the day, John Bigelow brought discouraging news. The vote was close, he told Jessie, but Buchanan was ahead. Concerned about Blair's health, she and Bigelow decided to postpone telling him until the next morning, after he had slept. They got him through an early dinner and an evening at the theater, though Blair could not understand their lack of enthusiasm for the play. When a prominent Democratic editor bowed and grinned at him from across the house, Blair nearly guessed why he looked so cheerful. The next day they learned they had lost Pennsylvania by three thousand votes, many of them probably fraudulent. Indiana, which voted the same day, went Democratic as well. It was a crushing blow.

"I heartily regret the defeat we have met and do not look for things to change for the better," Jessie wrote Lizzie afterward. "I wish the cause had triumphed—I do wish Mr. Frémont had been the one to administer the bitter dose of subjection to the South for he has the coolness & nerve to do it just as it needs to be done—without passion & without sympathy—as coldly as a surgeon over a hospital patient would he have cut off their right hand, Kansas, from the old unhealthy southern body." John faced the Pennsylvania defeat with his usual stoicism. "He bears it nobly," Jessie told Lizzie. "I do admire his self control." As for herself, she had little hope for November. "I don't think we will wear any but black feathers this year."[26]

Gradually the Frémont forces rallied, and as November

4 neared, Jessie regained a degree of optimism. Then in the midst of it all, seventeen-month-old Frank became gravely ill.

"He was perfectly well, good appetite, good digestion and gay as Charley," Jessie told Lizzie, "when suddenly Tuesday morning he was taken with a convulsion." For days he hovered between life and death, and Jessie, haunted by memories of her two dead babies, moved into the nursery to be near him. "He is so feeble looking yet it makes my heart ache," she wrote Lizzie. "Sleeping in the nursery & starting out of bed a dozen times a night do not improve my courage." The presidency scarcely mattered. "I don't care for the election. Let it go . . . although I dare say when Frank is well," she added with rueful self-knowledge, "I shall be less careless about it."[27]

Two days before the election, with Frank running about again, Jessie found she did care. Francis Blair was there to wait out the results, and they were again hopeful. "I don't dare say anything more than to tell you we may be successful," Jessie confided to Lizzie. Her problem was lack of sleep, for little Frank still wanted her with him. "He has grown so fond of me that I have to sleep with him the last half of each night in his own little bed," she explained to Lizzie. "He lies with his eyes open—screams if Mémé comes to him, but smiles on me & murmurs 'Mama . . . Baby' & so goes to sleep again. After the 4th I am going to make him give me up for it gives me too little sleep but I like him to love me so."[28]

November 4, 1856, dawned cold and rainy in New York City. Despite the foul weather the turnout was impressive. By evening huge crowds had gathered at the newspaper offices around Nassau Street to await the results as they trickled in by telegraph.

At first the news was encouraging. Frémont swept every New England state. His New York vote was also massive. In the West, he won impressive victories in Ohio, Michigan, Wisconsin, and Iowa. But there his drive faltered. Despite the efforts of Lincoln and other Republican speakers, Illinois, like Pennsylvania and Indiana, voted for Buchanan. From there south, Buchanan triumphed. Only Maryland stood apart, voting for the Know-Nothing candidate, Millard Fillmore.

When the results were tallied, Buchanan had 174 electoral votes, Frémont 114. In the popular count, Buchanan won 1.8 million votes, Frémont nearly 1.4 million. It was a stunning display for a new party running its first presidential candidate, but it was not enough.

John permitted himself little show of feeling, outwardly at least accepting the defeat with his usual reticent grace. But Jessie and Blair were devastated. At breakfast, Blair, who had put his whole heart into the campaign, broke down and cried. Lily, who had been dreaming of life in the White House, sobbed as well; and when she couldn't stop, Jessie wrapped a thick green veil around her tear-streaked face and sent her off on a long walk. Lily paced Washington Square until her tears finally stopped. When she returned home at last, her eyes red and swollen from weeping, Jessie sat her down for a talk. In later years, Lily would remember her mother's earnest words that day, as she spoke of the need for courage in the face of life's defeats. But in the months ahead, as her own anger and pain lingered on, Jessie would find it hard to follow her own advice.

19

If there is a word in our language sweeter than all the rest, whose mention thrills a chord in every bosom, it is the sweet word home.

The Mother's Assistant and Young Lady's Friend
1846

RETRENCHMENT

F OR THE REPUBLICAN PARTY in its first national campaign, the election could scarcely be called a defeat. From a party of thousands, it had swelled to more than a million supporters. "I have never seen a defeated party so full of vigor and enthusiasm," declared Connecticut editor Gideon Welles. Many were eager for Frémont to run again in 1860. "He will certainly triumph on another trial," young Frank Blair wrote enthusiastically to his father.[1]

Women pressing for their political rights were also elated by the Republican showing. At the seventh National Woman's Rights Convention held in New York City three weeks after the election, president Lucy Stone saw Jessie's prominence as an especially favorable sign. "The ballot has not yet been yielded; but it can not be far off when, as in the last Presidential contest, women were urged to attend political meetings, and a woman's name was made one of the rallying cries of the party of progress. The enthusiasm which everywhere greeted the name of Jessie was so far a recognition of woman's right to participate in politics." In a resolution the convention urged the new party to live up to the promises implicit in its campaign: "The Republican Party, appealing constantly, through its orators, to female sympathy, and using for its most popular rallying cry a female name, is peculiarly pledged by consistency, to do justice hereafter in those States where it holds control." Yet Stone remained skeptical enough of male politicians to urge her listeners to work for their own rights before supporting even the Republicans wholeheartedly. Her suspicions proved correct. During the next years, women would be asked to put aside their "curious doctrines," as the *New York Times* termed the convention's call for equal rights, for political priorities determined by men.[2]

The most ominous result of the election was the heightened antagonism between North and South. Southerners were deeply alarmed by the sweeping Republican vote in the North, where Frémont won eleven of the sixteen free states. Many predicted victory for the new party in 1860, and in that event, secession, even if it meant civil war.

"We are subsiding into former habits, not without some of the giddy feeling one has after having been a long while on ship board," Jessie reported to Lizzie two weeks after the election. John had thrown himself into his Mariposas affairs and was, she punned, "in full chase after his butterfly—this time with solid prospects of success." As usual she was less sanguine. "I am the most skeptical of mortals and until I see actual thousands I shall give small heed to the promised millions." The children were also thriving: "Frank fatten[ing] visibly" after his illness and Charley "exceedingly proud" of his first knee pants. The opera season was "charming," Jessie continued with determined cheerfulness, but as she described the scene to Lizzie, her own anger emerged. "I am quite a dividing attraction there & it amused me last night to see Belle Cass [the daughter of a political rival] wedged in among ladies & watching with her cold venomous eyes, the succession of clever & fashionable men who came to my box. We have upset her throne. She and Aunt Catron [wife of a southern politician] both have new white opera cloaks—they will wear them at the inauguration—see if they don't."[3]

Aside from such forgivable lapses, Jessie faced the defeat gallantly. Though her dreams were smashed, she managed an outward cheer. Yet her disappointment was intense. She believed the presidency would have "called out great qualities"[4] in John, and though she could scarcely admit it even to Lizzie, she had wanted it fiercely for herself as well.

For Jessie, brooding over the defeat and pondering an uncertain future, the next months would be a time of reassessment. She had been stunned by the viciousness of the campaign and profoundly wounded by her own father's opposition. She felt a deep need to draw her husband and children around her and settle permanently in one place. To Lizzie she put her options in geographical terms. Washington, that "semibarbarian latitude," was out, especially with the Buchanan administration in power. "Yourselves, Father & Susan comprise all my lovings there, & likings I have none." California also had little appeal. Jessie was wary of Las Mariposas entanglements, and the primitive life had lost its charm. Her choice was New York. "Mr. Frémont says I may live where I like & I like here," she announced.[5]

A week later, her priorities were reinforced when five-year-old Charley came down with scarlet fever. For ten days Jessie scarcely left his side. By late January the household was back to normal, and Jessie sought comfort in the quotidian. Lily was studying with a proper English governess, while the more lighthearted Nina had lessons in music and drawing. Jessie herself was helping with Charley's studies, though she admitted he was "not a rapid scholar except in fairy tales & Irish songs." John also seemed "remarkably well—positively fattening & very contented with things as they are." He was talking of a trip to California on Las Mariposas business, but Jessie clung to her new rootedness. "California has no attraction for me and I trust a stay of a few months may be all it requires of Mr. Frémont."[6]

At the end of January, Thomas Benton came to see the family. It was a difficult visit for them all, but Jessie was determined to make the best of it. "We're all dead men in the political world," she wrote Francis Blair afterward, "so we have all our talents free for private life and the hatchet is buried and we are ourselves again." But Blair was unwilling to forgive his old friend quite so easily. "It seems he deigned to spend a night at Col. Frémont's," he reported indignantly to his son Frank. "Jessie . . . is happy that he is willing to forgive her for desiring her husband's election to the presidency & banishes the thought that he greatly contributed to prevent it." Benton was unwell, he continued, softening. "His face is sharp & discolored by disease . . . he has lost probably 50 lbs. flesh, yet his spirit is buoyant—he talks strongly on politics—his whole soul bent on saving the Union."[7]

Over the next few months, Benton returned several times to see the family. "He comes and goes now with a cheerful informality that brings a choking sensation in my throat," Jessie wrote Lizzie in March. She was especially grateful to John for his courtesy to her father. "One might think Mr. Frémont had tried to defeat Father so much does he do to make him feel everything on the old footing. . . . Altogether he is as he ought to be in my house a most honored and welcome and contented guest, and you know what a relief it is to me."[8]

Jessie had managed to hold the family together, if precariously, but she herself was not well. At first she feared she was pregnant. "I have not had a sight of bloody menses since the fifteen of November," she confided to Lizzie, whom she asked to arrange for a nurse. "I am so old that there is a hope tis change of life—but a sick stomach & other familiar symptoms warns me I may want my good friend Matilda's services. . . . So tell her from the middle of August to the the 1st of October to hold herself disengaged. . . . I dread the ordeal."[9]

At thirty-two, it is unlikely that Jessie had reached menopause, but she was either wrong or miscarried, for she wrote nothing more of Matilda or her suspected pregnancy. Yet she remained unwell, suffering from a malaise she could not shake. Life seemed flat after the intensity of the campaign, but at the same time perilous and unpredictable. In her need to be alone, to escape the bustle and forced cheer of her household, she took long brooding walks, tramping miles each day through the crowded streets of New York. "I have a museum of shoes," she wrote Lizzie, making light of her excursions. "Some for frozen & some for thawed ground, and one devoted dress, short & cheap, and a cloak that defies rain or snow & so disguised I walk out entrenched."[10]

As spring came, she grew worse. The headaches, the spasms of the heart returned. She tried to keep busy. "We are at work on the book which is our baby and pet," she said of the memoir she was helping John begin. But this literary offspring paled beside Lizzie's astonishing announcement that after thirteen childless years of marriage, she was unexpectedly pregnant. "I am coming to see Lizzie and talk over the wonderful event," Jessie wrote gaily to Lizzie's mother. "With you and chloroform she will get through without knowing what pain is."[11] But when Lizzie, who was thirty-eight and frail, confessed her dread of childbirth, Jessie, sympathizing, admitted that she too felt depressed, though she couldn't explain why.

The strain of the past year provided reason enough for Jessie's malaise. But there may have been another cause. Shortly after the election, campaign biographer John Bigelow had come to believe that John had "debauched" a maid in the Frémont household. Shocked, Bigelow had abruptly broken with the family. Jessie, who felt a special rapport with him during the campaign, was puzzled and hurt by his sudden defection. Unaware of his motive, she blamed herself for some unintentional rudeness to his wife.[12]

Whether or not Jessie believed or even heard such rumors, she was nonetheless suffering from a profound sadness, a depression she could not shake. Her old rapport with her father had vanished, and her relationship to John had changed as well. During their fifteen years of marriage, the passionate intensity had seeped away. John had become more remote, his natural reserve heightened by the humiliations of the court-martial and the bitterness of the campaign. Whether his plan to go to California was escape as well as business, he himself may not have known. But it revealed deep differences in their temperaments. While Jessie craved a rooted family life, John still lacked "parental instinct," as she confided to Lizzie that spring.[13] While she sought comfort from the bruises of the campaign within the warming circle of family and friends, he remained apart, tending his wounds in private. When the election result was known, Jessie, Blair, and Lily mourned unabashedly. John bore it "nobly" but alone.

Jessie planned to spend the summer on Staten Island again, but in May she abruptly changed her mind. While John traveled to California, she and the children would go to Europe, where he could join them in the fall. Jessie's sudden decision suggests her own despair. Her restless husband was again heading west, while her father remained hurt and angry. She had struggled to recover her old closeness with Benton, but the campaign left a bitter residue that neither could ignore. Dining with Benton one Sunday that spring, Lizzie Lee found him angry and morose, "a lump of malignity." He "abuses everything & everybody but himself," she reported to her husband. "I was amused, rather disgusted . . . at his ferocity towards the Frémonts."[14]

Despite such displays, Benton invited Jessie to accompany him to a Virginia resort that summer. She refused. "I had enough of Virginia hospitality last year not to risk it again," she explained to Lizzie. "I wish I could add anything to his happiness—if I could I should have remained here this summer—but he will only see things his own way. . . . With him I should be meeting all the men who were personally malignant last year & with whom nothing can make me associate." Just before sailing, she asked Lizzie's husband to visit her father occasionally "and have a friendly talk with him—to keep his heart as gentle as possible to his old friends—and some young ones—who love him although he will not think so because of this political difference."[15]

In mid-June, accompanied by Nina, Lily, Charley, Frank, and her two loyal French maids, Jessie sailed for Europe. The sky was blue, the sea calm, and the ship "truly noble," she wrote Blair en route. Nonetheless, she was unhappy. "I have had the blues desperately," she confessed.[16]

They settled in a large country villa in St. Germain en Laye, ten miles from Paris, with a picturesque castle ruin in the foreground and a sweeping view of the Seine valley beyond. A retinue of skilled servants catered to their needs; "no pen can do justice to the cooking," Jessie exclaimed.[17] There were daily walks in the nearby forest, lessons for the children with Jessie or the new German governess, and expeditions to Paris to see the pictures at the Tuileries. In the evening they strolled along the town's fashionable promenade, admiring the distant spires of Paris while a band played military airs.

Despite the charms of the scene, Jessie was lonely. Writing to the Blairs, she continually urged them to come for a long stay. Even after she learned that Lizzie had succesfully delivered a healthy baby boy ("my grandson and your godson Preston Blair Lee," Francis Blair wrote her triumphantly), she persisted. "You should have tea out of my turquoise cup and a big wood fire and such other creature comforts as we like best," she wrote Lizzie as inducement.[18]

She thought often of her father. "When I saw how he was embittered last summer," she wrote Francis Blair, "it went to my heart that the injury, fancied as it was, should have come through me. I wanted success that I might put it at his feet and let him make use of it & feel his old power returned." But she now suspected that a victory would have alienated him permanently. "I am afraid I am not of the right stuff for a political woman," she told Blair.[19]

But it was John who dominated her thoughts. If Jessie had doubted her marriage during her postelection brooding, her separation clarified her feelings. Whatever her suspicions or fears, whatever her disappointments, she missed him desperately. "My sweetheart," she wrote him in July, "I spoil quantities of my pretty paper writing you things that begin well enough and then degenerate into the most selfish laments at not being with you. . . . I love you with all my heart and trust to you to give it health." Later in the month she wrote again: "Love me in memory of the old times when I was so dear to you. I love you now much more than I did then." In September she told him of "trying to make the sun go from west to east—that is trying to look young and pretty" to please him when he came. "I try . . . to follow all the rules" of diet and exercise, she said, "but one affectionate look from you will give me more life than all the rules. . . . We are all well and all look to your coming for the only real happiness we know. Most of all darling I love you and want you."[20]

In early September, while Jessie languished amid the civilized pleasures of St. Germain en Laye, Thomas Benton suffered a series of wrenching intestinal attacks that left him weak and emaciated. Though the old warrior would at first report merely an "obstinate constipation," he knew his disease was "mortal."[21] He was dying, slowly and painfully, of cancer of the rectum.

Benton was determined to hide the fact of cancer from Jessie, so she was informed only that he was seriously ill. Though she had already rented a large apartment in Paris for the coming year and reserved a box at the opera, her impulse was to go to him. Even when the Blairs wrote assuring her that her father's life was no longer in danger, her fears continued. In mid-October, frantic at the lack of further news, she decided to journey to America. As added inducement, John would be passing through New York in November, en route to join her in France, and with luck she could meet him there instead.

Jessie booked passage on the *Arago* for herself and six-year-old Charley, leaving Lily, Nina, and little Frank in the care of English friends. If all went well, she would see her father on November 4, exactly a year after the election. "How things fade," she wrote Lizzie as she set off. "I don't care two straws for the last fourth of November now—personally I mean. . . . This year I only hope that day will give me the sight of Father, in health, & quite free from any bad thoughts about me. I would go farther to cure him of a heart ache than of a bodily pain."[22]

The voyage was rough and Jessie so anxious that she was uncharacteristically seasick. But as the steamship approached New York, she was relieved to learn from newspapers brought from shore that her father had recovered enough to have gone for a brief horseback ride. When her ship docked, she found John, who had arrived from Panama just an hour before, waiting at the pier.

That night, ensconced with her husband at the Astor House, Jessie was too elated to sleep. Far into the night she savored "the strange coincidence" of meeting him at the pier, as well as her relief that her father was better. Half-ruefully, half-contentedly, she observed the inevitable changes that nearly half a year had brought. Both she, now thirty-three, and John, forty-four, were getting older. His dark hair had "silvered over, much, since the spring," while hers was "getting hard on to white," she told Lizzie, exaggerating the streaks of gray in her chestnut hair. Though John had a cold, they were nonetheless "both very well," she added, only hinting at her happiness.[23] Time had not dimmed her passion for this proud, reticent man, though the crush of events had made it fiercer, more protective. Reunited once more, she was determined to resist another separation.

John and Jessie established temporary quarters in New York City, but Jessie soon hurried on to Washington to see her father. She was shocked at the change in him. His flesh hung loosely on his once powerful frame, his voice was weak, his walk feeble. Nonetheless, he made light of his ailments and concealed his growing financial problems from her as well. With a fatal bravado, he was back at work on his latest project, an abridgment of congressional debates that he hoped would bring him the money he desperately needed.

As usual, Jessie found Washington inhospitable. At home, her sister Liz remained cool, while in society, the fashionable chattered of President Buchanan's charming young niece, Harriet Lane, who, as his White House hostess, filled the role Jessie might have played. Congressmen and diplomats, even the president himself, attended the teas and dinners of Jessie's old enemy, Rose Greenhow, returned from her California adventures as a glamorous widow. In the Cabinet, the South dominated, and within months, Buchanan—weak, vacillating, unimaginative—would fatally split his own party by recommending that Kansas, still the burning unsolved issue, be admitted as a slave state. Though she tried to forget the past, Jessie herself remained bitter. When a political enemy who had snubbed her tried to make amends, she refused. "I am a savage you know & don't turn the cheek twice," she confided to Lizzie.[24] Only at Silver Spring, where she went bearing a blue-ribboned box containing a Parisian christening dress for the new baby, did she feel the welcome was warm.

With her father recuperating, Jessie was eager to return to Paris, this time with John. She soon learned that her husband had other plans. John explained that he could not leave Las Mariposas long unattended. He must return to California, and he wanted her to come with him.

At first Jessie resisted. She stormed against California and Las Mariposas. She could live happily in New York or Paris, but a remote cottage in the Sierra foothills would be exile. Moreover, she remained dubious about its financial prospects and increasingly suspicious of her husband's associates, who tended to "do a little business for themselves" while ostensibly aiding him. But her rebellion was brief. "I refused so flatly to hear even of going to California that I suspected myself at the time," she admitted afterward to Lizzie, "& of course I am going. So is the whole caravan. We are only to stay six or eight months—to go immediately up to the Mariposas where Mr. Frémont will write as well as direct his work there."[25]

Jessie went to California reluctantly, with a vivid understanding of its difficulties. "No man can know what a wear & tear the detail of family life in a new country without servants is to a woman," she confided to Lizzie. John thought only of "the climate & the sunrise over the fine mountain scenery, the spring flowers & horseback rides that send him with a vigorous appetite to breakfast & a clear healthy mind to write.

I am to be ready to do that writing but I am to know & provide the component parts of that breakfast first—& I remember country life in California very accurately."

Jessie unabashedly preferred the civilized comforts of Paris or New York. "I think a stouter woman than myself might fall back dismayed from such an array of work" as housekeeping in California would bring. Only another woman could appreciate "the mysteries of washing and ironing," she continued her lament. "Think of Nina's skirts & mine & Lily's & two piggy boys to say nothing of Mr. Frémont's unbounded linen & we shall have 'open house' & if I don't do something extraordinary in the way of feeding & entertaining generally I will be called disdainful & proud & indifferent to Mr. Frémont's interests."

Despite her complaints, Jessie preferred the hardships of California with John to the pleasures of Europe without him, and she was determined to accompany him. "Now if I were to say any part of this to Mr. Frémont he would not let me go," she added, so "I look only at the good side with him & relieve my mind by this outpouring to you. . . . I assure you it does a great deal of good to talk it out."[26]

In late January, when Nina, Lily, and little Frank returned from France, another obstacle arose. Thomas Benton insisted that the two girls remain with him in Washington while the rest of the family went west. Jessie dreaded another fight with her father, but she and John agreed that the family must stay together. "I . . . shall come away from [Washington] all upset again by having to displease him," she wrote Lizzie just before visiting her father. "It is not easy to serve two masters and I would like so much to obey both of mine, but if I must choose it will be for the one that I think needs . . . me the most."

Benton, of course, acquiesced, but Jessie, deeply uneasy about leaving him, remained disturbed. Though he continued to put on a brave front when she was there, she feared he was dying. She felt guilty at her desertion, yet helpless to change her plans. She was haunted by the thought that he would die without her, as her mother had died without him.

"I often think with sickness at my heart of Mother's look as she held to Father's empty chair & leaned weeping upon me," she wrote Lizzie of that painful time three years before.

She saw him for the last time on March 14, 1858, his seventy-sixth birthday. Benton was well enough that day to point out jauntily in a note to young Frank Blair, "what a clean, neat hand I still write." Despite such glimmers of his old spirit, Jessie saw the pain in his face and heard it in his voice, now reduced to a rasping whisper. He spoke of the will he had made that fall and explained its provisions to her. Gingerly, they began to talk of their parting, but when he saw her anguish, he changed the topic, dreading to expose the emotions they both felt. "He knew he would not see me again," she said later, looking back.[27]

20

*We would assert that western women
display more fortitude and patient
endurance than their eastern sisters
ever have occasion to manifest, or
even imagine. They dwell in a new-
found land, peopled by the restless,
adventurous, excitable. Their companions
are smitten with the curse of gold.*

"Women of the West"
The Hesperian
March 1859

"THE LITTLE
WHITE HOUSE"

"YOU DON'T KNOW the beauty of cleanliness until you are
on a little thousand-ton ship with 772 passengers—such
pigs, the greater part of them," Jessie wrote Lizzie with
uncustomary asperity as the steamship *Star of the West* approached Panama. John and the children were elated to be
heading for California, but she felt sick and depressed. "I
broke down the second day, had fever & heart aches & af-
terwards seasickness & after three days of this dismalness
emerged to a weak satisfaction at being no longer in pain,"
she reported to Lizzie. She remained deeply concerned about
her father and haunted by their leave-taking. "Keep dear
Lizzie your promise to me and let me hear from some of you
about Father. He will write only the favorable side."[1]

Her gloom may have been enhanced by their large and
bustling entourage. Besides Charley, little Frank, Lily, Nina,
and two maids, they were accompanied by a retinue of aides—
lawyers, mining experts, business associates—some of whom
Jessie already suspected were less loyal or competent than
John wanted to believe.

Despite her malaise, Jessie appreciated the new ease of
the isthmus crossing. Carried swiftly through the jungle by
train (and given a "gorgeous" lunch on board, according to
young aide John Howard), they had only an hour in humid
Panama City before boarding the *Golden Age*, bound for San
Francisco.[2] Jessie's spirits lifted as they steamed up the calm
Pacific, and on the evening of April 12, 1858, with signal lights
gleaming and gun sounding, passed through the Golden Gate.

They set out almost immediately for Bear Valley, traveling by steamboat up the San Joaquin River to Stockton, then changing to a creaking stagecoach for the two-day, eighty-mile journey across the great Central Valley, warm and green-gold in the late spring sun. As they reached the foothills of the Sierra, where thousands of forty-niners once roamed, the land looked uprooted and abandoned, chewed and spit out by men hungry for gold.

Nearing Bear Valley, the hills were dotted with oak and digger pine, and knee-deep in grass and wildflowers "of a beauty and fragrance I never had met before," Jessie exclaimed. But such lushness couldn't hide the fact that the village of Bear Valley itself was a desolate little place of saloons and a few shabby boardinghouses on a ragged street. Even its chief ornament, the two-storied, pillared and porticoed Oso House Hotel, had interior walls of cotton sheeting. "Miners swaggered up and down . . . drinking, smoking, gambling," young John Howard observed with fascination. "Fighting . . . was a daily sport."[3]

As part of Frémont's seventy-square-mile Mariposas tract, Bear Valley was a company town. Frémont paid his miners $2.50 to $3.50 for their ten hours of daily labor, and pocketed half of the dollar they paid each night at one of the company boardinghouses.[4] The valley echoed with the steady clamor of his mill, crushing the gold-laden quartz ore that was his fortune.

The Frémont cottage, half a mile away, was a plain whitewashed structure set on a sloping lawn of wild geraniums and shaded by towering pines and live oaks. The Indians would soon begin to call it "the little White House," an irony not lost on Jessie or the rest of the local populace. Nearby were stables and a neglected garden overrun with cabbages, artichokes, and wild roses.

"All of us are well and very contented," Jessie wrote cheerfully to Lizzie a week after their arrival. "We have a fine pair of carriage horses and Lil has a horse of her own. She is teaching Charley & Frank to ride bare back. They are already browned with red cheeks & the baby [Frank] thrives on the fine milk & pure air." Jessie was planting honeysuckle and scarlet runner vine, and beginning to rejuvenate the vegetable garden. "We get quantities of milk, buttermilk, & fresh butter & eggs," she added, "& so you see my housekeeping goes on brilliantly."

John was caught in a tangle of legal battles over mining claims, but Jessie was optimistic. "His agents here took squatters claims over 100 acres over all the richest veins," she reported. Such seizures were bitterly resented by local miners, but Jessie, ignoring the rancor, pronounced the inhabitants friendly. To Jessie there were more obvious dangers than a few grumbling miners. In May she would write of a grizzly bear encountered on a horseback ride and of rattlesnakes found in the yard. "I used to fear caterpillars & spiders but I do not mind a housesnake or a chapparal snake now since I have seen the fresh trail of a rattlesnake crossing the patch to the kitchen," she remarked. Ensconced in her "little White House" in Bear Valley, musing on cabbages and gold, Washington seemed another world, one she claimed she wanted to forget. When you write, "you may put in a little politics but very little," she instructed Lizzie. "I've cut the shop & taken to farming."[5]

Two weeks after Jessie left Washington, her father suffered a final excruciating attack. Too feeble to sit upright, Thomas Benton took to his bed at last. By now he could eat only rice and milk, well chilled with ice. Nonetheless, he drove himself to finish the final pages of his book, dictating to his daughter Liz and son-in-law William Carey Jones in a strained whisper. When Francis Blair visited nim in early April, he found his old friend "in extremis," scarcely able to move his hands and feet, yet with his book and pen still by his side. "He has borne his pangs . . . with a stoicism almost superhuman," Blair wrote Van Buren that day. "He has kept his disease a secret for years . . . never complaining. . . . His patience and tenderness to attendants is amazing and love for his friends increases as his vitality decreases."

By the end of the first week in April, Benton completed his work. "I shall not trouble you much longer," he told his black nurse, Kitty, toward the last. "Do you hear that?" he asked, beckoning her to listen. "Kitty, that is the death rattle."[6] On April 10, 1858, two days before Jessie reached San Francisco, Thomas Hart Benton died.

Jessie suffered deeply from her father's death. Remembering her childhood, that tender, blissful time when she had been "his favorite scholar," she grieved that she had hurt him, that she could not repay his devotion as he grew old. Writing to Francis Blair, she spoke of her remorse at leaving her father for California. "It was a hard choice—one that left lasting regret." She could only hope he understood. "I had a letter from Father the day I left New York," she told Blair, struggling to soothe her guilt. Generously, Benton had urged her to go, telling her it was "not right for a family to be divided."[7] Still, she feared she had failed him in the end.

John postponed a journey to San Francisco to comfort her. "I remained with Jessie until I had got her through the first & worst two weeks," he reported to the Blairs in early June. "When I left she was in a more cheerful, or rather, less oppressed condition." Nonetheless, she fell ill ("this miserable weakness about heart," she explained tellingly), and later that month she joined him in San Francisco, where they hoped the sea breezes would improve her health and spirits. She tried not to dwell on the past. "I did not write the last mail because I wanted to keep my mind quite turned away from any thoughts that might agitate me," she wrote Lizzie from San Francisco. Nonetheless, she could not stop her anguish. "His memory and name are our care now."[8]

The remembrance was too sharp, the grief too fresh that summer, to bring her anything but pain, but in the years ahead, Jessie would find it far easier to tend her father's memory than the proud old man himself. Gradually, subtly, she would reshape the past, polishing and smoothing his image, molding the stubborn politician into a more pliant, more serviceable figure. Eventually, she would reconcile husband and father in memory, as she failed to do in life.

Wearing a black dress and black straw hat, Jessie returned with John to Bear Valley in early July. She had scarcely arrived when a crisis at the mines abruptly forced her thoughts to the present.

Las Mariposas, the wild tract of land John had inadvertently purchased from Juan Bautista Alvarado in 1847 for three thousand dollars, was a "floating" grant, whose boundaries were only vaguely defined as between the Merced, Chowchilla, and San Joaquin rivers and the Sierra Nevada. When gold was discovered, thousands of men swarmed over the land, rooting up the surface gold with pick and shovel. Later, some installed more elaborate equipment to extract the gold locked in the great quartz lode that ran like a giant backbone through the country. In 1855, when the Supreme Court in a split decision finally confirmed John's title to Las Mariposas, he drew its boundaries shrewdly—unscrupulously, some said—stretching them far up into the foothills to include rich mines claimed and worked by others. To many miners and settlers it was "an outrageous bare-faced piece of downright stealing." Though John's action would be confirmed by the courts, many found it profoundly unjust that one man should monopolize the wealth of the region. The bitterness was so widespread that in the 1856 election, Frémont received only six percent of the vote in Mariposa County and none at all in some mining precincts.[9]

Angry miners, some organized as the Hornitos League, vowed to defend their claims against Frémont's "aggressive, rapacious aims."[10] Among them, Jessie admitted, were a few idealists, "well meaning but foggy minded men, with vague ideas as to the rights in property and a much larger number . . . who believed in property, but only for themselves and preferred to acquire it by any method save earning it." The

driving force behind the Hornitos League was the Merced
Mining Company, which claimed valuable mines like the Pine
Tree and Josephine now included within Las Mariposas' swol-
len boundaries. In July, just after the Frémonts returned from
San Francisco, the Merced Company prodded the dissident
miners to act.[11]

July 9 was a night of almost unbearable heat. Unable to
sleep, Jessie sat by the open window, hoping to catch a breath
of the cooler air that came just before dawn. Suddenly she
heard hoofbeats. From the shadowy road that led up to the
mines, a man on horseback emerged. Galloping toward the
cottage, he reined his horse in the yard and in a low voice
relayed an urgent message: the Hornitos League had "jumped"
the Black Drift!

When Jessie repeated his words, John dismissed them
lightly. "Only mining work," he said. "You had best go to
sleep again." Obediently, Jessie returned to bed, but when
she woke again later that morning, John was gone. Questioning Isaac, their teamster and watchman, she learned that eighty
men had seized the rich Black Drift mine, three miles up the
ravine. John, with the few men he could muster, had ridden
up to confront them.

The next hours seemed endless to Jessie. She tried to
keep the children busy at their lessons, but everyone was on
edge. When one of John's agents arrived at the house, she
pointed dramatically to the remains of breakfast still on the
table and exclaimed, "You arrive at the end of the feast and
the beginning of the fray!"[12]

When John returned home safely late that morning, Jessie
felt numb with relief. She learned that after taking the Black
Drift, the Hornitos men had tried to seize the adjoining Pine
Tree mine. Six or seven of John's miners were inside. Ordered
out, they resisted. Barricading themselves in the tunnels behind a pile of rocks and tools laced with fused powder kegs,
they threatened to ignite them if anyone tried to enter.

Jessie was nearly overcome with fear for John's safety. She
pleaded with him not to return to the mines. But as the tension

continued, she pulled herself together. "I grew somewhat used to it," she reported to the Blairs later, "& whenever Mr. Frémont was in sight I was very brave."

The violence she dreaded nearly occurred that first day. John's force of less than thirty men was arrayed along the road and on the steep surrounding hillsides when John, wearing light summer clothing with a derringer concealed in his breast pocket, walked toward the angry men swarming about the tunnel mouth. Standing alone, an easy mark for the rifles pointed at him, he coolly asked them to explain their case. He was ready, he said, to listen fairly, and only asked the same of them.

As he hoped, they talked—bitterly, and at length. It meant, Jessie said later, "that they spent their first fierce intentions in the blank cartridges of 'speeches.' "

Toward evening a new crisis threatened. The besieging men intended to starve John's men out of the mine, but the wife of one of the trapped miners, slender young Elizabeth Ketton, who kept a local boardinghouse, insisted on bringing them food. "The little woman took a revolver & a basket of provisions & presented herself at the mouth of the mine," Jessie wrote the Blairs. "They refused her entrance. She said she would go & pushed on & told them if they 'offered to touch her she'd fire' & if she fired our men would have rushed in & fired also. . . . You see the carnage there would have been." Fortunately, the Hornitos men yielded. "After that she went in twice daily," Jessie concluded, "carrying food in her hands & under her clothes pistols & powder & caps."

John's men were outnumbered, and the sheriff was sympathetic to the Hornitos League, so John was forced to send for outside help. But when his messengers tried to leave the isolated valley, they found the league had blocked all roads and trails. At this juncture, Jessie and Lily recounted long afterward, Lily and young Douglass Fox, an English teenager who had accompanied the Frémonts to California, contrived their own solution. At dusk, Douglass stealthily led Lily's surefooted mountain-bred horse through the shadows of a dry creekbed behind the cottage and on up the chaparral-shrouded hillside. Once out of sight, he mounted and rode on to get aid at Coulterville, a friendly mining town twenty miles to the northeast.

That night, huddled in the cottage waiting for John to come home, "I was wild," Jessie remembered. Even after he had returned safely, she hardly slept, as angry men rode by the house, shouting, firing their guns in the air, exploding gunpowder in tin cans. "Lea and Isaac—our trusty colored men, both mountain men & good shots,—a fierce dog named Rowdy, & Mr. Frémont made the home force," Jessie wrote. "With pistols & double barrelled guns we had 32 shots."

The next day, Saturday, as the temperature rose to 115, a threatening note was delivered to the cottage. Jessie and the children had twenty-four hours to leave the region. If they refused, the house would be burned and they must "take the consequences." A reply was demanded by sundown. Jessie postponed her answer, hoping that somehow Douglass would summon aid. But her mood had changed: "a tide of anger had displaced the benumbing fear."

Toward sunset she spotted Douglass riding up the road, wearing a white sash wound around his head turban-style to signify victory. He had reached Coulterville, and its home guard was on the way. Messengers were also riding to Stockton, eighty miles away, to telegraph the governor for help.

"A spirit of mad exultation possessed me," Jessie recalled. She decided to confront the enemy. "With the half mad feeling of an officer who dresses in full uniform to go into battle I told Isaac to put to the best open wagon the carriage horses, with their blue rosettes on their harnesses, and himself dress up—while my French woman gladly went with me."

Jessie was in mourning for her father, but she now exchanged her plain black dress for a French gown of white muslin with lilac ribbons and a violet velvet bonnet trimmed with white lace. Dressed for heroics, she entered the carriage with her French maid, raised her white parasol defiantly, and ordered Isaac to drive to the village saloon, where the dissident miners had their headquarters. When they arrived, she called for Bates, the saloonkeeper, "a timid sort of publican." He emerged from the bar, followed by a crowd of hostile men.

Haughtily, Jessie returned the threatening note. There would be "no answer," she told the men. What they demanded was against the law. "You may come and kill us," she said scornfully, "we are but women and children, and it will be easy—but you cannot kill the Law." Help was coming, she told them. Their game was up.

Then she turned her back. "You can drive home, Isaac," she said. But as the carriage headed away, she felt cold terror. "I fully expected to be shot in the back."[13]

The siege continued for five hot, tense days. But gradually John's policy of patient talk paid off. The Hornitos men began to squabble among themselves: some wanted to attack, others to await word from the governor. The two sides began to exchange notes.

At first, Jessie had been able to do little more than wait at home. She had relieved some of her anxiety by writing her will—forty-four pages long, as she later admitted with some embarrassment to the Blairs. But when communications began, she was able to help. She "did great service . . . by suggestions during the negotiations," an aide reported, "and her fair hand wrote many a weary line, while by the supplies of bodily comforts to the men, and encouraging messages which she sent, they were much inspired and determined to stand by their guns till the last."[14]

On Monday, with the temperature a blistering 118 degrees, the league demanded that John abandon the Pine Tree mine until the courts determined who owned it. John refused. Tuesday passed tensely. On Wednesday, the league caved in, proposing a truce that left John in possession of the mine until Governor John B. Weller reached a decision. Correctly assuming that Weller, the widower of a Benton cousin, would support him, John agreed. The crisis was over.

The siege created support for the Frémonts in the Mariposa community. The violent tactics of the league, and especially their threats against the family, alienated many who agreed with their claims. "Our personal sympathies have always been with the citizens of Mariposa County, and against the present location of Frémont's claim," admitted the San Francisco *Evening Bulletin*, "but justice compels us to say that . . . the Merced Mining Company was in this case the aggressor."[15]

Not long after the crisis, a delegation of Mariposa women rode over to Bear Valley to see Jessie. Though they arrived on horseback, they wore their Sunday best, bonnets freighted with flowers and dresses with large hoop skirts that fit awkwardly over their pommels. The women had come to thank her for staying in Bear Valley during the crisis. "Had you given up and left the cottage," they told her, "our hills would have run blood."

For Jessie, the siege had been a terrifying yet strangely exhilarating experience. She had watched John, uneasy in the murky realm of politics, risk his life and take command. The siege had brought out his best qualities: his courage, his coolness in danger, his ability to arouse the loyalty of his men. To her, he must have seemed the young Frémont again, the hero she loved so recklessly at seventeen. "Slender, upright, elastic and tough as steel," aide John Howard remembered him that summer.[16]

Jessie too had shown her mettle. Writing to the Blairs after it was all over, John confessed that when the crisis began, he regretted that the family was with him. But on the whole, he said, "I think that I have been much more aided than put back by them." Then in a rare burst of feeling he added, "Jessie as usual was my best ally."[17]

The terrible events of the summer bound John and Jessie together. The mining crisis cemented their loyalty, but it was Thomas Benton's death that most altered their relationship. Though Jessie had chosen her husband over her father time and again, it was always with lingering regret. Despite Benton's bitter opposition during the campaign, she had struggled to prevent a final break. Wisely, John had understood and never demanded it of her. But deep down, he must have felt her love was incomplete. Benton's death changed all that. It freed Jessie's emotions and centered them irrevocably on her husband. His rival was dead.

Jessie too had gained. For years she had felt more loving than loved. It was she who yearned for closeness, John who resisted. In the months after her father's death, he began to cherish her more. "He finds time to take more care of me than ever in all the time we have been together," she wrote Francis Blair. At the same time, she became his ally in business as well. Jessie had long distrusted his advisers, men like lawyer Trenor Park and San Francisco banker Joseph Palmer. As events proved her right, John seemed to appreciate her shrewdness. "I am friend and adviser now," she wrote a month after the Pine Tree siege, "outwardly nothing is changed but to Mr. Palmer it is really very different—he finds an invisible obstacle & I am the confidante of his foiled plans."

At the same time, Jessie was growing wise about their differences, accepting them, moderating them. In temperament, she was volatile, both loving and hating more openly. John, in contrast, was cool, controlled, reserved. "I am so gusty by nature," she wrote Lizzie that August, "that . . . it is my steady instinct to avoid making him wince." Yet she believed it was her open warmth that drew him to her, for he needed "to be met two thirds of the way."

John seemed to be changing too. He had habitually escaped into the wilderness. Now, at forty-five, he appeared less restless. In isolated Bear Valley, he found his refuge at home. It was what Jessie longed for. "I have gone about like a stork with my young ones, building new nests summer & winter & rebuilding again & again as fast as they were abandoned or destroyed. All my energy—and I think I must have started with an unusual share for it to hold out yet—has gone to keeping a home & home feelings in our scattered little set." Through it all John had remained apart, resisting the closeness she and the children demanded. But at long last, she wrote Lizzie, "I am getting a great reward."[18]

The Frémonts spent the rest of the summer in San Francisco. Jessie was sick much of the time. Angry men and stolen children haunted her feverish dreams. She attributed her ailments to "morbid fears" brought on by the Pine Tree siege, but she may have had a relapse of malaria as well. "I live on quinine & iced watermelons," she reported in early October.[19]

Though her fever and nightmares gradually faded, John was reluctant to expose her again to the dangers lurking in Bear Valley. But Jessie would not be frightened away. "I refused out-and-out to stay in San Francisco." There was no divided loyalty now—no longing to return east. "I would go where he must be," she said simply. In the late fall of 1858, they returned to Bear Valley.[20]

Despite her genuine warmth and tolerance, there was more than a touch of queenliness in the colonel's lady reigning in her isolated kingdom. Some even suspected that she was the guiding force at Las Mariposas. "Frémont would never transact business without his wife being present, who had a much clearer head than he," an acquaintance claimed.[21] Despite her distaste for business, Jessie was thoroughly familiar with the mines. She continued to pen much of John's correspondence, and she inevitably discussed the business with him frequently. Still, it was John who rose at dawn to supervise the daily operations, and it was he, with his engineering skills and penchant for machinery, who planned new mills, a dam, even a small railroad—improvements he believed would finally make their little kingdom pay handsomely.

But legal fees still drained Las Mariposas profits, while John continued to borrow heavily to finance his improvements. By early 1859, Las Mariposas itself was in jeopardy. In March, John could not pay the interest on bonds held by eastern investors; in May, he was forced to lay off workers. That month Jessie gave up a camping trip to Yosemite to aid John in the emergency.

Two associates, Trenor Park and Joseph Palmer, were suing for a share in Las Mariposas. That May, in Jessie's hand,

John hinted darkly of "the enemy's machinations. . . . We have been attacked by the Park-Palmer faction & are now passing through a pretty heavy storm, which I think we shall weather." By then Las Mariposas was worth ten million dollars. "The contest," John said, has become "rather one for a principality than a private property." Though Jessie vowed that he would "sink the whole property before yielding," John was eventually forced to sign over a portion of Las Mariposas to Park. Bit by bit, its fabulous gold was slipping through his fingers.[22]

The Frémonts had no cash that year for a summer escape to cool San Francisco. By June it was so hot that they made leather shoes for the dogs to keep their paws from blistering and discovered that eggs buried in the dust would cook in eighteen minutes. "When it grew to be 104° and 107° at sunset in the most shaded & enclosed room of our Bear Valley cottage we grew desperate," Jessie wrote Francis Blair, "& out of the heat came a lightning flash of inspiration." The previous year, riding on nearby Mt. Bullion, they had spotted an oak-shaded spring just over its crest. Now, in the stifling heat, they suddenly remembered the spot. "Before sunrise next morning Lil & I were climbing the mountain—the stones rolling at every touch of our horses' hoofs—armed with a thermometer & a luncheon basket." When they reached the spring, they discovered the water was a cool fifty-five degrees and the breeze so sweet that "we went home like conquerors."

Within two days the whole family was installed at "Camp Jessie" in a huge tent open on three sides and furnished with mattresses filled with oak leaves and fragrant heather, laid "Oriental fashion" on the planked floor. "Sleeping is something fine," Jessie pronounced with satisfaction. The views were awesome. "We face an amphitheater of mountains. . . . The cliffs & chasms of Yosemite Valley are perfectly distinct." Their summer idyll ended abruptly in early August, however, when friendly Indians warned them that warriors from a neighboring tribe would be passing through and could cause trouble. They abandoned the camp the next morning.[23]

Jessie had scarcely settled back into cottage life when an old political ally, New York *Tribune* editor Horace Greeley, arrived for a visit. This was his first far-western journey, and while the gawky, earnest reformer was entranced with California's climate and fertility, he was appalled by its easy morals. Greeley had popularized the phrase "Go West, young man," but now in dispatches to the *Tribune* he informed his readers that what the state urgently needed were "virtuous, educated, energetic women." One hundred thousand, he claimed, would be useful.[24]

His visit to the Frémonts was in part political, and during country meals at the "little White House," he sounded them both out on another presidential contest. But John, determined to make Las Mariposas pay, was not tempted to reenter the political arena, and Jessie seems to have concurred. She had always been skeptical of Las Mariposas, she wrote their old political associate Nathanial Banks that month, "not to its capabilities but as to our profiting from them. Now I believe."[25]

During the fall and winter of 1859, Jessie and John remained optimistic about the mines. Another Frémont crushing mill was in operation, and they had won a final lawsuit against the Merced Company. The work evoked John's "old best qualities," Jessie wrote Lizzie. "They were rusting a little & his friends had not been good for him, but these keen winds of adversity have swept away all that were not hearts of oak." Most important, she and John had grown even closer. She was deeply moved when he told her that without her care and sharing of the anxieties that year, "he could never have endured it."[26]

Despite such rewards, Jessie longed for a more congenial life. Though she made the best of conditions and never complained, she was like an exile in Bear Valley, Lily remembered, for at heart "she was not interested in mines, horses, or chickens." By early 1860 their finances had improved so radically that John was able to pay forty-one thousand dollars in gold for a house and thirteen acres by the sea in San Francisco, which he put in Jessie's name.[27]

She was delighted. Her two years at Las Mariposas had been wearing. Her hair had turned "a queer tawny color," neither gray nor brown, and she feared she was losing her looks. "These years have had some points harder to bear than any we have known," she confided to Lizzie. Yet they evoked her best qualities—her pluck, her loyalty, her energy. Writer Richard Henry Dana, who visited the Frémonts at Bear Valley, pronounced her "a heroine equal to either fortune, the salons of Paris and the drawing-rooms of New York and Washington, or the roughest life of the remote and wild . . . Mariposa." Jessie herself put it more simply. She had learned, she said, "what one can do and what one can do without."[28]

In one respect she felt her Bear Valley sojourn had been "better than all the days of my life," for it had bound the family together. "When I knew I should never see Father again," she wrote Lizzie in the spring of 1860 just after settling in San Francisco, "I turned my whole heart into this house and sometimes I think I magnetized Mr. Frémont into home life. He takes part in & likes all the details of our household—the children's plays & witticisms & lessons—he looks after our comforts, & is in fact head of the house. No 'wild turkey' left. It's so easy to take care of children when two help. I feel now as if we were a complete & compact family. . . . Now we share & share and he is far the happier for it. As for me, you need no telling how satisfied my craving heart is."[29]

21

A few of my dear relatives or old friends about me would be very pleasant, especially during the long absences of my husband. But go friends or relatives, one & all, for the sake of this same dear husband—if I cannot have both. I left you all for him, & I would do the same thing again.

Persis Sibley Andrews
Journal
1845

SAN FRANCISCO IDYLL

I LOVE THE LIGHT and the sound and the smell of . . . water, and here on this point of land we have it on three sides," Jessie wrote rapturously to Lizzie from San Francisco in June 1860. "Mr. Frémont has found me here a 'house by the sea' that is more beautiful than any Sea Dream that Tennyson or any poet ever fancied." Perched on the tip of Black Point, a finger of land jutting into the bay where Fort Mason now stands, its views were magnificent, "a combination of every beauty in nature." A few miles to the west loomed the hills and cliffs of the Golden Gate; directly ahead was tiny Alcatraz Island, and beyond, across the sweep of water, the hills of Marin and Contra Costa. To the east, past shifting sand dunes, lay the flourishing city of San Francisco. "The flapping of the sails as the schooners round this point & the noise of their paddles as the steamers pass are household sounds," Jessie wrote. "It is like being on the bow of a ship."

For Jessie, California had become home, and Black Point her refuge. "If you don't come to see me I don't know when I shall see you," she wrote Lizzie that June.[1] She hoped that Las Mariposas would soon be in good enough shape to allow John to remain in San Francisco, where together they would write his much postponed memoirs. Commuting to Bear Valley, he was supervising the construction of his latest enthusiasm, a four-mile railroad that would carry quartz ore from the Pine Tree and Josephine mines down the steep mountainside to his new crushing mill on the Merced River.

A new president would be elected that fall, but to both Frémonts, in what John called their "underground condition," politics seemed remote, part of a world they had left behind.[2] John himself, obsessed with Las Mariposas, had done nothing to promote his candidacy. In part he may have been reacting to the lack of interest among party leaders. With a real prospect of victory in 1860, men like William Seward and Abraham Lincoln were themselves eager to run. Moreover, John's rumored dalliances had damaged his image among Republican insiders. Even the Blairs, who had heard—and perhaps begun to believe—the stories, were supporting another candidate. For Jessie, it was just as well. Though she disliked and distrusted the business of gold, the rigors of the 1856 campaign had made her equally leery of politics. What she sought in San Francisco, at Black Point, was an escape from both.

The Frémonts' new home was the most seaward of a cluster of five frame houses on the Point, and Jessie, fresh from the isolation of Bear Valley, found the little colony congenial. She hired a tutor to instruct Lily and the boys four hours a day, though she continued to do much of the teaching herself. Nine-year-old Charley was highly intelligent, she reported to Lizzie, although he was "like his Mother in fitfulness," while Frank, at five, was learning how to read. Jessie was more concerned about Lily, a stolid, plain-faced young woman with a slight stammer like her father and none of her mother's exuberant charm. Jessie was refurbishing Lily's wardrobe "for all the trotting out that 18 year olds have to do," though John made "great fun of her very long dresses & other insignia of young ladyism."[3] As for Lily, she seemed more interested in Chiquita, the little Spanish mare her father had given her for Christmas, than the social whirl Jessie hoped she would join.

For the moment such maternal concerns seemed minor as Jessie busied herself furnishing her new house from the riches of San Francisco, which she found "like Paris for beautiful things & at most reasonable prices."[4] Released from two years of Bear Valley austerity, she spent lavishly to refurbish the house and to add stables, walks, drives, and plantings of roses and fuchsias on their nearly thirteen acres of grounds.

To Jessie it was Black Point's combination of rural and urban pleasures that gave it such appeal. "We have cows, horses & dogs—in fact thorough country comfort with a city at our door & San Francisco is a true city in its resources," she wrote enthusiastically to Lizzie. With a population approaching eighty thousand, it was far more solid than the tent city she had known in 1849, or the disorderly, fire-ravaged town of 1851. There were schools and churches, ice cream parlors and opera. Families climbed the goat paths of Telegraph Hill to pick wild flowers on Sunday afternoons, took the ferry to picnic in rural Oakland, or paid twenty-five cents to see the seven-foot, four-inch "Arabian Giant" on display at Tucker's Music Hall.

"There is a very good opera here & lots of private parties," Jessie continued her paean, as if to convince a skeptical Lizzie. That June she could see *The Marriage of Figaro* or Verdi's *Ernani* from her ten-dollar box at Maguire's Opera House or Sheridan's *School for Scandal* at the Lyceum, where, the *Alta* admitted, the unsavory crowd of men who gathered outside to stare at the ladies as they left the theater was still a problem. Mrs. A. W. Ward was lecturing on the fashionable water cure; the controversial feminist, Eliza W. Farnham, was scheduled to speak on "Woman, her position and future rank in the community"; and the slight, boyish-looking Reverend Thomas Starr King, fresh from Boston, was drawing huge crowds each Sunday at the Unitarian church.

"Starr King, the new Unitarian clergyman, has been our event," Jessie informed Lizzie in mid-June.[5] Momentarily taken aback by this slight, homely man with lank hair and burning eyes, she had been overwhelmed by his eloquence and vigor as a speaker. Meeting him personally, she was delighted by his wit, his irreverent humor, and his buoyant good cheer. Though she was formally an Episcopalian, she purchased a pew in the Unitarian church.

Starr King liked to call himself a graduate of the Charlestown Navy Yard. Only fifteen when his father, a minister, died, he abandoned plans to attend Harvard and went to work as a schoolteacher and naval clerk to support his mother and five younger brothers and sisters. Off hours, he read avidly and mastered six languages. At twenty-one he assumed his father's old pulpit; two years later he became the popular minister of Boston's Hollis Street Unitarian Church. Despite his success, King sensed that as a self-educated man he would never be completely accepted in Boston. Proud, restless, and idealistic, he longed for challenge. In 1860, when he was thirty-five, he accepted the call to California.

From the first, King's thoroughly Bostonian wife, Julia, despised San Francisco. "The parish are pouring in upon us to congratulate me," King reported after his first sermon, "& to hear Julia pitch into the climate, the steamers, the city, & the whole Pacific shore generally." While the city's ubiquitous fleas never touched King, "she feels about a thousand a day."[6] In the fall the unhappy Julia injured her leg when she tripped over a loose board in one of the city's planked sidewalks, leaving her lame and housebound for most of the winter.

During these months, Jessie's friendship with King flourished. With John frequently at Bear Valley and Julia King marooned glumly at home, both welcomed the companionship. Writing a boyhood friend, King was frank in his enthusiasm. "I rode to Mrs. Frémont's, two miles off, & sat in her lovely cottage, hearing her talk & enjoying it hugely," he reported in September. "Yesterday I dined with Mrs. Frémont," he announced in January, "& walked bareheaded among roses, geraniums, vines & fuschias in profuse bloom." "Mrs. Frémont has staid [sic] to tea," he wrote in March. "We have had a glorious talk & time."[7]

But if there was potential for more than friendship, they resolutely ignored it. Both seemed unconscious of the implications of their joyous rapport. They continued to call each other "Mrs. Frémont" and "Mr. King," and Jessie always included Mrs. King and their daughter Edith in her greetings. To her, King was a loving friend, to whom she could not only speak her mind and heart but unleash her wit and intelligence.

It was a luxury she had seldom known. Yet Jessie never hid her devotion to her husband. When John received a medal from the Prussian government, she rushed over to show it to King. In contrast, King seldom mentioned John, whom he clearly thought unequal to Jessie. Referring to a suggestion that Frémont be appointed ambassador to France, he commented dryly: "*She* would have made a most brilliant and serviceable minister, & *he* can at least talk French."[8]

By the fall of 1860, Starr King was a fixture at Black Point gatherings. With its vistas and gardens, and Jessie's welcoming presence, it had become a kind of country salon—a meeting place for writers, artists, and politicians who came to stroll about the grounds and spend long, congenial hours at Jessie's hospitable table. Another regular guest, who rode out to the Point on horseback, was urbane, pipe-smoking Joseph Lawrence, a former newspaper man who was co-editor of San Francisco's literary journal, the *Golden Era*. It was through Lawrence that Jessie first met the young writer Bret Harte.

A shrewd judge of literary talent, Jessie had admired Harte's poems and sketches in the *Golden Era*, where the twenty-four-year-old author worked as a typesetter. Though Harte's efforts could be pretentious and overburdened with literary allusions, Jessie nonetheless recognized that this unknown young man was the most promising writer on the West Coast. When she asked to meet him, however, Harte at first demurred. Bright, intense, something of a dandy in his dress and manner, with curly black hair and a drooping mustache, he was proud, sensitive, "almost unhappy from want of success." He had arrived in California six years before, drifted about the gold region, then migrated to Humboldt County. In the spring of 1860 he moved to San Francisco, where he lived in a cheap room above a cousin's restaurant and wrote at night. "I had to insist this very shy young man should come to see me," Jessie remembered, "but soon he settled into a regular visit on Sunday . . . and for more than a year dined with us that day." Soon he was bringing his manuscripts to read aloud.[9]

The Black Point coterie pronounced Harte brilliantly clever, and within their lively and supportive circle, he thrived. The sketches, essays, and short stories he wrote for the *Golden Era*—at a dollar a column—grew steadily more vivid and accomplished, and he began to experiment with the California material that would become his true subject.

The first fragile blooms of a distinct California culture were emerging from the fertile soil of Black Point. Fluent in Spanish, Jessie was unusually sensitive to California's Hispanic heritage, and it was doubtless with her encouragement that Harte began to use Hispanic-California legends and stories in his work. But even more significantly, it was while he was reading his manuscripts regularly at Black Point that he wrote "The Work on Red Mountain," later expanded to become the celebrated "M' liss," the first of the mining camp stories that would make him famous.

Another Black Point visitor was a lively young commercial photographer, Carleton Watkins, who would later become one of the West's most distinguished landscape photographers. Even then, influenced in part by King's Emersonian view of nature, he was developing a distinct sense of the California landscape, a vision that began to emerge that year when the Frémonts hired him to produce a series of Las Mariposas scenes, his first important group of outdoor photographs. [10]

As for Jessie herself, frustrated in her hope of collaborating with John on his memoirs and still burdened by the dictum that women should inspire rather than create, she accepted her role as catalyst and muse, prodding and encouraging men like Harte and King to write and speak as she could not. Years later, when she did begin to write on her own, it was her California work that was most vivid, infused with a directness and vigor that her routine writing for parlor consumption often lacked.

Jessie was always an alert hostess, and when literary celebrities arrived in town, she lured them to Black Point. "I have just returned from Mrs. Frémont's where I have made a visit with Herman Melville, who is visiting San Francisco," King reported in October. The celebrated author of popular travel romances, Melville had recently produced two commercial failures, *Moby Dick* and *Pierre*. "The dollar has damned me," he said. "All my books are botches." Despairing, he left the East to recover his spirits and health on a sea voyage. By the time he reached San Francisco, however, he had resolved to return directly home, where he would spend the rest of his life in obscurity, working in the New York Customs House. But that day at Black Point he seems to have been cheerful enough. "We had a fine time with Mrs. F.," King wrote. "The Col. was at home. It is the 19th anniversary of her wedding—where all Washington was horrorstruck, as she said, because she had made 'such a foolish match.' Now that Frémont's mills turn out $16,000 a week in solid gold, I suppose Washington would pass a different judgment. She *is* a superb woman."[11]

While Jessie cultivated her Black Point salon, John was only a part-time participant. Far more than Jessie anticipated when she wrote Lizzie of his new domesticity, he continued to travel. In August, Lily represented the Frémont family at Bear Valley when his expensive and innovative new railroad was inaugurated. "Who . . . but a Frémont would have the nerve to expend the vast sums of money necessary to erect such a works in such a locality!" exclaimed an orator at the ceremonies. Meanwhile, John, in Los Angeles on business, was given a fifteen-gun salute and welcomed by Republican dignitaries. But he told the assembled notables that he would not "mingle actively" in the presidential campaign that year.[12] Reserved, perhaps embarrassed by his occasional stammer, he continued to shun public life.

Nonetheless, what Jessie called "the disturbing element" of politics had always been a lively part of the conversation at Black Point.[13] That fall, as the 1860 presidential election approached, the campaign talk grew obsessive. Republican prospects were far better than in 1856. Though the party nominee, Abraham Lincoln, was a compromise candidate, the Democrats were now hopelessly split into northern and southern factions. At a dinner Jessie gave in October, the Black Point circle had a chance to learn more about Mr. Lincoln from his former law partner, handsome, flamboyant Senator Edward Baker of Oregon, who had arrived in town to campaign for his old friend.

Three days earlier, Jessie and Starr King had sat in a private box in the packed American Theater to hear Baker address an enthusiastic Republican rally. During a pause in his impassioned speech, a young man, whom the newspapers would identify as "Mr. Harte," rushed to the footlights and led the audience in a rousing cheer.[14] San Franciscans later said the young man was Bret Harte and that Jessie Frémont had put him up to it, although she herself was silent on the subject.

While Jessie was impressed by Baker's powerful speech, Starr King was overwhelmed. "That is the true way to reach men," he exclaimed, pacing the box nervously. "How I envy him." Accustomed to writing out his words carefully beforehand, King did not believe he could move audiences by his spontaneous passion and wit. Jessie disagreed. That night she set out to convince him of his power. King listened, encouraged, flattered, bemused at her expanding ambition for him. "Mrs. F. is distressed that I have not lived longer in the state, so that she could have me elected *Senator* this winter," he reported afterward to an old friend.[15]

In mid-November, the Pony Express brought word that Abraham Lincoln had been elected president. In the South, the Republican victory provoked passionate defiance. "The revolution of 1860 has been initiated," declared the Charleston *Mercury*.[16] Despite her Republican sympathies, Jessie too must have found it hard to cheer the election of this awkward Springfield lawyer with his crude backwoods humor, knowing that if the Democrats had split four years earlier, her own husband would have been president.

At this crucial moment, John set out on a journey to the East Coast and Europe. Perhaps it was his old restlessness that propelled the journey, though its ostensible purpose was to raise additional capital for Las Mariposas, now more than a million dollars in debt. He sailed on January 1, 1861, accompanied by his urbane and expensive lawyer, Frederick Billings, and carrying with him the splendid set of Las Mariposas photographs made by Carleton Watkins to show potential investors. Jessie remained in San Francisco, awaiting the future.

The day John left, San Francisco papers reported that South Carolina had withdrawn from the Union. One by one, six other southern states followed. "The fear of what may be in store for us all if this cloud of civil war takes shape, makes me restless," Jessie wrote King as the news grew more alarming.[17] The upper South and border states teetered between union and secession. In Missouri, Francis Blair's son Frank struggled to hold it for the North.

In California, where there was a powerful southern faction, the governor talked loftily of a Pacific republic independent of both North and South, while rumors flew that secessionists were maneuvering to bring the state into the Confederacy. With California threatened, Starr King began to speak out. On February 22, Washington's birthday, he initiated his fiery campaign to keep California in the Union with an impassioned speech that thrilled the enthusiastic crowd jamming Tucker's Music Hall to hear him. Jessie pronounced it so good, King reported, that "she would like to hear it forty nights in succession."[18]

At the same time, Jessie became involved in her own small crusade. While she was still at Bear Valley, the family's long-time black servant, Albert Lea, had inexplicably murdered his estranged wife in San Francisco. That fall he was sentenced to death by hanging. Convinced that he was temporarily insane, the Frémonts managed to get a retrial, but Lea was again convicted. Their appeal to the governor to commute the sentence to life imprisonment was also refused. Then, in late February 1861, just before the scheduled hanging, the *Alta* published an account of the case that so outraged Jessie by its unfairness to Lea that she took what was an unusual step for a woman. Signing herself "J. B. F.," she wrote a spirited reply.[19]

Several days later the *Alta* published a rebuttal from the mother of Lea's murdered wife. To much of the public it was a morbid scandal, made more so by the involvement of two women brazen enough to make their views public. "You probably saw the controversy between Mrs. Frémont & Mr. Lea's wife's mother in the papers," a San Francisco man wrote Trenor Park. "It may lead to something serious,—as they are both fighting cusses."

On March 1, 1861, Lea was hanged in the jail yard. Jessie had visited him a few days beforehand and found him composed and ready for death. "It is not in mere words to give you the impression he made on me," she wrote Lizzie sorrowfully. "No knightly cavalier going to the block for his king & his cause ever had a more truly noble aspect."

Jessie believed that the governor had refused to reduce Lea's sentence because Lea was black. In the growing passions of civil war, others agreed. To show their sympathy for Lea, more than a thousand citizens attended his funeral. After his burial, Jessie placed a cross at the head of his grave.

A day later in Washington, D.C., Abraham Lincoln, heavily guarded by troops, was inaugurated president of a nation on the brink of civil war. Jessie knew she would soon be leaving San Francisco. John had written that he had talked with Lincoln in New York and expected to be given a command if war began. Five weeks later, on April 12, 1861, Confederate batteries fired on federally held Fort Sumter in Charleston Bay. The next day the beleaguered garrison surrendered. On April 15, President Lincoln called for seventy-five thousand volunteers to put down the insurrection.

Preparing to leave, Jessie arranged for Bret Harte's future. Knowing that he needed a secure income, she persuaded her old friend Edward Beale, the newly appointed surveyor-general of California, to give Harte a job in his office, where the leisurely pace would give him time to write. "If I were shipwrecked on a desert island," Harte wrote her gratefully, "I should expect to see a savage coming forward with a three-cornered note from you to say, I had been appointed Governor at a salary of twenty-four hundred dollars."[20]

In late April on steep Russian Hill, Jessie was thrown from a carriage when the horses bolted. "My head received the force of the fall," she reported, "& it has brought on constant spasms . . . in the back of the neck . . . often the whole spine thrills like a harp cord."[21] Bedridden for several weeks, she found only "chloroform rubbing" and warm baths relieved the pain. During her fretful convalescence, Starr King brought her books and what cheer he could. Her injury increased her restlessness. Her year at Black Point had been a kind of idyll, a respite in the rocky course of her life. Now she was eager to act.

In May, John wrote that he was returning at once from Europe and asked her to meet him in New York. He would soon be named a major general, commanding the Department of the West, encompassing Illinois and the region from the Mississippi to the Rockies, with headquarters in St. Louis. "We go to join Mr. Frémont & I will be with him everywhere—I will," Jessie wrote emphatically to an acquaintance. "I have not been so happy in years for him as now," she told their Mariposas accountant. "An army of cares has been boring into our lives these few years past, and I thank heaven for this noble chance in a great cause. . . . I am so glad I am going into an atmosphere where dollars and cents are not the first object."[22]

Jessie, Lily, and the boys left San Francisco on June 21. Seeing them off, Starr King gave Jessie a bouquet of violets and a volume of Emerson to read on the voyage east. But King understood her well enough to know she could not sit idle. "Have you met Mrs. Frémont?" he wrote an eastern friend later. "I hope so. Her husband I am very little acquainted with, but she is sublime, and carries guns enough to be formidable to a whole Cabinet—a she-Merrimack, thoroughly sheathed, and carrying fire in the genuine Benton furnaces."[23]

22

This conflict is one thing I've been waiting for. I'm well and strong and young—young enough to go to the front. If I can't be a soldier, I'll help soldiers.

Clara Barton
1861

I've often longed to see a war, and now I have my wish. I long to be a man.

Louisa May Alcott
1861

"GENERAL JESSIE"

S T. LOUIS IN THE SUMMER of 1861 was a tense, bitterly divided city, torn by the passions of civil war. When the Frémont family reached there on July 25, they found it ominously quiet. "Everything was changed," Jessie remembered. "There was no life on the river; the many steamboats were laid up at their wharves, their fires out, the singing, cheery crews gone." There were no flags, no bands, no cheering crowds to greet the new Union general and his celebrated wife. "As we drove through the deserted streets we saw only closed shutters to warehouses and business places; the wheels and the horses' hoofs echoed loud and harsh as when one drives through the silent streets late at night."

Though Missouri was a slave state, men like Congressman Frank Blair of St. Louis, the vigorous, outspoken youngest son of Francis Blair, had thus far managed to keep it in the Union. But the situation was precarious. Confederate troops had invaded southern Missouri and were threatening nearby Cairo, Illinois, strategically located at the junction of the Ohio and Mississippi rivers. Though Unionists probably outnumbered Confederates in the state, especially among the numerous German settlers, the governor, senators, and a majority of the state legislature supported the secessionist cause. In St. Louis, tenuously held by a small Union force, rebel soldiers were openly recruited at a St. Louis mansion that boldly flew the Confederate flag. To Jessie, viewing the shuttered houses and sullen people, "it was a hostile city and showed itself as such."[1]

John and Jessie were determined to hold Missouri for the North, and their mood was defiant. Writing to Thomas Starr King just before she left New York, Jessie had joked that John would prefer to make his headquarters in Charleston, his boyhood home in the heart of the Confederacy. "We shall not be able to indulge ourselves in burning Richmond," she added. "St. Louis is getting hot enough to be tempting."

Jessie and the children had reached New York on July 13 after an anxious voyage from Panama, chased by Confederate privateers. They found John harassed and preoccupied, busy recruiting his staff, buying arms and equipment, and maneuvering to wring more money and troops from the government. The next day Jessie plunged into work as "secretary and otherself," as she expansively defined her duties.

In the press of work, there was little time for intimacy. She and John had "really had no chance to have a talk," she wrote King from New York. Still, more than ever, she was committed to her husband. "I haunt around taking my chances of a word—sometimes it is only a look—but . . . it is enough."

The Blairs were urging her to settle in Washington while John went to St. Louis, but Jessie, impatient with her woman's role, was determined to play an active part in the war. The children and her sedate English maid were amazed at her "pace and contempt of bonnet boxes & extra wraps & such like," she reported exuberantly to King as the whole family set off by train for Missouri.[2]

When the Frémonts reached hostile St. Louis, they faced two immediate crises. The commander of the Union garrison downriver at Cairo was begging for reinforcements to meet an expected attack, while at Springfield, a market town in southwestern Missouri, short, wiry, red-headed General Nathaniel Lyon, dangerously outnumbered by rebel forces, was also pleading for aid. For weeks before the Frémonts reached St. Louis, Lyon had been urging Washington to send supplies and reinforcements. "Our troops are badly clothed, poorly fed, and imperfectly supplied with tents," he wrote. "None of them have as yet been paid." When he received no help from the Lincoln administration, the despairing general did not know whether to call it "imbecility or malice."[3]

Jessie was soon echoing Lyon's frustration. We have "an arsenal without arms or ammunition—troops on paper and a thoroughly prepared and united enemy. Thick and unremitting as mosquitoes," she wrote Lizzie two days after they reached St. Louis. They were desperate for troops to aid at Cairo and Springfield as well as to hold St. Louis, but the government was diverting regiments east to buttress beleaguered Washington, threatened by the South after the recent Union disaster at Bull Run. "The President is a Western man and not grown in red tape," Jessie told Lizzie. "If he knew the true defenceless condition of the West it would not remain so. I have begged Mr. Frémont to let me go on & tell him how things are here. But he says I'm tired with the sea voyage— that I shan't expose my health, and . . . that he can't do without me."[4]

"Mr. Frémont says send any thing in the shape of arms— but arms we must have," she pleaded with Lizzie's brother, Montgomery Blair, who as Lincoln's postmaster general was their conduit to the president. "I don't like this neglect," she added, "& I look to you & to the President to see that it has not a fatal effect. Just now the Potomac is so interesting that I do not blame every care for it but don't expect miracles on the M[i]ssi[ssippi]. . . . It is odd to feel in an enemy's country here in St. Louis but it is unmistakeably so."[5]

John was so eager for money to buy weapons and pay what troops he had that he notified Lincoln that he planned to seize the federal subtreasury in St. Louis, though its funds had not been allocated to him. "I am determined not to risk my character here for want of means within my reach," he informed Montgomery Blair grimly, "and what is needed I will take." Jessie fully backed her husband. "This is a day for men, not rules, to govern affairs."[6] The Frémonts' view was in part justified by the emergency they faced, a crisis the federal government had not fully grasped. But inevitably their impatience with rules and regulations, their disregard for governmental authority, would bring them into conflict not only with the federal bureaucracy but with the president himself.

While Jessie described their problems to Montgomery Blair, John, accompanied by nearly four thousand troops on a hastily assembled flotilla of eight steamboats, embarked for Cairo to relieve the beleaguered Union garrison. Though General Lyon near Springfield was also in desperate straits, John was convinced that he lacked the men, guns, and transportation to reinforce them both. Since Cairo was of greater strategic value, Lyon was left to fight or retreat as he saw fit.

John's Cairo mission proved effective, for the Confederate forces hastily retreated without fighting. When Jessie joined him, she got her first heady taste of Union enthusiasm as the soldiers, many already suffering from fever and dysentery in the summer heat, cheered for the new general. "The sound of the shouts with which we were welcomed at Cairo stays in my memory," she wrote Montgomery Blair when she returned to St. Louis. "Only a weak & threatened garrison seeing aid coming could make such sounds. . . . Undisciplined & untrained they are, but the volunteers are knights and crusaders of the best kind."[7]

Meanwhile at Wilson's Creek near Springfield, where General Lyon had rashly decided to fight rather than retreat, he seemed a crusader indeed as he led his five thousand men against a force twice their number. Riding ahead of his troops and swinging his hat, the fiery general plunged repeatedly into the fray until at last a bullet pierced his chest, killing him instantly.

Their leader dead, the Union troops retreated, and southern Missouri fell under Confederate control. The North was stunned. Just three weeks after Bull Run, it was the Union army's second major disaster. Many blamed Frémont for the defeat, claiming that he should have divided what troops he had and sent some to reinforce Lyon. But Frank Blair, returning to Missouri just after Lyon's death, defended Frémont. "Genl. Lyon died of red tape," he asserted grimly.[8]

The Frémonts established their St. Louis headquarters at

the opulent Brant mansion on Chouteau Avenue. Owned by Jessie's cousin, the widow Sarah Benton Brant, it was a splendid three-story villa surrounded by a walled garden. To Jessie, perhaps correctly, it seemed a practical arrangement that allowed the staff to live and work in the same building, but others grumbled that the six-thousand-dollar yearly rent was not only excessive but doubly suspect because it profited a relative.

The Brant basement served as a small armory where munitions were stored. Its first floor contained printing, telegraph, and staff offices. Upstairs, insulated from the hundreds of daily callers by guards and orderlies, John, Jessie, and the more intimate staff lived and worked. As usual Jessie was her husband's chief confidante and ally, attending to his secret correspondence, participating in staff discussions, seeing visitors for him. Though the situation was tense and the work exhausting, Jessie was never so fully alive as when she could channel her native vigor and drive into action. It was, she said afterward, "the most wearing and most welcome work of my life."[9]

Though the war was expanding women's opportunities, Jessie's position was unique. She worked intimately with her husband, sharing problems, offering solutions. Few other women had stepped so conspicuously outside their proper boundaries, and she was dangerously vulnerable. Rumors circulated about her role. According to one story, whenever John talked with a visitor, Jessie stood behind a large pier glass mirror in his office, where she could hear every word. Scandalized by her prominence, some began to call her "General Jessie."

While Jessie relished her active role and the power she wielded, she was aware of the dangers she faced. Stout now, well sheathed in stiff black mourning, she cultivated an outward womanliness almost southern in its appeal, though beneath she retained a vibrancy and directness that cut through any excessive cant. "She had a man's power, a man's education, and she did a man's work in the world," recalled writer

Rebecca Harding Davis, who knew her during the Civil War years, "but her wonderful charm was purely feminine."[10]

The Civil War allowed some women to serve as professional nurses and far more to work as volunteers. In St. Louis, Jessie comfortably became the liaison between her husband and the Western Sanitary Commission, a Red Cross precursor formed in the late summer by prominent civic leaders like the energetic Unitarian minister William G. Eliot, a friend of Starr King (and grandfather of the poet T. S. Eliot).

When the Wilson's Creek disaster brought hundreds of wounded men to St. Louis for care, Jessie was active in organizing makeshift hospitals and instrumental in bringing Dorothea Dix to St. Louis in September to inspect the new facilities. A tall, earnest, classically beautiful woman, Dix wore her hair swept back in two sleek wings and dressed somberly in black or gray, with a touch of white at her throat. Jessie had known her in Washington during the 1850s when Dix was lobbying to establish public institutions for the care of the insane, poor, and handicapped. Dix was now organizing an army nursing corps for the War Department. Deeply serious about her work, conscious of the boundaries she was crossing in bringing women into hospitals to care for men, she insisted that her nurses be over thirty and plain. "Their dresses must be brown or black," she announced, "with no bows, nor curls, no jewelry, and no hoop-skirts."[11] Determined to make nursing professional, she turned away as frivolous the wives and mothers who flocked to volunteer. While Jessie believed Dix's regulations were too restrictive, she felt a deep admiration and sympathy for this woman, who like herself was a controversial figure, already resented by male army personnel too ready to find her autocratic and domineering.

Through the torrid August heat, John and Jessie labored to turn the tide against the rebels in Missouri. "I am working here right up to my full capacity," John informed Montgomery Blair on August 12, "and although it is rough, the ship rides tolerably easy." Fortifications around the city were started, innovative iron-sheathed gunboats ordered, a new train depot

for troop transport erected, and brick army barracks begun.
The show of activity calmed St. Louis. Within three weeks
"everything was changed," reported the Reverend Mr. Eliot.
"The Union flag went up and the Confederate flag came down."
Attracted by Frémont's name, men rushed to volunteer, though
arms were still so scarce that many were forced to drill with
sticks instead of guns. "His name is a tower of strength to his
friends and a terror to his foes," exclaimed the *New York
Times* correspondent in St. Louis that month. Lizzie Lee was
equally confident. "Frémont has stirred up things in St. Louis
& given new life there," she reported to her husband. "If he
& Frank can't take care of Missouri I am mistaken in the
men."[12]

Despite such enthusiasm, the Frémonts faced a rising tide
of criticism. While Abraham Lincoln in the White House
shook hands with any citizen who came to call and ambled
unescorted through the streets of Washington, Missourians
grumbled that John was aloof and inaccessible, his headquarters guarded by a retinue of arrogant bodyguards in gaudy
uniforms and his staff composed of "foreigners"—California
cronies or Europeans with fancy titles who spoke heavily ac-
cented English or none at all. His office seemed disorganized
and inefficient, and a faint odor of corruption clung to his
California associates, who distributed lucrative contracts to
themselves and their friends without competitive bidding.
"Horse-dealers are making fortunes," a *Times* correspondent
observed cynically. "Some of his most intimate friends were
undoubtedly cheating and circumventing him," a disillusioned
aide later claimed. Though Frémont himself seemed personally honest, "he was no judge of men at all."[13]

The chaotic situation in Missouri required the talents of
an adroit politician, a skilled administrator, and an able soldier. But John was uneasy with the rough give-and-take of
politics, careless and impatient with the details of administration, and psychologically incapable of operating comfortably within a military chain of command. Jessie did have political savvy and a shrewd grasp of issues, and unlike John,

she was, aides agreed, "most practical." But forced to channel her ambition through a man, her loyalty was above all to her husband, and it warped her judgment dangerously. Still dazzled by the possibilities of his image, she worked tirelessly to promote him, insisting that he be treated as the hero she wanted him to be.

Though Jessie promoted her husband as a bold visionary, albeit misunderstood and abused, she privately saw him as a deeply vulnerable man in need of protection. In the 1856 campaign she had tried to shield him from attack. Now in St. Louis, she encouraged a tight circle of admirers who bolstered his wavering sense of self. More and more she judged men not on their abilities but on their loyalty to her husband.

John had always been an outsider, who chafed at all authority but his own. The pattern continued in St. Louis. Distrustful of West Point–trained officers since the court-martial, he staffed his headquarters with Hungarian and Italian exiles from the European revolutions of 1848–49, as well as old California friends like Black Point neighbor Leonidas Haskell, whom one young aide branded "a bird of ill omen . . . disliked by us all."[14] Together such men kept John isolated from the city and region he governed. Of his staff, Jessie alone probably knew or cared much about local politics. John lavished attention on the establishment of an elite cavalry unit of three hundred men, who served as his personal bodyguard. Commanded by the dashing Hungarian soldier Charles Zagonyi, they wore trim dark blue uniforms and white-plumed hats, carried fine German sabers and revolvers, and rode matched dark chestnut horses. Sweeping through the city with the lithe major general riding in their midst on his handsome gray horse, or protecting him from intrusion at the splendid Brant mansion, they seemed to many Missourians like the personal guard of a European prince.

A perceptive French army officer who visited the Frémonts in early September found their elaborate court startlingly different from the casual, democratic headquarters of the other generals he met that summer. John looked thin, dark, and tired, he thought, but his fiery glance illuminated his face. "I left with a very good impression of him," the Frenchman remarked, perhaps because John seemed profoundly different from most Americans. His character was "French, but revolutionary French," he noted. "His ardent, ambitious personality obviously is inclined to dictatorship."[15]

When Frank Blair returned to Missouri from his congressional duties in mid-August, he was quickly told of the problems at Frémont's headquarters. But the situation was so precarious that at first he brushed them aside. "I would advise that General Frémont be clothed with power to do just as he pleases & have all the money he wants and that he be held responsible for results," he informed President Lincoln, who had asked Blair to assess the situation.[16]

Jessie had known dashing Frank Blair since childhood, when he was the spoiled darling of the Blair family. Auburn-haired, with a red mustache and flashing gray eyes, he was a volatile, hard-drinking man, magnetic, generous, and outspoken in his stand against slavery. Trained in Thomas Benton's St. Louis law office, he had been devoted to the old man, managing the delicate task of supporting him in Missouri and Frémont nationally in 1856 while winning a congressional seat for himself. Like John Frémont, he was brave, impulsive, and so poor a manager of money that his father had to bail him out repeatedly. Like John he was also intensely ambitious. His family intended to make him president.

When Frank Blair reached St. Louis, John treated him deferentially. But John was temperamentally close-mouthed and unwilling to share his authority. He did not confide in Frank or welcome either his suggestions for the defense of Missouri or his more self-serving requests that his friends be given some of the lucrative contracts for beef, guns, and other supplies that were so liberally passed out at headquarters. Most insulting of all, though Frank wanted to be a major general in the Missouri militia, John appointed him only the commander of a brigade. Missouri had always been Frank

Blair's domain. Along with Nathaniel Lyon, he had kept it in the Union. Now, in the course of a month, it had become John Frémont's.

Within two weeks, Frank Blair's genuine doubts and fears about John, as well as his resentment at being superseded, came to a head. "I am beginning to lose my confidence in Frémont's capacity," he wrote his brother Montgomery on August 29. "He seems to occupy himself with trifles and does not grasp the great points of the business." He was aloof and inaccessible except to a chosen few. "Men come with affairs of Regiments and go away without seeing him or without an answer." When Frank urged him to set aside an hour a day to receive "all who come, without making them run the gauntlet of his desks & orderlies," John curtly refused. Frank suspected that he "feared some sort of rivalry with me. . . . I know very well that it will pain you to hear these things of Frémont," he concluded, "but I cannot be silent."

Writing again three days later, Frank was even more emphatic. "He talks of the vigor he is going to use, but I can see none of it. . . . Oh! for one hour of our dead Lyon," he exclaimed. By now Frank suspected that John had been negligent in not sending reinforcements to Lyon. "I could not think when I first returned here that any part of the blame could rest with him but my observations since have shaken my faith to the very foundation."[17]

While Frank Blair wrote his damning letters, John was mulling over an equally fateful act. Beyond St. Louis, Missouri was in chaos. Forty thousand citizens were actively fighting for the South, either in regular Confederate units or in guerrilla bands that roamed the countryside, burning bridges, cutting telegraph lines, destroying train tracks, and pillaging the farms of Union sympathizers. Wrestling with the problem one sultry night in late August, John reached a momentous decision.

The next morning at daybreak he summoned Jessie and one aide, Quaker abolitionist Edward M. Davis, the son-in-law of Lucretia Mott. He told them that he had decided to declare martial law in Missouri, and more important, to free the slaves of those who aided the rebel cause. Jessie and Davis warmly supported his decision, though Davis predicted that the Lincoln administration would never allow it. Nevertheless, without consulting the president, on August 30, 1861, John ordered the proclamation printed and distributed.

Frémont's emancipation proclamation, limited though it was to the slaves of Missouri rebels, electrified the nation. The war, thus far publicly justified by the Lincoln administration only as a means to preserve the Union, suddenly acquired a new purpose—freedom for slaves. It was the cause countless northerners longed to make the central purpose of the war, and Republican newspapers were enthusiastic. At political rallies throughout the North, Frémont's name was greeted with rousing cheers. Overnight he again found himself the leader of a great crusade against slavery.

Frémont's proclamation put Abraham Lincoln in an awkward position. If he endorsed it, he risked losing the support of moderates and conservatives in the North and border states who backed a struggle to preserve the Union but opposed the abolition of slavery. Moreover, he would be allowing an army subordinate to make a major policy decision affecting the entire nation. Yet most of his own party welcomed the proclamation, and Frémont was now a serious political threat.

The president's response reached St. Louis on September 8. Writing "in a spirit of caution and not of censure," Lincoln pointed out that the emancipation of rebel slaves would "alarm our Southern Union friends and turn them against us,—perhaps ruin our rather fair prospect for Kentucky," a border state still debating its course. He asked Frémont to rescind the order "as of your own motion."

Lincoln had given Frémont a way out of his unauthorized proclamation, but the proud, sensitive major general did not see it that way. "If I were to retract of my own accord," he wrote Lincoln that day, "it would imply that I myself thought it wrong." Instead he insisted that the president publicly revoke the proclamation.[18]

Was it genuine idealism, stubbornness, or a calculated attempt to defy the president for his own political gain that motivated John's response? Abraham Lincoln himself would never be quite sure. As for Jessie, she claimed she learned of John's decision to oppose the president only when he gave her his answer to copy. But she agreed with it wholeheartedly. Swept up in their own tight alliance, his decision was hers as well.

Nonetheless, Jessie sensed the danger in their situation, and she convinced John that she should go to Washington to talk with the president, to persuade him to support the proclamation. Naively, they both believed Lincoln would accept her as intermediary.

On September 8, accompanied by her English maid, Jessie boarded a train for Washington. For two days and two nights she sat up in the hot, crowded, creaking car, hurrying to see the president. On the evening of September 10, she arrived in the capital, soot-covered and exhausted but determined to defend her cause. She could not, of course, know that Frank Blair's damning letters about John would reach Lincoln before her and make her mission far more difficult.

23

It is injudicious for ladies to attempt arguing with gentlemen on political or financial topics. All the information that a woman can possibly acquire or remember on the subjects is so small that the discussion will not elevate them in the opinion of the masculine mind.

Eliza Leslie
The Behavior Book
1859

"QUITE A
FEMALE POLITICIAN"

WASHINGTON IN EARLY SEPTEMBER 1861 was a far different place from the careless southern town Jessie had last seen when James Buchanan was president. One hundred fifty thousand Union troops were camped around the city, and the stench, the noise, and the flies were everywhere. The streets swarmed with soldiers, whores, runaway slaves, lobbyists, and contractors eager to profit from the war. Jessie's old enemy, Rose Greenhow, was under house arrest at her home on Sixteenth Street for passing information to the Confederates. In Georgetown, Miss English's Female Seminary had been converted into a hospital.

But Jessie must have paid little attention to such changes as she hurried to Willard's Hotel, bent on her mission. When she arrived, she immediately dispatched a note to the president, asking when she might see him. After a short wait, she received his scribbled reply: "Now, at once, A. Lincoln."

Years later, Jessie wrote down her own detailed account of what followed:[1] "As I had not been able to undress or lie down since leaving St. Louis I had intended taking a bath and going to bed at once," she recalled. "But I walked over immediately just as I had been for two days and nights, in my dusty black mourning dress." She was accompanied by a friend, Judge Edward Coles of New York City, a staunch abolitionist.

To Jessie, the White House was a familiar place, and she entered confidently. She and Coles were asked to wait in the Red Room, lavishly refurbished by Mary Lincoln with crimson satin and gold damask upholstery, gilded cornices, and a grand piano. Eventually the tall, gaunt, ungainly president entered through a far door. As he came toward her, Jessie thought she saw the door set ajar, as though someone were listening behind it.

Lincoln bowed but did not speak. To Jessie he seemed strangely cold and hard. When she introduced Judge Coles, the president barely nodded. Coles then retreated to the doorway of the Blue Room, where he remained, pacing back and forth while Jessie and the president talked.

"Well?" Lincoln said impatiently. Hastily, Jessie handed him a letter from John. She explained that she had been sent to answer any questions he might have. Smiling grimly, Lincoln moved under a chandelier to read it.

Though Jessie knew she looked exhausted, he had not offered her a seat. "Instinct told me the President intended to discourage me, and I did not intend to appear nervous." Trembling with fatigue, she dragged a chair out from a row and sat down heavily.

When Lincoln finished reading the letter, he pulled up a chair beside her. "I have written to the General and he knows what I want done," he told her curtly. Jessie replied that she had been sent to explain her husband's position more fully, since he feared his viewpoint was opposed by men close to the president. Frémont believed it would be "long and dreadful work to conquer by arms alone," she told the president, "that there must be other consideration[s] to get us the support of foreign countries." England, France, and Spain "were on the eve of . . . recognizing the South; they were anxious for a pretext to do so; England on account of her cotton interest, and France because the Emperor dislikes us." Emancipation of the slaves would at once give the North a powerful moral edge and deter European nations from aiding the Confederacy.

Lincoln gave her a long, appraising look. "You are quite a female politician," he said.

Jessie understood then that he had already dismissed her because she was a woman. "I felt the sneering tone and saw there was a foregone decision against all listening," she recalled.

"The General ought not to have done it," Lincoln continued, speaking of Frémont's proclamation, this time rapidly and with less restraint. "He never would have done it if he had consulted Frank Blair; I sent Frank there to advise him and to keep me advised about the work. . . . The General should never have dragged the Negro into the war. It is a war for a great national object and the Negro has nothing to do with it."

"Then there is no use to say more," Jessie replied, "except that we were not aware that Frank Blair represented you—he did not say so openly." It was her first hint that Frank was in some way undercutting her husband.

But evidently Jessie did say more. "She . . . taxed me so violently with so many things that I had to exercise all the awkward tact I have to avoid quarreling with her," aide John Hay reported Lincoln telling him several years later. She had even implied that Frémont might challenge him in some way. To Jessie this was outrageous. "I have sense," she exclaimed when Hay published his version. "If I had a conspiracy on hand I would not tell of it."[2]

"Strange, isn't it," Jessie remarked later, "that when a man expresses a conviction fearlessly, he is reported as having made a trenchant and forceful statement, but when a woman speaks thus earnestly, she is reported as a lady who has lost her temper."[3]

No doubt Jessie was tired and overwrought when she saw the president, and she neglected to use her considerable charm. But she was also a clear and forceful speaker who expressed herself easily and well. Abraham Lincoln, like most men of his time, was unaccustomed to taking women seriously on political matters. Usually patient with visitors, even those who challenged him, he simply dismissed her, unable to recognize that at the least, she could have been a valuable firsthand source of information on conditions in Missouri. Two days later, ignoring her even as a messenger, he dispatched a letter directly to John ordering him to retract his emancipation decree. To the president, Jessie was simply a woman to be gotten rid of as quickly as possible.

The next day, Jessie faced an angry visitor. She had not seen old Francis Blair since she left for Las Mariposas in 1858, but he wasted little time in greetings. He was furious at John for defying the president and at Jessie for defending him. He had known her since she was a child, campaigned with her to elect John president, and now he did not hesitate to tell her exactly what he thought. " 'Who would have expected you to do such a thing as this, to come here and find fault with the President,' " Jessie remembered his angry words. At first she laughed, unable to comprehend his fury. "Look what Frémont has done; made the President his enemy!" Blair exclaimed.

For the next several hours Blair and Jessie argued. To Blair it was unseemly that she had become so involved in John's work. "It is not fit for a woman to go with an army," he told her. He reminded her of how much his family had done for John. "She bridled up at this," Blair reported to Lizzie afterward, "& put on a very *high* look." He was now convinced that the Frémonts would tolerate no rivals. "In a word they hate & fear Frank & are also hostile to everybody in the administration who is supposed to stand between them & imperial power. . . . I talked 3 hours & sounded her to the bottom," Blair reported, "her natural secretiveness [and] Benton cunning giving way under the passion I provoked."[4] But Blair too said far more than he intended. In his fury, he revealed that Frank had written to Montgomery, questioning John's competence, and that Montgomery had shown the letter to the president. In fact, Lincoln had just dispatched Montgomery to St. Louis to investigate the matter.

Suddenly, for Jessie, all the pieces fell into place. The Blairs had turned the president against her husband. Stunned at the betrayal, she threatened that John would challenge Frank to a duel. By the time the last bitter words were spoken, a friendship of thirty years was shattered.

The next day Jessie dispatched a note to Lincoln, demanding a copy of Frank's derogatory letter. The president refused. "I do not feel authorized to furnish you with copies of letters in my possession without the consent of the writers." He also explained that it was "not exactly correct" that he sent Montgomery Blair to St. Louis to "examine . . . and report" but simply "to see and converse with Gen. Frémont as a friend. . . . No impression has been made on my mind against the honor or integrity of Gen. Frémont," he claimed, "and I now enter my protest against being understood as acting in any hostility towards him."[5]

Despite the president's denial, Jessie was convinced that the Blairs were sabotaging her husband and that Lincoln backed them. She sent a coded dispatch to John to warn him of Montgomery's mission. "Things evidently prejudged. Collateral issues and compromises will be attempted but the true contest is on the proclamation. . . . Listen but remember our Salem witch. . . . Some true active friends here and the heart of the country with you everywhere."[6]

When Lizzie Blair learned of the controversy, she dreaded the consequences. She rightly perceived that emancipation was not the real issue for her fiery brother. "Frank is so radical that I can't think that the source," she wrote her father from Pennsylvania, where she had gone with her young son when Maryland rebels threatened Silver Spring. Frank and Frémont were both "firm brave men," she added. "A formal quarrel fills me with a terror I can't articulate."[7]

When Jessie returned to St. Louis, she found Montgomery Blair closeted with John. The cool, unbending postmaster general later claimed that during their talk John seemed "stupefied & almost unconscious, & . . . doing absolutely nothing." Jessie, however, had no such hesitancies. Montgomery was "working to '*modify*' and re-shape the General's course—but he had been listened to only and my arrival ended all attempts at concealing their real conduct. I did not speak to him then, or ever again."[8]

While Montgomery hurried back to Washington to recommend John's dismissal, John ordered Frank Blair, still a congressman, placed under arrest for "insidious and dishonorable efforts to bring my authority into contempt with the government." The Blairs were convinced that Jessie was behind the arrest. "I confess I have never been so entirely deceived in respect to a man's faculties," Montgomery claimed. "I do not vent upon him my indignation for Frank's arrest," he added. "That was as the phrase is 'Genl' Jessie's doing altogether. . . . I understand now that spies are set upon Frank by Jessie to see if she can't get hold of some talk to eke out the prosecution. . . . So we are to have a parcel of ridiculous lies trumped up to help out this woman's thirst for revenge. She is perfectly unscrupulous you know."[9]

The usually gentle Lizzie was equally venomous. She suggested to her father that John should "parade & drill some Reserve Corps about New York—there Jessie & he can play peacocks without such fearful consequences from it. The more I think of that couple, the more bitterly I feel my disappointment in them—it is so humiliating to have bolstered up such unworthy people for so long."[10]

The Blair-Frémont feud was soon public, and both sides used the press to present their side of the controversy. "When the Blairs go in for a fight," Lincoln himself was said to have repeated a common remark, "they go in for a funeral." In the Blairs' version of events, John was a brave but dangerously inept man flailing out of his depth, and Jessie, a clever and vindictive woman who had stepped beyond her sphere. The result of this unnatural intrusion into the male world was disaster. "Did you ever hear of such a superb jackass as 'John C. & Jessie Benton Frémont Major General Commanding,'" one Blair supporter jeered. "And poor Missouri has to suffer for their folly & crime."[11] The Blairs spread the story that John smoked opium, and more ominously, that he planned to set up a western republic with himself as ruler. In turn, the Frémonts asserted that Frank had turned against them because his friends had not been given the government contracts nor he the major general's appointment he demanded.

They suggested that Frank's drinking, his hot temper, and his fierce ambition were at the root of the controversy.

The North was thoroughly confused. Was Frémont a hero leading a great movement to free the slaves, or an ambitious and incompetent petty dictator eager to set himself up as "a sort of Mexican pronunciamento," as Francis Blair charged? Though the emancipation issue was not directly related to John's competence, people tended to support or condemn him according to their viewpoint on slavery. But gradually the Blairs' bruising campaign created suspicion even among longtime supporters. Though Horace Greeley in the *Tribune* stoutly defended John's proclamation, even he conceded that John might lack "experience, judgment, energy, and that insight into character which would be a safeguard against surrounding himself with dishonest men."[12]

Meanwhile, on September 21, disaster struck when hopelessly outnumbered Union troops surrendered to Confederate forces at Lexington, near Kansas City. More than three thousand soldiers were taken prisoner, and a hundred thousand dollars worth of supplies were seized. Many blamed Frémont for the catastrophe. Rumors flew that Lincoln would replace him, although the president, caught in the middle of the Frémont-Blair feud and well aware of Frémont's immense popularity, was stalling, hoping to give him more time to prove himself. Frank Blair, whom John had released, rearrested, and then freed again, furiously condemned "Old Abe" and the "poltroons & apes" of the Cabinet for the delay in removing John. "Jeff Davis and his whole crew have not done us half the harm that has been inflicted upon the country by the cowardice, ignorance, and stupidity of Lincoln's administration."[13]

John and Jessie themselves were desperate. They knew only a great victory could save them. "I am taking the field myself, and hope to destroy the enemy," John informed the administration. Acting swiftly, he gathered nearly forty thousand troops and began to move southwest, determined not only to drive the rebel army from Missouri but to follow it south. "My plan is New Orleans straight," he wrote Jessie from the field. "I think it can be done gloriously."[14]

While John pursued the enemy, Jessie was left in virtual command at their St. Louis headquarters. She worked tirelessly to muster the arms, transport, and supplies he continually requested. "See the Sanitary Committee, and tell them that the whole Surgical Department here is in a very bad condition," John wrote her on September 29. "Thank you for the sabres and guns," he wrote on October 15. "Send any such things forward as best you can." As always, Jessie was his closest ally. "I trust in you to do all that can be done."[15]

At the end of September, Jessie and Lily, nearly nineteen, along with many officers' wives, journeyed to Jefferson City to say a last good-bye to the army before it headed inland to pursue the rebel forces. They traveled on a heavily guarded troop train, for the country was still overrun with guerrillas. At Jefferson City, where the army's white tents dotted the hills, they stayed in a nearby farmhouse but spent their days at "Camp Lily."

Jessie found John deeply depressed. When the day's mail was brought to his tent, "he had no heart to open it." When she did, she found a poem written for him by the abolitionist poet John Greenleaf Whittier. Standing near the camp fire, she read it aloud, ending with the lines:

> Thy error, Frémont, simply was to act
> A brave man's part, without the statesman's tact. . .
> Still take thou courage! God has spoken through thee,
> Irrevocable, the mighty words *Be Free!*

John was overwhelmed. "I *knew* I was right," he exclaimed. Heartened by the poem and by Jessie's support, he told her he was ready to die for his cause.

Frémont's troops were poorly armed and clothed and living on half-rations, but led by Frémont and inspired by his emancipation order, they too were feeding on glory. The cry of the troops was "New Orleans, and home again by summer," Jessie said.[16]

While the troops were eager for battle, several of Frémont's field commanders were disturbed. They believed the army lacked the transportation and food supply for any real pursuit of the Southern forces. "I think Frémont crazy or worse," one of his generals, John Pope, wrote another, David Hunter. Bitterly, Pope asked if Frémont and his coterie should "be permitted to drag to destruction, or . . . unnecessary suffering, the 30,000 men of this army, for no other purpose than to save, if possible, their official lives?"[17] It was a question that President Lincoln, reading the damning reports of several officials sent to assess the situation, was also pondering.

The Frémonts were convinced that Pope and Hunter were deliberately dragging their feet to sabotage the campaign and force John's removal. Meanwhile in St. Louis, the army paymaster, claiming concern about contract irregularities, had cut off funds for weapons, forcing Jessie to arrange for private financing of an arms shipment to John. "This state of things, bad in time of peace, is simply treason in time of war," she wrote angrily to Ward Hill Lamon, a Lincoln confidant who had asked for information. "In view of the united front & bold policy of the enemy our distracted state here, encouraged by the silence of Washington . . . will lead simply to the destruction & massacre of the advance of the army."[18] By late October, she, like Frank Blair, was beginning to feel that the president's policy—neither removing John nor giving him the support he required—was the most dangerous course of all.

To Dorothea Dix she wrote poignantly of her distress. "My dear chief is doing his duty—he will do it for the country whatever he meets, but it's a shame & a crime to hamper & as far as they can disable him when so much depends on his success. There is nobody however to tell the President the truth & he is being ringed in by the evil-minded of the Cabinet. . . . I have not Mr. Frémont's patience & I get ill & heart sore. . . . I meant to write out one page only," she added contritely, "but have gone on talking to you it's such a relief to speak out."[19]

On October 25, Frémont's three-hundred-man body-guard, led by the dashing Hungarian Charles Zagonyi, made a daring attack on rebel-held Springfield, where General Lyon had been killed two months before. Shouting "Frémont and the Union," the guardsmen wrested the town from the two thousand rebels holding it. It was a splendid display, but the soldiers' shouts for Frémont disturbed the administration far more than the victory cheered them.

Frémont was moving rapidly now to catch the enemy, but time was running out. By the second of November he had massed his forces near Springfield, convinced—though others were not—that the Confederates would turn and fight. All was in readiness for a battle the next day when a messenger from Lincoln entered his tent. "I never can forget the appearance of the man as he sat there," the messenger reported afterward, "with his piercing eye and his hair parted in the middle. I ripped from my coat lining the document, which had been sewed in there, and handed the same to him, which he nervously took and opened."[20]

It was his dismissal.

When John's removal was announced to his troops, they came close to mutiny. Officers resigned and soldiers threw down their guns in disgust. With great dignity, John implored them to obey their next commander, and his words calmed the angry men.

When John reached St. Louis six days later, he was met by a tumultuous welcome from the large German and abolitionist population. Huge crowds chanting "Frémont and the Union" escorted him through the streets in a great torchlight procession. He was now the martyred leader of a growing portion of the North, men and women passionately convinced that the abolition of slavery must become the goal of the war.

The response overwhelmed Jessie. "I could not stand it," she confessed. "I went far up to the top of the house, and, in the cold night air, tried to still [my] contending emotions."

Her ambitions for her husband, her own desire to act, and her fierce opposition to slavery had all been thwarted, and her long intimate friendship with the Blairs was over. But the shouts of the crowd reaffirmed her belief that her cause was just. John's proclamation had ignited a great movement to make freedom the object of the war. "The President, the Cabinet, Genl. McClellan & their families and jobmen consitute an irresponsible body who appoint & remove, praise & censure, enrich or impoverish, imprison or release at their own pleasure without consulting or listening to the popular voice," she wrote her old friend Starr King. But Jessie, roused by that combination of ambition, idealism, and anger that had so often moved her father, was determined to fight them all. "This is a formidable body to combat," she told King, "but it's as exhilarating as a sea breeze to make head against. They are like all houses built on sand & we are on the rock."[21]

24

*It seems as though a few energetic
women could carry on the war
better than the men do it so far.*

Louisa May Alcott
October 1861

"THIS TENDERNESS TOWARDS SLAVERY"

THE FRÉMONTS LEFT ST. LOUIS in late November, weary and embittered. Uncertain what to do, they settled temporarily in New York City, where they were comforted by friends and supporters, who crowded into their Astor House suite to protest John's removal, condemn Lincoln's softness toward slavery, and suggest that John would make a far nobler president than the weak, temporizing prairie lawyer who occupied the White House.

Among their callers was Henry Ward Beecher, bringing violets for Jessie and inviting them both to attend a service at his Brooklyn church. "I have something to say and I want you to be there," he told them. When they arrived at Beecher's Plymouth Church on Sunday, they found crowds gathered in the street outside in the thin winter sunlight, waiting to greet and cheer them. The church was packed, and the congregation overflowed into the aisles and onto the altar steps. The atmosphere was electric as Beecher, a tall, lumbering, vital man with heavy jaws, thick lips, and searching eyes, spoke movingly of the national crisis and urged immediate emancipation. To him, Frémont's proclamation was a heroic measure. Turning to John dramatically, he predicted, "Your name will live and be remembered by a nation of *Freemen.*"[1]

Despite such moments, John remained moody and uncertain, reluctant to believe his support extended beyond a small coterie of radicals and abolitionists. Eager to restore his spirits—and perhaps to goad his ambition—Jessie persuaded him to go with her to hear the great abolitionist orator Wendell

Phillips at the Cooper Institute. The hall was crowded when the Frémonts slipped in unobserved. Phillips spoke eloquently against slavery, and when, as Jessie expected, he alluded to Frémont, the crowd cheered wildly. Amazed, moved, and embarrassed, John wanted to leave. But Jessie insisted that he stay to the very end.[2]

Throughout the North that first winter of the war, speakers like Beecher and Phillips praised Frémont's proclamation and condemned the Lincoln administration for what Charles Sumner called its "pious caution." In Washington, with President Lincoln and cabinet members Seward and Chase in attendance, Horace Greeley, lecturing on slavery at the Smithsonian, urged immediate emancipation. When he mentioned Frémont's name, the audience "stamped, clapped their hands, pounded with their canes, and yelled tremendously," an observer recorded. Lincoln, sitting on the platform, "turned quite pale and sunk down in his chair, as much as to say: 'Let me out of here.' "[3]

Jessie was heartened by such support, but it could not assuage her fury. She felt her husband had been deeply wronged, and her anger flared again and again. Her chief comfort, she wrote Starr King in December, was in the justness of their cause. "And good work we are doing," she said. "Perhaps serving to point the evils of this tenderness towards slavery."[4]

By now her genuine idealism was so entangled with her ambition and her anger that she could no longer separate the three. Her antislavery convictions and her dreams for her husband had merged. To her he was the leader of a great popular movement to free the slaves, a movement thwarted by petty politicians like the Blairs and Abraham Lincoln. "There is not much doubt now that slavery has found a Northern man to do her work," she said of Lincoln that winter. While the common people of the North longed to end slavery, the president resisted. "As in all great and lasting reformations the movement is from the roots up," she wrote King. The South was close to gaining recognition from Europe; the North was in disarray. "The rebels have numbers, skill, & fanatical enthusiasm on their side. We have only principle on ours." Yet the Lincoln administration—"the Washington Dictators," Jessie called them—refused to evoke that principle, which would transform the conflict from a sectional dispute into a moral crusade. The successes of the South, she believed, "could have been averted by two words—Be free—but they are not allowed to be spoken."[5] Possessed of a soaring political imagination, Jessie doubtless dreamed that John might replace Lincoln as president in 1864. More immediately, she was determined to explain and justify his controversial Missouri tenure to the public.

John's response to political adversity was characteristically silence and retreat; Jessie's was anger and action. Though as a woman she was limited in her choices, she hit on a brilliant ploy that would allow her to defend her husband and at the same time retain the appearance of womanly modesty. She would write a book whose ostensible subject was the poignant victory of John's much maligned bodyguard at Springfield and whose stated purpose would be to raise money for the fallen guards' families through its royalties. That the book would also be a subtle and skillful defense of John's Missouri tenure would be left unacknowledged. "For any personal object I should never use my name," she said in justification of her book, "but I think my father also would more than approve, when it is to do justice and to aid the widow and the orphan." If that rationale were not enough to excuse stepping from her proper sphere, like many women writers of the time, she dismissed her work as less than serious. "I am incapable of writing a book," she explained, "but I can tell what I know. . . . It is really nothing more than the fireside story of the Guard."[6]

Jessie planned and wrote *The Story of the Guard* in a blaze of energy in the weeks immediately after she left Missouri. By mid-January, despite many interruptions, she was promising to send the completed manuscript within a week to James Fields, the portly, genial editor of the *Atlantic Monthly* and partner in the prestigious Boston publishing firm of Ticknor and Fields. Though Jessie was deeply angry as she wrote, she nonetheless achieved a rhythmic and flowing tone, deliberately discursive, gentle, and meandering. As she explained to Fields, her intention was to tell the truth—or as much of it as was politic—so indirectly that it would be easy to swallow. "Don't be frightened—it's as soft as carded wool," she assured him.[7]

Beginning with a long, disarming digression on the pleasures of reading at Bear Valley, Jessie led her reader along an insidious path while ostensibly telling the simple and heroic story of the Guards' victory at Springfield. But the real focus of the book was John's aborted pursuit of the rebels, and its main purpose was to answer the charges of ostentation, incompetence, and corruption leveled against him. Jessie combined her own account with actual letters from John and two young officers on his staff, as well as the reminiscences of Guard commander Charles Zagonyi, whose broken Hungarian-English, as recorded by Jessie, became both engaging and moving. Jessie compiled her book adroitly, drawing her readers into sympathy with Frémont's efforts, almost convincing them that if only the Lincoln administration had not hobbled and finally stopped him, he would have taken New Orleans by New Year's. Charming, personal, seemingly haphazard, *The Story of the Guard* was powerful propaganda.

In her conclusion, Jessie returned to her anxiety at writing a book under her own name. "I think only the wife of a man much before the public can fully value the sacredness of home," she wrote in the cloying tones she hoped would be persuasive. "It has been a real sacrifice for me to lay open even so small a part of my life," and she asked her readers "not think this attempt to relieve suffering more unwomanly or less needed than any of the other new positions in which women are finding themselves during this strange phase of our national life." For Jessie, like countless other women, the Civil War provided an excuse to step beyond her narrow sphere—to write, to speak, to organize relief work, to nurse soldiers, even to replace men in traditional male occupations so they could go to war. "The restraints of ordinary times do not apply now," she wrote in justification of herself and other women.[8]

Jessie had originally hoped to publish her book by Christmas 1861, but because the subject was so controversial, she met resistance. Publisher George Childs refused, she claimed later, because he had a lucrative printing contract with the Treasury Department and found it "unprofitable to criticize the administration."[9] When she did reach a tentative agreement with Ticknor and Fields in December 1861, she herself decided to postpone publication because the book, with its subtle but nonetheless powerful indictment of the administration, might jeopardize John's hopes for another command.

That month, Congress, alarmed by Confederate victories and responsive to public criticism of Lincoln's "tenderness toward slavery," appointed a Committee on the Conduct of the War to investigate the administration record. Dominated by radical emancipationists like burly, aggressive Senator Benjamin Wade of Ohio, powerful Zachariah Chandler of Michigan, and the deeply sincere reformer Congressman George Julian of Indiana, the committee was sympathetic to Frémont. When it called him to testify in January, he and Jessie welcomed the opportunity to vindicate his record. "This is the end of our silence & now will come justice and retribution," Jessie wrote King as she and John set out for Washington. "Be glad for us dear friends for the cup has been full & every drop bitter & it was drunk in silence & without spilling a drop. . . . Now Fortune turn thy wheel."[10]

When she reached Washington in early January, Jessie did not try to see Lizzie. The two women had not corresponded since the break. In the early stages of the feud, Lizzie recognized that there was fault on both sides, that not only the Frémonts but her brothers and father had carried things too far: "I feel as if we were possessed about the Frémonts," she admitted to her husband. Unable to believe that John was the power-mad incompetent her brothers and father claimed, she found it easier to explain his "seclusion and torpor . . .

by the fact of his being an opium eater." But gradually her view of John—and Jessie—hardened. In the end, her loyalty was to her brothers and father, just as Jessie's was to her husband. "I cannot tell you how sorrowfully I think of Jessie," she wrote her husband just before John's dismissal. "No wonder she has run after her unhappy husband struggling to protect him against himself—& yet has such stormy temper—that she is as unfit to control him as herself—I do pity them—& the poor children more than all else."[11]

Jessie found Washington strange and alien without the Blairs to welcome her. Trying to accept her loss, she channeled her emotions into a passionate defense of her husband's cause. Never was she more like her father than during these months in Washington. "She has scarcely slept or rested," wrote the wife of a Republican official who met her in January. "To see her Husband vindicated, is the restless burning of her soul, and she is mistress of every statistic, every item, that can weigh for or against him."

Impressed though she was by Jessie's advocacy, this woman was disturbed by the escalating Republican battle, as moderates and radicals neglected their common enemy to fight among themselves over emancipation and the conduct of the war. "Within the same hour one is called on in Washington to listen to such opposite opinions!" she lamented. "My heart sickens. Where will all this end?"[12]

When the Lincolns announced a gala reception and ball for February 5, the Republican battleground extended to the White House itself.[13] To many radical Republicans, it seemed callous to entertain when soldiers were dying, and Jessie heard with satisfaction that more than eighty invitations had been refused. "Are the President and Mrs. Lincoln aware that there is a civil war?" Senator Benjamin Wade was said to have replied. "If they are not, Mr. and Mrs. Wade are, and for that reason decline to participate in dancing and feasting."

Smoldering over John's dismissal, the Frémonts were also reluctant to attend, but when Lincoln, anxious for party harmony, sent a special messenger to urge them to come, it seemed impolitic to refuse while John still hoped for another command.

When John and Jessie arrived at the White House, they found the Lincolns receiving their guests in the East Room, the president in a rumpled black broadcloth suit, Mrs. Lincoln coquettish in a low-cut white satin gown trimmed with black lace and equipped with a long train and headdress of black and white flowers. To many Northerners, Kentucky-born Mary Lincoln, with her extravagances in time of war, seemed a "vulgar doll," as abolitionist Lydia Maria Child condemned her. "I reckon the presence of 'our Jessie' in Washington will make her a little uncomfortable," Child wrote to a woman friend that winter.[14]

Mary Lincoln had hired Maillards, the fashionable New York caterer, to prepare a splashy display. "The tables fairly bent under expensive luxuries heaped one upon another," reported Greeley's *Tribune* disapprovingly. Among the scalloped oysters, truffle-stuffed turkey, and charlotte russe, glistened spun-sugar ornaments of a rococo patriotism, including a sugary model of Fort Sumter and a spun-sugar frigate equipped with forty candy guns and supported by cherubs draped in the Stars and Stripes.[15]

Despite the festive display, Jessie remembered Abraham Lincoln as worn and oppressed that night "A sadder face . . . I have rarely seen. He was . . . speaking to the people as they came, but feeling so deeply that he spoke of what he felt and thought, instead of welcoming the guests. To General Frémont he at once said that his son was very ill and that he feared for the result."

Jessie had learned that day from Dorothea Dix that ten-year-old Willie Lincoln had typhoid fever. Two weeks later he would die. Though the Lincolns announced that there would be no dancing because of their son's illness, "the Marine Band at the foot of the steps filled the house with music." Jessie nodded politely to the president when he greeted her, but deliberately did not speak. The Frémonts were soon surrounded by supporters, far more, to Jessie's biased eye, than the cluster around the president. To her the ball seemed "a ghastly failure." Prudently, she and John left early.

In January, John had testified several times before the sympathetic congressional committee investigating his Missouri regime, and in March he issued an extensive account of his tenure, replete with documents. Though Congressman Frank Blair branded his report "an apology for disaster and defeat" in a blistering house speech, John was skillfuly defended by congressional supporters. By now much of the Republican press was echoing Greeley's view that "the Government could hardly do . . . a thing more likely to be popular than to give Gen. Frémont another command."[16]

In March 1862, bowing to radical pressure, Lincoln named his difficult and alarmingly popular major general to command the newly created Mountain Department, encompassing western Virginia, eastern Kentucky, and a portion of Tennessee.

By the end of the month, John and Jessie had established their headquarters at the McClure Hotel in Wheeling, West Virginia. Lily and Frank accompanied them, while nine-year-old Charley attended school in Litchfield, Connecticut. As in Missouri, the wealthy of the region were secessionist or wobbly Unionists, Jessie reported to congressional ally George Julian, but "the working & middle class [are] all for emancipation & we are doing good political work here."[17]

Again John surrounded himself with a personal staff of European revolutionaries like Charles Zagonyi and California cronies like Leonidas Haskell, and again Jessie, stationing herself outside his office, acted as his principal assistant during the weeks he spent in Wheeling. The Frémonts immediately felt mistreated by the Lincoln administration. Four days after their arrival, John, in Jessie's hand, wrote Congressman George Julian asking for help in getting more troops. "People will think the delays are mine. None will believe that we are here with our hands tied because the Govt. delays to send troops or declines to give authority to use those in the West." In early May, as John left for the field, Jessie herself wrote to

Julian in words reminiscent of St. Louis: "Don't let troops be withdrawn from this Dept. They are trying to take away the Blenker Divison & that leaves nothing. It's hard enough to be shut up here *under restrictions* but too bad to have what little is promised withdrawn."[18]

During her month in Wheeling, Jessie found a friend in proud, shy, thirty-year-old Rebecca Harding, a writer just beginning to appear in the *Atlantic*. Her first story, the grimly realistic "Life in the Iron-Mills," was remarkably free of sentimental cant, but *Atlantic* editor James Fields was already urging her to add more "sunshine" to her work. Jessie was enthusiastic about her new acquaintance: "She remains the one agreeable result of my stay in Wheeling," she wrote Starr King afterward, "& she is an acquisition."

Rebecca Harding herself was fascinated by the Frémonts. Jessie had "wit and magnetic charm," while John seemed "the ideal soldier,—simple, high-bred, courteous." Perceptively, she saw that his own hatred of authority fueled his abolitionism. "He made of Freedom a religion. I don't know that he had any especial liking for the negro—very few Abolitionists [had]. But the slavery of the black man—of any man—was abhorrent to him."[19]

When John and his forces left for the field in May 1862, Jessie returned to New York, where she and the children settled temporarily at Little Neck, Long Island. Soon afterward Rebecca Harding came for a stay. "She has never seen the sea & I want to show it to her," Jessie explained to James Fields. Protective of this younger, less worldly woman, Jessie promised that she would "help her to a coat of armor" before sending her on to him and his "formidable sharpshooters circle" of Boston literati.[20]

Though Rebecca Harding's visit diverted her, it was an anxious time for Jessie as she waited for news from John. "It is so hard to have our body in one place when all one's heart & soul & strength are in another," she confided to a friend. She continued to work behind the scenes on John's behalf, encouraging sympathetic politicians like George Julian to defend him in Congress and journalists like *Tribune* editor Sydney Gay to promote him in the press. "My creed is short," Rebecca Harding heard Gay remark. "I believe in Almighty God, His Son, and John C. Frémont."[21]

Lincoln had three generals in the Virginia region: Irvin McDowell to protect Washington and eventually help slow-moving General George McClellan when he finally attacked Richmond; Nathaniel Banks, Frémont's longtime Massachusetts friend and supporter, to guard the Shenandoah Valley and prevent the Confederates from using it as a conduit to Washington; and Frémont, assigned the formidable task of marching over the mountains into eastern Tennessee to seize Knoxville, with its strategic rail line. It might all have worked if the opposing general had not been "Stonewall" Jackson, "the rebel Napoleon," as the press began to call him that spring. With half as many troops, he attacked Frémont's advance guard near Staunton and disrupted his preparations for invading Tennessee, then pursued Banks and routed him brutally at Front Royal and Winchester. Such lightning strokes left the Union forces in disarray. Alarmed that Jackson would attack Washington, the administration scrapped all previous plans and ordered its three generals to converge and trap him.

"Dear Jes," John wrote on May 26, 1862, from the field. "I have a moment to send you my love—all is going . . . well here. We march Eastward tomorrow, but already there are indications that Jackson is [in] retreat. Maybe we can catch him."[22] The tone of John's note was not that of a vigorous soldier determined to stop the enemy, and indeed his weary army moved too slowly to cut off Jackson's retreat. A week later when they clashed at Cross Keys, John's half-hearted attack failed to defeat him.

Two months after John assumed command, the president was thoroughly disillusioned with his glamorous major general. John's own mistakes and the Blair smear campaign had done their work. To Lincoln and many others, Frémont no longer seemed trustworthy. His image was appealing, but many now wondered what lay beneath. A *New York Times* correspondent who encountered John in West Virginia that spring found him immensely likable. "If you ask me why," he admitted, "the reply will be because he looks so splendidly on horseback." The earnest German-American reformer Carl Schurz, asked by Lincoln to evaluate Frémont's progress in West Virginia, had a similar reaction: "the whole personality appeared rather attractive—and yet, one did not feel quite sure."[23]

Jessie was alarmed by John's predicament. Piecing together the disappointing news from West Virginia, she was convinced that the Lincoln administration wanted him to fail. "It would be hard to say in which Capitol, Richmond or Washington, it would give most joy to have Mr. Frémont cut off," she wrote bitterly to a friend. "It tries me to the heart to see him cramped & thwarted & misrepresented," she told *Tribune* editor Gay. "If I could only see him—he has no one with him to whom he can rest his mind, & laying off that burden start again."[24]

Stonewall Jackson succeeded so brilliantly in part because there was no unified command among the Union forces in the Shenandoah, and in late June, Lincoln wisely decided to place one general over all three armies. Unfortunately, he chose glib, boastful John Pope, who would soon prove to be yet another of Lincoln's inept generals.

To Frémont personally, the appointment was a stunning rebuke. Convinced that Pope had sabotaged him while serving under him in Missouri, he saw no choice but resignation. "If he had stayed," Jessie bluntly wrote George Julian, "they would have prepared defeats & destroyed his reputation. . . . I think it was very good of him to give a technical military reason for resigning & not say as he was warranted in doing—this man you have put over me is my enemy. . . . I cannot trust him with my honor or the lives of my command so I retire knowing it to be useless to ask justice where he is a court favorite."[25]

As in the past, John came home to Jessie bitter and beaten. "Right or wrong, it was the crisis of his life, and he had lost," said Rebecca Harding, who was staying at the house when he arrived at midnight. Characteristically, he concealed his despair in a courteous reserve, and she remembered him as kind and thoughtful the next day as he drew a careful map of New York City and described the sights she should see. "He was the great man of my youth," she wrote sadly, long afterward.[26] For Jessie, horrified at what had happened, aching for her proud, reticent husband, every dream seemed shattered.

25

*Frémont, I am afraid, is a selfish
unprincipled adventurer. Since he
was removed from the command
in Missouri, his course seems to me
every way petty, selfish, and ignoble.
I have no confidence in him.*

Lydia Maria Child
July 1864

"THE LOST LEADER"

THE NEXT YEAR would be wearing for the Frémonts as John fruitlessly sought another command. He tried to resume management of Las Mariposas, but with its ever-mounting debts, it too seemed beyond his control. He found solace in long horseback rides in Central Park, often with Lily and Charles Zagonyi, the Hungarian commander of the Guards, who was also waiting impatiently for another assignment. "Isn't it a shame that such men have no higher use of their time than to train a girl to ride?" Jessie wrote bitterly to Starr King.

Though there was a touch of wry humor in Jessie's tone as she described her life that winter, she too was deeply weary. "I do a good deal of desultory work & in one way & another the General & the children fill the time," she reported to King. "In among it all we see many pleasant people & get snatches at some really good music & I can get a bunch of violets for ten cents & lots of new reading matter. That makes up decentish happiness don't it?"[1]

As her dreams collapsed around her, Jessie thought nostalgically of her Black Point friends. She was concerned about their welfare and eager to further their interests in the East. She tried to arrange a leave for King to give him time to rest and write, she promoted an exhibit of Carleton Watkins' photographs in New York City, and she brought Bret Harte to the attention of *Atlantic* editor James Fields. "He has something flaming in preparation for you," she informed Fields in early 1863.[2] When the manuscript arrived, Fields was impressed. In the fall Harte's stories and poems began to appear in the *Atlantic*.

Jessie's own literary endeavors were also bearing fruit. Once John had resigned his command, there was no reason to withhold publication of *The Story of the Guard*, and in October 1862, she turned the manuscript over to Fields. "Please shape it slenderly," she told him. "Dumpy books are so unsuggestive of elegance of thought or deep feeling. It's cruel enough to have lost my own slenderness without seeing that misfortune befall this child of my heart & memory." She still had doubts about the propriety of writing a book on her own. "I don't get reconciled to my name on the title page," she said. As publication neared, her anxiety grew. "Don't hesitate to draw your critical pen through anything that seems sentimental or stilted," she wrote bravely to Fields.[3]

Published in time for Christmas, *The Story of the Guard* was favorably received, although like Jessie herself, reviewers were eager to stress her womanliness. "Instead of being a labored and exhaustive defence of General Frémont by the fair Jessie, while her Benton blood was up, it is as mild and gentle as the heart of a woman," stated *The Hesperian*, a San Francisco woman's magazine. "The parts . . . by Mrs. Frémont are exceedingly well done and make the reader regret that the whole is not in her neat, compact and forcible style."[4]

The *Atlantic* reviewer, possibly Fields himself, seemed especially concerned not only to reaffirm Jessie's womanliness but to contradict rumors that she was a more talented writer than her husband. Her approach was "novel, but not ineffective," the *Atlantic* claimed. "Mrs. Frémont is a true woman, and has written a true woman's book. . . . Her style is full, free, vivid, with plenty of dashes and postscripts,—the vehicle of much genius and many noble thoughts; but in itself no style, or a careless and imperfect one." In contrast, John's letters reproduced in the book were "manly" in style, and despite stories to the contrary, it was he, not his wife, who was the real writer in the family. "We cannot be mistaken. The hand that penned the 'Story of the Guard' could not hold the pen of the [Emancipation] Proclamation or . . . the narrative of the Rocky-Mountain Expedition."[5]

Writing to King, Jessie was proud of her "bookling," and she asked him to promote its sale in California. "I get lots of compliments on it," she added, "but don't care for any but the General's, yours, & Mr. Harte's and Mr. Beale's."[6] Despite her show of modesty, she was eager to have it read widely. Concerned that the price was too high for a larger sale, she persuaded Fields to issue a cheap paperback edition "for soldiers" and arranged for a German translation as well.

For many idealists, Frémont remained the hope of the war, the man who should be president. Periodically, the Frémonts expected that John would be named to another post. Despite the pressure, Lincoln remained determined not to use a man whose competence he questioned and who was a formidable political rival as well. As the president's position became clear, the Frémonts and their supporters began to think more seriously of challenging him for the presidency.

At the same time, brooding over the accumulated injustices of the past, John was growing more cynical. During the next years his business and political schemes would be increasingly tinged with a dubious morality. Repeating a pattern, he surrounded himself with a protective clique of admiring supporters who served his interests and bolstered his flagging ego. Perhaps the most loyal was Leonidas Haskell, whose charming teenage daughter Nelly, Jessie and Lily had known and liked since Black Point days. Haskell had served John in St. Louis and West Virginia, and then followed him to New York. He was "simply a soldier of fortune," Haskell's young New York aide, Benjamin Brooks, claimed, "not to question why, just to do or do for his chosen captain." To Brooks, Frémont himself was attractive and intelligent, seemingly "blessed with the power to hypnotize his fellow men," yet strangely inaccessible. "He seemed to me a rare and perfect egoist. While unassuming in manner he . . . placed himself on a pedestal, an idol to which he not only offered perpetual incense himself but was ably assisted therein by his devoted adherents, some of whom doubtless did so in perfect good faith."[7]

Among these adherents, the most devoted was Jessie, who continued to believe passionately in both her husband and the abolitionist cause. On a special corner shelf she kept a treasured collection of antislavery books: *Uncle Tom's Cabin*, Wendell Phillips's speeches, Frederick Olmsted's *Slave States*, Whittier's poems, actress Fanny Kemble's scathing journal of life on a southern plantation, and abolitionist minister Theodore Parker's memoirs. Above them she placed a sculpture called "The Slave Auction" and a treasured fragment from a gun seized at Fort Wagner, the South Carolina stronghold that had been courageously but unsuccessfully charged by black Union soldiers.

Helplessly, Jessie watched the terrible events of the war. The corruption and inefficiency uncovered in Missouri seemed minor compared to the scandals and war profiteering in Washington itself. Observing Lincoln's tolerance of bungling generals, she was more convinced than ever that the president had not given John a fair chance to prove himself. To friends she bluntly called Abraham Lincoln "an ass."[8]

The war was indeed going badly for the North. By the late summer of 1863, the Union army under Ulysses S. Grant controlled the Mississippi, but in the East a series of floundering generals failed to reach Richmond. At Gettysburg in early July 1863, Union troops stopped Lee's invasion of the North but at a terrible cost. The death and destruction seemed endless.

In March 1863, the North had instituted a draft, but because the well-to-do could avoid it by paying three hundred dollars for a substitute, the burden fell on the poor. When the names of the first draftees were published in July, New York's poor exploded in protest. Gangs roamed the streets, sacking, burning, and looting; blacks were attacked and hanged. Because of the Frémonts' prominence in the war, their house was threatened. John's idle staff, who still clung to him, went eagerly to work to protect the family. Eight-year-old Frank

Frémont observed the activity with fascination: troughs were built on the roof "so inclined as to pitch a shell . . . into the middle of the street, where [it] would explode on impact; the ash barrel in the street . . . contained explosives connected with a battery in the cellar, the wires passed up through the coal hole; in the house there were sufficient rifles and shot guns to handle indoor fighting." During the four nights of rioting as many as thirty-five men camped in the hall and parlor. One former staff officer, whom Jessie dubbed "the Fire King," prepared "all kinds of 'hell-broths' " to be tossed among the rioters if they attacked the house.[9] Such concoctions proved unnecessary, however; perhaps because, as the Frémonts believed, the rioters noted their preparations and prudently stayed away.

In late July, Jessie was glad to escape to Nahant, a summer resort on the Massachusetts coast whose sedate residents shared her abolitionist sympathies. "Mrs. Frémont is next door to us, which is very pleasant," Henry Wadsworth Longfellow informed James Fields.[10] The children swam and boated with little Longfellows and Whittiers, and the whole family hiked, picnicked, and learned to play croquet.

When autumn came, Jessie was reluctant to return to New York and the brownstone mansion at 21 West Nineteenth Street they had recently bought, enlarged, and redecorated. "I'm afraid of 'tomorrow,' " she confessed to John Greenleaf Whittier as she prepared to leave Nahant. "The rule of our life . . . has been struggle & unrest. This summer has been so peaceful . . . that I am nervous about what must follow this lull in our stormy lives." But her energy was up and her political ambitions aroused. The day before, writing to Starr King, she had revealed her anger and hinted at her dreams. "I am hoping great things for the country from the growing knowledge of the President as he really is—a sly slimy nature."[11]

Jessie plunged into activity with a kind of frenzy. To one woman who met her during the winter of 1863–64, she seemed to be everywhere, an "enterprising ambitious woman" who never missed a cultural or charitable event in the city. "I am driving a four in hand team," she wrote Boston reformer Elizabeth Peabody, "society work, political work, sanitary comm[ission] work and the looking after my two big boys & home. . . . Throw in diphtheric sore throat for myself, runaway horses & wounded children [Lily and Charley had been injured in a carriage accident] & my sister's society & family duties . . . you can see I have no 'spare time.' "[12] She and her handsome sister Susy, whose husband, Baron Gauldrée Boilleau, was the French consul in New York, were holding weekly concerts in their homes (at two dollars a ticket) to raise money for the Sanitary Commission. But Jessie's main project was the commission's great fair in April.

The first sanitary commission fair, held in October 1863 in Chicago, had netted seventy-two thousand dollars for war relief, but the New York organizers were vastly more ambitious. Though the Sanitary Commission was a male-dominated organization, it reluctantly allowed women, organized into more than a hundred committees, to plan and manage the fair. Inevitably, this public outpouring of pent-up female energy caused alarm. General William T. Sherman wrote snippily to his wife that he didn't approve of "ladies selling things at a table." More, however, seemed to agree with the *Tribune* writer who asserted that "woman never appears to greater advantage than when she is engaged in the holy work of charity."[13]

Jessie, serving on the Arms and Trophies Committee, made it her special project to issue a series of small volumes of letters and memoirs related to the war, with profits benefiting the commission. A fellow committee member was Ellen McClellan, wife of the now-deposed Union general, who like Frémont was rumored to have presidential ambitions. Though politically at odds, by now the two women shared a common enemy in Abraham Lincoln. "We get on very civilly—even amicably," Jessie reported to Elizabeth Peabody. "On the opening night we shall all be in full bloom with generals attached."[14]

On April 4, 1864, crowds thronged the fair's main building at Fourteenth Street and Sixth Avenue for the grand opening. It was "a scene of fairylike magnificence and splendor," exclaimed the *Herald*. At hundreds of booths women, discreetly dressed in black with prim white linen collars and blue sashes, sold donated objects ranging from wax flowers to chips from Plymouth Rock contributed by the Plymouth Historical Society. Jessie, with her sample volumes and subscription book, sat in an upstairs gallery, where she took orders to be delivered by Christmas. The fair featured a restaurant serving ten thousand people a day, a "wigwam room" where Indians performed Iroquois dances, and a livestock department in a separate building that boasted a mammoth hog weighing 3,600 pounds and a five-horned sheep donated by P.T. Barnum. The "Floral Temple" on the main floor displayed a "hairy eagle" whose head, eyes, and backbone were made from President Lincoln's hair. Before it was all over, the New York women would raise more than a million dollars.

The fair program also included a lavish series of amateur theatricals. Jessie herself funded, organized, and directed a successful Cinderella, with thirteen-year-old Charley Frémont as the prince and two hundred children in fancy dress on stage for the ball scene. The extravaganza raised twenty-five hundred dollars for the commission. "You know I was built to last a hundred years & I may yet get to half of that," Jessie confided to Elizabeth Peabody not long before the fair opened. "But I think a little more of the present work would wreck me."[15] Then, in the midst of the hoopla, she learned that Starr King had died in San Francisco.

In the years since Jessie left San Francisco, Julia King had begun to enjoy the West. "All the troubles of a year or two ago have passed away: & with them much of her discontent with California," King wrote. "I really think I am more homesick than she." He had spent the war years traveling tirelessly about the state, raising money for war relief. It was mainly due to his efforts that California donated nearly a million and a quarter dollars, one fourth the national total, to the Sanitary

Commission. But King was a frail man, and his work exhausted him. In early 1864 he caught diphtheria and then pneumonia. On March 4, he died.

Jessie was stunned by the news. "I am heart sore for the loss of my friend," she wrote Elizabeth Peabody. "Dear and true and irreplaceable to me." It was another blow brought by the war. Grieving, she telegraphed that violets be put in his casket for her.[16]

To many northerners, by the spring of 1864, the war seemed a ceaseless slaughter, managed by clumsy generals and an inept administration. Though Abraham Lincoln had finally issued an emancipation proclamation, radical Republicans considered it a tardy and grudging concession to party pressure. Moreover, the president's proposals for reconstruction suggested that once the war was over, he would allow former slaveholders to dominate the South at the expense of black rights. In the *Tribune* Horace Greeley deplored the president's drifting policy toward slavery and suggested that another man should be the party candidate for president.

Meanwhile Frémont's supporters were quietly working for his nomination. They were a curious mixture of idealists and scamps. "I wish I had more influence with F. and that some men had less," Wendell Phillips admitted that summer to Elizabeth Cady Stanton, "but I believe in him." Years later, one associate claimed that when he and a group of supporters went to Frémont for his blessing, he replied by writing out a check for five thousand dollars. The whole campaign, the man added, "cost him a great deal of money."[17]

It was an irregular group of disaffected Republicans—"sly politicians from New York, impetuous hair-brained Germans from St. Louis, abolitionists, and personal friends and parasites of Frémont," as one opposition paper assessed them—who met in Cleveland on May 31, 1864, to nominate John Charles Frémont for the presidency. Leonidas Haskell's cynical young aide, Benjamin Brooks, found himself pressed into service as a delegate from California. "I could see nothing but preposterous nonsense in the whole affair," he said later.[18]

Whatever John and Jessie might have hoped, his candidacy evoked little public enthusiasm. Aside from Wendell Phillips and Elizabeth Cady Stanton, no prominent figures endorsed him. Rightly or wrongly, Frémont's reputation had been irrevocably damaged, even among dedicated reformers. The pro-Lincoln *New York Times* called him "the Lost Leader." In 1856 he seemed to represent "all that was noble and heroic" in the fight against slavery; now he was simply "a political adventurer of the most dangerous kind."[19]

Nonetheless, Abraham Lincoln was in political trouble. Renominated by party regulars at Baltimore on June 8, he received only lukewarm support. The North was gloomy over its lack of military success. The Confederates still held Richmond and the southern heartland, while Lincoln's new commanding general, Ulysses S. Grant, had lost nearly seventy thousand men in six weeks as he struggled grimly toward Richmond. Washington hospitals were choked with dying men, and the casualty lists in the newspapers sometimes ran to three columns daily.

Republican leaders, alarmed that Lincoln could not win, called for a new convention and cast about for another candidate—perhaps Ulysses S. Grant or Benjamin F. Butler. Jessie indicated that John would step aside for the right man. "Some one else must be put in [Lincoln's] place," she wrote John Greenleaf Whittier. "It must be some one firm against slavery. Everything hinges on that. And the General will thankfully retire & give his most active support to such a man." Lincoln himself was deeply discouraged. "You think I don't know I am going to be beaten," he was reported to say, "and unless some great change takes place beaten badly."[20]

But two great changes did occur. On August 29, another disaffected general—handsome, vain George McClellan—became the Democratic Party nominee. McClellan's nomination sobered Republicans. Suddenly it was clear that the party must unite to defeat this "peace" candidate, who proposed to end the war without abolishing slavery. Just days later, on September 2, General William T. Sherman, campaigning almost unnoticed in the deep South, marched into Atlanta. The North went wild. For the first time in the long, bitter war, the end was in sight.

Republicans abruptly dropped plans to field another candidate. Fearful that Frémont would split the Republican vote and give the victory to McClellan, Senator Zachariah Chandler and other radicals met with Lincoln in early September, then came to Frémont with a deal. If he would withdraw his candidacy, Lincoln would offer him a command and remove Montgomery Blair from the Cabinet. By now Blair was not only Frémont's personal enemy but too soft on slavery for most Republicans as well.

For several weeks John and Jessie brooded over the proposal. Wendell Phillips urged him to stay in the race, but John Greenleaf Whittier, stopping by their Nahant cottage, told Jessie that her husband must withdraw. "There is a time to act and a time to stand aside," she recalled him saying.

On September 22, 1864, in a public letter that was harsh toward the Lincoln administration but even harsher toward McClellan, John withdrew from the race. The next day Lincoln dismissed Blair from the Cabinet. John and Jessie always denied there had been a deal. "The safety of the Republican party was his one and only reason for accepting, or now, for withdrawing from the nomination," Jessie said.[21]

Abraham Lincoln won the election comfortably that November; and over the winter, Union superiority in manpower and manufacturing, aided by a grimly tenacious general, finally began to pay off. As for Jessie, despite her dashed hopes, she gamely continued her busy New York life. That winter, she and John attended a gigantic reception for General Grant, a small, seedy-looking man, now the idol of the nation. But privately, Jessie was deeply angry. "Jessie rages at all sorts of people, especially at Greeley, Beecher, and Garrison," reported Congressman George Julian, who had a long talk with her one April evening in 1865. "According to her, the General was shamefully betrayed by pretended radical and anti-Lincoln men who deserted him in time of greatest need, after encouraging him to stand in the breach."[22]

That spring the news came swiftly. On April 3, Union troops entered Richmond; on the ninth, Robert E. Lee surrendered to Grant at Appomattox Courthouse; on the fifteenth, sitting in his lace-and-flag-decorated box at Ford's Theatre, Abraham Lincoln was fatally shot. The man Jessie called "sly" and "slimy" was dead, but his place in history was assured. People forgot the blundering years, the mismanagement and corruption, the vacillating policy toward slavery. Lincoln's "cruel death silenced much truth," Jessie wrote many years later, "and since then he has been shaped and exalted . . . not content with his real greatness he has been made to appear incapable of error."[23]

The war left the Frémonts bruised and battered. Writing to young Nelly Haskell, Jessie recalled her first exhilarating years of marriage, "when I was young and more gay and happy than you can imagine me." In those long-gone days it seemed that fate was hers to seize and shape. But repeatedly she found herself powerless to influence the rushing course of events. She married a man who dreamed greatly, yet in some inexplicable way, failed again and again. She tried to explain his lapses: "It has never been his allotted part to go with the current." Though she strove to boost him, she was beginning to see that as a woman she had little real control. Trying to accept her powerlessness, she admitted that whenever she saw "a hot generous nature blindly striking out and trying to hold to some vanishing joy," she saw herself as she had been long before. "It was not natural to me or easy for me to bend my pride," she told Nelly. "I am sure if it was all written out in a book it would grieve any one to see how I got broken in."[24]

26

*About the age of forty-five to fifty
years, the menstrual flux is suppressed,
the breasts lose their fullness and the
uterus loses its organic capacity. The
body itself does not long delay entering
into decrepitude, and soon we see the
woman—once so favored by nature when
she was charged with the duty of repro-
ducing her species—degraded to the
level of a being who has no further duty
to perform in the world.*

Dr. Augustus K. Gardner
Conjugal Sins
1870

RETREAT TO POCAHO

I N APRIL OF 1865, as the war ended and the North mourned its dead president, the Frémonts purchased a massive gray stone mansion overlooking the Hudson near Tarrytown, New York.[1] Surrounded by more than a hundred acres of orchards, woods, and fields, Pocaho, as they called it, adopting the local Indian name, would become their sanctuary. Exhausted by the passions and disappointments of the war, Jessie would spend the next decade in luxurious retreat.

"It is only an hour from town & this is our true home," she wrote Lizzie's husband, Phillips Lee, that fall. Forsaking politics and politicians, she cultivated the blander society of the wealthy old families—Schuylers, Aspinwalls, Phelpses, Peabodys—whose great estates lined the river. "We have a lovely home here among people who are glad to have us. My visiting list for the summer is just twenty-five miles long for the Hudson is a great street & people dine & visit by rail when they are past driving limits."

Yet Jessie was haunted by the past. For her, one of the tragedies of the war was the rupture of her friendship with the Blairs, and especially with Lizzie. "Often in going over the grounds & planning walks & opening views & bringing all the brooks into one, my old walks at Silver Spring come to me," she wrote Lizzie's husband, who had unexpectedly called at their New York townhouse while they were at Pocaho. Responding to his gesture of partial reconciliation, she wrote openly of her sadness. "A gulf like death lies between that time & now but all that went before that time died is very green in my memory. . . . All of you were always so good to me. I never have & never tried to alter any part of the feeling of that time."

Though Jessie accepted the severing of ties, a terrible regret permeated her letter. "One gets used to nearly everything," she wrote sorrowfully. Knowing that Lee would show her letter to Lizzie, she also relayed the family news she hoped that Lizzie, despite the rupture, would still want to hear. Charley, who was Lee's godson, was at the Peekskill Academy, a military school twelve miles north of Pocaho. "He keeps his passion for the sea," she wrote. "He is a very big boy—very strong & active and healthy and when he is over his cub days—he is only fourteen now—he will be splendidly handsome in a manly way. Frank is more delicate in health—more delicate in tastes & mind too but equally manly, but he is & always will be a beauty." Lily was less well, still nervous from the carriage accident more than a year and a half before, though the scars on her face had disappeared. As always, John, despite the vicissitudes of fortune, retained his "firm health & youthful looks except that his hair is all grey. I am the most changed," Jessie added, "for I am much fuller in figure than I like & my hair is almost entirely white. . . . When the color was taken out of my life in that hard first year of the war, it was natural enough the color should leave my hair too. But when one has to give up a dear hope the very struggle leaves a calm. I am really peaceful and happy again for in these stone walls I centre the only remaining interests of my life. . . . I used to get so tired thinking & never came to a resting place."[2]

Lee, a high-ranking career naval officer, tactfully responded to her letter in his role as concerned godfather by encouraging Charley to attend the Naval Academy at Annapolis. But if Jessie hoped for a direct response from Lizzie, she was disappointed. During the next years, the two women would neither correspond nor see each other, although they would keep in tenuous touch through Lee. "Thank Lizzie for her good will for my boy," Jessie wrote him in reply, "and give her my love for auld lang syne."[3]

Jessie's retreat was total. House, garden, children, and society absorbed her energy during the next years, almost as if in penance for her forays into the male realm of politics, war, and business. When the movement to give black men the vote encouraged women to demand the same right, she remained aloof. In the winter of 1865–66, Elizabeth Cady Stanton called to ask her to sign a petition for woman's suffrage. Jessie refused. "Oh, no. I do not believe in suffrage for women," she said. "I think women in their present position manage men better." Stanton responded sharply that she doubted whether it was woman's business to "manage men." Later, reporting Jessie's answer to a friend, Stanton felt "out of patience with men, women, and fate," clearly disappointed in the woman whose name had meant so much to her and other women during the 1856 campaign. Jessie was actually far more ambivalent about the issue than she revealed to Stanton. Several months later, replying to a request from Susan B. Anthony for a financial contribution, she admitted, "I can not see the subject as you do." Nonetheless, she enclosed money for the cause.[4]

Jessie had repeatedly experienced the repercussions of stepping beyond her sphere. Collaborating with John on his reports, working on his presidential campaign, or aiding him at Las Mariposas, she had escaped censure only as long as she remained discreetly in the background. In St. Louis it had all exploded in her face. She was condemned as "General Jessie," her alliance with her husband branded an unnatural, two-headed monster. The Blairs saw her as a brazen woman, a camp follower who had boldly interfered in the male world. Her visit to Abraham Lincoln had become a minor scandal.

Jessie felt bruised and disillusioned. To advocate the vote for women would damage her position still further and she wanted no more controversy. Temporarily, she had lost her nerve.

Settling in at Pocaho, she no longer sought out strong interesting women like Dorothea Dix, Elizabeth Peabody, or Rebecca Harding Davis. Her new friends were staid married women with money, children, and few political interests. For nearly a decade, until circumstances smashed the padded world she created at Pocaho, she practiced a lavish domesticity iron- ically reminiscent of Cherry Grove, the Virginia plantation she once found so confining. A retinue of well-trained ser- vants—maids, grooms, coachmen, gardeners, even a French chef—smoothed their lives. Orchards, vegetable gardens, a dairy, henhouse, and duckpond provided them with produce. From their ample greenhouse more than three thousand cut- tings were set out one verdant year. There were horses and dogs, carriages and boats. Teenaged Charley had his own yacht, given to him as a reward for progress in Latin.

While Jessie savored such rural largesse, she and the fam- ily at first continued to return to their New York townhouse for the winter season—to shop, to visit and entertain friends, to attend concerts and the opera, to explore the picture gal- leries. Postwar New York was a crude, hectic, vital place. New millionaires were building opulent marble palaces up Fifth Avenue while the immigrant poor crowded into dark tenements on the Lower East Side. It was a time of feverish enterprise, of speculation and easy deals, of loose banking, cheap money, and growing corruption. The city throbbed with a vulgar gaiety. During the first social season after the war, the wealthy spent an estimated seven million dollars to give and attend balls.

During these first glittering postwar years, the Frémonts' own fortune seemed secure. In 1862, when John resigned his West Virginia command and turned again to Las Mariposas affairs, he found them more entangled and encumbered than before. "Why when I came to California, I was worth noth- ing," he was said to have remarked at this time, "and now I owe two million dollars."[5] In 1863 he relinquished control of Las Mariposas to a company of wily businessmen who ma- nipulated the transaction so that he was left with far less than he expected. Nonetheless, he remained an immensely wealthy man and free from the everyday cares of Las Mariposas.

But John was irresistibly drawn to speculative enterprises,

and he soon sank their money into railroads. Envisioning a great southern line spanning the continent from Norfolk to San Diego, in 1866 he became a partner in the unbuilt Memphis, El Paso, and Pacific Railroad. Again there would be complications: tainted transactions, tangled finances, scandal, and interminable lawsuits. But years would pass before it would all fall apart.

Meanwhile there was Pocaho. To an impressionable young woman who visited the Frémonts during these years, it seemed an enchanted place. Writing afterward to her sister, she described the winding drive to the house through a walnut forest thick with wild ferns, flowers, mosses, and shrubs. She found the house spacious, its large, airy rooms filled with flowers, books, pictures, and beautiful furniture. Albert Bierstadt's painting of the Golden Gate hung on one wall, a portrait of Jessie by Giuseppe Fagnani on another. The Frémonts' fine library, augmented by the collection of the German naturalist Alexander von Humboldt, purchased at his death, lined the walls of a magnificent twenty-by-thirty-foot room.

Jessie and Lily's quarters were especially luxurious, like "fairy bowers" to the awed young woman. She arrived early in the morning, to find Jessie still *en deshabille*, for she and Lily lived "English-style," with early tea in bed followed by a morning nap. Nonetheless, she was welcomed with generous hospitality. Breakfast was ample and handsomely served. "We had tea or coffee, broiled fish and hot rolls, after which came down delicious asparagus and radishes." Lily, who poured the tea, seemed charming, and Jessie was, of course, fascinating. But there were cracks in the picture, though the young woman scarcely saw the implications. Lily was "short, stout and not stylish," she recorded, and typically, "the Gen. was not home."[6]

Lily was twenty-two when the Civil War ended, and much of Jessie's postwar socializing was doubtless done so her daughter could meet eligible young men. During the war itself, Jessie seems to have encouraged a match with Congressman George Julian, a shy, intense widower in his mid-forties who shared the family's radical Republicanism and found Lily herself "a charming girl." Jessie cultivated his friendship, inviting him to family suppers and to go riding with Lily in the park. "Lily is not a pianist but she is a horsewoman," she wrote him gaily.[7] While the lonely congressman may have been attracted, in the midst of the war he married another young woman, plain like Lily, but a suffragist educated in the lively, progressive atmosphere of Oberlin and Antioch colleges.

Lily was often a bridesmaid during the next years, as friends and acquaintances married. "Dr. Van Buren's daughter . . . is to have six bridesmaids all in white tulle with blue trimmings & Miss Van Buren promises that I shall have a pleasant groomsman—I dare-say I shall have a pleasant time of it," she wrote cheerfully to Nelly Haskell not long after the war. But gradually, for quiet, reserved Lily, who felt more comfortable with animals than people, the social scene soured. Like her father, she was reticent and undemonstrative; unlike him, she was also practical and unimaginative. She seems never to have fallen in love. By the time she and two young friends attended an Annapolis ball with Jessie as chaperone, she was twenty-eight and neglected, despite her green silk dress and coral jewelry. "I came away before supper," she reported to Nelly Haskell, "but Mother staid with the two Maggies she was chaperone to till 5am!"[8]

Lily never married. Perhaps she, or Jessie, expected too much—an extraordinary man for the only daughter of the wealthy and proud Frémonts. She preferred to stay at Pocaho, where she gradually took over the household management from Jessie and supervised Frank's studies as well. Her joys were solitary—reading, pressing wild flowers in her scrapbook, riding her horse.

Lily's withdrawal was a dark comment on her parents' relationship, on her mother's distress when John was away, in danger, or aloof. Reacting to the extravagant passions of their marriage, she sought the peace and safety of subdued emotions. Jessie had never spared herself life. Her daughter chose to avoid it.

As Lily settled into spinsterhood, Jessie focused her maternal energy on her two boys. Encouraged by Phil Lee, Charley wanted to attend the Naval Academy, though at first Jessie was leery, having heard not only that the climate was bad but that it was "the fashion as well as a habit to drink there."[9] Phil Lee evidently soothed her fears, for Charley entered Annapolis in 1868. Jessie visited frequently, not only to see that her son remained healthy and sober but because she enjoyed the society of the boisterous and spirited cadets, some of whom liked her so much that they corresponded with her for years afterward.

Frank was the more scholarly of the two boys, and Jessie was convinced he could be "eminent in any lettered profession." Instead he chose West Point. Though Jessie had resented West Pointers since the court-martial, she recognized that without such a "latch key" there was "no entering the service of our country."[10]

Like Lily, the two boys would live unflamboyant lives. Following safe and regular paths, both would become middle-level career officers within a secure and ordered system. If Jessie was disappointed, she kept it to herself, perhaps because she did not want her sons to pay the price she and John had suffered for their ambition and stubborn nonconformity.

During these years at Pocaho, John was often away. He stayed regularly in New York, where his main office was located, and frequently spent weeks or months in Washington or the West on railroad business. Jessie was always elated "when he made time for a day at home." But Lily saw the pain. "Father has gone to Washington. . . . Mother isn't particularly well," she reported to Nelly on one occasion. "Mother [has been] a little down," she wrote on another, "but as Father comes up on the five o'clock she'll be all right tonight."[11]

Jessie was approaching fifty. Her hair was white, her figure stout. Seeking peace, she cosseted herself at Pocaho, but her pampered life cramped her active temperament and stifled her natural energy. During the bitter Civil War years, she had experienced sporadic headaches. At Pocaho they became commonplace.

Jessie had no useful work. Her domestic duties were few. Sheltered and protected, she was lonely. Lily, mutely devoted, was nonetheless an alien temperament, while John, as always, remained elusive. Though Jessie had long since accepted his nature and was fiercely loyal, it left an emptiness. A warm, hospitable woman, she filled the house with guests— cheerful cadets, visiting dignitaries, New York society friends— but the headaches, the sadness, continued.

Beneath it all was a brooding anger. Jessie remained deeply bitter over the injustices to John. She struggled to accept the failure of their dreams, to resign herself to what life had brought. But in some deep part of herself she still burned for vindication.

During these years Jessie often thought nostalgically of her youthful years in Washington when, passionately in love, filled with hope and ambition, surrounded by family and friends, her life "was all filled with energetic action." In March 1868, such memories came flooding back when she saw Kit Carson again. Accompanied by several Ute Indian chiefs, Carson had come east in connection with his work as superintendent of Indian affairs in Colorado Territory. When he reached New York, Jessie hurried down from Pocaho to see him. Though she knew the fifty-eight-year-old Carson was ill, she was unprepared for the feeble old man, leaning heavily on the shoulder of her son Frank, who tottered in to greet her. All about him "was the dignity of coming death," she said.

Jessie was overwhelmed with sadness. "But Carson was only troubled by my emotion," she recalled. When she pressed him to come to Pocaho to recuperate, he refused, explaining that he only wanted to reach his home before he died. He was too sick to talk much, and their visit was brief. Later, knowing she would not see him again, Jessie sent violets to his hotel.[12]

Two months later, on May 23, 1868, Kit Carson died at

Fort Lyon, Colorado. To Jessie, who early sensed and promoted his mythic qualities, he would always be an American
knight—gentle, brave, and honorable—and even more a beloved friend, one of the few who remained loyal to the end.

During these years, John and Jessie shunned any real
political involvement. When Ulysses S. Grant was elected
president, they attended his inauguration in March 1869, mainly
to establish government contacts for John's railroad enterprise. Three months later they were on their way to Europe—
John to make money, Jessie to spend it.

On June 12, the Frémonts (minus Charley, who was on
a naval cruise) embarked on the *Ville de Paris*. They traveled
in luxury, occupying the ship's bridal suite and sumptuous
adjoining rooms. When they reached Paris ten days later, they
settled into opulent quarters at the Hotel de Jardins de Tuileries, opposite the palace gardens. While fourteen-year-old
Frank went rowing on the lake in the Bois de Bologne and
John attended to railroad business, Jessie and Lily embarked
on a grand shopping spree; then, in a whirl of trunks and
bonnet boxes, they set off by train for Germany and Denmark.
In late August they toured the Austrian Alps, traveling in two
carriages and preceded by a green-suited postilion who blew
a brass horn as they passed through mountain villages. "Bowing was so continual it was like a drive up 5th Ave. to the
Park," Lily said. [13]

John was with them only sporadically. Though the family's
lavish style belied it, his Memphis, El Paso, and Pacific Railroad was in trouble. Earlier that year the company had begun
to sell bonds in Paris to raise money for railroad construction,
but its French promoters, who included the Frémonts' brother-
in-law, Baron Gauldrée Boilleau, misrepresented the company's situation, claiming that it was already a transcontinental
line controlling land from Norfolk to San Diego, and that the
federal government had guaranteed a fixed interest rate on
its bonds. Even in a time of extravagant puffery, such claims
were flagrant. The company had land grants only in Texas,
and those were shaky; and the U.S. government had neither

given it subsidies (though John had lobbied hard for them) nor guaranteed its bonds. By the time the Frémonts reached Paris, several French newspapers had branded the venture a fraud, and the American ambassador, alarmed at the advertisements, had urged the U.S. government to investigate.[14]

Though John later claimed that he knew nothing in advance of the French promotion, he was slow in revealing the true situation to the public. Meanwhile the company's chief engineer, James Daniel, who accompanied the Frémonts to Paris, found him suspiciously close-mouthed about the bond sale. Reluctantly, he came to believe that John was deliberately holding millions in Europe under his control instead of sending the money to Texas for railroad construction. "The same mystery exists here about all transactions that existed . . . in N.Y.," Daniel wrote company president Benjamin H. Epperson in alarm. "I am not allowed to investigate the company books or contracts."[15]

It was not only the railroad imbroglio that kept John occupied in Paris that summer. He had begun a flirtation with a young American sculptor, Vinnie Ream, a beautiful twenty-two-year-old woman with long dark curls, brown eyes, and a rushing enthusiasm for life.

Vinnie Ream began her sculpting career in Washington, D.C., where Abraham Lincoln himself, charmed by the talented young woman, sat for his bust for half an hour a day for five months despite Mary Lincoln's objections. When Lincoln was assassinated, Ream, backed by influential congressmen, won a competition to do a statue of the martyred president, though some protested that she was an inexperienced girl who was more adept at coquetry than sculpture. In 1869, chaperoned by her parents, she went to Europe to sculpt her Lincoln statue in marble.

For a brief period in September, while Jessie and the children were traveling, John saw her daily.[16] In late September, he joined the family for a week of Austrian travel, but when he returned to Paris before them, he resumed his visits. Vinnie Ream and her parents were leaving soon for Rome, and John wrote ostensibly to outline the costs of the various routes. "This is my little bulletin of business for you this morning my darling," he concluded. "If I should be happy enough to see you tonight I will make it clearer—otherwise tomorrow. I feel disturbed & disquieted this morning. Frémont." Writing again the next day, he discussed baggage arrangements. "What I have been at to you here looks like the letter of a business agent," he added, "but, although you may not see it, it is a love letter."[17]

At fifty-six, John Frémont was still a handsome man. "He holds his own better than you do, my dear," a blunt old woman told Jessie during the war. He was also wealthy and famous, with a glamorous intensity that must have impressed the young woman. Yet the relationship seems to have been essentially innocent—one of several flirtations Vinnie Ream maintained with susceptible older men. During her Paris interlude, she had many distinguished callers, though John was the most frequent. At the same time she amassed a collection of flattering letters from a raft of admirers eager to boost her career, ranging from friendly notes from Frank Blair and General William T. Sherman to gushing pages from the elderly southern lawyer-poet Albert Pike, who also addressed her as "darling." A working woman, supporting her parents by her sculpture and dependent on wealthy patrons for her income, she seems to have understood both the advantages of her charm and the dangers of sexual entanglement.

When Jessie, Lily, and Frank returned to Paris, they immediately visited Ream at her studio, where Jessie posed for a bust, then stayed on for lunch. Several days later Ream finished the bust, received a last visit from John, and started for Munich and Rome with her family.

Whatever his feelings, there is no indication that John ever continued his romance. While Jessie was too perceptive a woman not to have sensed his infatuation, her own visits to Ream indicate her confidence in them both—or perhaps an attempt to monitor the situation. Although it was undoubtedly painful to see John entranced by a woman as fresh, young, and vibrant as she had once been, outwardly her devotion remained unshaken.

On November 13, 1869, after ten days in London, John and Jessie sailed from Liverpool on the *Java*. Lily, Frank, and a maid remained in Dresden for the winter, where Frank would be tutored in German, Latin, arithmetic, fencing, and music, while Lily planned to perfect her German and learn to paint flowers on china.

After a brief stay at Pocaho, John and Jessie headed for Washington, "where the General has a Railroad to protect & foster," Jessie explained. The Paris bond scandal had prompted a congressional investigation, and they sailed into a storm of controversy as John attempted to defend his increasingly dubious railroad. Though old congressional friends like Charles Sumner and Nathaniel Banks supported him, the public seemed to agree with Senator Jacob M. Howard, the chief congressional investigator, who called the bond promotion a "stupendous fraud" and found Frémont in "suspicious proximity to foul and fraudulent transactions."[18]

Much of the bond money was never accounted for. Despite the millions raised, by January 1871, only three miles of Memphis and El Paso track had been laid and less than twenty-five miles graded. Frémont's brother-in-law, Boilleau, was shown to have received $150,000 for "services"; John himself may have reaped more than a million dollars in commissions. "Frémont's name stinketh in Paris," reported his long-disillusioned 1856 campaign aide John Bigelow.[19]

The Memphis and El Paso was destroyed by the scandal. A shrewd manipulator, John A. C. Gray, moved in to gain control of the company through bankruptcy proceedings, then slowly began to force John out. Meanwhile, John joined the backers of yet another proposed southern transcontinental line, the Texas and Pacific. Again he was outmaneuvered. By the spring of 1873, the Frémonts were pressed for money.

Living in splendor at Pocaho, Jessie had tried to remain aloof from John's tangled business affairs. But that spring, as his fortune began to slip from his grasp, she became involved: writing business letters, accompanying him to Philadelphia and Washington to see lawyers and agents, participating in long grueling conferences as they struggled to resolve their financial dilemma. They tried to remain optimistic, reassuring themselves that they still had investments and property. But in the welter of suits and countersuits, of negotiations and deals, they were caught in a deepening morass.

At Pocaho, there was no obvious retrenchment. They were tended and pampered by a retinue of servants; house guests perceived no change in their abundant hospitality; as usual, there were summer pilgrimages to Saratoga Springs, Newport, or Bar Harbor. But beneath the careless luxury, everything seemed precarious. Their lives were suffused with a vague and terrible dread.

That spring their most distressing concern was a lawsuit brought by Memphis and El Paso bondholders in France. In March in a Paris courtroom, John and his French promoters were charged with swindling, "by the sale of fraudulent and worthless bonds to the extent of $6,000,000." The trial made news everywhere. For Jessie it was particularly painful because it involved not only John but her sister Susy's husband, Boilleau, who had helped promote the bonds in France.

After weeks of testimony, all of the defendants were convicted of swindling. Boilleau, sentenced to three years in jail, was led off amid the taunts of the angry French bondholders who crowded the courtroom. John, who had pleaded insufficient notice and prudently remained in the United States, received a five-year sentence in absentia.[20]

Convinced that John was innocent, Jessie brooded obsessively about the case. That summer the whole family was unwell from the strain: John suffering from a relapse of malaria, Lily from eye trouble, and Jessie from exhaustion and depression that erupted in vague aches and pains.

Eighteen-year-old Frank came down with a lingering pneumonia. He had been worn and tired since marching in his summer uniform in freezing weather at Ulysses S. Grant's second inauguration in March. By midsummer he was seriously ill. "Frank has been spitting blood—almost a hemorrhage," Lily wrote Nelly in mid-August from Bar Harbor, where they had gone in hopes that the bracing air would cure him.[21] To Jessie, it suggested the fatal Benton ailment, tuberculosis. Doctors urged that he spend the winter in a warm climate. It seemed improbable that he would ever return to West Point.

Then another blow fell. On September 18, 1873, the great Wall Street banking firm of Jay Cooke & Company collapsed, plunging the nation into financial panic. Within months five thousand large firms—including eighty-nine railroads—failed. Hundreds of thousands of workers lost their jobs. For the Frémonts, it meant the downward spiral spun faster. Most immediately, Frank's winter journey was jeopardized.

"We had houses and lands and stocks and no money for unpremeditated uses," Jessie explained. But in their dilemma she saw a chance to act. Determined to raise cash for Frank's journey, she contacted New York *Ledger* editor Robert Bonner, who had once asked her to write some sketches for his popular weekly newspaper. "I had refused then, because I did not wish to do anything to be talked of. Yet now I had more than enough motive to brave all criticisms." Without consulting the family, she arranged to write a series of reminiscences for the *Ledger*. In return, Bonner agreed to pay her one hundred dollars a column.[22]

Jessie set to work on her sketches, turning them out rapidly in the course of an intense three-week period. "I am very pleased with myself for I have four columns all finished," she wrote gleefully to Nelly. It was the first time she had ever been paid for her work and she was jubilant. "$400 this week already, and now it runs easily for my mind is settled as to what it ought to be. Charley, Frank & Lil listened last night to the whole and each approved."[23]

Under the title "Distinguished Persons I Have Known," Jessie produced a series of rambling reminiscences, devoting columns to such notables as Andrew Jackson, Hans Christian

Andersen, Kit Carson, Martin Van Buren, and Starr King. For the most part her work—like the *Ledger* itself—was sentimental and cloying, displaying little of her native wit and verve. Only occasionally, as in her sketch of Kit Carson, was there freshness and feeling. But her readers evidently relished such drawing-room chatter, almost as if the celebrated Mrs. Frémont herself were sitting beside them, whispering charming tales of the great and near-great.

Jessie's feelings were deeply ambivalent as she began what would be twenty years of writing for a living. Like other women writers of her time, she was exhilarated by the power to earn money, yet anxious to minimize such a bold step out of her proper sphere. Over the years she would strive to maintain the illusion that her work was simply a casual pastime that happened to pay—so much so that her son Frank would remember little about her work except that "as a writer, she always disclaimed any special flair or genius . . . 'fine writing' she did not aspire to nor care for."[24] Yet the writing and the money that resulted were both profoundly important to Jessie. They gave her, after years of working behind the scenes, a sense of direct power and control. Over time, the experience would change her view of the world.

Jessie used her *Ledger* earnings to send Frank off to Nassau that fall. Though she and Lily had hoped to accompany him, "panic & business" prevented their journey. "It's a pull to let the boy go without any of us," Lily told Nelly, "but it can't be helped."[25]

By January they had scraped together enough cash to join him. But Jessie felt depressed as she left John, looking gaunt and harassed, to face their financial problems alone. The first night on board the steamer, she went "sadly to bed . . . not sea sick but heart sick," she wrote Nelly, who with her new husband, George Browne, had promised to look after him. "My Nelly, it comforted me to know you and the General were left to each other as we slid away. . . . He is so solitary, so lonely, my poor dear darling—you know how tender hearted he is & he has no one now."

Arriving in Nassau, Jessie found the weather balmy and Frank recuperating. "It was right to come," she told Nelly. But she continued to brood about John. "You must keep me fully posted about his looks. I must know if he gets ill," she wrote. "I think sometimes I could step over the sea so yearning for the General do I get."[26]

Returning to New York in May 1874, Jessie faced the further disintegration of their finances. They had no money for mortgage payments or taxes. Humiliation followed humiliation.

"The Tax collector is here—says he can levy on anything moveable," Jessie wrote desperately to Nelly's husband, George Browne, from Pocaho during this terrible time. "The collector is at the stable now looking at horses, carriages etc. with a view to moving them into the village, advertising for six days &, if not redeemed, selling them." Jessie managed to put him off temporarily, "on condition . . . nothing should be spirited away out of the stable—of the contents of which he took a list."[27]

Frantic for cash, she met with the president of the Texas and Pacific Railroad, trying in vain to persuade him to repay a $142,000 debt John claimed.[28] They sold California land and then, bit by bit, the horses, the boats, Charley's yacht, the beloved Bierstadt painting of the Golden Gate. In January 1875, Jessie was forced to offer their magnificent Humboldt book collection at half its assessed value. "I cannot wait," she wrote urgently to an acquaintance who promised to help.

By now she knew that Pocaho too would have to be sold. It was a bitter task she would endure alone. "The General has been so tired and hurt by the undeserved griefs of these two hard years that, to spare him, I have to do many things I hardly understand."[29]

By late 1875 Pocaho was gone and they were living in a rented house at 924 Madison Avenue, unfashionably far uptown. Jokingly, Jessie called it "poverty flat." A few loyal friends like Nelly and George Browne remained. But others had dropped away, as if their humiliation were some dread disease. Bitterly, they experienced what Jessie called "the silence that falls around those who are struggling with great calamities."[30]

During this difficult time, John went west to sell what California property they still had. Now in his early-sixties, he was deeply weary. Journeying by train, following the same route he had explored so joyfully with his band of mountain men thirty years before, he was overcome by despair. As the train climbed through the Rockies, he began to scribble a poem on the back of an envelope. "Long years ago I wandered here/ In the mid-summer of the year/ Life's summer too," he wrote. But the rapture, the freedom, the dazzling hopes had vanished. His life was filled with "hateful strife and thwarted aim." Everything he touched had turned to ashes, and he felt profoundly helpless. Gazing bleakly at the darkening mountains, he saw no way out. Only death, "the brief day's close," lay ahead.

When John sent his nine stanzas to Jessie, she read them with an aching sadness, as a "de profundis cry from him to me." Characteristically, she wanted to share his poem with the world, and she sent it to *Littell's Living Age*, where it was published anonymously. "The General knew nothing of this until I gave him the number with the lines in print," she told Whittier. "He was very pleased. But his is the most reserved and shy nature I ever met."[31]

During these years, Jessie never doubted—at least publicly—John's essential innocence in the scandals and failures that rained upon him. To her, he remained a hero, "more great in his silent acceptance of undeserved calamity than in the days men praised him."[32] She believed that he was the victim of unscrupulous men who had taken advantage of his trusting nature. At the same time she was convinced that the bond scandal had been exploited by political enemies to punish him for his strong antislavery views during the war.

Seeking to vindicate him, she corresponded with writer James Parton about doing a popular article that would justify John's part in the Memphis and El Paso imbroglio. Despite their shaky finances, Jessie was willing to pay for such a piece. "Because I am Mr. Frémont's wife I cannot speak for him," she explained, but she was determined to restore his image. "So far from reconsidering or giving up," she wrote firmly, "this is the business of my life and the lives of my two sons."[33]

Jessie's faith in this weary man was fierce now, and she felt passionately the unfairness of his fate. Over the years, as she saw how wounded, how beleaguered he was, her love had become protective, almost maternal, the love of a mother for a child who is mocked and misunderstood by the world. And though she scrupulously preserved the outward forms of obeisance to "the General," as she proudly called him, their adversity made her strong as it weakened him.

The crisis brought out her latent energy, an enduring optimism that nothing could completely quench. If John could not defend himself, she would. If he could not support the family, she must try. "I am like a deeply built ship," she told Nelly Haskell Browne, "I drive best under a strong wind."[34]

Beneath the surface courtesies, Jessie seemed more than ever the dominant force, the one with energy and strength. Yet it was not that simple. She needed John's love more than he needed hers, and so in a deeper sense, it was he who controlled their relationship. Elusive, fleeing, always just out of reach, he held her fast.

27

*I like women who are not annihilated
when "the girl" goes off in a huff;
who could preside at the White House
or scrub the kitchen floor, who are
not afraid to travel a few miles alone,
and who, moreover, if plunged into the
depths of poverty, would fight their own
way out of it, asking help of no man.*

Mary Kyle Dallas
"Be Independent"
New York *Ledger*
1875

ARIZONA REPRIEVE

THEIR FINANCIAL CRISIS gave Jessie a legitimate motive for working, one she lacked during her Pocaho years. Writing at a tiny desk in their gloomy, charmless house on Madison Avenue, she began to produce what would be her best work. Delving into her past, she wrote of her California gold-rush experiences at the request of *Harper's Magazine*. While her sketches for the *Ledger* had been hasty and choppy, her work for *Harper's* was polished and assured. Her writing was intensely personal, her style studded with precise details as she touched on her migrating childhood in St. Louis, Cherry Grove, and Washington, and then skillfully evoked the loneliness and wonder of her first journey to California.

In the late fall of 1876, she finished a first draft, and John stayed home one day to hear Lily and a friend take turns reading it aloud. A year later, it appeared as a three-part series in *Harper's*, for which she was apparently paid five hundred dollars per installment. The following spring *Harper's* bought Jessie's interest in the copyright for a hundred dollars and that summer issued *A Year of American Travel* in book form. Cloth-bound, it probably sold for a dollar a copy; with a paper cover it was twenty-five cents. Like *The Story of the Guard*, the work was well received. But again some detected an ulterior purpose. "She can't make much of a Hero out of her husband," grumbled one old forty-niner who read it. "He is and was an unmitigated fraud and bilk of the first order."[1]

Despite Jessie's literary successes, the Frémonts had less money each year. In late 1877 they moved to a rented house on the Staten Island esplanade, another step down to a still cheaper rent. That fall they were also forced to sell more paintings, books, and furniture to pay off debts. Mercilessly, a *New York Times* reporter described the curious throng who crowded the auction gallery one October night to probe, poke, and bargain for the Frémonts' worldly goods: Thomas Buchanan Read's portrait of John and Fagnani's of Jessie, a marble bust of Benton, a Steinway piano, ebony and ormolu-encrusted furniture, sets of French and English china, a stuffed American eagle with outstretched wings.[2]

In their shame, the family drew closer. In his reserved way, John became as protective of Jessie as she was of him. Writing to Nelly Haskell Browne from San Francisco, where he had gone again with business hopes, he showed his concern. "I am doubtful if at home they will tell me truly how Mrs. Frémont is and how she gets along, so will you write and tell me, Nell? I am going to rely upon you to do so."[3]

By the spring of 1878 the Frémonts were desperate. When Rutherford B. Hayes, who as an idealistic young lawyer had supported Frémont in his 1856 campaign, became president himself, they grasped at the chance for a new start. In May they traveled to Washington to negotiate a federal appointment.

Jessie was relentless as she made her political rounds, while John, writing to Zachariah Chandler, the Michigan senator who had arranged his withdrawal in 1864, at last asked the party to fulfill its promise of a political appointment, if it were not "out of date."[4]

President Hayes proved willing to help out his old hero. First he offered the governorship of Idaho Territory, but John turned this down. Arizona seemed more alluring. John had already been in contact with mining investors there. Beyond the twenty-six-hundred-dollar-a-year governor's salary, he glimpsed the possibility of another fortune.

For both Jessie and John, the Arizona appointment was a last chance to restore the power, wealth, and prestige they had lost. As Jessie prepared to journey west after a seventeen-year absence, her imagination soared. John had never been "such a hero as now in these long years of silence under wrong," she wrote a friend. "But the day is breaking."[5]

"We are in full blast of going out," Jessie wrote Nelly jubilantly from San Francisco four months later, "praises, invitations, flowers, fruits, books . . . driving in four-in-hands & in landaus & coupees & etc. The wheel has turned you see."

The Frémont party—John, Jessie, Lily, Frank, their long-time Irish maid Mary, and their beloved staghound Thor— had reached San Francisco on September 12, 1878, after a week-long journey across the continent by train. For Jessie, the journey west had been a kind of vindication. After years of mockery and neglect, John was treated like the hero she believed him to be. She found it both exhilarating and exhausting, "like a long dream," she wrote young Sandy Morton, their New York doctor and friend. "And I keep telling over my rosary of blessed points—the justification—the public recognition of a wrong done—the gathering stream . . . of friendly and indignant sympathy—it has been a regular widening gulf-stream since we struck Chicago."

In San Francisco it reached a crescendo. A committee from the Society of California Pioneers escorted them to the swank new Palace Hotel, where they were given a lavish corner suite ("four bedrooms, two parlors, two bathrooms & our own hall," Lily recorded) as guests of its flamboyant millionaire owner, William Sharon. They were greeted enthusiastically by old friends and associates. Even long-time enemies were cordial. "Lots of old hatchets were buried and pipes of peace . . . offered in their place," Jessie said.[6] More privately, they were reunited with Jessie's sister Liz and her three children, who had been struggling to survive in California since the death of William Carey Jones. Without Jones's poisoning presence, their reunion was warm, though Jessie found her niece Betty, who like many fashionable young San Francisco women wore face powder and crimped her bangs, rather racy by eastern standards.

Continuing south, they stopped for a rousing welcome in Los Angeles before heading east to Fort Yuma, the end of the rail line, where they boarded three mule-drawn army ambulances for the journey to Prescott, Arizona's capital, 230 miles beyond across the desert. For eight days they jolted through a sterile landscape, camping at night at meager oases. Ascending at last into the cool, pine-covered mountains near Prescott, they were met by outgoing Governor John P. Hoyt (who was gamely going off to govern Idaho Territory) and Secretary of State John J. Gosper, an ambitious, wooden-legged man eager to be governor himself. Frémont and Hoyt entered Prescott triumphantly, riding in the town's only barouche, with Jessie and the others following in less elegant vehicles. Prescott's several thousand citizens turned out to greet them. "All the piazzas were crowded," Jessie said, "cheers & flags & such."[7]

Nestled in a pine-forested valley surrounded on three sides by granite peaks, Prescott's setting was magnificent. The light was dazzling, the sunsets spectacular. The town itself was less imposing. While it could boast of a new theater and two-story brick school, its center was a dirt plaza lined with saloons and stores, its capitol a rough-hewn log building that also housed a brewery and a general store.

John, gray and worn when he reached Prescott, collapsed with nervous exhaustion. Four days later, however, he was well enough to accompany Jessie to a gala supper and dance in their honor, an occasion the local *Arizona Miner* pronounced "the most brilliant social event that ever transpired within the boundaries of Arizona." A Prescott lawyer gallantly set the tone when he claimed he had come not so much to "see the General, but to honor Jessie, the governor's queenly wife."[8]

The hoopla was heartening, but Jessie found it a strain as well. "I have been only seeing the days and hours as they came and had to be met," she confessed to Morton. "And what was required of me was to be pleased and astonished and receptive, and sometimes it was easy and sometimes it was not but I was taught my trade of society well in the early days, so it is second nature."

The trip west had restored John's confidence, and Jessie was determined to preserve his new optimism and will. "The General would find it exile but for me," she confided to Morton. "With me he feels it a term of voluntary labor from involuntary causes and together we make the labor light, but oh so much of it is uncongenial. Never mind, we will succeed. . . . When I see the General flagging a little under new discomforts or old memories, I get my chance and warm his heart again. So he is now very well and sees his way clear. . . . And people like me for coming (as if I could keep away when the General has his hands full—I *never* was so needed.)"⁹

The Frémonts lived in temporary quarters for six weeks before finding a six-room cedar and pine house to rent at ninety dollars a month, forty percent of their salary. Located a block from the plaza, it overlooked the Camp Verde and Santa Fe road, frequented by heavy freight wagons drawn by twenty-mule teams and prospectors trudging to and from the mines with their pack-laden burros. Before moving into their house, they had its plank walls scoured with boiling lye to remove vermin, then re-covered with cotton sheeting and wallpaper. Pressed for money, Jessie sewed the curtains herself, with the help of Lily and Mary, and filled the house with Indian pottery and a changing array of wild flowers, delighting in such exotic effects as satiny yellow and ruby cactus blossoms in the red-papered parlor. Housekeeping proved easy with Lily supervising Mary and Ah Chung, a dignified Chinese who came from California on a year's contract. The local market provided ample beef, game, and vegetables, but there were omissions. "We are four days travel from a lemon," Jessie sighed.¹⁰

From the beginning, Jessie felt well in Prescott's high desert climate, but John's binding mountain headache" only gradually wore off, while for weeks Lily, now seriously overweight, gasped for breath whenever she exerted herself. But soon Prescott was invigorating them all. Frank, whose incipient tuberculosis still worried the family, was "fattening steadily" and John had "a clean pink-tinged smooth skin, filled out so that fifteen years are off his looks." Jessie herself was "splendidly well," she announced, "and ready to take hold of Fortune's wheel, and pull it to the place I would have it 'stick.' "[11]

Prescott's upper crust—lawyers, mining engineers, merchants, army officers from nearby Fort Whipple—soon swept the govenor's family into a busy round. "We are going to be quite gay next week," Lily informed Nelly in late November, "a dinner, the Post hop, & a theatrical performance in which Frank acts." But the social whirl impressed Jessie far less than the simple strength and endurance of the women she met. "Some of the quiet-faced women here tell me of things you would feel impossible for women to live through."[12]

Unabashedly, the Frémonts were in Arizona for a purpose, and from the beginning John devoted more time to his business schemes than to his gubernatorial duties. The possibilities were glittering. The Frémonts had arrived in the midst of a mining boom: rich deposits of gold and silver had been discovered along the Colorado River and in the mountains of the interior. Boomtowns like Tombstone were attracting eastern capital, as well as the likes of Doc Holliday and Wyatt Earp. John soon found a willing partner for his dreams in Charles Silent, a territorial supreme court judge living in Prescott. Eager to believe, Jessie pronounced Silent "a Daniel for judgment & reliableness, and skill too."[13]

That fall John and Judge Silent traveled by horseback to inspect potential mines, and by the time the territorial legislature adjourned in late winter, they were ready to head east to seek backing for their ventures. They left Prescott in February 1879, accompanied as far as San Francisco by Frank, who was in desperate need of a dentist. John's trip was financed by a two-thousand-dollar appropriation from the legislature, which had commissioned him to go to Washington to arrange the settlement of a controversy regarding the Salt River Indian Reservation. At the last minute, a suspicious opponent spoke sneeringly of federal carpetbaggers and tried to substitute another man. Though his motion was defeated, it revealed the beginnings of a festering resentment toward the new governor.

With John and Frank gone, Jessie and Lily settled into a quiet provincial routine. Jessie's most invigorating activity was the regular Friday afternoon history class she taught at the local public school to an audience of awed adolescents dressed in their Sunday best to hear the celebrated Mrs. Frémont. A New York *Tribune* correspondent once called Jessie one of the four or five great conversationalists of his lifetime, but this was her first chance to speak in public, and she reveled in the opportunity. When townspeople began to drop in to hear her as well, she was all the more delighted. With her low musical voice, her wit, and her gift for anecdote, she doubtless charmed them all. Her aim, she said, was to give flesh and color to the dry bones of history, to show that all humanity was made "from the same elements and that pain and sorrow and death certainly come to all."[14]

John had promised to return in April, but inevitably, scrambling to push his projects in the East, he was delayed. To Jessie the summer seemed long and dreary. She was anxious about John and fretful that she could do so little to promote their fortune. Lily was far more contented with their life of luncheons, teas, and evenings at the fort, listening to the army band or gossiping over the latest stage robbery, mining strike, or local marriage. Exhausting a neighbor's supply of French novels, Jessie began Motley's *Dutch Republic*, while Lily plodded through a three-volume history of Scotland.

"We had a pretty solitary pull of it the six months of the General's absence," Jessie admitted to Nelly when John returned in late August, "but all's well that ends well." In the East he had managed to recruit a group of businessmen, including Colonel Charles King Rogers, President Hayes's personal friend and private secretary, who were prepared to invest in the mines he selected. Characteristically, John was euphoric about their prospects. "I think that in the course of a few months we shall have the control of some mines that I believe equal to any on the continent," he reported enthusiastically to Rogers soon after his return.[15]

John had hired two German-trained mining experts to advise him, and in the early fall he and Frank accompanied them on a tour of inspection. On his return, with Jessie's help, John scrambled to complete the annual territorial report for the government. "I am J.C.F.'s pen," Jessie said. At the same time, he was planning yet another journey to the mines. Blatantly now, the Frémonts were out to rebuild their fortune. Aging, frightened, they lived on a desperate optimism.

"Mother & I will have a very quiet spell while they are gone," Lily wrote complacently to Nelly that October, which "we have planned to devote to the manufacture of winter nightgowns & returning visits!"[16] But Jessie was no longer willing to wait passively in Prescott. John's mining schemes seemed at the point of fruition, and he needed someone he could trust in New York to manage his interests. Since he could not easily leave his gubernatorial duties, Jessie proposed that she go east as his agent. Specifically, she would set up a company to finance their most promising mine, the Silver Prince. Years later Lily, perhaps embarrassed by her mother's active role, would claim that Jessie left Prescott because the altitude made her sick, but the truth was, Jessie was remarkably well in Prescott. She was simply eager to act. Suffering from the strain of her isolated existence, she longed to be of use to the family. With a fortune so close, she was determined to grasp it.

By early November 1879, just a year after she left New York, Jessie was back in the city, staying temporarily at the Everett House and hard at work promoting their mining schemes. Determined to succeed, she would tolerate no opposition. In a letter to Rogers in Washington, she urged the dismissal of the territorial secretary of state, John Gosper, a "thwarting official" who was interfering with their plans. "There are several things I would rather tell than write you," she confided. "I know it will please the President when I tell him of my fortune restored."[17]

In December, despite a severe case of bronchitis, she launched the Silver Prince venture, in which she and Charles Silent each owned a quarter share. "We have everything arranged for the management and development of our own mine," she reported jubilantly to Rogers. "And I go back early in the spring." John would prefer to give up his governorship and pursue his mining interests exclusively, she added, "but to resign now would give the power next winter when the Legislature meets again, to unknown people and interests. And if he continues there he will prevent and veto any vexatious legislation regarding mines and railroads." Jessie asked Rogers to give John leave to come east "to make his own arrangements for his own interests—and for friends who have helped him wear through the dark eleventh hour. . . . We are neither of us in the class of 'friends remembering not,'" she concluded pointedly. A month later, however, Jessie's investors backed out and she was forced to find others. In a stridently political letter to Rogers, she blamed John Gosper for the failure. "It has been a battle against influences chiefly hidden," she wrote. "But I have won."[18]

Meanwhile in Prescott, John and Charles Silent continued their alliance. "We have such comfort in Judge Silent—Father & I each in our way," Lily wrote Nelly. "We should have had a fearfully lonesome winter without him; you know how like a strange cat Father behaves unless he thoroughly likes his surrounding & he has been never quite at home in this town & misses Mother immensely."[19]

Jessie eventually succeeded in obtaining leave for John, and in March 1880 he came east again. In New York he and Jessie promoted their enterprises—not only mines but a Sonora cattle ranch (in which John had been promised a half interest if he could persuade the Mexican government to verify the grant) and a railroad franchise from Tucson to Point Lobos on the Gulf of California (if only he could obtain congressional support). "The General . . . wants a thorough talk with you on the railroad connection and that Mexican property generally," Jessie informed Rogers in June. Meanwhile in Prescott criticism of the absentee governor was growing, and even long-suffering Lily was restive. "I am beginning to think that Father's return to Prescott will take place on the same day when the real sea-serpent is captured," she said.[20]

In October 1880, John reluctantly returned to Arizona for the winter legislative session, again leaving Jessie to manage their affairs in New York. The opposition continued its attacks, but John scarcely seemed to care. When the legislature adjourned in March, he abruptly moved with Lily to Tucson. As soon as Lily was settled at 245 Main Street, he headed east again, ostensibly to obtain weapons for local militia to use in fighting the Apaches but in reality to promote his own ventures.

Over the summer of 1881, the Frémonts' plans fluctuated. For a while John talked of settling the family on a ranch near Tucson, with Charley and Frank to help him run it. Earlier they had pulled strings to get twenty-three-year-old Frank an army commission, and he was now at Fort Missoula, Montana. Charley, who married just before the rest of the family left for Prescott, was a naval officer stationed in New York. Jessie longed for the whole family to be together. "It is two years since we have been 'living in trunks.' "[21]

But their plans continued to go awry. John's poor business reputation doubtless deterred investors. "The Eastern capitalist remembers John Charles's magnificent Mariposa & Memphis & El Paso projects," remarked one cynical Arizonan, "and he has not forgotten what miserable fiascos they were."[22] Gradually, John and Jessie talked less of mines and ranches and more of the railroad as the great venture that would restore their fortune. But it too would fizzle.

By now the new Chester Arthur administration was under pressure to force John's resignation. He was like "a hen on a hot griddle," an opponent complained, "popping from Arizona to New York and Washington . . . in a bewildering manner."[23]

Arizona Secretary of State Gosper flatly demanded that he either return or resign.

On October 11, 1881, John bowed to the pressure and tendered his resignation. Lily soon returned east, settling with Jessie in rural Suffern in Rockland County, New York. "Both Mother & Father have been a little under the weather, both literally & from the long strain they have been under," she confided to Nelly a month later.

The Frémonts' Arizona sojourn was a desperate and tawdry episode that left them no better off than before. Seeing no alternative, John would continue to peddle his mining schemes among New York investors, still hoping for a change in fortune. Jessie tried to maintain an outward cheer. Writing to Nelly that month she spoke of her hopes for renting "a pretty flat in town" next year, when one of their ventures paid off. Meanwhile, "each move in the General's work goes forward as he planned it." By the following winter "our 'harvest' will be in."[24]

Despite her words, Jessie doubtless sensed their waning hopes, for quietly and steadily she was pursuing her own writing as well. For the next decade it would be their most reliable source of income.

28

*I have always regarded it as a
better ambition to be a true woman
than to become a successful writer.*

Lucy Larcom
A New England Girlhood
1889

FIRESIDE HISTORY

I AM WRITING so quietly since we are alone here—when my mind is a little more assured I will write *well*," Jessie reported earnestly to Nelly in April 1882. But like many women, she found it hard to give her work priority: family duties—the needs of John, Lily, or Charley and his family living nearby at Sing Sing—inevitably came first. "It's a luxury to be alone," she sighed.[1]

Jessie was working on a series of reminiscences for *Wide Awake*, a popular children's magazine whose name, derived from a prewar Republican antislavery group, gave it a subtle political cast she no doubt found congenial. *Wide Awake* was a spritely, determinedly uplifting amalgam of fiction, biography, essays, and poetry. Its contributors, predominantly women, included Sarah Orne Jewett, Harriet Beecher Stowe, and Helen Hunt Jackson, as well as occasional male authors like John Greenleaf Whittier and Edward Everett Hale. Its most successful series was the much loved *Five Little Peppers and How They Grew*.

Jessie had always told stories and reminiscences to her own children and later to Nelly's three boys as well, and she found it easy to transmute her tales into manuscript. Moreover, for a woman still leery of overstepping her boundaries, such stories seemed appropriately domestic. "As soon as the illustrations are ready something I have written will be published in *Wide Awake*," she announced to Nelly in August 1882. But in the margin she cautioned Nelly not to spread her news: "This for yourself," she warned.[2]

Though Jessie would publish more than fifty stories and articles and three books in the next decade, she would consistently downplay her writing to her family and rarely mention it to friends. Uneasy about the propriety of working for pay and painfully conscious of John's sensitivity and pride, she did not want it widely known that she was becoming the family breadwinner.

By early 1883, Jessie was working steadily on a series of reminiscences for *Wide Awake*—"memoirs in aid of future histories," as she described them. History itself was "too large for me," she explained. Instead she called her sketches "fireside" history—personal reminiscences about presidents and congressmen, diplomats and socialites, that commented only indirectly on the issues of the time. Jessie admitted that her stories were deliberately " 'harmless'—a nursery pudding without hurtful ingredients of complete facts."[3] Nonetheless, in the background, shining faintly in the indirect light, were the two heroes of her life—Benton and Frémont. If her message was unstated, readers nonetheless caught the gleam.

When *Souvenirs of My Time*, a collection of her *Wide Awake* sketches, was published as a book in 1887, it was well received. *The Nation* called it "an unfailing source of entertainment. . . . Mrs. Frémont has the art of brief narration, apparently as a gift of nature." *Souvenirs* is preeminently "a woman's book," its critic stated approvingly. "The womanly element pervades it ." *The Atlantic* was similarly enthusiastic. "The whole book is so bright and winning, and displays such good taste and wise reserve, that we heartily wish Mrs. Frémont might be persuaded to write in earnest the full *memoires* of her life."[4]

Over the next decade, Jessie continued to produce the "harmless puddings" she knew would both sell and preserve her womanly aura. She churned out a steady stream of historical sketches, juvenile fiction, and fairy tales, most of which were first published in *Wide Awake*. But she was reluctant to experiment or express her real feelings directly. Though she obtained immense satisfaction from her work—from the craft itself and from the sense of power and control she felt in earning money—she deliberately limited her scope to non-controversial writing that she knew would pay. Whether she had novels in her—or poetry—she would never know.

While Jessie wrote steadily for *Wide Awake*, Lily puttered about the garden and orchard, and tended the chickens and cow. Following an old pattern, John moved in and out of their lives. Still hoping to peddle his business schemes, he spent much of his time in New York City, retreating to Suffern on Sundays for rest and encouragement.

Seventy years old in 1883, John was a beaten man. His dreams of restored fortune and fame had collapsed. He could no longer steadily support his family. Ashamed and humiliated, he retreated even more into himself. Though he depended on Jessie's love and comfort, he must have found it hard at times to face this strong, energetic, resourceful woman, who seemed to believe in him more than he did in himself.

As for Jessie, though she once hoped for steady intimacy in their marriage, she now accepted, perhaps even needed, a certain distance. Her love had become a curious mixture of adoration and pity. While her heart went out to the shattered man, she still clung to the hero inside. Such devotion was a strain for them both, and at times she too had to escape. John's persistent absences may have relieved her as well.

Yet she remained deeply vulnerable to this sad, aloof, tarnished man. Writing to Sandy Morton after John returned from Arizona, she compared herself to a bittersweet country chrysanthemum. "It is a good brave enduring plant and blooms on after drought and frost have each done their worst—and a very little sunshine uncurls its innermost petals, and out shines the heart with ever so little encouragement."[5]

By the summer of 1883, John and Jessie were temporarily together again in a furnished apartment at 218 West Fifty-ninth Street, in a German neighborhood overlooking New York's Central Park. Poignantly, for they had no furniture themselves now, Jessie discovered an old sofa she had owned in Pocaho years among the furnishings. When the landlady told her she could buy it back when she was able, she took it as "a good omen that small as well as great things were being restored to us."[6]

To Jessie, her family and a narrowing circle of loyal friends had become central: "the rest . . . a play on which one looks without interfering." That year twenty-eight-year-old Frank, back on a brief leave from army duty in Montana, married Carrie Townsend, the daughter of longtime family friends. Jessie, approving, called it "a thoroughly good congenial marriage." Generously maternal, she liked her daughters-in-law and adored her grandchildren.[7]

That summer an old friend who had once been as close to Jessie as her own family stepped briefly into her life again. In late July, Lizzie Blair Lee, visiting in New York, unexpectedly came to see her. Lizzie's visit may have been prompted by an unsettling report she heard from a mutual friend who had called on Jessie and found her looking "hungry—they are so poor." The friend added that "Jessie's infatuation about Frémont, his power over her," was still in full force.

A number of Jessie's old friends were disturbed about the Frémont marriage. Lizzie herself had long since dismissed John as morally shabby and financially irresponsible, and she was dismayed by Jessie's blindness to his faults. Jessie's sister, Liz, agreeing, called her devotion "Jessie's insanity." She and Lizzie could not understand how Jessie could allow John to "gamble away his own & her children's bread over & over again . . . and he too faithless even to pretend to live with her." To them both, Jessie's loyalty seemed humiliating and excessive. "She belongs to him body & soul," Lizzie said, "& he does with [her] as he pleases as much as he does with his own right hand."[8]

When Lizzie called on Jessie that July, the two women, once so intimate, seem to have skirted around such dangerous topics. Seeing Lizzie again, Jessie was overwhelmed by memories of a happier, more hopeful time. Too proud to admit her present problems, she prattled on about her children and grandchildren, keeping up a gallant facade. Writing afterward to thank Lizzie for her visit, she came close to revealing her despair. Recalling Lizzie's tender concern when five-month-old Anne died at Silver Spring many years before, she wrote bitterly, "I knew it, dimly, then—I know it surely now, that for the death of a baby girl there should be no sorrow for life is hard on women."

Jessie ended her letter to Lizzie with a promise to visit whenever she was near, to "tell you better than a letter can . . . that I am always your old friend."[9] But far too much lay mutely between the two women for their friendship to bloom again. Jessie had cast her lot with John long before, an act of will she would never repent. She knew the inner man, shy and insecure, as Lizzie and others could not. Moreover, she had wrapped her own identity so tightly around the heroic image she helped him create, that though it might be shattered in others' eyes, in hers it would always remain intact.

It was a difficult time for Jessie as she floundered between resignation and a natural activism that surged repeatedly. For the first few years after their return from Arizona, the Frémonts had remained outwardly hopeful. But by the time of Lizzie's visit, their situation was bleak. Though Jessie's writing continued to bring a modest return, it was never enough to repay their mounting debts. Meanwhile, John's ventures continued to fail.

By now they were willing to pursue every path. They promoted a tenuous claim to Alcatraz Island in San Francisco Bay and continued a long-standing campaign to win compensation from the government for its seizure of Black Point during the Civil War. In the spring of 1884 they traveled to Washington to push a bill that would give John a military pension for his services as an explorer and Civil War general. Though Jessie did not hesitate to enlist old friends in her cause, the bill remained locked in congressional committees and no vote was taken. There were some who still despised John Frémont, and others who were simply indifferent.

Toward the end of 1883, to save money, the Frémonts moved to a furnished house at New Brighton on Staten Island.

Though Jessie praised the sea views, it was an anxious household, as their schemes and hopes continued to collapse. When Charley left on a three-year cruise in August 1884, Jessie fell seriously ill. Her disease, she informed Nelly, was rheumatism "on top of nervous prostration—my useful right hand swollen & warped out of shape and service—my knees so stiff I got up and down stairs on all fours." Cod liver oil and "electrical medical treatment" administered by Dr. Morton were apparently effective. By January she could write again "with queer handling of the pen" and was regularly walking two miles a day. But she feared poverty, illness, death. "I thought my use was ended," she confided to Nelly.[10]

In December 1884, in the midst of their worries, the Frémonts were interviewed at their Staten Island home by a twenty-nine-year-old Harvard philosophy instructor named Josiah Royce, who had been asked to write a history of California for Houghton Mifflin's American Commonwealth series.

Royce was a brilliant, ambitious, homely little man with a pudgy, child's face. By what he called "odd fortune," he had been born in California. His parents had journeyed west by covered wagon in 1849, "guided," his mother recorded, "only by the light of Frémont's *Travels*."[11] The trek had been a grueling ordeal, but life in California proved as hard. Royce's father, eccentric and ineffectual, failed at one job after another. His deeply religious mother, appalled by the crudity of the mining towns, taught her precocious son at home.

When Royce—redheaded, freckled, priggish, and unaccustomed to boys' games—entered school at eleven, he was tormented by his schoolmates. Eventually he became a teacher at the new college at Berkeley, but when Harvard called, Royce gladly abandoned his native state. "He had never got used to the sunshine," philosopher George Santayana observed, "he had never tasted peace."[12] Royce would eventually become a pillar of the Harvard philosophy department, but at the time he interviewed the Frémonts, he was merely an instructor, poorly paid and immensely insecure.

Royce had spent the previous summer in San Francisco, browsing among historian Hubert Howe Bancroft's magnificent collection of Californiana and talking with his librarian and ghost-writer, Henry Lebbeus Oak. For Royce's own family, the California promise had been fraudulent. The gold rush of his childhood was far different from the one romanticized by writers like Bret Harte, who glossed over the violence, squalor, and despair. Now Royce began to suspect that much of what passed for California history was equally false. As he investigated what he came to call the "Myth of the Conquest," he discovered that while Frémont accepted the accolade "Conqueror of California," he was always vague, evasive even, about his actual role. Royce was determined to find out the truth. The Frémonts, naive and unsuspecting, would be no match.

Royce found the Frémonts cordial. John was "well-preserved, a pleasing old gentleman, quiet, cool, self-possessed, patient [but] not too communicative." Jessie—"very enthusiastic, garrulous, naïvely boastful"—was less appealing.

Jessie began by speaking grandly of "the great policy of my Father," but Royce quickly zeroed in on the specifics of the Gillespie mission and Frémont's role in the Bear Flag episode.[13] Part of the "Myth of the Conquest," as Royce saw it, was that Frémont had acted under secret orders from the government. But among Bancroft's papers Royce had seen a document that contradicted this claim: the original government instructions from Polk and Buchanan that Archibald Gillespie had carried to both American Consul Thomas Larkin and John forty years before. These instructions urged Larkin peacefully to encourage the Mexican Californians to join the Union and to use "the greatest vigilance" in preventing any English takeover. They clearly did not order a revolt.

In response to Royce's probing, John admitted he "took a risk" in joining the Bear Flaggers, knowing his government might "disavow" him. But to Royce, looking for an Achilles' heel, John's most stunning admission was that he knew nothing about Larkin's secret instructions. Jessie seconded her husband. "Absurd! Impossible!" she exclaimed. The government would never have entrusted the ignorant, tactless Larkin with such a mission. Royce, with a copy of Larkin's instructions in his pocket, could hardly express his glee. He had cornered the Frémonts. It was, he confessed later, "one of the keenest delights of my life."[14]

After the interview Royce wrote up his notes and sent them to Jessie for correction. Clearly, she had become the family spokesperson, the apologist. Royce continued to find her attitude irritating. She had "a curious loftiness of mind" that allowed her to ignore the contradictions and confusions in her husband's testimony. Committed to his heroic image, she was "grandly elevated above the level of the historical." To her the government's view could be summarized in a single sentence: "since England intends to take California, we must see that she does not." Scribbling on the margin of Royce's notes, she also repeated, in circuitous language, the theme of a secret code. The letters from her father that Gillespie carried to John "were in a manner in family cipher," she explained, "so full were they of prearranged reference to talks & agreements known only at home." These letters, John himself told Royce, were much stronger and fuller than the dispatch—"stronger and fuller to the one point of taking and holding possession of California in the event of any occurrence that would justify it."[15]

That was the crucial point. Did the situation in California justify John's course? With historical hindsight, his impulsive plunge into action suggested a man too eager to be a hero. Larkin's persuasive diplomacy seemed the wiser course. But for Josiah Royce such a conclusion was not enough.

In August 1885, Royce paid one more visit to the Frémonts. Again they were hospitable: John dignified and charming, "the good Jessie . . . calm and sunny and benevolent in her easy chair." But to Royce their story seemed hopelessly muddled. John still maintained that Larkin's mission was a mystery to him and that his own instructions, given orally by Gillespie and reinforced by Benton's letter, were far stronger.

Royce refused to see it as a lapse in memory about Larkin's part and a difference in judgment about whether force had been necessary at the time. To him, John was lying, "unmistakably, unmitigatedly, hopelessly."[16]

Royce's *California*, published the following year, covered the state's history from the conquest to 1856, but its focus was the Bear Flag episode and its target John Charles Frémont. To Royce, the Bear Flag action was a "sinful undertaking" by lawless men who prevented what otherwise would have been a peaceful transfer of the province to the United States and began a pattern of abuse toward Mexican-Californians. Moreover, Frémont acted in direct contradiction to government orders because he preferred "personal glory to obedience." Afterward he allowed the nation to treat him as a hero, when in reality he was merely a disobedient officer. "And so a reputation was made whose only foundation was a culpable blunder and a perversion of history."[17]

Royce's historical detective work was brilliant, but his concern with John was curiously obsessive. To Royce and his family, the promise of California was a lie and Frémont a fraud. This was the psychological core of his indictment. In *California*, Royce struck back at the grim experiences of his own California childhood.

While the Frémonts struggled against poverty and to defend their past, the equally penniless Ulysses S. Grant, who had also lost his money in dubious postwar business ventures, was writing his memoirs. Published in two volumes in the summer of 1885, just as Grant died of throat cancer, his work, sensitive and reflective, became a national best-seller. Grant's bereaved family reaped nearly half a million dollars.

As the Frémonts monitored the astounding success of Grant's memoirs, a new source of wealth suddenly seemed within reach. Jessie had long urged John to write his memoirs, and sporadically in the mid-1850s, he had begun. Now, with the Grant example glittering before them, they began to ponder the idea again.

In May 1885, the Frémonts moved again, this time to a furnished brownstone at 130 East Sixty-fourth Street, a "philistine" place, Jessie admitted, with tasteless paintings—"child & flowers . . . child asleep against dog"—but nonetheless comfortable enough.[18] Sitting at her desk before the bay window of her bedroom, she continued to write her harmless children's stories. But Royce's assertions—and Grant's success—preyed on her mind.

Jessie was now sixty-one years old. Her strong, heavy features more and more resembled her father's. And the drive, the ambition, the gnawing energy were still there. She remained deeply angry at the injustices to John. "As yet not one public expression of notice or thanks has been given to the General—not even a vote of thanks from Congress," she remarked bitterly.[19] In her own writings she reined her desire to vaunt him, but she dreamed of producing a book that would make him a hero again. More than fortune, she wanted to restore his name, his image, the one she had glimpsed at sixteen and never let go.

During the next year the book—"the dear book that secures fame and brings fortune"—would become the focus of their lives. It was Jessie who planned this "labor of love." In a long, rambling memorandum to an acquaintance familiar with publishing, she outlined its sweeping theme: "the part had by my Father and Mr. Frémont in shaping and carrying forward the growth of the West." Eventually a publisher, Belford, Clarke & Company of Chicago and New York, emerged, offering what Jessie called a "most liberal" contract. "It will be a most beautiful book," she wrote enthusiastically. "The publishers mean it to be, they say, '*the* American book of the 19th Century.' Paper, size, type, illustrations—all will be of the best order."[20]

By the late spring of 1886, John, Jessie, and Lily were living in Washington, D.C., where they could consult government archives. Their advance was sizable enough to allow them to rent a charming small house at 1310 Nineteenth Street, overlooking the grounds of the British Embassy. "By taking it for a year we get it much lower and it gives us time to get in our money," Jessie wrote optimistically, "and at our leisure look up one to buy. For this is our place." Their Washington reception had been heartening. Southern relatives in the capital were surprisingly cordial, and President Grover Cleveland, though a Democrat, was gracious, "sending . . . personal messages, invitation to his receiving of the Diplomatic Corps, then again the Army & Navy. . . . Everyone shows a consideration and respect, which is most comforting and gratifying."[21]

Despite such social blandishments, the Frémonts quickly settled into a disciplined routine. As in the past, John talked out his story, and Jessie wrote down his words. "We are all up early," Lily described their day, "teas & coffees over by 8–½ at the latest; then Father & Mother go at their work & no interruption is allowed till our noon breakfast comes, after which they rest till half past one when they go at it again till five—but very often till Mary goes up & forces them into coming down to the cooling soup."[22]

There was a poignant glow—a genuine happiness—in the Frémont family during this hopeful time. For Jessie, working with John in their second-story study, it must have seemed like the long-ago "happy winter," when together they wrote the report that made him famous. "I think it has been a pull to work so steadily through all the summer," she confessed to a friend, "but it's worth suffering for. I am in love with the book."[23]

Lily too seemed more alive. It was her job to check data at government offices and the Library of Congress ("where all the librarians know me now & help me hunt up references") and to make a final clean copy for the printer from Jessie's scribbled drafts. At first Lily wrote in longhand, but the work was so tedious that she daringly decided to learn to type. "Father is charmed," she reported happily after she had mastered the strange new machine, "as it makes his work of revision so much easier."[24]

On her own, Jessie was also working on her "first venture

of serious writing," a long biographical essay about her father to be included in the memoir. "He seems very present to me these days as we talk of him and write of him, here where we were all together," she wrote to her father's old colleague, former navy secretary George Bancroft.[25] In her essay, she would deftly solder the bond between father and husband that had been so fragile in real life.

Memoirs of My Life . . . A Retrospect of Fifty Years was published in early 1887. A bulky six-hundred-fifty-page affair, it covered John's life only through the conquest of California. The court-martial, the 1856 presidential campaign, and the Civil War were left for a promised second volume. Josiah Royce, hinting at Jessie's participation, recognized "a noble literary touch" in the account of the early Washington years. But for the most part the book was long, tedious, and unrevealing. More than half was taken almost word for word from the previously published first and second reports. John's childhood memories were skimpy, while Royce rightly called the Frémonts' explanation of John's part in the conquest "disappointingly unenlightening."[26] Though John and Jessie had made an effort to get information from the aging George Bancroft, the result was still vague and unsatisfactory. Offered at prices ranging from $5.75 to $12.50 according to the quality of the binding, and largely ignored by the press, the book did not sell. Few Americans were interested in the rewarmed adventures of a tarnished hero. There would be no second volume.

29

I begin to think there can never come much happiness to me from loving: I have always had so much pain mingled with it. I wish I could make a world outside it, as men do.

George Eliot
Daniel Deronda
1876

"CALIFORNIA, OF COURSE"

IN THE EUPHORIA of writing the book that would restore fame and fortune, Jessie had hoped to settle permanently in Washington. But by June of 1887, when their lease expired, Washington was a luxury they could no longer afford. They retreated to a modest cottage at Point Pleasant on the New Jersey coast, where Jessie gamely wrote Nelly of the fragrant pine and sea air, and the fine strawberries and potatoes she found in the local market.

Despite her determined cheerfulness to Nelly, it was a despondent household. Lily puttered about the little cottage, Jessie resumed her *Wide Awake* work, and John, traveling frequently to New York, peddled his tired business schemes. In turns they were all sick. Jessie, feverish for weeks in the late spring, only gradually recovered over the long, warm summer. In the fall Lily developed a steady hacking cough. By Thanksgiving John had severe bronchitis.

John was on the verge of pneumonia, and their physician advised a warm climate. Jessie had often dreamed of wintering in California—when they had money again—but with the eastern winter closing in, she did not feel they could wait. As added inducement, their old Arizona friend, Charles Silent, was now living in Los Angeles and involved in a real estate venture that John could join. Although John protested that he could not immediately leave his New York business, Jessie, deeply alarmed by his persistent cough and fever, brushed aside his objections and hurried into New York to make what arrangements she could. They had no ready cash for tickets, and she knew she would have to beg.

She went to see an old acquaintance, Collis P. Huntington, the shrewd, energetic Connecticut peddler who had been with her on the *Crescent City* to Panama in 1849 and now ran the Central and Southern Pacific railroads. Swallowing her fierce pride, she told him of John's frightening illness and his need for a warm climate. Huntington was known as a tough man who guarded his money, but he reacted unhesitantly. He promised to take care of everything. "You should have my private car," he apologized, "but it is lent." The next day he came to the house where Jessie was staying, bearing tickets, letters for officials along the route, and a generous amount of money for expenses.

Triumphant, Jessie hurried back to their chilly seaside cottage. But when she told John what she had done, he was humiliated and angry. Ignoring his cold fury, she swept them all up—John, Lily, and their old servant, Mary—and off to California. They planned to stay only through the winter.

Scribbling a hurried note to Nelly as they left for New Orleans and Los Angeles, Jessie was jubilant. "*I!* have been the active one, getting the tickets! Seeing business people and making all ready. I . . . had not a leisure breath so it is only this written goodbye. . . . Write to us sometimes, just Los Angeles, California."

John remained grimly taciturn until their train reached Kentucky and sunshine. "Towards evening," Jessie remembered, "he beckoned me across to his section, and holding my hand said, 'You were right to come. I feel better already.' Whereupon I cried heartily."[1]

"The General says he is '*perfectly*' well," Jessie wrote cheerfully to a young California friend several months later. "He is *serene* and sleeps and eats in his wholesome natural way." To Collis Huntington she also reported his improved health. "I was very unhappy when I saw you last—that is all changed now."[2]

The Frémonts had arrived in Los Angeles on a balmy

Christmas Eve and soon settled at the Marlborough, a residential hotel, for the season. They found the weather "delicious," and by February, Jessie, sixty-three, and John, seventy-five, were feeling so well they were walking three to five miles a day. "The sea is near," Jessie wrote to an eastern friend, "and various lines of railway take us quickly out of town and into the most lovely green hills and blossoming orchards of apricot and peach as well as orange."[3]

The Frémonts found themselves far more celebrated in California than in the East. Not only were John's financial failures scarcely known, but most Californians, unlike the waspish Josiah Royce, were eager to mythologize their past, and there were tenuous moments of glory for the aging "Conqueror of California."

In May the Frémonts traveled north to the Santa Cruz Mountains, where a grove of towering redwood trees was dedicated as the "General Frémont Grove." A photograph marking the occasion shows the family posing by one of the giant trees: John, leaning against it, hat in hand, his eyes wary; Jessie, alert and smiling close beside him; Lily, standing four feet away, heavy, patient, and staid.

In Los Angeles John was asked to give the opening address at the annual Flower Festival, whose proceeds financed a home for working women. "When the old explorer and Indian fighter . . . feebly stepped forward," reported the Los Angeles *Times*, "the cheers that arose from the vast audience fairly made the building tremble. It was a glorious tribute to the old General, and he felt it." But when John tried to speak, his throat was sore, his voice weak, and the audience restless before he finished. Still those in front heard him recall the hardships of his first winter trek over the Sierra and his descent into springtime California. And they heard him say he planned to make the state his home "to the end of his days."[4]

During those first hopeful months, even their financial problems seemed solvable. The Frémonts arrived in Los Angeles at the crest of a great real estate boom. The population, eleven thousand in 1880, would reach fifty thousand by 1890.

Thousands of easterners, suffering from chronic ailments or wanderlust, had been lured to southern California by cheap railway fares and the promise of a benign climate. Between 1886 and 1888, when the Frémonts arrived, fifty new towns had been laid out near Los Angeles by eager developers. John, still dabbling in dreams, was soon writing an eastern associate to arrange for a colony of Belgians to settle on southern California land. The property he had in mind "could be cut up and resold for four or five times as much as we now give for it, and this within a year," he predicted with his usual optimism.[5]

Through Charles Silent, who unlike John had made money in Arizona mines and was now a wealthy Los Angeles entrepreneur, the Frémonts became involved in the development of the new town of Inglewood on the southwest outskirts of Los Angeles. When Inglewood's promoters, in exchange for the Frémonts' help in selling lots, proposed to build them a modern Eastlake-style house in the raw little town, where residential lots were selling for two to five hundred dollars each, they eagerly accepted.

By the summer of 1888, the boom had collapsed. There were far more towns and homesites than potential buyers. Though Inglewood's developers hoped the Frémont name would be a lure, the little town at its peak attracted only three hundred people. Its fancy new hotel, its planned College of Applied Sciences, and its five real estate offices all closed. The failing developers even tried to take the Frémonts' house from them, and it was probably Charles Silent who stopped them. John and Jessie pronounced the town too "remote and lonesome" to live in, but they did acquire a small income by renting their new house.[6]

By fall, John decided to return east to promote his business ventures and again appeal to Congress for a pension. Perhaps he was restless as well, anxious to escape the vigor and energy of his formidable wife. Or perhaps, as he and Jessie told each other, he was only reluctantly doing what he felt necessary to earn money for the family. Promising to return in a few months, he left Jessie and Lily to pursue their own lives.

"We are in bliss here," Jessie wrote to Nelly from Los Angeles the following spring. She and Lily had rented "a dot of a cottage but charmingly planned and furnished . . . set apart in what was an orchard of pear, apple and orange trees all in bloom. . . . The strong sea wind sweeps up over a dozen miles of grain and clover and really the result is enchanting." From their cottage they could see elegant tree-lined Adams Street with its long row of villas, and St. James Park, "carved out of an orange orchard and bounded by old pepper & eucalyptus trees in double lines." And everywhere, Jessie wrote enthusiastically, there were "fine cement sidewalks."[7]

Amid such suburban pleasures, she was writing steadily and well. Inspired by her return to California, she was working on a series for *Wide Awake* about her experiences at Bear Valley. Her style was natural and unaffected, with none of the sentimentality that marred her Eastern- and European-inspired reminiscences. The result, published first in *Wide Awake* and then by D. Lothrop as *Far West Sketches* in 1890, was one of her most attractive books.

Despite her satisfaction with her work, Jessie was lonely. John had remained in New York through the winter, and she missed him as well as her children and grandchildren in the East. Her "transplanting" to California, she admitted, caused her a "hard bout of home-sickness" that year.

By April she was eagerly awaiting John's return. "His stay in New York was far longer than we thought for but it is not to be regretted," she wrote Nelly. "And the winter there was marvelous. So he is well, as well as contented." A month later, he still had not come. "We look all the time now for the General," she told Nelly. John returned to Los Angeles that summer, but his stay was brief. In the fall of 1889 he returned to New York and Washington, where he had renewed hopes of receiving a military pension from a more hospitable Congress.

Jessie was gradually making a life for herself, and at times the bitterness of the past seemed to slip away. "Here on this far shore where the serene climate gentles even hard memories I seem to look back into another life—its strifes ended—only its results in good cherished," she said. "We have many pleasant friends, and take our part in some of the good works of the town. . . . And I write."

She was in fine health: "Rheumatism and bronchitis have become plagues of the past."[8] Her widening circle of friends included the young artist John Gutzon Borglum, whom she met when he painted a portrait of John. Impressed by his work, she provided him with a barrage of encouragement and frank advice, as well as useful introductions to potential patrons like Leland Stanford and H. M. De Young. But her closest friend was Caroline Severance, a national leader in the women's rights movement.

Over the next years, these two strong, active women would see each other almost daily. Their lively, warm friendship reflected how much Jessie had changed since her retreat to Pocaho, when she refused to sign a petition for women's suffrage. Poverty and the necessity of earning a living had altered her views. Severance pronounced her "brilliant, spontaneous, and original."[9]

Four years older, Severance herself was a woman of immense energy and idealism. Since the 1850s in Boston she had been an abolitionist and a suffragist, writing, speaking, and organizing for both causes. In 1875 when she and her husband moved to Los Angeles because of his incipient tuberculosis, she continued to work for suffrage and launched a successful movement to make kindergartens a regular part of the public school system. Jessie was soon involved in her projects. When the regal and witty Julia Ward Howe came to Los Angeles to lecture on women's issues, it was at Jessie's house, "dressed with flowers," that she spoke.[10]

Jessie was also writing prodigiously—several tales set in France or Nassau, stories like "The Deck Hand" with its bitter condemnation of slavery—another Kit Carson piece—many of which would be collected in *The Will and the Way Stories*, published in 1891 by D. Lothrop. In one unusual *Wide Awake* piece, "Play and Work," Jessie revealed her changing views on women and work. Perhaps influenced by Caroline Severance's growing interest in socialism, she described a suddenly impoverished New York woman who started a successful jam and preserves business, run as a women's cooperative with profit-sharing among her female employees. Even after the woman earned enough to retire, she continued to work simply because she liked it. Although Jessie had always been reluctant to admit she enjoyed her work and the money it brought, she was now able, at least vicariously, to exult in the process.

In March 1890, John telegraphed the glad news that his pension bill had at last passed the House, granting him a major general's retirement income of nearly six thousand dollars a year for life. "You will have seen the honoring vote of the House," Jessie wrote joyously to Nelly, "150 *for*, to 7. . . . It was a delightful gratifying triumph. The Senate vote is *sure* and will be soon."[11]

But even after the Senate confirmed their pension, John stayed on in the East, working on an account of the California conquest requested by *Century* magazine. At the same time, he was trying to gain a commission by arranging for the sale of some California property to English investors. He was still short of funds. Pressed by an old friend who had loaned him money, John was forced to explain that the first installment of his new pension had been "promptly swallowed up by the long dearth."[12]

Jessie missed John steadily. Writing in early July, she thanked him for a recent telegram with its "comforting promise" of imminent good news from the English investors. "It is so slow this writing," she sighed. " 'If' I could I would telegraph all the time. But then we could be together so there would be no need for telegrams."[13]

But John's hopeful message was premature. In his regular letters to Jessie, he recorded the disheartening lack of progress in his English transaction. "If the Guiseppi fails," he concluded glumly on July 11, referring to yet another dangling venture, "I have no confidence in anybody here. My love to home. Frémont."[14]

Perhaps not wanting to alarm her, John did not mention that he was sick. Three days before, on a hot Tuesday, he had felt dizzy and exhausted. By Friday, when he wrote to Jessie, he was seriously ill. The Frémonts' longtime family physician, Sandy Morton, was alarmed at his condition, and the next day, though John protested, he notified Charley at his home in Sing Sing. When Charley reached his father's Twenty-Fifth Street boardinghouse late that afternoon, John was feverish and in pain, and his pulse was dangerously weak. Dr. Morton had diagnosed his condition as peritonitis, inflammation of the bowels, probably from eating contaminated food.

Early Sunday morning John began to vomit. The disease seemed suddenly to overwhelm him. Fearing the worst, Charley sent a telegram to warn Jessie. "The three hours previous to the end he was completely out of his head," Charley wrote Lily afterward, "and he was insensible for the last half hour. The end came painlessly, and without knowledge to him. It was blessedly quick and easy."

Before he lapsed into unconsciousness, John murmured something about going home. "Home?" Morton asked. "What do you call home?"

"California, of course."

Writing that day to Lily, Charley confessed that he felt no regret at his death. The last years of his father's life had been painful, burdened by failures and humiliations, and a futile struggle for money. "As I looked at him lying there so still and peaceful I questioned whether it was not heartless, for I could find no sorrow or pity for him at all—but a feeling of relief that his life was over. . . . Of what the effect is going to be on mother, I don't dare think," he added. "And when I do think—I doubt whether the cruellest result would not be the kindest. They lived in each other so that I don't think there is any life for the one left."[15]

Jessie received the first warning telegram that same Sunday. "Father is seriously ill. Charley."

At once Lily hurried down to the telegraph office to try to find out more. While she was gone, a second telegram reached the house. "Like a bolt from a clear sky the blow fell, Jessie said afterward. "It seemed to fairly shrivel up my arm." Tearing it open she read the fatal message: "Father is dead."[16]

Jessie was completely unprepared for the shock. For the first thirty-six hours she was so stunned that the doctor Lily hastily summoned feared paralysis. Finally, she managed to send a telegram to Charley, asking that he put her miniature portrait, which John still kept with him, and a telegraphed message in the casket. "I folded up the telegram and wrapped it and the miniature in the ribbons which were tied to it," Charley replied. "And I want to tell you that he looked peaceful and so quiet."

The ceremony had been simple, he wrote, "for he was not a man of parade and display." Charley had turned down any "grand army and society offers. They could not get up a *fitting* funeral of that kind; any other would be a mockery," he remarked. "I am hoping the Los Angeles papers have told you of it all—only the simple church service . . . and a few of us took him to where I had to leave him—the Trinity Receiving Vault at 135th St." His body would remain there until Jessie decided where he should be buried.[17]

For more than a week after John's death, Jessie continued to receive his letters. "Of the sadness . . . I cannot tell," she said later. "It has been so hard, & yet so dear to receive my Father's letters right along," Lily wrote her cousin, Carey Jones. "The last we had were dated Friday 11 & in them there was not the least intimation or sign of coming illness—just his regular daily letter home with its cheering love permeating all the necessary business matters."

After the first stunned days, Jessie threw herself into a

frenzy of activity. She seized on the idea that she must finish John's article for the *Century*, and she wrote Sandy Morton to forward it to her. Lily recognized her artificial condition: "Mother is better," she wrote Carey Jones three weeks after John's death, "but it is still a surface better."

All during August, Jessie struggled to finish the *Century* article by the September 1 deadline. Still unable to face John's death directly, she made the article an obsession. Originally, John had been asked to write an account of his part in the California conquest, particularly in light of the charges made by Royce, who was serving as an informal adviser on the California series the *Century* was planning. But Jessie, dizzy with grief, lacked all perspective. "It was a very heavy pull on her to do it at this time," Lily wrote Carey Jones, "& there were days when I thought she would not be able to go through with it."[18]

Jessie barely managed to finish her work by the deadline. Then she collapsed. The anguish she tried to ignore overwhelmed her. During most of September she was gravely ill—"a blur of bodily and mental suffering." For nearly two months she was too weak to walk upstairs.[19]

At the same time, a torrent of cares rained down upon her. When John died, his new pension ceased. Charley struggled to unravel his father's affairs, but it was quickly clear there were only debts. As a solution, he urged Jessie and Lily to return east to live with him.

Jessie was forced to borrow money from Los Angeles friends to meet immediate expenses and the word leaked out. "Frémont's Family Destitute," headlined the San Francisco *Call*; "Mrs. Frémont's Poverty," reported the *New York Times*. When several groups began to solicit contributions for her support, Charley and Frank indignantly announced that they could provide for their mother. "Neither my brother nor myself would permit her to suffer in that way," Charley told a reporter, "though I am free to confess she is poor." Proudly, Jessie refused to accept any charity.

"If Mrs. Frémont is without a dollar in the house it is a

consuming reproach to the thousands of wealthy people of California," declared an eastern newspaper. "The first intimation of such a condition should have brought prompt and generous relief from the many men who have become many time millionaires, while the founder of California died in abject poverty."[20] The furor reached Congress, and on September 24, it passed a special bill granting Jessie a widow's pension of two thousand dollars a year. At the same time, Caroline Severance developed a tactful plan that would enable Jessie and Lily to stay in Los Angeles as they wished. Severance and a group of women proposed to raise money to buy them a house as a "gift from the women of California and a memorial of our regard for General Frémont." Realizing that if she died and her pension ceased, Lily would have nothing, Jessie accepted. Practical, reasonable Lily understood the necessity. "Everyone is so wonderfully kind," she wrote her cousin, "but oh Carey, isn't it just God's own great mercy that Father was allowed to pass into his eternal rest in quiet peace with no knowledge that all this was about to become necessary for Mother, it would have been such anguish to his dear heart."[21]

A second strain was the growing problem with *Century* magazine, which had returned her manuscript with heavy editorial changes. Jessie was indignant, possibly because by then she had seen yet another of Josiah Royce's merciless attacks in the October *Atlantic*. "I can, and will set out facts so definitely that no error can stand," she wrote Carey Jones. "I have my own opinion of the [*Century*] editors but I intend to *use* them. I had a full day's hard & angry thinking—restoring the General's own words, ideas, and punctuation. . . . only Lily, and you now know what resistance, what persistence, what complete 'fight' this rouses in me."[22]

Even harder for Jessie to bear was the controversy that erupted over John's burial site. A campaign had begun to bring his body to California for burial at Lone Mountain overlooking the Golden Gate. The idea "has taken hold of Mother's heart," Lily said, "& its accomplishment would bring her sustaining strength. . . . We want Father in this state—for every reason—but of course the decision lies in other hands than ours." But when the state legislature was asked to fund the project, a vociferous group opposed it, charging Frémont was a false hero of California. Deeply wounded, unable to face more controversy, Jessie quickly accepted the offer of a gravesite at Rockland Cemetery across the Hudson from Pocaho, "where we shall *all* join him," she emphasized. There he would be "surrounded in death . . . by loving hearts. . . . I would not bring him from such loving memory . . . to be subjected to discussion."[23]

Over the next months, Jessie continued to grieve. Though she was a strong woman, she had channeled her energy and passion into her husband's life. Everything she did, even her writing, was shaped to aid and promote him. At the same time, she had always been deeply vulnerable to him as a man. When he died, she felt empty and purposeless, bereft. Scarcely able to eat or sleep, she lost weight, and her fine oval face, with its high cheekbones and luminous dark eyes, became more striking. "It was," she admitted, "work to keep alive."[24]

30

Whatever the theories may be of woman's dependence on man, in the supreme moments of her life he cannot bear her burdens. In the tragedies and triumphs of human experience, every mortal stands alone.

Elizabeth Cady Stanton
"Solitude of Self"
1892

Jessie Benton Frémont, 1895. Photograph by Charles F. Lummis. *Courtesy of Southwest Museum, Los Angeles.*

AN AFFINITY
FOR "TOMATOES, OLIVES,
AND THE SEA"

THE HEALING CAME SLOWLY. By late October Jessie was going for walks again, "not yet alone for I need Lil's arm, dear good child—a quarter of a mile. And daily I take an hour or two hours sometimes on the cable cars—they glide so smoothly they tire me less than a carriage—and then I am not obliged to speak, or say thank you as I must even to Mrs. Severance, who is the only one I have seen. I get home tired, but wholesomely tired now. At first it was depressing. But there are unexplored depths in us that only solitude of heart can find—a weary exploration but leading nearer to Divine strength."[1]

That fall and winter Caroline Severance and a committee of California women raised eighty-five hundred dollars to purchase a lot and build a home for Jessie and Lily. By early 1891, architect Sumner Hunt was supervising the construction of a two-story redwood house on the corner of Hoover and Twenty-eighth streets. Jessie had requested a modern house, simple and comfortable, without Victorian affectations. "No prettiness—no gingerbread," she declared.[2]

In July 1891, Jessie and Lily moved into their spacious new house set among a grove of thirty-two orange trees. They were delighted with its four bedrooms (to allow room for Charley and Frank and their families), second-floor bath, and screened porches at the front and rear positioned to trap the sun. Caroline Severance was just four blocks away on Adams, and a streetcar line on Hoover, for which they received perpetual passes, connected them with the whole city.

Newspapers described the house and the campaign that had financed it. "Mrs. Senator Hearst and Mrs. C. P. Huntington made donations of $500 each, and several other ladies gave $100 each," reported the *New York Times*. It was charity and it was humiliating, but Caroline Severance helped Jessie believe it was done out of loving concern. "Real, heartfelt sympathy *does* bring healing," Jessie said that year, "and helps to give strength for the inevitable endurance of what seems unendurable."[3]

"We furnished the house ourselves," she reported cheerfully six months later to the artist Borglum, "and the papering I paid for with a check for . . . writing." Her favorite room was the "boudoir-parlor" with its handsome oiled redwood fireplace surrounded by handmade tiles. She had filled the room with books, pictures, china, bronze, Indian baskets—the "wreckage from our old days." Her portrait by Thomas Buchanan Read ("the General especially liked the eyes and mouth," she told Borglum) hung on one wall, while Borglum's own portrait of John hung above her desk. "It is our true shrine. There are violets before it now—we keep flowers there always."[4]

In her memory, John had become the unchanging hero she had always wanted him to be, and she was determined that the world share her vision. Within weeks after his death, laboring over the *Century* article, she had begun to think again of completing his memoirs. This time she planned to tell his story in part from her point of view, using her own lighter reminiscences as "an entering wedge" to draw the reader into the more serious sections in which John's life would be explained and justified. "I think I know the public. And I want it with me. I want it to find me *interesting*. Then, well established, I can say more sharply to facts. . . . Feminine courtesy, and deference are the crutches the public expects a woman to use. I must be firmly on my seat of authority before I drop them."[5]

Jessie began the memoir in April 1891, with the help of

Frank, who arranged leave from the army to come to California with Carrie and their baby for a long visit. That summer, in the new house, they worked rapidly despite Jessie's shaken nerves. "My son is a tireless worker but I have to lie by often," she reported. "Still over half our writing is in the publisher's hands already." The work obsessed and exhausted her. "We had to examine, sift, verify and read up masses of collateral writings and records—to condense without losing a point or becoming diffuse either."[6]

Despite her periodic fatigue, in six months she and Frank produced more than four hundred densely typed pages that included an exhaustive defense of John's role in the California conquest, the court-martial, the Civil War, and the Memphis and El Paso scandal. But despite Jessie's lighter interpolations, it was, like the published first volume, long, detailed, and partisan.

Though Jessie had evidently reached a tentative agreement with a publisher, the second volume would never appear. "The public *hate* a controversy," she herself remarked while working on the memoir. "Nobody cares so much about us as we care for ourselves."[7] But in their eagerness to justify John's career, she and Frank had ignored her words. Nonetheless, in an era of fawning and long-winded memoirs, their failure was an anomaly, indicative most of all of how stained and faded John's reputation had become.

Jessie must have been crushed. "There is a time for each thing," she wrote several years later, trying to understand. "The General's name will grow to mean much more to our people as time clears away interested writers who mystify simple facts for their own ends." Gradually, she accepted the failure. "I do not think the General is forgotten—I have too many and varied proofs of that, but one cannot keep uppermost a long past name. . . . Except indeed to the *one*."[8]

Dredging up the past—the joys as well as the bitterness—had been an ordeal Jessie felt compelled to complete. And though she would not have explained it as such, it served a hidden purpose. Begun in grief to hold him fast, the process had purged and freed her to live again for herself.

Before John died, Jessie had begun to build a life in California. His sudden death and her long adjustment stalled this late California flowering. But gradually over the next years she would reach a genuine contentment.

Part of it was California itself. "I took naturally to tomatoes, olives and the sea," she remarked. She had always said she lacked "the puritan streak," and California's warm Mediterranean atmosphere—a state of mind as well as weather—suited her temperament.[9]

She shared her delight in California with a new friend, Charles Lummis, who, fleeing Harvard and the confining East, had walked southwest to New Mexico and California. In 1894 Lummis founded *Land of Sunshine*, a southern California magazine dedicated to fostering an emerging Anglo-Hispanic culture. Flamboyant and compelling, often dressed as a Spanish caballero, Lummis was Josiah Royce's opposite, a romantic committed to the Frémont legend. He and Jessie felt an immediate affinity of temperament and interest, and he persuaded her to contribute several articles to *Land of Sunshine*. Jessie found Lummis an "unusually quick, brave, comprehending, interesting person." He called her "the most interesting woman I ever met."[10]

By the mid-1890s, Jessie was thriving again. "I am so thankful no longer to feel morbid in any way," she remarked. "I am out a great deal," she described her life in March 1895, when she was seventy. "In this loveliest fresh season it is good to breathe open air all day, if one can. Lil and I are rarely in (except for meals) and always for our good home evenings which she too finds pleasant with books and nice people often until nearly eleven. We are both wonderfully well. . . . I can, and do, walk my daily mile or mile and a half in the morning."[11]

She sat for her bust by her friend Borglum, received tourists who came by to "Kodak" her house and talk about "the

General," and gaily rode the electric cars (which came "every seven minutes," she reported) all over town. She enjoyed long visits from her children and grandchildren, and yearly stays at a Long Beach cottage (off season when the rate was only thirty dollars a month), where she savored the seafood gumbo, fresh fruits, and ocean views from her hammock on the veranda.

She was also a member of the Friday Morning Club, a lively and progressive women's group founded in 1891 by Caroline Severance, who in Boston more than twenty years before had established the first women's club in America. Members of the Friday group, which swelled to two hundred by 1893, spearheaded the first southern California suffrage campaign, and in 1896 welcomed Susan B. Anthony to Los Angeles to speak for a state amendment to give women the vote. (California women would gain the vote in 1911.) The club also supported a cooperative exchange where women could sell their work, secured the appointment of a first woman to the Los Angeles school board, and helped establish a juvenile court. At the same time, in the tolerant, often unconventional Los Angeles atmosphere, members discussed and advocated ideas ranging from dress reform (thirty-five members admitting at one meeting that they no longer wore corsets) to municipal ownership of utilities and international disarmament. Jessie herself presented several talks to the group.

Such activities invigorated her. "Sunday is my seventy-second birthday," she wrote Borglum in May 1896, "and it is not reasonable to be so thoroughly—unconsciously, well as I am, but it is so." Sending a photograph of herself to a friend, she claimed the wrinkles in her face had not yet entered her soul, "though they look in the picture like iron threads."[12]

Despite her vitality, Jessie was a tiny, fragile old woman, increasingly conscious of her mortality. "My machine is again in perfect condition," she said after a brief illness in 1897. "I am wonderfully well. But after seventy it seems like living on reprieves."[13] Her greatest concern was now Lily's future, and her best hope, Black Point.

For thirty years, in lawsuits and private bills in Congress, she and John had tried to get compensation for the government's seizure of their Black Point property during the Civil War. After John's death, Jessie intensified the campaign, explaining the case in an emotional article, "A Home Found and Lost," in *Home Maker* magazine, and enlisting the help of politicians and publicists like Lummis. Occasionally, she could put the situation wryly: "I hope to see Lil provided for and then I shall cease to feel like a trust-fund that must be saved and administered exclusively for the one object of not dying and so stopping my pension."[14] But neither she, Lily, nor their descendants, who would continue the case in the courts for years, would ever be compensated for Black Point.

Reaching her mid-seventies as the century closed, Jessie suffered from occasional bouts of rheumatism and growing deafness. More and more, she began to evoke the privileges of age, refusing to spend time with dull visitors or make tedious social calls to people who bored her. "We are cranks about being to ourselves," she declared. "Mrs. Severance . . . comes often to see me and pities my 'forced seclusion.' I only go out for a daily walk out of the delight of escaping interruptions and wearisome commonplaces!" Writing, too, had become drudgery. "I can't see just why for I am absolutely well," she confessed to Nelly, "but I hate it. And write only to the boys and their families." Yet her vitality continued to bubble, and a month later, despite her professed aversion, she was writing enthusiastically to Vice-President Theodore Roosevelt, "You are an inspiration. I am very—*very* much pleased with you, if you will allow me to say so?—at seventy-six one speaks." Yet as the century ended, though she suffered "fewer troubles to health than the majority," she admitted, "I feel Time heavily enough sometimes."[15]

In June of 1900, Jessie suffered a severe attack of rheumatism, then fell and fractured her hip. "For six weeks I knew nothing but torture." As the pain lessened, she was able to move into a wicker wheelchair during the day. But when she tried to read, "the nerves of the spine had had too serious a wrench and I could not see. Therefore, for months longer, I sat in darkness."[16]

As if in compensation, her mind seemed preternaturally active. In the enforced stillness, her thoughts returned repeatedly to the past she had half-buried during her last years in Los Angeles. Charles Lummis as well as others had long urged her to write her own memoirs, and now, sitting in darkness, she began to plan out whole chapters.

Gradually she regained her sight, but she remained an invalid. "I cannot yet stand alone," she admitted to an acquaintance ten months after her fall. Fifty-eight-year-old Lily, with a trained nurse to assist her, stepped in to order her mother's life. She insisted that Jessie have perfect peace. "I never open a letter first . . . nor am told anything which can agitate me," Jessie said. "My daughter watches over me tenderly and I do try to be braver but there are so many hours in ten months."[17]

Imprisoned by her own body and by her overly protective daughter, Jessie sought escape in her memoirs, the remarkable mental flowering of a woman struggling against pain and decay. As her eyes improved, she began to write down the chapters in her head, and they poured out almost effortlessly, as if "under dictation."

They were a strange amalgam of honesty and myth. In one area Jessie was forthright. Helped by the times and her own stronger sense of self, she no longer tried to gloss over her rebellion at Miss English's Female Seminary or the scandal she caused when she dressed like a boy at her cousin Sally's wedding. As she recalled her childhood, her father became alive again, fully his tender and irascible self. But when she reached her married years, John remained strangely remote, always the hero but scarcely human. The myths they had created together entrapped her still, and she could not break free even at the end.

In the spring of 1901, Jessie faltered. Perhaps it was the pain of her injury or Lily's subtle discouragement. She put her work aside, leaving unfinished her remembrances of the bitter Civil War years and all that followed. Perhaps more than anything she could not bear to record John's decline—the long years of humiliation and failure. Though for her the post-Pocaho years, despite their difficulties, had been a kind of late blooming, her memoirs, like her life, were still bound by his.

Charles Lummis sought a publisher for her, but she was a fading figure and her discursive style less fashionable. Her memoirs, like those she and Frank had written for John, would never be published.

"I am a cripple from a broken leg—broken badly, which with rheumatism often added, is torture," she remarked bluntly a year and a half after her fall. Despite her pain, she remained concerned about John's memory. After years of debate, a committee of friends had commissioned a young woman sculptor, Clio Hinton Huneker, to create a statue for his grave at Rockland Cemetery. But Jessie, with all of her old spirit, indignantly turned it down. "My old friend, Mr. Whiton, sent me a photograph of what *she calls* a statue. A short, well fed man, shading his eyes with his hand. For a man of five feet ten, meeting all sorts of privations—until he looked *disemboweled*, as my mother said—this is a cardinal deviation from the truth. . . . Myself, I should be really sorry to have her concerned *in any way*, with the memory of the General." Yet Jessie despaired that she herself could do so little. "I understand his grave is quite overgrown with weeds and brambles. You saw my helpless state last year—I am as helpless now as then and need a skilled nurse. I have no money to attend to this grave. The General would be the last person to allow me to neglect the living for the dead. But, if I get repayment for [Black Point], then I intend placing there a simple slab."[18]

The household was now quiet and orderly. In the evenings Lily and the nurse played solitaire. Lily had always believed that survival depended on muted emotions, and she carefully monitored her mother's life. Yet Jessie had never asked to be protected from feeling, and spiritedly, poignantly, she tried to resist her daughter's rule as best as she could, refusing to drink her medicinal tonic or to have the red flannel wrappings on her leg changed.

When Charles Lummis stopped by to see her, he found her "wrinkled, tremulous, deaf, tied to her chair," yet still infused with vitality. When she was near fifty Jessie had told her sons, "I am 'very old and very wise' and I have been alive all the days of my life."[19] It was still true at seventy-eight.

Only in her last autumn did she withdraw into herself. Wrapped in a white shawl, she sat on the sunny porch where she could see the beds of violets she loved and the orange trees with their ripening fruit.

On Christmas morning, 1902, she suddenly grew weaker. Before night, she lapsed into unconsciousness. Toward evening two days later, December 27, 1902, her breath became shorter. About seven o'clock, she died.

On the morning of December 30, little Christ Episcopal Church on the corner of Pico and Flower streets was filled long before the service began, and those who could not enter stood on the sidewalks outside. The newspapers noted many old pioneers among the mourners. At ten thirty, as the organist played Chopin's Funeral March, the pallbearers carried the casket—unexpectedly pearl-gray, trimmed with silver, and covered with clusters of fresh violets—into the church.[20]

Neither Charley or Frank, both stationed in the Philippines, were able to attend their mother's funeral, but Charley's son John Charles, a midshipman on the flagship *New York* lying off Santa Barbara, was there, dressed in fatigues, with Lily leaning heavily on his arm. In later years Charley would become an admiral and commander of the Boston Navy Yard. Frank, less fortunate, would be court-martialed three times and eventually dismissed from the army for financial irregularities and insubordination. As for Lily, she would remain in the Los Angeles area, a sad, quiet woman, helped financially by old friends. "Thank you Dear Nelly for the check which I am having changed into a black street suit," she would write in 1911. Protective of the family image, Lily burned most of her parents' letters. "It is not a cheerful task that of going over and destroying old letters and papers," she said, "but it is better than having them get into wrong hands. . . . it is very hard to burn up the letters of those we love."[21]

Jessie had left instructions for her funeral on a half sheet of paper in her security box in the Union Bank and Savings vault. She requested a simple service with the sons of long-time friends—Seymour Severance, Edward Silent, and others—as pallbearers.

As the California sun glinted through the church windows, the pallbearers carried her casket to the chancel rail. The minister intoned the traditional service for the burial of the dead and read from Paul's First Epistle to the Corinthians: "O Death, where is thy sting? O grave, where is thy victory?"

' In her instructions, Jessie asked to be cremated, probably to save money for Lily. When the service ended, her body was taken to Rosedale Cemetery, and after a final prayer, placed in the crematory. Later her ashes would be sent to Rockland Cemetery overlooking the Hudson, where they would be placed, as she wished, beside John.

NOTES

Published works are cited by author and short title. Full references appear in the bibliography. The following abbreviations are used in these notes:

JBF	Jessie Benton Frémont
JCF	John Charles Frémont
EBF	Elizabeth Benton Frémont
THB	Thomas Hart Benton
EBL	Elizabeth Blair Lee
FPB	Francis Preston Blair
NHB	Nelly Haskell Browne
FP	Frémont Papers, Bancroft Library, University of California, Berkeley
B-L	Blair-Lee Papers, Princeton
BP	Blair Papers, Library of Congress
LC	Library of Congress

Prologue
The View From Los Angeles

1. JBF, *Year*, 25.
2. JCF, *Memoirs*, 67.
3. Phillips, *JBF*, 292.
4. JBF, "Great Events," 271, FP; JBF to Dr. William J. Morton, Oct. 7, 1878, FP.
5. JBF to Dr. William J. Morton, Christmas [1881], FP.
6. JBF's first account: *Souvenirs*, 38–51; second account: untitled typescript (henceforth JBF, Memoirs), 34, 46/47 (old draft), FP. Jessie's sister remarked that Preston Johnston was "so like Jessie, they could have passed for twins." See Elizabeth Benton Jones to EBL, June 18, 1888, BP.

Chapter One
"The Place a Son Would Have Had"

1. Phillips, *JBF*, 29.
2. JBF, *Year*, 25.
3. JBF, Memoirs, 5, FP.
4. Jefferson City, Missouri, *Journal*, n.d., Jones Papers, California and Western Manuscripts Collection, Stanford; JBF, Memoirs, 21.
5. JBF, Memoirs, 7.
6. E. Smith, *Magnificent Missourian*, 22.
7. JBF, Memoirs, 12/15 (old draft); JBF, "Biographical Sketch," 13.
8. For documents of the brawl, see A. Jackson, *Correspondence* 1:309–18; Parton, *Jackson* 1:386–98.
9. B. Davis, *Old Hickory*, 194.
10. S. Miller, "The Prestons," 127; JBF, Memoirs, 5.
11. JBF, Memoirs, 17.
12. Capers, *Memphis*, 53; JBF, Memoirs, 18.
13. JBF, *Souvenirs*, 148.
14. JBF, Memoirs, 3–4.

Chapter Two
Washington Childhood

1. M. Smith, *Washington Society*, 294.
2. Quoted in Parton, *Andrew Jackson* 3:169.
3. M. Smith, *Washington Society*, 293–94.
4. Ibid., 294.
5. Ibid., 296; Story, *Life and Letters* 1:563.
6. Quoted in B. Davis, *Old Hickory*, 195.
7. Hall, *Aristocratic Journey*, 165; Martineau, *Retrospect* 1:160.
8. Trollope, *Domestic Manners*, 226.
9. Ibid., 230; Alcott, *The Young Wife*, 83; Kendall, *Autobiography*, 280.
10. Darby, *Personal Recollections*, 184.
11. JBF, *Souvenirs*, 317.
12. JBF, Memoirs, 24, FP.
13. Ibid., 26.
14. Sally McDowell to Susan McDowell, Mar. 7, 1837, McDowell Family Papers, Univ. of Va.
15. JBF, Memoirs, 38 (old draft).
16. Clay, "Children," 52, 49; Martineau, *Society* 3:166, 177.

Chapter Three
The Lessons of Geography

1. JBF, Memoirs, 15, FP; JBF, *Souvenirs*, 131; JBF, *Year*, 21. For an excellent study of antebellum Rockbridge County, see Kellar, "Rockbridge County."

2. JBF, Memoirs, 23, 16.
3. See JBF, "Uncle Primus and Dog Turban," *Wide Awake* 21 (June 1885):37–39; JBF, "William-Rufus," *Wide Awake* 21 (Aug. 1885):162.
4. Ms. inventory of James McDowell estate, Nov. 9–10, 1835, McCormick Papers, State Historical Society of Wis.; JBF, *Year*, 92–93.
5. Robert, *Road from Monticello*, 81, 103.
6. JBF, Memoirs, 19–20.
7. Trollope, *Domestic Manners*, 303.
8. JBF, *Year*, 16.
9. Trollope, *Domestic Manners*, 15; Audubon quoted in McDermott, *Before Mark Twain*, xxiii.
10. Trollope, *Domestic Manners*, 18; Hamilton, *Men and Manners* 2:178.
11. JBF, *Souvenirs*, 133.
12. Ibid., 142.
13. Ibid.
14. Ibid., 136.
15. Ibid., 157–58; *Republican* quoted in Missouri Historical Society, *Glimpses*, 47, 54.
16. JBF, *Souvenirs*, 160.

Chapter Four
Miss English's Female Seminary

1. M. Smith, *Washington Society*, 370.
2. Fairfield, *Letters*, 64.
3. Hone, *Diary* 1:128; Benton quoted in Schlesinger, *Age of Jackson*, 125.
4. Sally McDowell to Susan McDowell, June 13, 1836, McDowell Family Papers, Univ. of Va.
5. THB, *View* 1:735.
6. JBF, Memoirs, 30, FP; JBF, *Souvenirs*, 13.
7. The account of the May Queen/Bodisco episode is based on JBF, *Souvenirs*, 12–33, and her far more revealing Memoirs, 30–32.
8. Hone, *Diary* 2:522.
9. Poore, *Reminiscences* 1:372.
10. Douglas, *Feminization of Am. Culture*, 50. For the role of women in Jacksonian America see Lerner, "The Lady and the Mill Girl," 5–15.

Chapter Five
The Young Lieutenant

1. For information on JCF's parents see rejected ms. divorce petition of John Pryor, Dec. 1, 1811, with attachments, Va. State Library; JBF's [1856] notes in Bigelow Papers, N.Y. Public Library; Bigelow, *Memoir*, 11–23 (information supplied by JBF); JCF, *Expeditions* 1:xxi–xxiv; and Nevins, *Frémont*, 2–10. Anne Pryor Fremon's name is variously spelled Ann, Anne, and Anna. JBF spells it Anne.

2. Quoted in Goodwin, *Frémont*, 2.
3. Anna Pryor to John Lowry, Aug. 28, 1811, copy in Pryor divorce petition, Va. State Library.
4. In early adulthood JCF signed himself "C. Frémont" and was addressed as "Charley" or "Charles." About the time he married JBF, he began to sign himself "J. C. Frémont," and alternately, from the later 1840s, "John C. Frémont."
5. Bigelow, *Memoir*, 25.
6. JCF, *Memoirs*, 19, 21; Charleston College faculty journal quoted in Nevins, *Frémont*, 16.
7. JCF, *Memoirs*, 24; Nevins, *Frémont*, 25; Charles A. Geyer to Joseph N. Nicollet, Jan. 1, 1840, Lownes Collection, Brown.
8. JCF, *Memoirs*, 30.
9. Ibid., 65.
10. Ibid., 66.
11. Ibid., 67.
12. JBF, *Souvenirs*, 63.
13. JCF, *Memoirs*, 67.
14. Rowson, *Charlotte Temple*, 26, 27.
15. JCF, *Memoirs*, 68; JBF, *Souvenirs*, 37; JBF, Memoirs, 33, FP.
16. JBF, Memoirs, 34.
17. JCF, *Expeditions* 1:98.
18. JBF, Memoirs, 46 (old draft).
19. Eaton, *Autobiography*, 18; JBF quoted in Thomas Starr King to Randolph Ryers, Oct. 19, 1860, King Papers, Bancroft.
20. JBF to EBL, July 23, [1856], B-L.
21. Ibid.
22. Marriage records, Superior Court of D.C.
23. JCF, *Expeditions* 1:102.
24. Rachel Walker to Maria Preston Pope, Jan. 1842, Preston Family Papers, Filson Club.
25. Moody, "Here Was a Woman," 171.
26. Sarah S. Thompson to Nathaniel Hart, Jan. 19, 1842, Edmund T. Halsey Collection, Filson Club.
27. Rachel Walker to Maria Preston Pope, Jan. 1842, Preston Family Papers; James McDowell III to James McDowell, Jr., Dec. 18 [1841], McDowell Family Papers, Univ. of Va.

Chapter Six
The Making of a Hero

1. Adams, *Memoirs*, 11:48.
2. Coleman, *Priscilla Cooper Tyler*, 92–93.

3. JCF, *Memoirs*, 71; Gouverneur, *As I Remember*, 192; Eaton, *Autobiography*, 83.
4. Coleman, *Priscilla Cooper Tyler*, 88.
5. Bidwell, *In California*, 9.
6. THB, *View* 2:474.
7. JCF, *Expeditions* 1:116.
8. JBF, Memoirs, 38, FP.
9. JBF, *Year*, 24.
10. JBF, Memoirs, 41.
11. THB to James McDowell, Jr., Dec. 12, 1842, James McDowell II [Jr.] Papers, Duke; Edward Dobyns, ms. on Susan Benton Boilleau, Jones Collection, Stanford.
12. JCF, *Expeditions* 1:132. Lily's birthdate has been given as Nov. 13, but JBF and Lily cite it as Nov. 15. See JBF to EBL, Nov. 14, 1851, B-L; and EBF to NHB, Nov. 16, 1876, FP. No birth record exists.
13. JBF, Memoirs, 41.
14. Ibid.; JCF, *Memoirs*, 163.
15. Nevins, *Frémont*, 101.
16. JCF, *Expeditions* 1:185, 262, 180, 269–70.
17. Preuss, *Exploring with Frémont*, 41, 46, 50.
18. JBF, Memoirs, 42.
19. Longfellow, *Life* 2:65–66.
20. Garrard, *Wah-To-Yah*, "introductory"; J. Miller, quoted in Goetzmann *Exploration*, 243–44.

Chapter Seven
Waiting

1. JBF, Memoirs, 41, FP.
2. JBF, "The Origin of the Frémont Explorations," 768.
3. JCF, *Expeditions* 1:346n.
4. JBF's main account of the howitzer incident, quoted here unless otherwise cited, is Memoirs, 43–6. See also JBF, "The Origin of the Frémont Explorations," 768–70, and JCF, *Memoirs*, 167–68.
5. JCF, *Expeditions* 1:345–46.
6. THB, *View* 2:579; JCF, *Expeditions* 1:358.
7. JBF, "The Origin of the Frémont Explorations," 769.
8. Corroborating one aspect of JBF's story, Derosier is not on a list of expedition members made on May 27, just before they started west, but he is mentioned as with the party on July 26. See Talbot, *Journals*, 7, 28. For an insightful analysis of the incident, see D. Jackson, "The Myth of the Frémont Howitzer."
9. JBF, "The Origin of the Frémont Explorations," 768.

10. JBF, Memoirs, 46.
11. Talbot, *Journals*, 17.
12. JCF, *Expeditions* 1:352.
13. JCF, *Expeditions* 1:354–55.
14. Ibid., 357; JBF, Memoirs, 50.
15. JCF, *Expeditions* 1:356–57.
16. Ibid., 357.
17. Ibid., 626.
18. THB, *View* 2:568; Fairfield, *Letters*, 330.
19. JCF, *Expeditions* 1:360.
20. JBF to Adelaide Talbot, April 21, 1844, Talbot Papers, LC.
21. Larkin, *Papers* 2:94; THB to James McDowell, Jr., June 21, 1844, James McDowell II [Jr.] Papers, Duke.
22. JCF, *Expeditions* 1:361.
23. JCF's homecoming: JBF, *Souvenirs*, 163–65; JBF, Memoirs, 50.

Chapter Eight
"The Happy Winter"

1. JBF, Memoirs, 46–47, FP.
2. Preuss, *Exploring with Frémont*, 120.
3. JBF, Memoirs, 54 (old draft).
4. JBF to EBL, n.d. [spring 1857] and June 2, 1860, B-L; JBF, Memoirs, 54 (old draft).
5. JBF, Memoirs, 47.
6. Howe, *Bancroft* 1:259–60.
7. Graebner, *Empire*, 76.
8. Chambers, *Benton*, 275–76.
9. Ibid., 279.
10. Ibid., 281.
11. Adams, *Memoirs* 12:140, 57.
12. W. E. Smith, *Blair Family* 1:222.
13. Adams, *Memoirs* 12:179; *Globe*, Mar. 4, 1845; *Times* quoted in Pletcher, *Diplomacy of Annexation*, 238.
14. JCF, *Expeditions* 1:484, 460, 687.
15. Ibid., 430, 473–74.
16. Ibid., 442, 516, 543.
17. Schlissel, *Women's Diaries*, 14. For recent interpretations of pioneer women, also see Faragher, *Overland Trail*; Jeffrey, *Frontier Women*; and Myres, *Westering Women*.
18. JBF, *Year*, 3.
19. JCF, *Expeditions* 1:501.
20. Ibid., 528, 541.

21. Ibid., 645, 660.
22. Ibid., 709–10.

Chapter Nine
The Vagaries of Reputation

1. JCF, *Expeditions* 1:396.
2. Fairfield, *Letters*, 367; V. Davis, *Jefferson Davis* 1:223; Polk, *Diary* 4:355 and 3:402–4.
3. *Union*, May 7, June 2, 1845; Abert quoted in JCF, *Expeditions* 1:422.
4. JCF, *Expeditions* 1:407.
5. Ibid., 420.
6. St. Louis *Missourian* quoted in *Union*, June 14, 1845.
7. See Becker, *Plains & the Rockies*, 246–56.
8. *Southern Literary Messenger* 15 (Sept. 1849):529.
9. *Union*, Aug. 28, 1845; *United States Magazine and Democratic Review* 17 (July 1845):75, 77, 68.
10. Schlissel, *Women's Diaries*, 28.
11. McKinstry, *Gold Rush Diary*, 207; Holliday, *World Rushed In*, 222; Larkin, *Papers* 5:291.
12. JCF, *Expeditions* 2:148–50.
13. Emerson, *Journals* 9:431.
14. JCF, *Expeditions* 1:375; Gray to John Torrey, Saturday morning [Mar. 8, 1845], Torrey Correspondence, N.Y. Botanical Garden; Preuss, *Exploring with Frémont*, 128.
15. JCF, "Notice to the Reader," *Globe*, May 20, 1845.
16. Polk's account of the discussion, as described here, appears in *Diary* 1:68–72.
17. Larkin, *Papers* 3:266.
18. Ibid., 4:44–47.
19. THB to James McDowell, Jr., Oct. 3 [1845], James McDowell II [Jr.] Papers, Duke.
20. JCF, *Expeditions* 2:148.
21. JBF to EBL, Apr. 15, 1847, BP.
22. EBL to S. P. Lee, July 20, 1846, B-L; JBF to EBL, Apr. 15, 1847, BP.
23. For descriptions of Blair's estate, see *Union*, Aug. 4, 1845, and Blair, "Annals of Silver Spring," 164–67.
24. JBF to EBL, Apr. 15, 1847, BP.
25. For the Thomas scandal, see Eliza Benton to Sally McDowell, Dec. 8, 1839, and Sally McDowell to Susan McDowell, Apr. 2, 1836, McDowell Family Papers, Univ. of Va.; Chambers, *Benton*, 301–3; H. Linn to Mrs. Linn, April 1844, Lewis F. Linn Papers, Missouri Historical

Society; THB to James McDowell, Jr., Aug. 15, 1843, Dec. 26 and 30, 1845, James McDowell II [Jr.] Papers, Duke; *Union*, Mar. 11, 1847.

Chapter Ten
"I Have No Sympathy for the War"

1. Pletcher, *Diplomacy of Annexation*, 376; *National Intelligencer*, Nov. 6, 1845.
2. See JBF ms. notes on the Mexican War prepared for Josiah Royce, n.d. [1885], Huntington: JCF, *Memoirs*, 421; Wamsley, *Idols*, 115.
3. *Union*, June 6, 1846.
4. JCF, *Expeditions* 2:48; *National Intelligencer*, May 15, 1846.
5. *Union*, May 9, 1846; Polk, *Diary* 1:390.
6. Sellers, *Polk* 2:418.
7. For documents on the Gabilan incident, quoted here, see Larkin *Papers* 4:228–49.
8. JCF, *Expeditions* 2:130.
9. Ibid., 181.
10. Larkin, *Papers* 4:289.
11. THB, *View* 2:682–84.
12. JCF, *Expeditions* 2:147–50.
13. JCF, *Memoirs*, 486.
14. Ord, *Occurrences*, 58.
15. Larkin, *Papers* 4:340–41, 348.
16. JCF, *Expeditions* 2:470.
17. Ibid., 139; Kern to Richard Kern, July 27, 1846, in Lewis, *California in 1846*, 45.
18. Proclamation reprinted in Larkin, *Papers* 4:354.
19. Larkin, *Papers* 4:410.
20. JCF, *Expeditions* 2:469.
21. Ibid., 182.
22. Ibid.
23. Rosaliá Vallejo Leese, ms. "History of the Bear Party," June 27, 1874, Bancroft.
24. Larkin, *First and Last Consul*, 73. See also Larkin, *Papers* 6:225.
25. JCF, *Expeditions* 2:155–57.
26. Bidwell, *In California*, 108
27. *Union*, Nov. 9, 1846. For varying interpretations of the Bear Flag episode see Harlow, *California Conquered*; Hawgood, "John C. Frémont and the Bear Flag Revolution"; Hussey, "The Origin of the Gillespie Mission"; Stenberg, "Polk and Frémont"; Tays, "Frémont Had No Secret Instructions"; and Wiltsee, "The Truth about Frémont."
28. See Pletcher, *Diplomacy of Annexation*, 592–95, and Larkin, *Papers* 4:408–10.

29. Polk, *Diary* 2:228.
30. Bodisco quoted by Adams, *Memoirs* 12:187.
31. JBF to Torrey, Mar. 21, 1847, Torrey Correspondence, Library, N.Y. Botanical Garden.

Chapter Eleven
"A New and Painful Epoch"

1. *Union*, May 8, 9, 1847.
2. Polk, *Diary* 2:445.
3. JCF, *Expeditions* 2:269.
4. Griffin, *Diary*, 70.
5. Polk, *Diary* 3:52–53.
6. *Union*, June 15, 1847; EBL to S. P. Lee, June 16, 1847, B-L. An excerpt from the Carson article, probably furnished by JBF, appears in Bigelow, *Memoir*, 139–41.
7. JCF, *Expeditions* 2:442.
8. EBL to S. P. Lee, May 24, 1847, B-L; *Union*, June 15, 1847; JCF, *Expeditions* 2:370.
9. *Union*, Sept. 16, 1848.
10. JBF's account: "Great Events," 51–52, FP.
11. *Republican*, Aug. 30, 1847; N.Y. *Herald*, Sept. 9, 11, 1847.
12. N.Y. *Herald*, Sept. 9, 11, 1847.
13. JCF, *Expeditions* 2:405.
14. Anne Fremon had married a Mr. Hale, probably after JCF left home, but Hale evidently died before she did. See Cornish, "Diary," 75.
15. JCF, *Expeditions* 2:388.
16. Ibid., 404.
17. Polk, *Diary* 3:197–98.
18. Ibid., 202–3.
19. Ibid., 204, 210.
20. Quoted in EBL to S. P. Lee, Oct. 23, 1847, B-L.
21. JBF, Memoirs, 53.

Chapter Twelve
"The Proud Lonely Man"

1. N.Y. *Herald*, Nov. 4, 1847.
2. JCF, *Expeditions* 2, supplement, 39.
3. JBF, "Great Events," 59, FP.
4. Ibid.
5. N.Y. *Herald*, Dec. 5, 1847.
6. JCF, *Expeditions* 2, supplement, 197–98.
7. JCF, *Expeditions* 2:343; D. Clarke, *Kearny*, 358.

8. N.Y. *Herald*, Nov. 19, 1847.
9. JCF, *Expeditions* 2, supplement, 326–27.
10. N.Y. *Tribune*, Jan. 12, 1848; N.Y. *Herald*, Jan. 19, 1848.
11. Blair to Van Buren, Jan. 23, 1847 [1848], Van Buren Papers, LC.
12. JCF, *Expeditions* 2, supplement, 446.
13. Ibid., 337–41.
14. Ibid., 447; JBF, "Great Events," 75, 77.
15. JBF, "Great Events," 60; N.Y. *Herald*, Aug. 8, 1848.
16. JBF, *Year*, 2.
17. JBF, Memoirs, 52–53, FP.
18. JCF, *Expeditions* 3:15.
19. JBF, Memoirs, 59.
20. Quoted in EBL to S. P. Lee, Aug. 8, 1848, B-L.
21. *Union*, Sept. 21, 1848.
22. N.Y. *Tribune*, July 15, 1856; Lecompte, "A Letter from Jessie to Kit," 263.
23. N.Y. *Tribune*, July 8, 1856.
24. N.Y. *Herald*, Oct. 13, 1848; Lecompte, "A Letter from Jessie to Kit," 263.
25. JBF, "Great Events," 78.
26. Bigelow, *Memoirs*, 360.
27. JBF, *Year*, 9; JBF, "Great Events," 79.
28. For the Kearny deathbed controversy, see JBF, Memoirs, 59, and "Great Events," 80; THB letter in *National Intelligencer*, Dec. 13, 1848; D. Clarke, *Kearny*, 383–86.
29. *National Intelligencer*, Dec. 22, 1848.
30. JBF, *Year*, 10–11.
31. FPB to Van Buren, Dec. 30, 1848, Van Buren Papers; JCF, *Expeditions* 3:72.
32. JBF, "Great Events," 77.
33. JBF, *Year*, 12–13.
34. JBF, "Great Events," 78.

Chapter Thirteen
Voyage to El Dorado

1. Caughey, *Gold Is the Cornerstone*, 40–41.
2. Paul, *California Gold Discovery*, 97.
3. Time-Life, *Forty-Niners*, 43.
4. See N.Y. *Herald* and N.Y. *Tribune*, Mar. 1849, passim; Time-Life, *Forty-Niners*, 43–47.
5. JBF, *Year*, 10–12; JBF, "Great Events," 102, FP.
6. For the *Crescent City* departure, see Gardiner, 18–22; N.Y. *Herald*, Mar. 15, 16, 1849; JBF, "Great Events," 102, FP.

7. JBF, Memoirs, 61–62, FP; JBF, "Great Events" 102.
8. JBF, Year, 14.
9. For JBF's isthmus crossing, quoted below, see her "Great Events," 103–5, and Year, 26–34.
10. JBF, Year, 38.
11. JCF's Taos letter, as quoted here, appears in JBF, Year, 42–54.
12. JBF, "Great Events," 84.
13. Preuss, Exploring with Frémont, 144–45.
14. JBF, Year, 56–57; JBF, "Great Events," 107.
15. JBF, Year, 56.
16. Ibid., 58.
17. Transcript of Panama Star, May 13, 1849, Beale Papers, LC.
18. JBF, Year, 59.
19. For details of the Panama voyage, unless otherwise cited, see JBF, Year, 59–64, and "Great Events," 108–9.
20. Re-union of the Pioneer Panama Passengers, 16, 28; Alta California, June 7, 1849.
21. Talbot, Journals, 93.

Chapter Fourteen
California Metamorphosis

1. Larkin, Papers, 8:238.
2. JBF, Year, 66.
3. Larkin, Papers 8:245; JBF, Souvenirs, 187.
4. JBF, Year, 69.
5. Drury, "The Jeffers-Willey Wedding," 16; Browne, Letters, 123.
6. JBF, Year, 71.
7. JBF, "Great Events," 119, FP.
8. JBF, Year, 91, 82.
9. Ibid., 85–86.
10. Crosby, Memoirs, 42.
11. EBF, Recollections, 27; Drury, "The Jeffers-Wiley Wedding," 15. For JBF's presence and role at the convention, see Drury, 15; JBF, Year, 92–96, and "Great Events," 126.
12. JBF, "Great Events," 126, and Year, 94.
13. Colton, Three Years in California, 374.
14. See B. Taylor, Eldorado, 144.
15. JBF, Year, 96; Browne, Letters, 126.
16. See B. Taylor, Eldorado, 153, 155.
17. JBF, Year, 96–97.
18. JBF, "Great Events," 124–25; Crosby, Memoirs, 35.
19. JBF, "Great Events," 127.
20. JBF, Year, 103.

21. B. Taylor, *Eldorado*, 233.
22. JBF, *Year*, 100–101.

Chapter Fifteen
Brief Triumph

1. THB, *View* 2:750–51; Chambers, *Benton*, 361.
2. JBF, "Great Events," 153, FP.
3. JBF, "Dining Out," Bixby Collection, Missouri Historical Society.
4. Quoted in S. Miller, "James McDowell," 182–85.
5. Stewart, *Adolph Sutro*, 21.
6. JBF to EBL, Nov. 14, 1851, B-L.
7. JBF to FPB, Aug. 14, 1851, B-L.
8. JBF to EBL, Nov. 14, 1851, B-L.
9. Greenhow, *My Imprisonment*, 147.
10. Chambers, *Benton*, 372, 377, 383.
11. For JBF's account of the fires, quoted below, see "Great Events," 156–61.
12. JBF to EBL, Aug. 14, 1851, B-L.
13. JBF to FPB, Aug. 14, 1851, B-L.
14. JCF, *Expeditions* 3:267n, xlix.
15. JBF to FPB, Aug. 14, 1851, and Apr. 11, 1851, B-L.

Chapter Sixteen
The Restless Years

1. JBF, Memoirs, 65, FP.
2. Ibid., 66–67, *N.Y. Times*, Apr. 19, 1852.
3. See Spence, "David Hoffman," for a valuable account of Frémont's London agent.
4. Spence, "David Hoffman," 385; JCF, *Expeditions* 3:207n.
5. JCF, *Expeditions* 3:355.
6. Ibid., 358.
7. *N.Y. Times*, Apr. 29, 1852; JCF, *Expeditions* 3:351.
8. FPB to Van Buren, Apr. 3, 1852, Van Buren Papers, LC.
9. JBF, "Great Events," 174, FP.
10. Ibid., 178.
11. Benton quoted in Chambers, *Benton*, 397; JBF, "Great Events," 179.
12. JBF, "Great Events," 179.
13. JBF to EBL, Oct. 14 [1853], B-L.
14. FPB to Van Buren, Nov. 27, 1853, Van Buren Papers.
15. Seward, *Seward at Washington*, 216–17.
16. JCF, *Expeditions* 3:422.
17. Ibid., 442.

18. JBF most fully described what she considered a psychic experience in "How the Good News Came from the West," *Wide Awake* 28 (Dec. 1888):21–23.
19. JBF to FPB, [Apr.] 13 [1854], B-L; JBF to EBL, Apr. 18 [1856] and Monday mg. [spring 1854], B-L.
20. Blair to Minna Blair, Apr. 17–18, 1854, BP.
21. JBF, "Great Events," 191; JCF, *Expeditions* 3:488.
22. JBF, Memoirs, 89–90.
23. Ibid., 90; Benton interviewed in *Globe*, Feb. 28, 1855.
24. JBF, Memoirs, 92; JBF, "Senator Thomas Hart Benton," 244.
25. JBF, Memoirs, 92.
26. Frémont biographers have given Francis Preston Frémont's birth year as 1854, but convincing internal evidence (e.g., JBF to EBL, Jan. 12 1856 and June 8, 1857, B-L) and the *Official Register . . . U.S. Military Academy*, 1873, all indicate it was 1855.
27. JBF to EBL, Saturday morning [July 1855] and n.d. [after May 17, 1855], B-L.
28. JBF to EBL, Saturday morning [July 1855], B-L.
29. JBF to EBL, Aug. 17 [1855], B-L.
30. JBF, "Great Events," 203–4. See also JBF, Memoirs, 92–93.

Chapter Seventeen
The Sound of Cheering

1. JBF to FPB, [Aug.] 27 [1855], B-L.
2. FPB to Van Buren, Jan. 25, 1856, Van Buren Papers, LC.
3. JCF to Messrs. Carpenter, Oct. 26, 1855, Dreer Collection, Historical Society of Pa.; JBF to FPB, Oct. 21 and Nov. 3, [1855], B-L.
4. See EBL to S. P. Lee, Nov. 17 and 30, 1855, B-L.
5. THB to Van Buren, Sept. 1, 1855, Van Buren Papers.
6. JBF to EBL, Nov. 21 [1855], B-L; Joseph Palmer to Montgomery Blair, May 31, 1855, BP.
7. JBF to FPB, Nov. 3 [1855], B-L.
8. Ibid.; JBF to EBL, undated note [Dec. 7, 1855?], B-L.
9. JBF to EBL, [Dec.] 14 [1855] and Jan. 12, 1856, B-L.
10. Sumner to George Bancroft, Apr. 22, 1846, Bancroft Papers, Mass. Historical Society.
11. JBF to EBL, Mar. 7, Mar. 8, and Apr. 18 [1856], B-L.
12. JBF to EBL, Apr. 17 [1856] Apr. 18 [1856], and Mar. 8 [1856], B-L.
13. JBF to EBL, Apr. 18 [1856], B-L.
14. JBF to EBL, Apr. 25 [1856], B-L.
15. JBF to EBL, Apr. 29 [1856], B-L.
16. Bigelow to FPB, Apr. 1856, BP.
17. N.Y. *Tribune*, Apr. 9, 1856.

18. Nevins, *Ordeal*, 2:446n.
19. JBF to EBL, June 9 [1856], B-L.
20. THB, *View* 2:787–88.
21. Halstead, *Trimmers*, 22, 35.
22. N.Y. *Tribune*, June 6, 1856.
23. Isely, *Greeley*, 164; Koerner, *Memoirs*, 14; N.Y. *Tribune*, June 11, 12, 1856.
24. JCF to FPB, [June] 17 [1856], Bigelow Papers, N.Y. Public Library.
25. Isely, *Greeley*, 171.
26. EBL quoted in E. Smith, *Blair*, 231; FPB to Frank Blair, Jr., July 1, 1856, BP.
27. N.Y. *Tribune*, June 26, 1856; Abbott, *Reminiscences*, 107–10.

Chapter Eighteen
"Frémont and Our Jessie"

1. Julian, *Political Recollections*, 153; Farnham quoted in *California Chronicle*, Oct. 2, 1856; Thoreau, *Correspondence*, 436.
2. Whitman, *Complete Poetry*, 604, 600.
3. N.Y. *Tribune*, July 22, June 26, 1856.
4. N.Y. *Tribune*, July 8, 11, 1856.
5. Child, *Letters*, 290.
6. Lovejoy, "Letters," 138.
7. Goodwin, *Frémont*, 204: G. Clarke, *Julian*, 175.
8. JBF, "Great Events," 205, FP; Bigelow *Retrospections* 1:144.
9. *Union*, July 12 and 31, 1856.
10. Bigelow, *Memoirs*, 12, 20, 21.
11. JBF note, n.d., Bigelow Papers, N.Y. Public Library.
12. N.Y. *Tribune*, June 24, 1856.
13. *Dispatch* clipping, n.d., Bigelow Papers, N.Y. Public Library; transcript of Charleston *Courier*, Aug. 27, 1856, FP; Wise quoted in *California Chronicle*, Oct. 1, 1856.
14. N.Y. *Tribune*, July 4, 1856.
15. Quoted in Pitt, *Decline*, 199–200. For similar rumors see ms. statement of Stephen C. Foster, Alcalde of Los Angeles, 1847–48, Bancroft; Bell, *Reminiscences*, 38; Hollingsworth, "Journal," 236–37; and Ord, *The City of the Angels*, 23–24.
16. Clark, *Beecher*, 125; Child, *Letters*, 290; Toombs quoted in *Union*, Aug. 2, 1856; Lincoln, *Collected Works* 2:355; Klein, *Buchanan*, 258.
17. JBF to EBL. July 2 [1856], B-L; JBF to Dr. John Roberton, June 30, 1856, Benton Papers, Missouri Historical Society.
18. JBF to EBL, July 23 and Aug. 12 [1856], B-L.
19. N.Y. *Tribune*, June 27, 1856; Oliphant, "Recollections," 434; Collier, "Recollections," 140.

20. JBF to EBL, Aug. 12, [1856], B-L.
21. JBF to EBL, Aug. 20 [1856] and n.d. [late Aug.-Sept. 1856], B-L.
22. JBF to FPB, Aug. 25 [1856], BP.
23. EBL draft letter, n.d. [late Aug. 1856], B-L.
24. JBF to EBL, n.d. [late Aug.-Sept. 1856], B-L; FPB to Van Buren, Sept. 22, 1856, Van Buren Papers, LC.
25. JBF to EBL, Aug. 12 [1856], B-L; Nichols, "Papers," 257; JBF to EBL, Aug. 20 [1856], B-L; JBF, "Great Events," 206.
26. JBF to EBL, Oct. 20 [1856], B-L.
27. JBF to EBL, n.d. [Oct. 1856], B-L.
28. JBF to EBL, Nov. 2 [1856], B-L.

Chapter Nineteen
Retrenchment

1. Niven, *Welles*, 275; Frank Blair to FPB, Nov. 16, 1856, BP.
2. Stanton et al., *Woman Suffrage* 1:633; *N.Y. Times*, Nov. 26, 1856.
3. JBF to EBL, Nov. 18 [1856], B-L.
4. JBF to EBL, Oct. 20 [1856], B-L.
5. JBF to EBL, Aug. 14 and Nov. 18 [1856], B-L.
6. JBF to EBL, Jan. 23 [1857], B-L; JBF to FPB, Jan. 31 [1857], B-L.
7. JBF to FPB, Jan. 31 [1857], B-L; FPB to Frank Blair, Feb. 5, 1857, BP.
8. JBF to EBL, Mar. 1, 1857, B-L.
9. JBF to EBL, n.d. [early 1857], B-L.
10. JBF to EBL, Jan. 23 [1857], B-L.
11. JBF to Mrs. Eliza Blair, May 4, 1857, B-L.
12. For speculation on JCF's rumored affair see Gideon Welles to FPB, Apr. 9, 1860, BP; Preston King to Welles, Mar. 3, 1860, King to Welles, Apr. 9 and 21, 1860, Welles Papers, LC. JBF puzzles about Bigelow's defection in JBF to FPB, Jan. 8, 1858, BP.
13. JBF to EBL, n.d. [spring, 1857], B-L.
14. EBL to S. P. Lee, Apr. 11, 1857, B-L.
15. JBF to EBL, June 2 [1857], and to S. P. Lee, June 9 [1857], B-L.
16. JBF to FPB, Thursday night, Halfway [June 1857], B-L.
17. JBF to EBL, July 19, 1857, B-L.
18. JBF, quoting back to FPB, Aug. 30 [1857], B-L; JBF to EBL, Sept. 23, 1857, B-L.
19. JBF to FPB, Aug. 30 [1857], B-L.
20. JBF to JCF, July 25, 29 and Sept. 23 [1857], FP.
21. Chambers, *Benton*, 434.
22. JBF to EBL, Oct. 13 [1857], B-L.
23. JBF to EBL, Nov. 4 [1857], B-L.
24. JBF to EBL, Dec. 18 [1857], B-L.

25. JBF to FBP, Christmas day [1857], B-L; JBF to EBL, Dec. 15 [1857], B-L.
26. JBF to EBL, Jan. 11, 1858, B-L; JBF to FPB, Christmas day [1857], B-L.
27. JBF to EBL, Feb. 1 and Mar. 3, 1858, B-L; THB to Frank Blair, Mar. 14, 1858, BP; JBF to FPB, May [1858], B-L.

Chapter Twenty ˒
"The Little White House"

1. JBF to EBL, Mar. 28 [1858], B-L. See also N.Y. *Herald*, Mar. 20, 1858.
2. Howard, *Remembrance*, 78.
3. JBF, *Mother Lode*, 32; Howard, *Remembrance*, 80. *Mother Lode Narratives* contains most of JBF's letters to the Blairs written from Bear Valley, along with selections from her *Far West Sketches*.
4. *Mariposas Estate*, 38–39, 50.
5. JBF, *Mother Lode*, 32–33, 38.
6. FPB to Van Buren, Apr. 2 and 12, 1857, Van Buren Papers, LC.
7. JBF, *Mother Lode*, 36, 39.
8. JCF to FPB, June 4, 1858, B-L; JBF, *Mother Lode*, 36; JBF to EBL, July 4 and May 28 [1858], B-L.
9. S.F. *Bulletin*, May 27, 1858, quoted in Crampton, "Mariposa," 236–37; Gates, "Frémont-Jones Scramble," 38.
10. S.F. *Herald*, Jan. 28, 1857, quoted in Crampton, "Mariposa," 243.
11. For JBF's accounts of the siege, as quoted here, see "Great Events," 207–13, FP; Memoirs, 99–104, FP; *Mother Lode*, 41–72.
12. Bosqui, *Memoirs*, 85. See also S.F. *Bulletin*, July 14–19, 1858.
13. JBF described this confrontation only in her unpublished memoirs. While she may have dramatized the story, Lily, eighteen at the time, corroborates it in her *Recollections*, adding that she accompanied her mother to the tavern.
14. "Iota" [John Howard, Sr.], "The Riot on Frémont's Mariposa Ranch," N.Y. *Evening Post*, Aug. 12, 1858.
15. S.F. *Bulletin*, July 15, 1858.
16. Howard, *Remembrance*, 82.
17. JCF to FPB, July 16, 1858, BP.
18. JBF, *Mother Lode*, 36; JBF to EBL, Aug. 17, 1858, B-L.
19. JBF, "Great Events," 213; JBF, postscript to FPB, Oct. 4, 1858, BP.
20. JBF, *Mother Lode*, 61; JBF, "Great Events," 213.
21. Galen Clark, ms. *Reminiscences*, 1880, 6, Bancroft.
22. JCF to Nathaniel Banks, May 16, 1859, Banks Papers, LC; JCF to J. J. Dix, May 18, 1859; FP; JBF, *Mother Lode*, 90.
23. JBF, *Mother Lode*, 89–91.

24. Isely, *Greeley*, 207–8.
25. JBF to Banks, Aug. 20, 1859, Banks Papers, LC.
26. JBF, *Mother Lode*, 97.
27. EBF, *Recollections*, 87. See JCF, *Expeditions* 3:1xxiii, and Rather, *Jessie Frémont at Black Point*, 23–30, for details of the property and its purchase.
28. JBF, *Mother Lode*, 97, 62; JBF to EBL, June 2, 1860, B-L; Dana, "Twenty-four Years After," 453.
29. JBF to EBL, June 2, 1860, B-L.

Chapter Twenty-One
San Francisco Idyll

1. JBF to EBL, June 14 [1860) and June 2, 1860, B-L.
2. JCF to Montgomery Blair, Mar. 4, 1860, BP.
3. JBF to EBL, June 2, 1860, and June 14 [1860], B-L.
4. JBF to EBL, June 2, 1860, B-L.
5. JBF to EBL, June 14 [1860], B-L; *Alta* and S.F. *Bulletin*, Mar.-June 1860, passim.
6. King to Randolph Ryers, May 4, 1860; King to Mrs. King, Sr., June 1, 1860, King Papers, Bancroft.
7. King to Ryers, Sept. 10, 1860, Jan. 31 and Mar. 10, 1861, King Papers, Bancroft.
8. King to Henry Bellows, Sept. 30, 1861, Mass. Historical Society (photocopy, Bancroft).
9. JBF, "Great Events," n.p. [following 215] FP; JBF, *Souvenirs*, 204.
10. See Palmquist, *Watkins*, for Carleton Watkins's early California career.
11. King to Ryers, Oct. 19, 1860, King Papers, Bancroft.
12. *Alta*, Aug. 10, 1860; S.F. *Bulletin*, Aug. 7, 1860.
13. JBF, "Great Events," n.p. [following 215].
14. S.F. *Bulletin*, Oct. 27, 1860.
15. JBF, "Starr King," N.Y. *Ledger*, Mar. 6, 1875; King to Ryers, Oct. 29, 1860, King Papers, Bancroft.
16. McPherson, *Ordeal*, 129.
17. JBF to King, Tuesday mg.[early 1861], King Collection, Society of Calif. Pioneers.
18. King to Ryers, Mar. 10, 1861, King Papers, Bancroft.
19. For the Lea controversy, see *Alta*, Feb. 26–28, Mar. 1–3, 1861; Calvin Park to Trenor Park, Mar. 2, 1861, Park-McCullough House; JBF to EBL, Mar. 10 [1861], B-L.
20. JBF, "Great Events," n.p. [following 215].
21. JBF to Anderson, May 28 [1861], Kansas State Historical Society.
22. JBF to Anderson, May [June] 11 [1861], Kansas State Historical Society; Nevins, *Frémont*, 472.

23. King to Henry Bellows, Mar. 18, 1862, Bellows Papers, Mass. Hist. Society (photocopy, Bancroft).

Chapter Twenty-Two
"General Jessie"

1. JBF, *Souvenirs*, 166.
2. JBF to King, July 20 [1861], King Collection, Society of Calif. Pioneers; Pickard, *Whittier* 2:462.
3. Nevins, *Frémont*, 485.
4. W. E. Smith, *Blair Family* 2:59.
5. JBF to M. Blair [July 28 1861], BP.
6. JCF to M. Blair, July 31 [1861], BP; W. E. Smith, *Blair Family* 2:59.
7. JBF to M. Blair, Aug. 5 [1861], BP.
8. Frank Blair to M. Blair, report to Lincoln, Aug. 24, 1861, BP.
9. JBF, *Guard*, 44.
10. R. Davis, "In Remembrance," 239.
11. Wilson, *Dix*, 273.
12. JCF to M. Blair, Aug. 12, 1861, BP; Eliot quoted in JBF, "Great Events," 318, FP; *N.Y. Times*, Aug. 18, 1861; EBL to S. P. Lee, Aug. 20, 1861, B-L.
13. *N.Y. Times*, Aug. 30, 1861.
14. Tracy, "Frémont Pursuit," 177.
15. Ferri Pisani, *Prince Napoleon*, 239.
16. Frank Blair to M. Blair, report to Lincoln, Aug. 24, 1861, BP.
17. Frank Blair to M. Blair, Aug. 29 and Sept. 1, 1861, BP.
18. Lincoln, *Works* 4:506; JBF, "Great Events," 262–63.

Chapter Twenty-Three
"Quite a Female Politician"

1. JBF's version of the Lincoln interview and quarrel with FPB, quoted here, appears in her ms. account, April 10, 1890, FP, and in "Great Events," 269–74, FP.
2. Hay, *Diaries and Letters*, 133.
3. Phillips, *JBF*, 253.
4. FPB quoted in EBL to S. P. Lee, Sept. 17–18, 1861, B-L.
5. Lincoln, *Works* 4:519.
6. JBF to JCF, n.d. [Sept. 11, 1861?], Chicago Historical Society.
7. EBL to FPB, Sept. 15, 1861, BP.
8. E. Smith, *Blair*, 301; JBF, ms. account of Lincoln interview, April 10, 1890, FP.
9. JBF, "Great Events," 278; M. Blair to W. O. Bartlett, Sept. 26, 1861, BP.

10. EBL to FPB, Sept. 27, 1861, BP.
11. Barton Bates to Edward Bates, Oct. 10, 1861, Bates Papers Missouri Historical Society.
12. FPB to Bigelow, Oct. 26, 1861, BP; N.Y. *Tribune*, Nov. 7, 1861.
13. W. E. Smith, *Blair Family* 2:83–84.
14. Nevins, *Frémont*, 529; JBF, *Guard*, 85.
15. JBF, *Guard*, 50–51, 88, 195.
16. Pickard, *Whittier* 2:462–63; JBF, *Guard*, 46.
17. JBF, "Great Events," 294–95.
18. JBF to Ward Hill Lamon, Oct. 30–31 [1861], Huntington.
19. JBF to Dix, n.d. [fall, 1861], FP.
20. Nevins, *Frémont*, 540.
21. JBF, *Guard*, 202; JBF to King, Dec. 29, 1861, King Collection, Society of Calif. Pioneers.

Chapter Twenty-Four
"This Tenderness Toward Slavery"

1. JBF, "Great Events," 325–26, FP.
2. See N.Y. *Tribune*, Dec. 20, 1861, and I. Bartlett, *Wendell and Ann Phillips*, 52.
3. N.Y. *Tribune*, Nov. 28, 1861; Hollister, *Colfax*, 184.
4. JBF to King, Dec. 29, 1861, King Collection, Society of Calif. Pioneers.
5. JBF to James T. Fields, Jan. 19 [1862], Fields Papers, Huntington; JBF to King, Dec. 29, 1861, King Collection, Society of Calif. Pioneers.
6. JBF, *Guard*, vii, xi–xii.
7. JBF to Fields, Oct. 8, 1862, Fields Papers.
8. JBF, *Guard*, 222–23.
9. JBF to Henry Preston Child, Oct. 18, 1897, Filson Club.
10. JBF to King, Dec. 29, 1861, King Papers, Society of Calif. Pioneers.
11. EBL to S. P. Lee, Oct. 7 and Oct. 22, 1861, B-L.
12. Kasson, "An Iowa Woman in Washington," 65.
13. JBF's main account of the Lincoln gala, quoted here, is in "Great Events," 327–29.
14. Child, *Letters*, 396, 400.
15. N.Y. *Tribune*, Feb. 6, 1862.
16. E. Smith, *Blair*, 306; N.Y. *Tribune*, Feb. 5, 1862.
17. JBF to George Julian, May 1, 1862, Giddings-Julian Papers, LC.
18. Ibid., Apr. 2 and May 1, 1862.
19. JBF to King, Feb. 27 [1863], King Collection, Society of Calif. Pioneers; R. Davis, *Bits*, 116, 175.
20. JBF to Fields, May 22 [1862], Fields Papers.
21. JBF to Annie Fields, May 29 [1862], Fields Papers; R. Davis, *Bits*, 175–76.

22. Note to JBF in JCF to Frank Frémont, May 26, 1862, Fremont Papers, Huntington.

23. Andrews, *North Reports*, 259; Schurz, *Reminiscences* 2:344.

24. JBF to Biddle Boggs, June 27 [1862], Calif. State Library; JBF to Sydney Howard Gay, June 21 [1862], Gay Papers, Rare Book and Manuscript Library, Columbia.

25. JBF to Julian, Jan. 16 [1864], Giddings-Julian Papers.

26. R. Davis, *Bits*, 180.

Chapter Twenty-Five
"The Lost Leader"

1. JBF to King, n.d. [winter, 1862–63], King Collection, Society of Calif. Pioneers.

2. JBF to Fields, Feb. 20 [1863], Fields Papers, Huntington.

3. JBF to Fields, Oct. 22 and 30 [1862], Fields Papers.

4. *Hesperian* 9 (1863):636.

5. *Atlantic* 11 (1863):143.

6. JBF to King, n.d. [winter 1862–63], King Collection, Society of Calif. Pioneers.

7. Benjamin H. Brooks, typescript, A Transcript . . . upon the Tablet of Memory, circa 1925, 76, 80–81, Bancroft.

8. JBF quoted in Lucretia Mott to Martha Wright et al., Aug. 1, 1862, Osborne Family Papers, Syracuse.

9. Frank Frémont, Memorandum for Allan Nevins, FP; EBF to NHB, July 26, 1863, FP.

10. Longfellow, *Letters* 4:351.

11. JBF to Whittier, Oct. 17 [1863], Houghton Library, Harvard; JBF to King, Oct. 16 [1863], King Collection, Society of Calif. Pioneers.

12. Daly, *Diary*, 276; JBF to Peabody, Mar. 20 [1864], Horace Mann Papers, Mass. Historical Society.

13. Young, *Women and the Crisis*, 310; N.Y. *Tribune*, Apr. 8, 1864.

14. JBF to Peabody, Mar. 20 [1864], Mann Papers.

15. N.Y. *Tribune* and N.Y. *Herald*, Mar.-Apr. 1864, passim; JBF to Peabody, Mar. 20 [1864], Mann Papers.

16. King to Ryers, Mar. 22, 1863, King Papers, Bancroft; JBF to Peabody, Monday mg. [spring 1864], Mann Papers.

17. I. Bartlett, *Wendell Phillips*, 272; *N.Y. Times*, July 15, 1890.

18. R. Bartlett, *Frémont*, 104; Brooks, "A Transcript . . . upon the Tablet of Memory," 85, Bancroft.

19. *N.Y. Times*, July 2, 1864.

20. JBF to Whittier, Aug. 22 [1864], Central Mich. Univ.; R. Bartlett, *Frémont*, 119.

21. JBF to Samuel T. Pickard, May 28, 1893, Houghton Library, Harvard.

See also W. E. Smith, *Blair Family* 2:284–92 and JBF, "Great Events," 390–92.

22. Julian, "Journal," 330.
23. JBF to Pickard, May 28, 1893, Houghton Library, Harvard.
24. JBF to NHB, Nov. 1 [1864?], FP; JBF to Whittier, Aug. 22 [1864], Central Mich. Univ.

Chapter Twenty-Six
Retreat to Pocaho

1. *N.Y. Times*, May 14, 1865.
2. JBF to S. P. Lee, Oct. 25, 1865, B-L.
3. JBF to S. P. Lee, Jan. 27, 1866, B-L.
4. Stanton, Letters 2:112; Stanton et al., *Woman Suffrage* 2:911.
5. Crampton, "Mariposa," 271.
6. Sara K. [Upton] Edwards to Louisa Finlay, May 20, 1872, Bancroft.
7. Julian, "Journal," 330; JBF to Julian, April 10 [1863], Giddings-Julian Papers, LC.
8. EBF to NHB, Jan. 16, 1867, and Jan. 8, 1871, FP.
9. JBF to S. P. Lee, May 12 [1868], B-L.
10. Ibid.; JBF to S. P. Lee, Jan. 27, 1866, B-L.
11. JBF to Whittier, Mar. 5, 1868, New-York Historical Society; EBF to NHB, [Jan.?] 27 [1867?] and April 22, 1873, FP.
12. JBF, "Kit Carson," N.Y. *Ledger*, Feb. 20, 1875; EBF to NHB, Mar. 20 [1868], FP.
13. EBF to NHB, Sept. 12, 1869, FP.
14. See *N.Y. Times*, Aug. 3, 4, 11, 12, 1869.
15. Daniel to Epperson, July 24, 1869, Epperson Papers, Barker Texas History Center, Univ. of Texas at Austin.
16. See Ream journal, Sept. 1869, passim, Ream Papers, LC.
17. JCF to Ream, Saturday mg. [Oct. 2, 1869] and n.d. [Oct. 3, 1869], Ream Papers.
18. JBF to Whittier, Dec. 22, 1869, Central Mich. Univ.; V. Taylor, *Franco-Texan*, 59.
19. V. Taylor, *Franco-Texan*, 39–41, 51, 72; Bigelow, *Retrospections* 4:399.
20. *N.Y. Times*, Mar. 4, 15, 28, and April 10, 1873.
21. EBF to NHB, Aug. 19 [1873], FP.
22. JBF to A. K. McClure, June 25, 1877, Gratz Papers, Historical Society of Pa.
23. JBF to NHB, Thursday mg. [1873], FP.
24. Frank Frémont, Memorandum for Allan Nevins, FP.
25. EBF to NHB, Wednesday mg. [fall, 1873], FP.
26. JBF to NHB, Monday noon [Jan. 19], Jan. 25, and Feb. 9, 1874, FP.
27. JBF to George Browne, Monday afternoon [1874–75], FP.

28. See Thomas Scott to Jeremiah Black, Sept. 30 [1874], Black Papers, LC. A series of letters to lawyer Black during this period reveal JBF's continual financial anxiety.

29. JBF to George W. Childs, Jan. 24, 1875, Dreer Collection, Historical Society of Pa.

30. JBF to Dr. William Morton, Apr. 18, 1877, FP; JBF to Whittier, Jan. 21–22 [1880], Houghton Library, Harvard.

31. Poem in JBF, "Great Events," n.p., FP; JBF to Whittier, Jan. 21–22 [1880], Houghton Library, Harvard.

32. JBF to Whittier, Jan. 21–22 [1880], Houghton Library, Harvard.

33. JBF to Parton, Jan. 9, 1874, Houghton Library, Harvard.

34. Phillips, *JBF*, 292.

Chapter Twenty-Seven
Arizona Reprieve

1. Buck, *Yankee Trader*, 266.

2. *N.Y. Times*, Oct. 10, 1877.

3. JCF to NHB, Feb. 16, 1878, FP.

4. JCF to Chandler, May 23, 1878, LC.

5. JBF to Albert Tracy, May 16, 1878, Tracy Papers, N.Y. Public Library.

6. JBF to NHB, Monday [Sept. 1878], FP; JBF to Dr. William Morton, Oct. 7, 1878, FP; EBF to NHB, Thursday mg. [Sept. 1878], FP.

7. JBF to Morton, Oct. 7, 1878, FP.

8. Spence, "Jessie Benton Frémont . . . Arizona," 64.

9. JBF to Morton, Oct. 7, 1878, FP.

10. JBF to Geordie Browne, Nov. 14, 1878, FP.

11. EBF to NHB, Oct. 14 [1878] and Oct. 24, 1878, FP; JBF to Morton, Nov. 23, 1878, FP.

12. EBF to NHB, Nov. 24 [1878], FP; JBF to Stanton, Aug. 13, 1879, Douglass Library, Rutgers.

13. JBF to NHB, n.d. [fall-winter, 1878–79], FP.

14. Richardson, *Secret Service*, 195; JBF to Morton, Nov. 23, 1878, FP. See also JBF, "My Arizona Class."

15. JBF to NHB, Oct. 3, 1879, FP; JCF to Rogers, Sept. 3, 1879, FP.

16. JBF to NHB, Oct. 3, 1879, FP; EBF to NHB, Oct. 2 [1879], FP.

17. JBF to Rogers, Nov. 9, 1879, FP.

18. JBF to Rogers, Dec. 2, 1879, and Jan. 8, 1880, FP.

19. EBJ to NHB, Jan. 13, 1880, FP.

20. JBF to Rogers, n.d. [June 18, 1880], FP; EBF to NHB, Aug. 8, 1880, FP.

21. JBF to Sydney Howard Gay, Oct. 27 [1880?], Gay Papers, Rare Book and Manuscript Library, Columbia.

22. Wagoner, *Arizona Territory*, 189.

23. Ibid.

24. EBF to NHB, New Year's Day [1882], FP; JBF to NHB, Friday night [Jan. 1882], FP; JBF to George Browne, Mar. 24 [1882], FP.

Chapter Twenty-Eight
Fireside History

1. JBF to NHB, Apr. 3 [1882] and Friday night [late summer, 1881], FP.
2. JBF to NHB, Aug. 16 [1882], FP.
3. JBF to Whittier, Feb. 27 and Mar. 13, 1883, Houghton Library, Harvard; JBF to Charles Nordhoff, n.d., FP.
4. *Nation* 44(1887): 216; *Atlantic* 60 (1887):133.
5. JBF to Morton, Nov. 3, [1881], FP.
6. JBF to NHB, June 17 [1882], FP.
7. JBF to Whittier, Mar. 13, 1883, Houghton Library, Harvard; JBF to NHB, Oct. 8 [1883], FP. For the marriage, see *N.Y. Times*, Nov. 15, 1883.
8. EBL to S. P. Lee, July 21, 1883, B-L.
9. JBF to EBL, July 29 [1883], B-L.
10. JBF to NHB, Jan. 27 [1885], FP.
11. J. Royce, *Letters*, 93; S. Royce, *Frontier Lady*, 3. See Kevin Starr, *California Dream*, 142–71, for a brilliant overview of Royce and California.
12. Santayana quoted in introduction to J. Royce, *California*, xv.
13. J. Royce, *Letters*, 142.
14. Ibid., 142, 144.
15. J. Royce, *Letters*, 142, 152; J. Royce notes on Frémont interview with JBF marginalia, Oak Papers, Bancroft.
16. J. Royce, *Letters*, 171.
17. J. Royce, *California*, 119, and "Frémont," 552, 555.
18. JBF to NHB, July 16 [1885], FP.
19. JBF ms. notes, Monday Nov. 30 [1885], Misc. Ms. Coll., LC.
20. Ibid.; JBF to George Browne, n.d. [mid-1886], FP.
21. JBF to George Browne, n.d. [mid-1886], FP.
22. EBF to NHB, Oct. 7, [1886], FP.
23. JBF to Mary Beale, n.d. [fall, 1886], Beale Papers, LC.
24. EBF to NHB, Oct. 7, [1886], FP.
25. JBF to Bancroft, n.d. [received July 7, 1886], Bancroft Papers, Mass. Historical Society.
26. J. Royce, "Frémont," 557, 548.

Chapter Twenty-Nine
"California, of Course"

1. JBF, Memoirs, n.p., FP; JBF to NHB, Sunday [Dec. 1887], FP.
2. JBF to Julia Boynton Green, Mar. 21, 1888, Green Collection, Hun-

tington; JBF to Huntington, Mar. 30, 1888, Huntington Papers, Arents Research Library, Syracuse.

3. JBF to Charles de Arnaud, Feb. 12 [1888], Huntington.
4. L.A. *Times*, Apr. 18, 1888.
5. JCF to de Arnaud, Mar. 12, 1888, Boston Public Library.
6. JBF to NHB, Apr. 28 [1889], FP. See also Robinson, *Ranchos*, 140–43 and Dumke, *Boom of the Eighties*, 61–63.
7. JBF to NHB, Apr. 28 [1889], FP.
8. JBF to Whittier, Nov. 19, 1889, New-York Historical Society; JBF to NHB, Apr. 28 [1889] and May 31, 1889, FP; JBF to Jane Waterman, Feb. 15 [1890?], Waterman Papers, Bancroft.
9. Ruddy, *Severance*, 127.
10. Tharp, *Three Saints*, 355. See also Jensen, "Caroline Severance in Los Angeles."
11. JBF to NHB, Mar. 25, 1890, FP.
12. JCF to A. A. Selover, June 1, 1890, New-York Historical Society.
13. JBF to JCF, July 7, 1890, FP.
14. JCF to JBF, July 11, 1890, FP.
15. JCF, Jr., to EBF, July 13, 1890, FP; JBF, Memoirs, n.p., FP. See also Dr. William Morton to JBF, July 22, 1890, FP.
16. JBF, Memoirs, n.p.
17. JCF, Jr., to JBF, July 17, 1890, and to EBF, July 14, 1890, FP.
18. JBF, Memoirs, n.p.; EBF to Carey Jones, July 21 [1890], Aug. 8 and Aug. 30, 1890, Jones Papers, California and Western Manuscripts Collection, Stanford.
19. JBF to Jones, Oct. 28, 1890, Jones Papers.
20. S.F. *Morning Call*, Sept. 17, 1890; *N.Y. Times*, Sept. 18, 1890; Charley quoted in S.F. *Morning Call*, Sept. 24, 1890.
21. EBF to Jones, Aug. 8, 1890, Jones Papers.
22. JBF to Jones, Nov. 7, 1890, Jones Papers. The article appeared in the April 1891 issue of *Century*.
23. EBF to Jones, Aug. 8, 1890, and JBF to Jones, Dec. 8 [1890], Jones Papers.
24. JBF to John G. Borglum, Jan. 3, 1891 [1892], Borglum Papers, LC.

Chapter Thirty
An Affinity for "Tomatoes, Olives, and the Sea"

1. JBF to Carey Jones, Oct. 28, 1890, Jones Papers, Stanford.
2. JBF to John G. Borglum, Jan. 3, 1891 [1892], Borglum Papers, LC.
3. *N.Y. Times*, July 26, 1891; JBF to Whittier, Feb. 8, 1891, Central Mich. Univ.
4. JBF to Borglum, Sunday Jan. 17, 1891 [1892], Borglum Papers.
5. JBF to Carey Jones, Oct. 28, 1890, Jones Papers.

6. JBF to Borglum, July 6, 1891, and Jan. 3, 1891 [1892], Borglum Papers.
7. JBF to Borglum, Jan. 3, 1891 [1892], Borglum Papers.
8. JBF to Samuel Pickard, May 28, 1893, Houghton Library, Harvard; JBF to Charles de Arnaud, Dec. 11, 1899, George N. Meissner Papers, Washington Univ., St. Louis.
9. JBF to Kate Field, Jan. 17, 1896, Boston Public Library.
10. JBF to French Tipton, Aug. 3, 1897, Eastern Ky. Univ.; Fiske and Lummis, *Lummis*, 157.
11. JBF to Whiton, July 29, 1895, Southwest Museum; JBF to NHB, Mar. 18, 1895, FP.
12. JBF to Borglum, May 25, 1896, Borglum Papers; JBF to NHB, Sept. 28, 1897, FP.
13. JBF to Borglum, July 3, 1897, Borglum Papers.
14. JBF to Borglum, Aug. 1, 1897, Borglum Papers.
15. JBF to Borglum, Jan. 13, 1897, Borglum Papers; JBF to NHB, Aug. 15, 1899, FP; JBF to Theodore Roosevelt, Aug. 24, 1899, Roosevelt Papers, LC; JBF to de Arnaud, Dec. 11, 1899, Meissner Papers.
16. JBF to Edward Bok, Apr. 4, 1901, Bok Papers, LC; JBF, Memoirs, preface, FP.
17. JBF to Bok, Apr. 4, 1901, Bok Papers.
18. JBF to Mrs. Elizabeth [Whittier] Pickard, Feb. 12, 1902, Houghton Library, Harvard; JBF to John Colton, Jan. 16, 1902, Huntington.
19. *Out West*, 18 (1903): 92; JBF to Dr. William Morton, Oct. 17 [1873], FP.
20. *L.A. Times*, Dec. 31, 1902.
21. *N.Y. Times*, Jan. 4 and Mar. 25, 1909; EBF to NHB, Mar. 20, 1911, FP; EBF to Sallie Preston, Aug. 6, 1907, Preston-Johnston Papers, Univ. of Ky.

BIBLIOGRAPHY

Major Manuscript Collections

Bancroft Library, University of California, Berkeley: Frémont Papers (includes JBF, Memoirs [1901–02]. JBF and Francis Preston Frémont, "Great Events During the Life of Major General John C. Frémont . . . and of Jessie Benton Frémont" [1891]); Thomas Starr King Papers.
James S. Copley Library, La Jolla: Frémont Papers.
Duke University: James McDowell II Papers.
Huntington Library: James T. Fields Papers; Frémont Papers.
Library of Congress: Blair Papers; John Gutzon Borglum Papers; Giddings-Julian Papers; Vinnie Ream Hoxie Papers; Van Buren Papers.
Massachusetts Historical Society: Elizabeth Peabody Correspondence in Horace Mann Papers.
New York Public Library: John Bigelow Papers.
Princeton: Blair-Lee Papers.
Society of California Pioneers, San Francisco: Thomas Starr King Collection.
Stanford: William Carey Jones Papers.
University of Virginia: McDowell Family Papers.

Frémont material from the following sources was also useful: Archives of American Art (Smithsonian Institution), Boston Public Library, Brown University, California State Library (Sacramento), University of California at Los Angeles, Central Michigan University, Chicago Historical Society, Columbia University, Connecticut Historical Society, Cornell University, Eastern Kentucky University, Filson Club (Louisville, Kentucky), Rutherford B. Hayes Presidential Center (Fremont, Ohio), Historical Society of Pennsylvania, Harvard University, Johns Hopkins University, Kansas State Historical Society, University of Kentucky, Knox College, Minnesota Historical Society, Missouri Historical Society, Newberry Library (Chicago), New York Botanical Garden Library, New-York Historical Society, Notre Dame, Park-McCullough House (North Bennington, Vermont), Pierpont Morgan Library, University of the Pacific, Mabel Smith Douglass Library of Rutgers

University, Sharlot Hall Museum (Prescott, Arizona), Southwest Museum (Los Angeles), Stowe-Day Foundation, Syracuse University, University of Texas at Austin, Trinity College, U.S. Military Academy, Virginia State Library, Wisconsin State Historical Society, and Yale University.

Books, Articles,
and Dissertations

Abbott, Lyman. *Reminiscences.* Boston: Houghton Mifflin, 1915.

Adams, John Quincy. *Memoirs . . . 1795 to 1848.* Edited by Charles Francis Adams. 12 vols. Philadelphia: J. B. Lippincott, 1874–77.

Alcott, William A. *The Young Wife, or Duties of Woman in the Marriage Relation.* 1837. Reprint. New York: Arno, 1972.

Andrews, J. Cutler. *The North Reports the Civil War.* Pittsburgh: University of Pittsburgh Press, 1955.

Barker-Benfield, Graham John. *The Horrors of the Half-Known Life: Male Attitudes Toward Women and Sexuality in Nineteenth-Century America.* New York: Harper & Row, 1976.

Bartlett, Irving H. *Wendell and Ann Phillips: The Community of Reform, 1840–1880.* New York: W. W. Norton, 1979.

———. *Wendell Phillips: Brahmin Radical.* Boston: Beacon, 1961.

Bartlett, Ruhl J. *John C. Frémont and the Republican Party.* 1930. Reprint. New York: Da Capo, 1970.

Becker, Robert H., ed. *The Plains & the Rockies: A Critical Bibliography of Exploration, Adventure and Travel in the American West, 1800–1865.* 4th ed. San Francisco: John Howell Books, 1982.

Bell, Horace. *Reminiscences of a Ranger; or, Early Times in Southern California.* Los Angeles: Yarnell, Caystile, & Mathes, 1881.

Benton, Thomas Hart. *Thirty Years' View; or, a History of the Working of the American Government . . . from 1820 to 1850.* 2 vols. New York: D. Appleton, 1854–56.

Berg, Barbara J. *The Remembered Gate: Origins of American Feminism: The Woman and the City, 1800–1860.* New York: Oxford University Press, 1978.

Bidwell, John. *In California Before the Gold Rush.* Los Angeles: Ward Ritchie, 1948.

Bigelow, John. *Memoir of the Life and Public Services of John Charles Frémont.* New York: Derby & Jackson, 1856.

———. *Retrospections of an Active Life.* 5 vols. New York: Baker & Taylor, 1909–13.

Billington, Ray Allen. *The Far Western Frontier, 1830–1860.* New York: Harper & Brothers, 1956.

Blair, Gist. "Annals of Silver Spring." *Records of the Columbia Historical Society* 21 (1918): 155–85.

Bode, Carl. *Antebellum Culture*. Carbondale: Southern Illinois University Press, 1970.

Bosqui, Edward. *Memoirs*. Oakland, Calif.: Holmes Book Company, 1952.

Briggs, Carl, and Clyde Francis Trudell. *Quarterdeck & Saddlehorn: The Story of Edward F. Beale, 1822–1893*. Glendale, Calif.: Arthur H. Clark, 1983.

Browne, J. Ross. *J. Ross Browne: His Letters, Journals, and Writings*. Edited by Lina F. Browne. Albuquerque: University of New Mexico Press, 1969.

Buck, Franklin A. *A Yankee Trader in the Gold Rush: The Letters of Franklin A. Buck*. Compiled by Katherine A. White. Boston: Houghton Mifflin, 1930.

Capers, Gerald M., Jr. *The Biography of a River Town: Memphis: Its Heroic Age*. Chapel Hill: University of North Carolina Press, 1939.

Carter, Harvey Lewis. *'Dear Old Kit': The Historical Christopher Carson*. Norman: University of Oklahoma Press, 1968.

Caughey, John W. *Gold Is the Cornerstone*. Berkeley: University of California Press, 1948.

Chambers, William N. *Old Bullion Benton: Senator from the New West*. Boston: Little, Brown, 1956.

Child, Lydia Maria. *Lydia Maria Child: Selected Letters, 1817–1880*. Edited by Milton Meltzer and Patricia G. Holland. Amherst: University of Massachusetts Press, 1982.

Clark, Clifford E., Jr. *Henry Ward Beecher*. Urbana: University of Illinois Press, 1978.

Clarke, Dwight L. *Stephen Watts Kearny: Soldier of the West*. Norman: University of Oklahoma Press, 1961.

Clarke, Grace Julian. *George W. Julian*. Indianapolis: Indiana Historical Commission, 1923.

Clay, George R. "Children of the Young Republic." *American Heritage* 11 (April 1960): 46–53.

Coleman, Elizabeth Tyler. *Priscilla Cooper Tyler and the American Scene, 1816–1889*. University: University of Alabama Press, 1955.

Collier, L. T. "Recollections of Thomas H. Benton," *Missouri Historical Review* 8 (1914): 136–41.

Colton, Walter. *Three Years in California*. 1850. Reprint. Edited by Marguerite Eyer Wilbur. Palo Alto, Calif.: Stanford University Press, 1949.

Conrad, Susan P. *Perish the Thought: Intellectual Women in Romantic America, 1830–1860*. New York: Oxford University Press, 1976.

Cornish, John Hamilton. "The Diary of John Hamilton Cornish, 1846–

1860." Edited by R. Conover Bartram. *South Carolina Historical Magazine* 64 (1963): 73–85; 145–57.

Crampton, C. Gregory. "The Opening of the Mariposa Mining Region, 1849–1859, with Particular Reference to the Mexican Land Grant of John Charles Frémont." Ph.D. dissertation, UC, Berkeley, 1941.

Crosby, Elisha O. *Memoirs . . . 1849 to 1864*. Edited by Charles Albro Barker. San Marino, Calif.: Huntington Library, 1945.

Daly, Maria Lydig. *Diary of a Union Lady, 1861–1865*. Edited by Harold E. Hammond. New York: Funk & Wagnalls, 1962.

Dana, Richard Henry. "Twenty-Four Years After." In *Two Years Before the Mast*. Boston: Houghton Mifflin, 1887.

Darby, John F. *Personal Recollections*. 1880. Reprint. New York: Arno, 1975.

Davis, Burke. *Old Hickory: A Life of Andrew Jackson*. New York: Dial, 1977.

Davis, Rebecca Harding. *Bits of Gossip*. Boston: Houghton Mifflin, 1904.
———. "In Remembrance." *The Independent*, Jan. 29, 1903.

Davis, Varina. *Jefferson Davis . . . A Memoir*. 2 vols. New York: Belford, 1890.

Degler, Carl N. *At Odds: Women and the Family in America from the Revolution to the Present*. New York: Oxford University Press, 1980.

DeVoto, Bernard. *The Year of Decision: 1846*. Boston: Little, Brown, 1943.

Douglas, Ann. *The Feminization of American Culture*. New York: Alfred A. Knopf, 1977.

Drury, Miriam, ed. "The Jeffers-Willey Wedding." *California Historical Society Quarterly* 35 (1956): 11–21.

Du Bois, Ellen Carol. *Feminism and Suffrage: The Emergence of an Independent Women's Movement in America, 1848–1869*. Ithaca, N.Y.: Cornell University Press, 1978.

Dumke, Glenn S. *The Boom of the Eighties in Southern California*. San Marino, Calif.: Huntington Library, 1944.

Eaton, Peggy. *The Autobiography of Peggy Eaton*. New York: Charles Scribner's Sons, 1932.

Egan, Ferol. *Frémont: Explorer for a Restless Nation*. Garden City, N.Y.: Doubleday, 1977.

Ellet, Elizabeth F. *The Queens of American Society*. Philadelphia: Porter & Coates, 1867.

Emerson, Ralph Waldo. *Journals and Miscellaneous Notebooks*. 16 vols. Edited by William H. Gilman et al. Cambridge: Harvard University Press, 1960–82.

Fairfield, John. *The Letters of John Fairfield*. Edited by Arthur G. Staples. Lewiston, Me.: *Lewiston Journal*, 1922.

Faragher, John Mack. *Women and Men on the Overland Trail*. New Haven, Conn.: Yale University Press, 1979.

Farrar, Eliza W. R. *The Young Lady's Friend*. 1836. Reprint. New York: Arno, 1974.

Fender, Stephen. *Plotting the Golden West: American Literature and the Rhetoric of the California Trail*. Cambridge, England: Cambridge University Press, 1981.

Ferri Pisani, Camille. *Prince Napoleon in America, 1861*. Bloomington: Indiana University Press, 1959.

Fink, Augusta. *Monterey: The Presence of the Past*. San Francisco: *Chronicle*, 1972.

Fireman, Bert M. "Frémont's Arizona Adventure." *American West* 1 (winter 1964): 8–19.

Fiske, Turbesé Lummis, and Keith Lummis. *Charles F. Lummis, The Man and His West*. Norman: University of Oklahoma Press, 1975.

Flexner, Eleanor. *Century of Struggle: The Woman's Rights Movement in the United States*. Rev. ed. Cambridge: Harvard University Press, 1975.

The Forty-Niners. New York: Time-Life, 1974.

Frémont, Elizabeth Benton. *Recollections . . .* Compiled by I. T. Martin. New York: F. H. Hitchcock, 1912.

Frémont, Jessie Benton. "Biographical Sketch of Senator Benton . . ." In John Charles Frémont, *Memoirs of My Life*. Chicago: Belford, Clarke, 1887.

———. "California and Frémont." *Land of Sunshine* 4 (Dec. 1895): 3–14.

———. "Distinguished Persons I Have Known." New York *Ledger*, Jan. 2, 9, 16, 23, 30, Feb. 6, 13, 20, Mar. 6, 27, Apr. 3, 17, 1875.

———. "Dolores." *Land of Sunshine*. 7 (1897):3–4.

———. "Kit Carson." *Historical Society of Southern California Quarterly* 42 (1960): 331–34. Reprinted from *Land of Sunshine*, Feb. 1897.

———. *Mother Lode Narratives*. Edited and annotated by Shirley Sargent. Ashland, Ore.: Lewis Osborne, 1970.

———. "My Arizona Classroom." In *How to Earn and Learn* by Jessie Benton Frémont, Ella Farman Pratt, et al. Boston: D. Lothrop, 1884.

———. "The Origin of the Frémont Explorations." *Century* 41 [N.S. 19] (March 1891): 766–71.

———. *Far West Sketches*. Boston: D. Lothrop, 1890.

———. "Senator Thomas H. Benton." *The Independent* 55 (Jan. 29, 1903): 240–44.

———. *Souvenirs of My Time*. Boston: D. Lothrop, 1887.

———. *The Story of the Guard: A Chronicle of the War*. Boston: Ticknor and Fields, 1863.

———. *The Will and the Way Stories*. Boston: D. Lothrop, 1891.

———. *A Year of American Travel*. 1878. New ed. Introduction by Patrice Manahan. San Francisco: Book Club of California, 1960.

Frémont, John Charles. "The Conquest of California." *Century* 41 [N.S. 19] (Apr. 1891): 917–28.

———. *The Expeditions of John Charles Frémont: Travels from 1838 to 1844.* Vol. 1. Edited by Donald Jackson and Mary Lee Spence. Urbana: University of Illinois Press, 1970.

———. *The Expeditions of John Charles Frémont: The Bear Flag Revolt and the Court-Martial.* Vol. 2. Edited by Mary Lee Spence and Donald Jackson. Urbana: University of Illinois Press, 1973.

———. *The Expeditions of John Charles Frémont: Proceedings of the Court-Martial.* Vol. 2, Supplement. Edited by Mary Lee Spence and Donald Jackson. University of Illinois Press, 1973.

———. *The Expeditions of John Charles Frémont: Travels from 1848 to 1854.* Vol. 3. Edited by Mary Lee Spence. Urbana: University of Illinois Press, 1984.

———. *Memoirs of My Life* . . . Chicago: Belford, Clarke, 1887.

Gardiner, Howard C. *In Pursuit of the Golden Dream: Reminiscences* . . . *1849–1857.* Edited by Dale L. Morgan. Stoughton, Mass: Western Hemisphere, 1970.

Garrard, Lewis. *Wah-To-Yah & the Taos Trail.* 1850. New ed. Introduction by Carl I. Wheat. Palo Alto, Calif.: American West, 1968.

Gates, Paul W. "The Frémont-Jones Scramble for California Land Claims." *Southern California Quarterly* 56 (1974): 13–44.

Gobright, L. A. *Recollection of Men and Things at Washington.* Philadelphia: Claxton, Remsen & Haffelfinger, 1869.

Goetzmann, William H. *Exploration and Empire: The Explorer and the Scientist in the Winning of the American West.* New York: Alfred A. Knopf, 1966.

Goodwin, Cardinal. *John Charles Frémont: An Explanation of His Career.* Palo Alto, Calif.: Stanford University Press, 1930.

Gouverneur, Marian. *As I Remember: Recollections of American Society during the Nineteenth Century.* New York: D. Appleton, 1911.

Graebner, Norman A. *Empire on the Pacific: A Study in American Continental Expansion.* New York: Ronald Press, 1955.

Green, Constance M. *Washington: Village and Capital, 1800–1878.* Princeton, N.J.: Princeton University Press, 1962.

Greenhow, Rose. *My Imprisonment.* London: Richard Bentley, 1863.

Griffen, John S. *A Doctor Comes to California: The Diary of John S. Griffen, Assistant Surgeon with Kearny's Dragoons, 1846–1847.* Edited by George W. Ames, Jr. San Francisco: California Historical Society, 1943.

Guild, Thelma S., and Harvey L. Carter. *Kit Carson: A Pattern for Heroes.* Lincoln: University of Nebraska Press, 1984.

Hafen, LeRoy R., and Ann W. Hafen, eds. *Frémont's Fourth Expedition.* Glendale, Calif.: Arthur H. Clark, 1960.

Hall, Margaret H. *The Aristocratic Journey . . . 1827–1828.* Edited by Una Pope-Hennessy. New York: G. P. Putnam's Sons, 1931.

Halstead, Murat. *Trimmers, Trucklers and Temporizers: Notes of Murat Halstead from the Political Conventions of 1856.* Edited by William B. Hesseltine and Rex G. Fisher. Madison: State Historical Society of Wisconsin, 1961.

Hamilton, Thomas. *Men and Manners in America.* 2 vols. Edinburgh: William Blackwood, 1833.

Harlow, Neal. *California Conquered: War and Peace on the Pacific, 1846–1850.* Berkeley: University of California Press, 1982.

Hawgood, John A. "John C. Frémont and the Bear Flag Revolution: A Reappraisal." *Southern California Quarterly* 44 (1962): 67–96.

Hay, John. *Lincoln and the Civil War in the Diaries and Letters of John Hay.* Edited by Tyler Dennett. New York: Dodd, Mead, 1939.

Hellerstein, Erna O., Leslie P. Hume, and Karen M. Offen, eds. *Victorian Women: A Documentary Account of Women's Lives in Nineteenth-Century England, France, and the United States.* Stanford, Calif: Stanford University Press, 1981.

Holliday, J. S. *The World Rushed In: The California Gold Rush Experience.* New York: Simon and Schuster, 1981.

Hollingsworth, John McHenry. "Journal." *California Historical Society Quarterly* 1 (1922–23): 207–70.

Hollister, O. J. *Life of Schuyler Colfax.* New York: Funk & Wagnalls, 1886.

Hone, Philip. *Diary . . . 1828–1851.* Edited by Allan Nevins. 2 vols. New York: Dodd, Mead, 1927.

Howard, John Raymond. *Remembrance of Things Past.* New York: Thomas Y. Crowell, 1925.

Howe, M. A. DeWolfe. *The Life and Letters of George Bancroft.* 2 vols. New York: Charles Scribner's Sons, 1908.

Hubbell, Thelma Lee, and Gloria R. Lothrop. "The Friday Morning Club: A Los Angeles Legacy." *Southern California Quarterly* 50 (1968): 59–90.

Hussey, John. "The Origin of the Gillespie Mission." *California Historical Society Quarterly* 19 (1940): 43–58.

Isely, Jeter A. *Horace Greeley and the Republican Party, 1853–1861.* Princeton, N.J.: Princeton University Press, 1947.

Jackson, Andrew. *Correspondence . . .* Edited by John S. Bassett. 6 vols. Washington: Carnegie Institution, 1926–33.

Jackson, Donald. "The Myth of the Frémont Howitzer." *Bulletin* of the Missouri Historical Society 23 (1966–67): 205–14.

Jeffrey, Julie Roy. *Frontier Women: The Trans-Mississippi West, 1840–1880.* New York: Hill and Wang, 1979.

Jensen, Joan M. "After Slavery: Caroline Severance in Los Angeles." *Southern California Quarterly* 48 (1966): 175–86.

Johnson, Kenneth M. *The Frémont Court Martial*. Los Angeles: Dawson's Book Shop, 1968.

Julian, George W. "George W. Julian's Journal—The Assassination of Lincoln." *Indiana Magazine of History* 11 (1915): 324–37.

———. *Political Recollections*. Chicago: Jansen, McClurg, 1884.

Kasson, Mrs. John A. "An Iowa Woman in Washington, D.C., 1861–65." *Iowa Journal of History* 52 (1954): 61–90.

Kellar, Herbert A. "Rockbridge County, Virginia, in 1835: A Study of Ante-Bellum Society." In Louis J. Paetow, ed., *The Crusades and Other Historical Essays*. New York: F. S. Crofts, 1928.

Kelley, Mary. *The Unconscious Rebel: Studies in Feminine Fiction, 1820–1880*. Ph.D. dissertation, University of Iowa, 1974. Photocopy. Ann Arbor, Mich.: University Microfilms, 1975.

Kemble, John H. *The Panama Route, 1848–1869*. Berkeley: University of California Press, 1943.

Kendall, Amos. *Autobiography . . .* Edited by William Stickney. Boston: Lee and Shepard, 1872.

Kennerly, William Clark. *Persimmon Hill: A Narrative of Old St. Louis and the Far West*. As told to Elizabeth Russell. Norman: University of Oklahoma Press, 1948.

Klein, Philip S. *President James Buchanan*. University Park: Pennsylvania State University Press, 1962.

Koerner, Gustave. *Memoirs . . . 1809–1896*. Edited by Thomas J. McCormack. 2 vols. Cedar Rapids, Iowa: Torch, 1909.

Kune, Julian. *Reminiscences of an Octogenarian Hungarian Exile*. Chicago: p.p., 1911.

Larkin, Thomas O. *First and Last Consul: Thomas Oliver Larkin . . . A Selection of Letters*. 2d. ed. Edited by John A. Hawgood. Palo Alto, Calif.: Pacific Books, 1970.

———. *The Larkin Papers*. 10 vols. Edited by George P. Hammond. Berkeley: University of California Press, 1951–64.

Lavender, David. *Westward Vision: The Story of the Oregon Trail*. New York: McGraw-Hill, 1963.

Lecompte, Janet. "A Letter from Jessie to Kit." *Bulletin* of the Missouri Historical Society 29 (1972–73): 260–63.

Lerner, Gerda. "The Lady and the Mill Girl: Changes in the Status of Women in the Age of Jackson, 1800–1840." In Nancy F. Cott and Elizabeth H. Pleck, eds., *A Heritage of Her Own: Toward a New Social History of American Women*. New York: Simon and Schuster, 1979.

Lewis, Oscar, ed. *California in 1846*. 1934. Reprinted in *The United States Conquest of California*. New York: Arno, 1976.

Lincoln, Abraham. *The Collected Works*. Edited by Roy P. Basler. 8 vols. New Brunswick, N.J.: Rutgers University Press, 1953.

Longfellow, Henry Wadsworth. *The Letters of Henry Wadsworth Long-fellow*. Edited by Andrew Hilen. 6 vols. Cambridge, Mass: Harvard University Press, 1966–82.

———. *Life of Henry Wadsworth Longfellow with Extracts from His Journals and Correspondence*. Edited by Samuel Longfellow. 2 vols. Boston: Ticknor and Fields, 1886.

Lotchin, Roger W. *San Francisco, 1846–1856*. New York: Oxford University Press, 1974.

Lovejoy, Julia Louisa. "Letters . . . Part One, 1856." *Kansas Historical Quarterly* 15 (1947): 127–42.

McDermott, John Francis, ed. *Before Mark Twain: A Sampler of Old, Old Times on the Mississippi*. Carbondale: Southern Illinois University Press, 1968.

McKinstry, Byron N. *The California Gold Rush & Overland Diary of Byron N. McKinstry, 1850–1852*. Edited by Bruce L. McKinstry. Glendale, Calif.: Arthur H. Clark, 1975.

McPherson, James M. *Ordeal by Fire: The Civil War and Reconstruction*. New York: Alfred A. Knopf, 1982.

The Mariposas Estate. Prepared by John C. Frémont and Frederick Billings. London: Whittingham and Wilkins, 1861.

Marti, Werner H. *Messenger of Destiny: The California Adventures, 1846–1847, of Archibald H. Gillespie*. San Francisco: John Howell-Books, 1960.

Martineau, Harriet. *Retrospect of Western Travel*. 2 vols. London: Saunders and Otley, 1838.

———. *Society in America*. 3 vols. London: Saunders and Otley, 1837.

Miller, Joaquin. *Overland in a Covered Wagon*. New York: D. Appleton, 1930.

Miller, Sally C. P. "Col. James McDowell." *Washington and Lee Historical Papers* 3 (1892): 95–115.

———. "James McDowell." Ibid. 5 (1895): 37–210.

———. "The Prestons." Ibid. 4 (1893): 117–28.

Miller, Robert E. "Zagonyi." *Missouri Historical Review* 76 (1981–82): 174–92.

Missouri Historical Society. "Cholera Epidemics in St. Louis." *Glimpses of the Past*. Vol. 3, no. 3. St. Louis, 1936.

Moody, Charles A. "Here Was a Woman." *Out West* 18 (1903): 169–85.

Myres, Sandra L. *Westering Women and the Frontier Experience, 1800–1915*. Albuquerque: University of New Mexico Press, 1982.

Nevins, Allan. *Frémont: Pathmarker of the West*. New York: Longmans, Green, 1955.

———. *Ordeal of the Union*. 2 vols. New York: Charles Scribner's Sons, 1947.

Nichols, Clarina I. H. "The Forgotten Feminist of Kansas: The Papers of

Clarina I. H. Nichols, 1854–1885." Part 2, 1855–56. Edited by Joseph G. Gambone. *Kansas Historical Quarterly* 39 (1973): 220–61.

Niven, John. *Gideon Welles: Lincoln's Secretary of the Navy*. New York: Oxford University Press, 1973.

Oliphant, John A. "Recollections of Thomas H. Benton." *Missouri Historical Review* 14 (1920): 433–35.

Ord, Angustias de la Guerra. *Occurrences in Hispanic California*. Translated and edited by Francis Price and William H. Ellison. Washington, D.C.: Academy of American Franciscan History, 1956.

Ord, Edward O. C. *The City of the Angels and the City of the Saints; or, A Trip to Los Angeles and San Bernadino in 1856*. Edited by Neal Harlow. San Marino, Calif.: Huntington Library, 1978.

Palmquist, Peter E. *Carleton E. Watkins, Photographer of the American West*. Albuquerque: University of New Mexico Press for the Amon Carter Museum, 1983.

Parton, James. *Life of Andrew Jackson*. 3 vols. Boston: Houghton Mifflin, 1859–60.

Paul, Rodman W. *California Gold: The Beginning of Mining in the Far West*. 1947. Reprint. Lincoln: University of Nebraska Press, 1965.

———. *The California Gold Discovery: Sources, Documents, Accounts and Memoirs*. Georgetown, Calif.: Talisman, 1967.

Phillips, Catherine Coffin. *Jessie Benton Frémont: A Woman Who Made History*. San Francisco: John Henry Nash, 1935.

Pickard, Samuel T. *Life and Letters of John Greenleaf Whittier*. 2 vols. Boston: Houghton Mifflin, 1895.

Pitt, Leonard. *The Decline of the Californios: A Social History of the Spanish-Speaking Californians, 1846–1890*. Berkeley: University of California Press, 1966.

Pletcher, David M. *The Diplomacy of Annexation: Texas, Oregon, and the Mexican War*. Columbia: University of Missouri Press, 1973.

Polk, James K. *Diary . . .* Edited by Milo Milton Quaife. 4 vols. Chicago: A. C. McClurg, 1910.

Poore, Ben Perley. *Perley's Reminiscences of Sixty Years in the National Metropolis*. 2 vols. Philadelphia: Hubbard Brothers, 1886.

Preuss, Charles. *Exploring with Frémont: The Private Diaries of Charles Preuss, Cartographer*. Translated and edited by Erwin G. and Elizabeth K. Gudde. Norman: University of Oklahoma Press, 1958.

Rather, Lois. *Jessie Frémont at Black Point*. Oakland, Calif.: Rather Press, 1974.

Re-union of the Pioneer Panama Passengers on the Fourth of June, 1874. San Francisco: printed at the Stock Report Office, 1874.

Richardson, Albert D. *The Secret Service, the Field, the Dungeon, and the Escape*. Hartford: American Publishing, 1865.

Robert, Joseph Clarke. *The Road from Monticello: A Study of the Vir-*

ginia Slavery Debate of 1832. Durham, N.C.: Duke University Press, 1941.

Robinson, W. W. *Ranchos Become Cities.* Pasadena, Calif.: San Pasqual, 1939.

Rolle, Andrew. "Exploring an Explorer: Psychohistory and John Charles Frémont." *Pacific Historical Review* 51 (1982): 135–63.

Rowson, Susanna. *Charlotte Temple.* 1791. New York: John Lomax, 1832.

Royce, Josiah. *California from the Conquest in 1846 to the Second Vigilance Committee in San Francisco: A Study of American Character.* 1886. Reprint. Introduction by Robert Glass Cleland. New York, 1948.

———. *The Letters of Josiah Royce.* Edited by John Clendenning. Chicago: University of Chicago Press, 1970.

———. "Frémont." *Atlantic Monthly* 66 (1890): 548–57.

Royce, Sarah. *A Frontier Lady: Recollections of the Gold Rush and Early California.* Edited by Ralph Henry Gabriel. 1932. Reprint. Lincoln: University of Nebraska Press, 1977.

Ruddy, Ella Giles, ed. *The Mother of Clubs: Caroline M. Seymour Severance.* Los Angeles: Baumgardt, 1906.

Ryan, Mary P. "American Society and the Cult of Domesticity." Ph.D. dissertation. UC, Santa Barbara, 1971. Photocopy. Ann Arbor, Mich.: University Microfilms, 1974.

Schlesinger, Arthur M., Jr. *The Age of Jackson.* Boston: Little, Brown, 1945.

Schlissel, Lillian. *Women's Diaries of the Westward Journey.* New York: Shocken, 1982.

Schurz, Carl. *The Reminiscences of Carl Schurz, 1852–1863.* Vol. 2. New York: McClure, 1907.

Sellers, Charles. *James K. Polk.* 2 vols. Princeton, N.J.: Princeton University Press, 1957–1966.

Seward, Frederick W. *Seward at Washington . . . 1846–1861.* New York: Derby and Miller, 1891.

Silber, Irwin. *Songs America Voted By.* Harrisburg, Pa.: Stackpole Books, 1971.

Smith, Elbert B. *Francis Preston Blair.* New York: Free Press, 1980.

———. *Magnificent Missourian: The Life of Thomas Hart Benton.* Philadelphia: J. B. Lippincott, 1958.

Smith, Margaret Bayard. *The First Forty Years of Washington Society.* Edited by Gaillard Hunt. New York: Charles Scribner's Sons, 1906.

Smith, William Ernest. *The Francis Preston Blair Family in Politics.* 2 vols. New York: Macmillan, 1933.

Smith-Rosenberg, Carroll. *Disorderly Conduct: Visions of Gender in Victorian America.* New York: Oxford University Press, 1985.

Songs for Freeman: A Collection of Campaign and Patriotic Songs for the People. Utica, N.Y.: H. H. Hawley, 1856.

Spence, Mary Lee. "David Hoffman: Frémont's Mariposa Agent in London." *Southern California Quarterly* 60 (1978): 379–403.

——. "The Frémonts and Utah," *Utah Historical Quarterly* 44 (1976): 286–302.

——. "Jessie Benton Frémont: First Lady of Arizona." *The Journal of Arizona History* 24 (1983): 55–72.

Stanton, Elizabeth Cady. *Eighty Years and More: Reminiscences, 1815–1897.* 1898. Reprint. New York: Schocken, 1971.

——. *Elizabeth Cady Stanton as Revealed in Her Letters, Diary, and Reminiscences.* Edited by Theodore Stanton and Harriet Stanton Blatch. 2 vols. New York: Harper & Brothers, 1922.

Stanton, Elizabeth Cady, Susan B. Anthony, and Matilda J. Gage. *The History of Woman Suffrage.* Vols. 1–2 [1848–1876]. New York: Fowler & Wells, 1881–82.

Starr, Kevin. *Americans and the California Dream, 1850–1915.* New York: Oxford University Press, 1973.

——. *Inventing the Dream: California Through the Progressive Era.* New York: Oxford University Press, 1985.

Stenberg, Richard R. "Polk and Frémont, 1845–1846." *Pacific Historical Review* 7 (1938): 211–27.

Stewart, Robert E., Jr., and Mary Frances Stewart. *Adolph Sutro: A Biography.* Berkeley, Calif.: Howell-North, 1962.

Story, Joseph. *Life and Letters . . .* Edited by William W. Story. London: John Chapman, 1851.

Talbot, Theodore. *Journals . . . 1843 and 1849–52.* Edited by Charles H. Carey. Portland, Ore.: Metropolitan, 1931.

——. *Soldier in the West: Letters . . . 1845–53.* Edited by Robert V. Hine and Savoie Lottinville. Norman: University of Oklahoma Press, 1972.

Taylor, Bayard. *Eldorado.* 1850. New ed. Introduction by Robert Glass Cleland. New York: Alfred A. Knopf, 1949.

Taylor, Virginia H. *The Franco-Texan Land Company.* Austin: University of Texas Press, 1969.

Tays, George. "Frémont Had No Secret Instructions." *Pacific Historical Review* 9 (1940): 157–71.

Tharp, Louise Hall. *Three Saints and a Sinner: Julia Ward Howe, Louisa, Annie and Sam Ward.* Boston: Little, Brown, 1956.

Thompson, Gerald. *Edward F. Beale and the American West.* Albuquerque: University of New Mexico Press, 1983.

Thoreau, Henry David. *The Correspondence . . .* Edited by Walter Harding and Carl Bode. New York: New York University Press, 1958.

Tompkins, Edmund P. *Rockbridge County, Virginia: An Informal History.* Edited by Marshall William Fishwick. Richmond, Va.: Whittet & Shepperson, 1952.

Tracy, Albert. "Fremont's Pursuit of Jackson . . . The Journal of Colonel Albert Tracy, March–July 1862." Edited by Francis F. Wayland. *Virginia Magazine of History and Biography*. 70 (1962): 165–93, 332–54.
———. "Missouri in Crisis: The Journal of Captain Albert Tracy, 1861." Edited by Ray W. Irwin. *Missouri Historical Review* 51 (1956–57): 8–21, 151–64, 270–83.

Trollope, Frances. *Domestic Manners of the Americans*. 1832. New ed. Edited by Donald Smalley. New York: Alfred A. Knopf, 1949.

Van Buren, Martin. *Autobiography*. Edited by John C. Fitzpatrick. American Historical Association *Annual Report*, 2, 1918. Washington: Government Printing Office, 1920.

Wagoner, Jay J. *Arizona Territory, 1863–1912*. Tucson: University of Arizona Press, 1970.

Walker, Franklin. *San Francisco's Literary Frontier*. New York: Alfred A. Knopf, 1939.

Wamsley, James S. *Idols, Victims, Pioneers: Virginia Women from 1607*. Richmond: Virginia State Chamber of Commerce, 1976.

Watkins, T. H., and R. R. Olmsted. *Mirror of the Dream: An Illustrated History of San Francisco*. San Francisco: Scrimshaw, 1976.

Welter, Barbara. *Dimity Convictions: The American Woman in the Nineteenth Century*. Athens: Ohio University Press, 1976.

Wendte, Charles W. *Thomas Starr King, Patriot and Preacher*. Boston: Beacon, 1921.

Whitman, Walt. "The Eighteenth Presidency!" In *Complete Poetry and Selected Prose and Letters*. Edited by Emory Holloway. London: Nonesuch, 1938.

Wilson, Dorothy Clarke. *Stranger and Traveler: The Story of Dorothea Dix*. Boston: Little, Brown, 1975.

Wiltsee, Ernest A. *The Truth about Frémont: An Inquiry*. San Francisco: John Henry Nash, 1936.

Winslow, Charles. "Nantucket to the Golden Gate in 1849." Edited by Helen Irving Oehler. *California Historical Society Quarterly* 29 (1950): 1–18, 167–72.

Young, Agatha. *The Women and the Crisis: Women of the North in the Civil War*. New York: McDowell, Obolensky, 1959.

INDEX